Exploring canadian sociology a reader

Exploring canadian sociology

a reader

Edited by Bruce Ravelli
Mount Royal College

PEARSON
Prentice Hall

Toronto

National Library of Canada Cataloguing in Publication

Exploring Canadian sociology : a reader/edited by Bruce Ravelli.

ISBN 0-13-177625-8

   1. Canada—Social conditions. 2. Sociology—Canada. I. Ravelli, Bruce Douglas, 1963–

HM586.E96 2005   301'.0971   C2004-900009-8

ISBN 0-13-177625-8

Vice President, Editorial Director: Michael J. Young
Executive Acquisitions Editor: Jessica Mosher
Signing Representative: Lise Mills
Executive Marketing Manager: Judith Allen
Associate Editor: Patti Altridge
Production Editor: Söğüt Y. Güleç
Copy Editor: Cheryl Cohen
Proofreader: Lesley Mann
Production Coordinator: Peggy Brown
Page Layout: B.J. Weckerle
Art Director: Julia Hall
Cover and Interior Design: Miguel Acevedo
Cover Image: Nonstock/Stock4b

Statistics Canada information is used with the permission of the Minister of Industry, as Minister responsible for Statistics Canada. Information on the availability of the wide range of data from Statistics Canada can be obtained from Statistics Canada's Regional Offices, its World Wide Web site at **http://www.statcan.ca**, and its toll-free access number 1-800-263-1136.

   3 4 5   09 08 07 06 05

Printed and bound in the United States.

For Sacha.

Contents

Preface

EXPLORING AS A METAPHOR FOR SOCIOLOGY

"Exploring" is an apt metaphor for the sociological endeavour generally and the reader specifically. Sociologists are dedicated to investigating our society in much the same way as the early explorers set out to discover new worlds. Seeing our society through the eyes of an explorer might allow the sociologist to examine society from a more insightful and analytical position. Students, by their nature, are also explorers, travelling through the curriculum and hoping to find topics that they would like to visit more extensively later. Hopefully, both teachers and students will use these readings as the staging point for their journey through the sociological landscape.

BRIEF READER CONCEPT

Many Canadian college and university courses are offered during a single academic semester. In their short time together both teachers and students want to explore as much of the discipline as possible. For teachers, a reader allows them to expose students to the rich diversity of sociology. For students, a reader helps expand their interest as it offers diverse sociological perspectives through the original writings of practising sociologists. A brief reader also allows the teacher and his or her students to use the majority of the text during the semester and, by doing so, maximize their investment.

HOW THE ARTICLES WERE SELECTED

Introductory courses are intended to offer a panoramic view of how a discipline investigates our world. As I was preparing this reader, I kept in mind the teachers who want their students to engage with the insights of the sociological tradition as well as the students who appreciate readings that apply to what they are interested in. Trying to please both audiences was certainly a challenge, and one I am sure I can improve upon, but I am convinced that these articles are both intellectually challenging and a stimulating snapshot of how sociologists explore the social world. (All articles are reproduced with their original spelling. References have been edited to ensure stylistic consistency.)

ORGANIZATION OF THE READER

Part 1: Setting the Sociological Compass

These readings introduce the field of sociology. At its most basic, sociology is a tool that we can use to explore how individuals are influenced by society, and how individuals in turn shape society. Sociology, as described by Mills and Johnson, attempts to explore the dynamic relationship between individuals and their society. For me, Mills's writings define what good sociology is all about, while Johnson provides a glimpse at how the sociological perspective can be used to understand society, and ourselves, better. The final article in this first section describes the defining features of Canadian sociology and highlights its unique character and historical influences.

Part 2: Social Interaction

This selection of readings explores how the dynamic forces of human interaction define our social world. For example, the Albas and Albas article on the extraordinary lengths students will go to when they are trying to demonstrate that they are not cheating is an intriguing view into how some students respond to the stresses of writing exams. Next, Fertile explores her early fascination with "dumpster-diving" as one mechanism by which we can all learn more about our society's infatuation with con- sumerism and shopping. Her insights demon- strate that the best sociology often begins with a personal experience. In Matthews's analysis, the author interviews adolescent girls and how they perceive beauty and their physical selves. Matthews's research establishes the powerful influence of peer groups during this important period of social development. Beagan's research continues and enhances our understanding of how medical students make the transition from student to doctor. Often, as students and teach- ers, we overlook the importance of moving from

one status to another (e.g., medical student to doctor). As the reading confirms, there is much more to being a doctor than knowing anatomy. The final article, by Winslow, is a disturbing look into the rites of passage and group bond- ing by the now-defunct Canadian Airborne Regiment and how it assimilated members into its elite military culture.

Part 3: Social Diversity

Deutschmann begins the social diversity section with an investigation of deviance in Canada. Once we appreciate that deviant acts vary across time and space, we are in a better position to explore social dynamics and how they influence what society deems as deviant. Through her practical and theoretical examination we are able to uncover, and hopefully understand, these social dynamics. Nielsen's discovery of the inter- personal terrain of lesbian communication is a fascinating account of the richness of human communication. In her work, Nielsen reviews the many ways that lesbians identify each other and how they secretly share support for each other while interacting within the larger hetero- sexual community. The final two articles in the section uncover the rewarding, and at times dangerous, benefits of using the participant- observer research method. Wolf's article reviews his field research with the motorcycle gang the Rebels, while Adler discusses the experiences she has had with drug dealers and smugglers.

Part 4: Social Inequality

Sociologists are generally reflective social scien- tists who try to improve the lives of those who are less fortunate. As you will see after reading the articles, ethnicity plays a key role in explain- ing social inequality in Canada. Anderson and Frideres provide a theoretical overview of how sociologists explore the intersection of poverty and ethnicity. Their analysis reveals the com- plexity of ethnic relations and the role it has played in the development of Canada. Lian and

Matthews continue the exploration of historical processes when they investigate whether or not John Porter's concept of the *vertical mosaic* applies to ethnicity and income in Canada. Their findings offer little support for Porter's earlier assertions, but they do confirm how visible minority status continues to negatively influence ethnic populations' earning potential. The research by Kazemipur and Halli reinforces the negative influence of ethnicity and reveals that if migrants come to Canada during their adolescent years, they suffer from unusually severe poverty conditions. Restoule's article concludes this section with a personal account of how our ethnicity defines our identity as well as the recognition of the social significance of *identifying* with that definition.

Part 5: Social Institutions

Matthews begins the exploration of social institutions by looking at how the Canadian family has changed over time. She also investigates the economic, cultural, and technological forces that she believes will continue to inspire changes in the future. Wotherspoon's analysis of the role of public education in the knowledge economy is a thoughtful reflection of how traditional views of knowledge and information are being transformed to suit economic interests. For Wotherspoon, the new educational landscape may expand opportunities for some but it may also restrict access to others as new educational requirements marginalize rather than enable. Finally, Bibby's investigation into Canadian religiosity uncovers some interesting challenges to religious participation in Canada. Bibby suggests that while churches have faced many challenges recently, they remain a stable and valued part of the Canadian social landscape. Religion, even today, provides many Canadians with purpose and continuity from generation to generation.

Part 6: Urbanization/Globalization

Bryant and Joseph begin by offering an overview of the demographic factors influencing rural communities across Canada. Their research suggests that migration patterns as well as an aging population will continue to exert pressure on small towns as communities try to meet the changing needs of their citizens. For Bryant and Joseph there are important roles for provincial and the federal governments to play in helping these communities respond to the many challenges they face. Clairmont and Magill review the experiences of a black community in Halifax (Africville) that was subjected to a forced relocation program in the 1960s. The authors describe the experience of this small community and introduce the problems associated with any forced relocation program. Today, Africville continues to hold strong symbolic value for the black community. Hedley's article explores the information age and the role it plays in global economic and social development. He suggests that while technology shows great potential for assisting global economic development, so far the benefits have flowed only to the developed nations. Giddens continues this theme in his article on globalization. Giddens concludes both this section and this reader, by investigating how globalization is changing the very fabric of our lives.

TEACHING FEATURES

This reader offers two features to enhance student learning. First, a brief introduction precedes each selection and helps students focus on what is most significant. Second, all readings are followed by three "Navigating the Concepts" questions, which are intended to help the student take the key concepts from the reading and apply them to their own exploration of the social world.

INTERNET RESOURCES

See Pearson Education Canada's Sociology Supersite at:

http://www.pearsoned.ca/sociology

This site is full of information about the discipline including the theory, major theorists, and key concepts; links to sociology news and research sites; a listing of Canadian and world-wide graduate programs; and more. Content also created by Bruce Ravelli.

Instructor's Test Item File

Pearson Education also supports *Exploring Canadian Sociology: A Reader* with a Test Item File. For each of the 23 selections in this reader, the Test Item File provides instructors with 6 multiple-choice questions (with answers) and essay questions for easy test creation.

NOTE: This supplement can be downloaded from Pearson Education Canada's protected Instructor Central Web site at:

www. pearsoned.ca/instructor

To obtain an access code, please call your PEC Sales and Editorial Representative.

ACKNOWLEDGEMENTS

I am grateful to many people for their help in preparing this reader. First, I would like to recognize the administration and my colleagues at Mount Royal College who continue to value and support teaching excellence. Second, the efforts of the acquisition and editorial staff at Pearson Education have been invaluable. In particular, I would like to mention Jessica Mosher, executive acquisitions editor, who championed my belief that Canadian teachers and students needed a brief introductory reader. As well, Patti Altridge, associate editor, and Söğüt Güleç, production editor, were both instrumental in keeping the project focused and moving ahead. Thanks also to Cheryl Cohen and Lesley Mann for their meticulous editing of the manuscript. Third, the following reviewers of my manuscript warrant special appreciation:

Jane Grekul, University of Alberta
Sue Dier, Camosun College
Lorraine McNeil, Fanshawe College
Ronald Lambert, University of Waterloo
Shirley Pettifer, Vanier College
Carolyn Taylor, St. Lawrence College.

I would also like to thank all my students (past, present, and future) for their enthusiasm and their desire to learn more about the world—all of you inspire me to become a better teacher and sociologist. And last, I would like to thank my family and friends for their confidence in me and their love.

I welcome all faculty and students to share their thoughts and reactions to this reader with me in whatever form they find most convenient. You can write to me at:

Bruce Ravelli
Department of Behavioural Sciences
Mount Royal College
4825 Richard Road SW
Calgary AB T3E 6K6

You can send me an email at:
bravelli@mtroyal.ca

Exploring canadian sociology
a reader

PART 1

Setting the Sociological Compass

Sociologists see the social world differently than the average person. A firm understanding of this unique perspective is necessary before you begin your journey through sociology.

Chapter 1

The Promise of Sociology

C. Wright Mills

Source: From *The Sociological Imagination* by C. Wright Mills, copyright 1959, 2000 by Oxford University Press, Inc. Used by permission of Oxford University Press, Inc.

For many sociologists, the *sociological imagination* defines what sociology is all about—helping us understand the individual's relationship with society. C. Wright Mills outlines how our view of the world changes once we begin to explore the ways in which our lives are influenced by the social forces that surround us all. As you read the chapter, try to consider how significant events in a person's life often lead to changes in the way that person sees the world.

Nowadays men often feel that their private lives are a series of traps. They sense that within their everyday worlds, they cannot overcome their troubles, and in this feeling, they are often quite correct: What ordinary men are directly aware of and what they try to do are bounded by the private orbits in which they live; their visions and their powers are limited to the close-up scenes of job, family, neighborhood; in other milieux, they move vicariously and remain spectators. And the more aware they become, however vaguely, of ambitions and of threats which transcend their immediate locales, the more trapped they seem to feel.

Underlying this sense of being trapped are seemingly impersonal changes in the very structure of continent-wide societies. The facts of contemporary history are also facts about the success and the failure of individual men and women. When a society is industrialized, a peasant becomes a worker; a feudal lord is liquidated or becomes a businessman. When classes rise or fall, a man is employed or unemployed; when the rate of investment goes up or down, a man takes new heart or goes broke. When wars happen, an insurance salesman becomes a rocket launcher; a store clerk, a radar man; a wife lives alone; a child grows up without a father. Neither the life of an individual nor the history of a society can be understood without understanding both.

Yet men do not usually define the troubles they endure in terms of historical change and institutional contradiction. The well-being they enjoy, they do not usually impute to the big ups and downs of the societies in which they live. Seldom aware of the intricate connection between the patterns of their own lives and the course of world history, ordinary men do not usually know what this connection means for the kinds of men they are becoming and for the kinds of history-making in which they might take part. They do not possess the quality of mind essential to grasp the interplay of man and society, of biography and history, of self and world. They cannot cope with their personal troubles in such ways as to control the structural transformations that usually lie behind them.

Surely it is no wonder. In what period have so many men been so totally exposed at so fast a pace to such earthquakes of change? That Americans have not known such catastrophic changes as have the men and women of other societies is due to historical facts that are now quickly becoming "merely history." The history that now affects every man is world history. Within this scene and this period, in the course of a single generation, one-sixth of mankind is transformed from all that is feudal and backward into all that is modern, advanced, and fearful. Political colonies are freed; new and less visible forms of imperialism installed. Revolutions occur; men feel the intimate grip of new kinds of authority. Totalitarian societies rise, and are smashed to bits—or succeed fabulously. After two centuries of ascendancy, capitalism is shown up as only one way to make society into an industrial apparatus. After two centuries of hope, even formal democracy is restricted to a quite small portion of mankind. Everywhere in the underdeveloped world, ancient ways of life are broken up and vague expectations become urgent demands. Everywhere in the overdeveloped world, the means of authority and of violence become total in scope and bureaucratic in form. Humanity itself now lies before us, the super-nation at either pole concentrating its most coordinated and massive efforts upon the preparation of World War III.

The very shaping of history now outpaces the ability of men to orient themselves in accordance with cherished values. And which values? Even when they do not panic, men often sense that older ways of feeling and thinking have collapsed and that newer beginnings are ambiguous to the point of moral stasis. Is it any wonder that ordinary men feel they cannot cope with the larger worlds with which they are so suddenly confronted? That they cannot understand the meaning of their epoch for their own lives? That—in defense of selfhood—they become morally insensible, trying to remain altogether private men? Is it any wonder that they come to be possessed by a sense of the trap?

It is not only information that they need—in this Age of Fact, information often dominates their attention and overwhelms their capacities to assimilate it. It is not only the skills of reason that they need—although their struggles to acquire these often exhaust their limited moral energy.

What they need, and what they feel they need, is a quality of mind that will help them to use information and to develop reason in order to achieve lucid summations of what is going on in the world and of what may be happening within themselves. It is this quality, I am going to contend, that journalists and scholars, artists and publics, scientists and editors are coming to expect of what may be called the sociological imagination.

The sociological imagination enables its possessor to understand the larger historical scene in terms of its meaning for the inner life and the external career of a variety of individuals. It enables him to take into account how individuals, in the welter of their daily experience, often become falsely conscious of their social positions. Within that welter, the framework of modern society is sought, and within that framework the psychologies of a variety of men and women are formulated. By such means the personal uneasiness of individuals is focused upon explicit troubles and the indifference of publics is transformed into involvement with public issues.

The first fruit of this imagination—and the first lesson of the social science that embodies it—is the idea that the individual can understand his own experience and gauge his own fate only by locating himself within his period, that he can know his own chances in life by becoming aware of those of all individuals in his circumstances. In many ways it is a terrible lesson; in many ways [it is] a magnificent one. We do not know the limits of man's capacities for supreme effort or willing degradation, for agony or glee, for pleasurable brutality or the sweetness of reason. But in our time we have come to know that the limits of "human nature" are frighteningly broad. We have come to know that every individual lives, from one generation to the next, in some society, that he lives out a biography, and that he lives it out within some historical sequence. By the fact of his living he contributes, however minutely, to the shaping of this society and to the course of its history, even as he is made by society and by its historical push and shove.

The sociological imagination enables us to grasp history and biography and the relations between the two within society. That is its task and its promise. To recognize this task and this promise is the mark of the classic social analyst. It is characteristic of Herbert Spencer—turgid, polysyllabic, comprehensive; of E. A. Ross—graceful, muckraking, upright; of Auguste Comte and Emile Durkheim; of the intricate and subtle Karl Mannheim. It is the quality of all that is intellectually excellent in Karl Marx; it is the clue to Thorstein Veblen's brilliant and ironic insight, to Joseph Schumpeter's many-sided constructions of reality; it is the basis of the psychological sweep of W. E. H. Lecky no less than of the profundity and clarity of Max Weber. And it is the signal of what is best in contemporary studies of man and society.

No social study that does not come back to the problems of biography, of history, and of their intersections within a society has completed its intellectual journey. Whatever the specific problems of the classic social analysts, however limited or however broad the features of social reality they have examined, those who have been imaginatively aware of the promise of their work have consistently asked three sorts of questions:

1. What is the structure of this particular society as a whole? What are its essential components, and how are they related to one another? How does it differ from other varieties of social order? Within it, what is the meaning of any particular feature for its continuance and for its change?

2. Where does this society stand in human history? What are the mechanics by which it is changing? What is its place within and its meaning for the development of humanity as a whole? How does any particular feature we are examining affect, and how is it affected by, the historical period in which it moves? And this period—what are its essential features? How does it differ from other periods? What are its characteristic ways of history-making?

3. What varieties of men and women now prevail in this society and in this period? And what varieties are coming to prevail? In what ways are they selected and formed, liberated and repressed, made sensitive and blunted? What kinds of "human nature" are revealed in the conduct and character we observe in this society in this period? And what is the meaning for "human nature" of each and every feature of the society we are examining?

Whether the point of interest is a great power state or a minor literary mood, a family, a prison, a creed—these are the kinds of questions the best social analysts have asked. They are the intellectual pivots of classic studies of man in society—and they are the questions inevitably raised by any mind possessing the sociological imagination. For that imagination is the capacity to shift from one perspective to another—from the political to the psychological; from examination of a single family to comparative assessment of the national budgets of the world; from the theological school to the military establishment; from considerations of an oil industry to studies of contemporary poetry. It is the capacity to range from the most impersonal and remote transformations to the most intimate features of the human self—and to see the relations between the two. [At the b]ack of its use there is always the urge to know the social and historical meaning of the individual in the society and in the period in which he has his quality and his being.

That, in brief, is why it is by means of the sociological imagination that men now hope to grasp what is going on in the world, and to understand what is happening in themselves as minute points of the intersections of biography and history within society. In large part, contemporary man's self-conscious view of himself as at least an outsider, if not a permanent stranger, rests upon an absorbed realization of social relativity and of the transformative power of history. The sociological imagination is the most fruitful form of this self-consciousness. By its use men whose mentalities have swept only a series of limited orbits often come to feel as if [they have] suddenly awakened in a house with which they had only supposed themselves to be familiar. Correctly or incorrectly, they often come to feel that they can now provide themselves with adequate summations, cohesive assessments, comprehensive orientations. Older decisions that once appeared sound now seem to them products of a mind unaccountably dense. Their capacity for astonishment is made lively again. They acquire a new way of thinking, they experience a transvaluation of values: In a word, by their reflection and by their sensibility, they realize the cultural meaning of the social sciences.

Perhaps the most fruitful distinction with which the sociological imagination works is between "the personal troubles of milieu" and "the public issues of social structure." This distinction is an essential tool of the sociological imagination and a feature of all classic work in social science.

Troubles occur within the character of the individual and within the range of his immediate relations with others; they have to do with his self and with those limited areas of social life of which he is directly and personally aware. Accordingly, the statement and the resolution of troubles properly lie within the individual as a biographical entity and within the scope of his immediate milieu—the social setting that is directly open to his personal experience and to some extent his willful activity. A trouble is a private matter: Values cherished by an individual are felt by him to be threatened.

Issues have to do with matters that transcend these local environments of the individual and the range of his inner life. They have to do with the organization of many such milieux into the institutions of an historical society as a whole, with the ways in which various milieux overlap and interpenetrate to form the larger structure of social and historical life. An issue is a public matter: Some value cherished by publics is felt to be threatened. Often there is a debate about what that value really is and about what it is that really threatens it. This debate is often without focus if only because it is the very nature of an issue, unlike even widespread trouble, that it cannot very well be defined in terms of the immediate and everyday environments of ordinary men. An issue, in fact, often involves a crisis in institutional arrangements, and often too it involves what Marxists call "contradictions" or "antagonisms."

In these terms, consider unemployment. When, in a city of 100,000, only one man is unemployed, that is his personal trouble, and for its relief we properly look to the character of the man, his skills, and his immediate opportunities. But when in a nation of 50 million employees, 15 million men are unemployed, that is an issue, and we may not hope to find its solution within the range of opportunities open to any one individual. The very structure of opportunities has collapsed. Both the correct statement of the problem and the range of possible solutions require us to consider the economic and political institutions of the society and not merely the personal situation and character of a scatter of individuals.

Consider war. The personal problem of war, when it occurs, may be how to survive it or how to die in it with honor; how to make money out of it; how to climb into the higher safety of the military apparatus; or how to contribute to the war's termination. In short, according to one's values, to find a set of milieux and within it to survive the war or make one's death in it meaningful. But the structural issues of war have to do with its causes; with what types of men it throws up into command; with its effects upon economic and political, family and religious institutions, with the unorganized irresponsibility of a world of nation-states.

Consider marriage. Inside a marriage a man and a woman may experience personal troubles, but when the divorce rate during the first four years of marriage is 250 out of every 1,000 attempts, this is an indication of a structural issue having to do with the institutions of marriage and the family and other institutions that bear upon them.

Or consider the metropolis—the horrible, beautiful, ugly, magnificent sprawl of the great city. For many upper-class people, the personal solution to "the problem of the city" is to have an apartment with private garage under it in the heart of the city and, forty miles out, a house by Henry Hill, garden by Garrett Eckbo, on a hundred acres of private land. In these two controlled environments—with a small staff at each end and a private helicopter connection—most people could solve many of the problems of personal milieux caused by the facts of the city. But all this, however splendid,

does not solve the public issues that the structural fact of the city poses. What should be done with this wonderful monstrosity? Break it up into scattered units, combining residence and work? Refurbish it as it stands? Or, after evacuation, dynamite it and build new cities according to new plans in new places? What should those plans be? And who is to decide and to accomplish whatever choice is made? These are structural issues; to confront them and to solve them requires us to consider political and economic issues that affect innumerable milieux.

Insofar as an economy is so arranged that slumps occur, the problem of unemployment becomes incapable of personal solution. Insofar as war is inherent in the nation-state system and in the uneven industrialization of the world, the ordinary individual in his restricted milieu will be powerless—with or without psychiatric aid—to solve the troubles this system or lack of system imposes upon him. Insofar as the family as an institution turns women into darling little slaves and men into their chief providers and unweaned dependents, the problem of a satisfactory marriage remains incapable of purely private solution. Insofar as the overdeveloped megalopolis and the overdeveloped automobile are built-in features of the overdeveloped society, the issues of urban living will not be solved by personal ingenuity and private wealth.

What we experience in various and specific milieux, I have noted, is often caused by structural changes. Accordingly, to understand the changes of many personal milieux, we are required to look beyond them. And the number and variety of such structural changes increase as the institutions within which we live become more embracing and more intricately connected with one another. To be aware of the idea of social structure and to use it with sensibility is to be capable of tracing such linkages among a great variety of milieux. To be able to do that is to possess the sociological imagination....

NAVIGATING THE CONCEPTS

1. Can you think of a personal experience that made you see the world differently? Apply Mills' concepts of *quality of mind* and *sociological imagination* to help explain your experience.

2. Give three examples of *troubles* that you experience as well as three *issues* facing your community and/or school. According to Mills, why do personal troubles rarely become issues?

3. Do you believe that our ability to gain the sociological imagination might be influenced by our gender, social class, minority status, or where we live? Why? Why not?

Chapter 2

The Perspective of Sociology

Allan G. Johnson

Source: From "Introduction", by Allan G. Johnson as it appears in *The Forest and the Trees: Sociology as Life, Practice and Promise,* by Allan G. Johnson. Reprinted by permission of Temple University Press. © 1997 by Allan G. Johnson. All Rights Reserved.

Allan G. Johnson outlines his approach to sociology and how it influences his perception of the world around him. His passion for sociology is evident in his writing, as is his commitment to bettering the lives of those less fortunate than himself. Johnson's article also demonstrates how individual life histories influence personal opinions and prejudices.

I am a practicing sociologist. This book is about what it is that I practice and what it means and why it matters to practice it. This book is about how the practice finds its way into almost every aspect of life, from headlines in the morning paper to the experience of growing older to the ravages of social oppression in the world. It is about things small and things large, things simple and things complex well past what we can imagine.

I practice sociology in many ways. I practice it when I think about how social life works, when I write, when I work with people trying to see what's going on in the world and our lives in it. I practice as a consultant in corporations to help solve the dilemmas of a diverse and difficult world in which race, gender, sexual orientation, and other issues of difference cast dark shadows over people's lives. I practice when I walk down a street, shop in a market, or sit in a sidewalk restaurant, sip a cup of coffee, and watch the world go by and wonder what life *really* is all about, what this stream of interconnected people's lives consists of, what knits it all together and what tears it apart, and what, as my students would say, it's got to do with me.

I practice sociology for many reasons. I practice it because there is so much unnecessary suffering in the world, and to do something about it we need to understand where it comes from. In this sense, practicing sociology has a profoundly moral dimension. I don't mean this in the sense that it's about being good instead of bad. I mean it in a deeper and broader sense of morality that touches on the essence of what we're about as human beings and what our life together consists of. It is impossible to study social life for very long without coming up against the consequences that social life produces, and a lot of these consequences do such damage to people's lives that, unless we find ways to deny or ignore the reality of it, we feel compelled to ask "why?" And once we ask that question, we need tools to help make sense of where it leads and to imagine how we might go from there toward something better. We can't help but be part of the problem; practicing sociology is a way to also be part of the solution. This not only helps the world, but makes it easier to live in, especially given how crazy a place it can seem. It helps to be able to see how one thing is connected to another, and, in that, how to find ways to make some small difference. We can't change the world all by ourselves, but we can make informed decisions about how to participate in it, and how that can help turn the world toward something better, even if it's just in our neighborhoods or families or where we work.

I wouldn't do all this if I didn't believe something better was possible, so I have to add faith to my list of reasons for practicing sociology. I believe that the choices we make as individuals matter beyond our lives more than we can imagine, that things don't have to be the way they are, but that they won't get better all by themselves. We need to do something, and what we do needs to be based on more than hunches and personal opinion and prejudice. We need systematic ways to figure things out, and that's what sociological practice offers.

I also practice sociology because it helps to keep me in touch with the essence of my own life in the world, for sociology isn't simply about some larger world "out there." It's also about us in the world and the connection between the two, which means it can take us toward basic truths about who we are and what our lives are about. I practice it because it reminds me that for all that we think we know about things, beneath that is all that we don't know, which is good reason to feel awed from time to time. On some level, for example, I'm amazed that social life works at all, that we're able to live and work together as much as we do, to talk, dream, imagine, fight, and create. There is something miraculous about the simplest conversation, miraculous in the sense that there is a core truth about how it happens that we can never get to. We can contemplate the miracle of things by taking ourselves

toward the limit of what we can know. And we can feel the fringe of core truths and how our lives are part of them. So, while my practice is usually "about" understanding the world, it is also about keeping myself in touch with the essentially unknowable essence of human existence that lies beneath.

Practicing sociology is a way to observe the world and to think about and make sense of it. It is a way to be in the world and *of* the world, to play a meaningful role in the life of our species as it shapes and reshapes itself into the mystery of what's going on and what it's got to do with us....

THE ONE THING

If sociology could teach everyone just one thing with the best chance to lead toward everything else we could know about social life, it would, I believe, be this: *We are always participating in something larger than ourselves, and if we want to understand social life and what happens to people in it, we have to understand what it is that we're participating in and how we participate in it.* In other words, the key to understanding social life isn't just the forest and it isn't just the trees. It's the forest and the trees and how they're related to one another. Sociology is the study of how all this happens.

The "larger" things we participate in are called social systems, and they come in all shapes and sizes. In general, the concept of a system refers to any collection of parts or elements that are connected in ways that cohere into some kind of whole. We can think of the engine in a car as a system, for example, a collection of parts arranged in ways that make the car "go." Or we could think of a language as a system, with words and punctuation and rules for how to combine them into sentences that mean something. We can also think of a family as a system—a collection of elements related to one another in a way that leads us to think of it as a unit.

These include things such as the positions of mother, father, wife, husband, parent, child, daughter, son, sister, and brother. Elements also include shared ideas that tie those positions together to make relationships, such as how "good mothers" are supposed to act in relation to children or what a "family" is and what makes family members "related" to one another as kin. If we take the positions and the ideas and other elements, then we can think of what results as a whole and call it a social system.

In similar ways, we can think of corporations or societies as social systems. They differ from one another—and from families—in the kinds of elements they include and how those are arranged in relation to one another. Corporations have positions such as CEOs and stockholders, for example; but the position of "mother" isn't part of the corporate system. People who work in corporations can certainly be mothers in families, but that isn't a position that connects them to a corporation. Such differences are a key to seeing how systems work and produce different kinds of consequences. Corporations are sometimes referred to as "families," for example, but if you look at how families and corporations are actually put together as systems, it's easy to see how unrealistic such notions are. Families don't usually "lay off" their members when times are tough or to boost the bottom line, and they usually don't divide the food on the dinner table according to who's the strongest and best able to grab the lion's share for themselves.[1] But corporations dispense with workers all the time as a way to raise dividends and the value of stock, and top managers routinely take a huge share of each year's profits even while putting other members of the corporate "family" out of work.

What social life comes down to, then, is social systems and how people participate in and relate to them. Note that people *participate* in systems without being *parts* of the systems themselves. In this sense, "father" is a position

in my family, and I, Allan, am a person who actually occupies that position. It's a crucial distinction that's easy to lose sight of. It's easy to lose sight of because we're so used to thinking solely in terms of individuals. It's crucial because it means that people aren't systems, and systems aren't people, and if we forget that, we're likely to focus on the wrong thing in trying to solve our problems.

Thinking of systems as just people is why members of privileged groups often take it personally when someone points out that society is racist or sexist or classist. "The United States is a racist society that privileges whites over other racial groups" is a statement that describes the United States as a social system. It does *not* thereby describe me or anyone else as an individual, for that has more to do with how each of us participates in society. As an individual, I can't avoid participating and can't help but be affected and shaped by that. But how all that plays out in practice depends on many things, including the choices I make about *how* to participate. Born in 1946, I grew up listening to the radio shows of the day, including *Amos and Andy,* which was full of racist stereotypes about blacks (the actors were white). Like any other child, I looked to my environment to define what was "funny." Since this show was clearly defined as "funny" from a white perspective in a white society, and since I was born white, I laughed along with everyone else as we drove down the highway listening to the car radio. I even learned to "do" the voices of "black" characters and regaled my family with renditions of classic lines from the show.

More than forty years later, those racist images are firmly lodged in my memory; once they get in, there's no way to get them out. With the benefit of hindsight, I see the racism in them and how they're connected to massive injustice and suffering in the society I participate in. As an individual, I can't undo the past and I can't undo my childhood. I can, however, choose what to do about race and racism *now*. I can't make my society or the place where I live or work suddenly nonracist, but I can decide how to live as a white person in relation to my privileged *position* as a white person. I can decide whether to laugh or object when I hear racist "humor"; I can decide how to treat people who aren't classified as "white"; I can decide what to do about the consequences that racism produces for people, whether to be part of the solution or merely part of the problem. I don't feel guilty because my country is racist, because that wasn't my doing. But as a white person who *participates* in that society, I feel responsible to consider what to do about it. The only way to get past the potential for guilt and see how I can make a difference is to realize that the system isn't me and I'm not the system.

Nonetheless, systems and people are closely connected to each other, and seeing how that works is a basic part of sociological practice. One way to see this is to compare social systems to a game such as Monopoly. We can think of Monopoly as a social system. It has positions (players, banker); it has a material reality (the board, the pieces, the dice, play money, property deeds, houses and hotels); and it has ideas that connect all of this together in a set of relationships. There are values that define the point of the game—to win—and rules that spell out what's allowed in pursuit of winning, including the idea of cheating. Notice that we can describe the game without saying anything about the personalities, intentions, attitudes, or other characteristics of the people who might play it. The game, in other words, has an existence that we can describe all by itself. "It" exists whether or not anyone is playing it at the moment. The same is true of social systems. We don't have to describe actual basketball players in order to describe "a basketball team" as a kind of system that has characteristics that distinguish it from other systems.

I don't play Monopoly anymore, mostly because I don't like the way I behave when I do. When I used to play Monopoly, I'd try to win, even against my own children, and I couldn't resist feeling good when I did (we're *supposed* to feel good) even if I also felt guilty about it. Why did I act and feel this way? It wasn't because I have a greedy, mercenary personality, because I know that I don't behave this way when I'm not playing Monopoly. Clearly I am *capable* of behaving this way as an individual, which is part of the explanation. But the rest of it comes down to the simple fact that I behaved that way because winning is what Monopoly is about. When I participate in that system, greedy behavior is presented to me as a path of least resistance. As defined by the game, it's what you're supposed to do; it's the point. And when I play the game, I feel obliged to go by its rules and pursue the values it promotes. I look upon the game as having some kind of authority over the people who play it, which becomes apparent when I consider how rare it is for people to suggest changing the rules ("I'm sorry, honey," I say as I take my kid's last dollar, "but that's just the way the game is played"). If *we* were the game, then we'd feel free to play by any rules we liked. But we tend not to see games—or systems—in that way. We tend to see them as external to us and therefore not ours to shape however we please....

IT'S ABOUT US AND IT'S NOT ABOUT US

If we start from the idea that we're always participating in something larger than ourselves and that social life flows from this relationship, then we have to consider that we're all involved—even if only indirectly—in the social consequences that result, both the good and the bad. By definition, if I participate in a racist society—no matter what my race—then I'm involved in white privilege and racist consequences. As an individual, I may not feel or act in racist ways and in my heart I may even hate racism; but that's beside the core sociological point. I'm *involved* in one way or another by virtue of my participation in society itself.[2] If someone takes what I say more seriously because I'm white, then I've received a benefit of racism whether I'm aware of it or not, and in doing so, I've unwittingly participated in racism. This raises the question of how society works *and* how I participate in it—whether I actively defend white privilege or let people know I'm against racism or just go about my business and pretend there's no problem to begin with.

In diversity training sessions, this simple insight can dramatically alter how people see potentially painful issues and themselves in relation to them. This is especially true for people in privileged groups who otherwise resist looking at the nature and consequences of privilege. Their defensive resistance is probably the biggest single barrier to ending racism, sexism, and other forms of social oppression. Most of the time it happens because, like everyone else, they're stuck in an individualistic model of the world and can't see a way to acknowledge racial privilege as a fact of social life without also feeling personally blamed and guilty for it. And the people who are most likely to feel this way are often the ones who are otherwise most open to doing something to make things better. When they look at a problem like racism sociologically, however, they can see how it's both about them and not about them. It's not about them in the sense that they didn't create the racist society we all live in. As I was growing up white, no one asked me if it was OK with me for white people to use *Amos and Andy* to make fun of black people and keep them in their place beneath white privilege. And if they *had* asked me, I doubt that as a child I'd have known enough to object. In this sense, white people who've grown up in a racist environment have no reason to feel guilty when they hear anger about the existence of white racism and the harm and suffering it causes.

Racism *is* about me personally, however, because whether or not I'm conscious of it, I'm always making choices about how to participate in a society that is organized in racist ways and that makes behavior that perpetuates white privilege a path of least resistance. Regardless of how I behave, as a white person I have privileges that are at the expense of people of other races. Race privilege is built into the system itself, which means I don't have to like it or believe in it or even do anything to receive it. When I go shopping at the mall, sales people and store detectives don't follow me around as if I was going to steal something. They don't swoop down on me and pointedly ask "Can I help you?" as if I was a suspicious character or something other than a serious customer. But black people are mistreated this way all the time, and it usually doesn't matter how well they dress or how much money they have to spend.[3] Most people would agree that everyone should be treated decently, but when some are and some aren't simply because of which group they belong to, then social privilege is at work. And whether I like it or not, as a white person I benefit from that by getting something of value that's denied to them. Once I see this, it's hard to avoid asking about how I participate in the system that produces such racist consequences. What are my responsibilities? What could I do differently that would contribute to different outcomes? How can I be part of the solution to racism rather than merely part of the problem?

In other words, by making me aware that I'm involved in something larger than myself, sociological practice gets me off the hook of personal guilt and blame for a world that I didn't create and that isn't my fault. At the same time, however, it makes me aware of how I choose to participate in that world and how and why that matters. I have no reason to feel guilty simply because I'm white; but I also don't have the luxury of thinking that racism and race privilege have nothing to do with me.[4]...

NAVIGATING THE CONCEPTS NOTES

1. Has your own life history (for example, family structure, ethnic background, income level, gender) influenced the way you see the world? How?

2. "What social life comes down to, then, is social systems and how people participate in and relate to them." Discuss this quotation from Johnson and how it relates to your role as a student at your school.

3. Johnson reviews his own childhood experience with racist imagery from the media. With evidence from contemporary media (preferably Canadian), do you feel media imagery is more racially sensitive today than in the past? If yes, what do you feel is responsible for the change? If no, why have the media not responded more proactively to image equality?

1. There are of course numerous examples of cultures and historical periods where families have behaved in this way, especially in relation to daughters. But in places like the United States where organizations are routinely likened to families, this is not how normal family life is viewed.

2. For more on this way of looking at racism, see David T. Wellman, *Portraits of White Racism*, 2nd ed. (New York: Cambridge University Press, 1993).

3. See, for example, Ellis Cose, *The Rage of a Privileged Class* (New York: HarperCollins, 1993); Joe R. Feagin, "The Continuing Significance of Race: Antiblack Discrimination in Public Places," *American Sociological Review* 56, 1 (1991): 101–16; and Joe R. Feagin and Melvin P. Sikes, *Living with Racism: The Black Middle-Class Experience* (Boston: Beacon Press, 1994).

4. For useful perspectives on how white people can become more aware of how they're connected to a racist society on a personal level, see Paul Kivel, *Uprooting Racism: How White People Can Work for Racial Justice* (Philadelphia: New Society Publishers, 1996).

Chapter 3

Defining Features of Canadian Sociology
Bruce Ravelli

Source: Ravelli, Bruce. (2004). Defining Features of Canadian Sociology (Chp. 3). In Macionis, John J., Nijole B. Benokraitis, and Bruce Ravelli (eds.). *Seeing Ourselves: Classic, Contemporary, and Cross-Cultural Readings in Sociology* (Canadian Edition). Toronto: Pearson Education. Reprinted with permission by Pearson Education Canada Inc.

In this brief review, Bruce Ravelli offers a look into some of the defining features of Canadian sociology. The idea is to inspire you to think about Canadian society itself and whether or not you believe it is reflected in Canadian sociology.

Canadian sociology often mirrors the nature of Canada itself: a diverse landscape where Canadians struggle to find their unique voice within a chorus dominated by Americans. In fact, some analysts suggest that Canadian sociology is a product of its experiences with, and at times its resistance to, the larger and more dominant American sociological tradition (see Brym & Saint-Pierre, 1997; Hiller, 2001; Hiller & Di Luzio, 2001). The dominance of the American sociological tradition in Canada is largely due to its longer history[1] and its sheer size.[2] However, at least four elements influence the presence of a distinctly Canadian sociology:

1. Canada's physical geography, defined by its vast and often challenging physical environment, and its regionalism, evidenced in the important role Quebec plays in Canadian sociology's intellectual development

2. Canadian sociology's focus on the political economy

3. The Canadianization movement of the 1960s and 1970s in response to the number of American faculty in our postsecondary institutions

4. The radical nature of Canadian sociology

CANADA'S GEOGRAPHY AND REGIONALISM

Canada, the world's second-largest country—in terms of total area, not population—(Countries of the World, 2002), is blessed with rich natural resources and a beautiful and diverse landscape. As we will see, these environmental factors have influenced Canadian sociology. According to Hiller (2001), Canadian sociology is not simply a culmination of the varieties of sociology practised in Canada; it is instead the product of Canadian sociologists' efforts to understand the Canadian experience. For Hiller (2001), one of Canadian sociology's defining pursuits has been the attempt to understand a changing national society. Everett Hughes asserted in 1959 that Canadian sociology should be grounded in its own societal context: as society changes, so too should its sociology (cited in Hiller, 2001).

Sociology "should reflect both the unique aspects of the society's character as well as the evolution of that society" (Hiller, 2001: 262).

External and internal forces help to shape and define a Canadian sociology. The particular nature of the relationship between Canada's physical landscape and Canadian sociology is seen clearly in Brym and Saint Pierre (1997). They suggest that one defining characteristic of Canadian sociology is its survivalism (1997: 543) and propose that a core theme of Canadian sociology is the development and maintenance of a community in the face of hostile elements (e.g., geographically, socially) and outside forces (i.e., political and intellectual pressures from the United States and American sociologists). One inside force defining Canadian sociology is the role that regionalism plays in our country's development (e.g., west versus east) and, in particular, Quebec's influence. Quebec has a unique linguistic and cultural influence on Canadian society generally and on Canadian sociology specifically.

The teaching of Canadian francophone sociology began in 1943, when the Faculty of Social Sciences was established at Laval University in Quebec City. Although francophone sociology is comparatively young, it experienced explosive growth from the 1960s to the 1980s, as demonstrated by rising student enrolment and the wealth of research produced by francophone sociologists (Brym & Saint-Pierre, 1997: 544). During the 1960s, a social movement in Quebec called the Quiet Revolution saw the influence of the Catholic Church diminish, replaced by an expanded provincial bureaucracy and, ultimately, a resurgence in nationalistic sentiments (seen in the rising popularity of the separatist movement and the growing influence of the Parti Québécois and its then-leader, René Lévesque).

The Quiet Revolution not only inspired changes in Quebec society and politics, but it also influenced sociologists to focus on issues of social class and social policy (see Brym & Saint-Pierre, 1997; Hiller, 2001). In fact, some Quebec sociologists have played leadership roles in the transformation of francophone society as senior advisors and civil servants for the provincial government (Brym & Saint-Pierre, 1997: 544). This is consistent with Southcott's (1999: 459) position that francophone sociologists are more likely to see themselves as "agents of change" than are their anglophone colleagues. Again, we see that the society in which sociologists work affects their approach to the discipline. One of those approaches involves an interest in the political economy.

CANADIAN FOCUS ON THE POLITICAL ECONOMY

Wallace Clement (2001), a leading figure in Canadian sociology, believes that one of the defining elements of Canadian sociology is its interest in the political economy. The political economy encompasses politics, government, and governing, as well as the social and cultural constitution of markets, institutions, and actors (Clement, 2001: 406). For Clement, this intellectual pursuit is characterized by the attempt to uncover tensions and contradictions within society and use them as the bases for social change.

Arguably, the first Canadian sociologist to investigate Canada's political economy was Harold A. Innis in *The Fur Trade in Canada* (1970/1930) and *The Cod Fisheries* (1954/1940). In these works, Innis develops what has been termed the *staples thesis*, which contends that Canada's development was based on the exploitation of raw materials sent back to European countries to satisfy their industrial thirsts. Innis suggests that each staple (e.g., commercial: cod, fur, timber; industrial: pulp and paper, minerals) had its own characteristics that imposed a particular logic on its individual development (Clement, 2001: 407). As Canada grew and these economic developments continued, these raw materials were sent abroad, refined into more valuable commodities (e.g., furniture, automobiles), and returned to Canada at vastly inflated prices. Innis suggests that since Canada's economic position was subordinate to Britain and to the United States, Canadians were seen as "hewers of wood, drawers of water"—people who performed menial tasks. Certainly, the historical development of Canada's natural resources suggests that Canadian society has been, at least in part, defined by the realization that Canada is not one of the world's major economic or social forces. This underdog mentality was evident in the attempt by Canadian universities in the 1960s and 1970s to Canadianize our postsecondary education system.

THE CANADIANIZATION MOVEMENT

The development of Canadian anglophone sociology was influenced by American sociology as practised at the University of Chicago (see Brym & Saint-Pierre, 1997; Eichler, 2001; Hiller, 2001; Hiller & Di Luzio, 2001; Langlois, 2000; McKay, 1998).

Founded in 1892 by Albion Small, the department of sociology at the University of Chicago defined the American sociological tradition for much of the early twentieth century. The Chicago School of sociology was dominated by the symbolic-interactionist approach, focusing on social reform and collective social responsibility. The Chicago School's influence was most profound on early francophone sociology in Quebec, particularly at Canada's founding department of sociology, McGill. In fact, many influential sociologists in Canada trained at the University of Chicago (such as C. A. Dawson, Everett Hughes, Harold

Innis, A. C. McCrimmon, and Roderick D. McKenzie). The Chicago School was instrumental in defining Canadian sociology, but in the 1950s and 1960s, a movement to increase the number of Canadian faculty teaching at Canadian universities began.

During the late 1960s, Connors and Curtis (1970, cited in Hiller & Di Luzio, 2001: 494) found that more than 60 percent of sociologists in Canada had received their highest degree from a foreign institution. Even in 1971, Hedley and Warburton (1973: 305, cited in Hiller & Di Luzio, 2001: 494) found that in large Canadian sociology departments (those with more than 20 faculty members), more than 50 percent of instructors were American, 20 percent were from other countries, and 30 percent were Canadian. These finding were important as they emphasized the need to hire and train more Canadian sociologists if we ever hoped to investigate and understand Canadian society.

The discipline's Canadianization movement was also prompted by the explosion in the number of university enrolments in Canada beginning in the 1950s. In 1962–63, full-time university enrolment in Canada was 132 681, while only 10 years later (1972–73) it had more than doubled to 284 897. Ten years later (1982–83) the number had reached 640 000 (Hiller & Di Luzio, 2001: 491), and at the end of 1999, the number of full-time Canadian university enrolments hovered around 580 000 (Statistics Canada, 1999). Clearly, the need for Canadian-trained sociologists to teach students about Canadian society was a pressing one. This sentiment was clearly expressed when the Association of Universities and Colleges of Canada appointed a Commission on Canadian Studies in 1972, which resulted in The Symons Report (1975).

The report called on the Canadian academic community to increase its efforts to contribute to the knowledge of their own society. The reaction to this report came in an increase in the number of Canadian society courses taught by sociologists across the country, as well as in an increased focus on publishing sociological materials for Canadian sociology students. The assertion that these measures have worked has some support in the number of part- and full-time students who are undergraduate majors in sociology: the figure rose from 13 638 in 1982–83 to 21 028 in 1996–97 (Hiller & Di Luzio, 2001: 493). These students are making a sociological analysis of their own society, and they are also learning about the comparatively radical nature of Canadian sociology.

THE RADICAL NATURE OF CANADIAN SOCIOLOGY

Brym and Saint-Pierre (1997) suggest that one of the defining features of English-Canadian sociology is its radical nature, seen in its focus on the political economy and feminist ideas and perspectives. The important distinction these authors add, however, is how little of this radicalism is seen by the public (1997: 546). Certainly, Quebec sociologists are more focused on the policy ramifications of their endeavours, but Brym and Saint-Pierre recognize that many leading English-Canadian sociologists (such as Margrit Eichler, Graham Lowe, and Susan McDaniel) are mindful of the impact their ideas have on the larger society (1997: 546). Their investigations into the political economy was instrumental in showing that Canadian sociology was not afraid to uncover the hidden power structures that influence and guide society. Canadian feminist sociologists continue this tradition by looking at how gender acts as a locus of oppression and domination.

Margrit Eichler (2001) suggests that the simultaneous emergence of the Canadianization movement and the feminist movement led to a politics of knowledge that proved helpful to both groups. By expanding university departments by adding Canadian academics during the 1960s and 1970s, the feminist movement found a new voice on university campuses. In Eichler's paper *Women Pioneers in Canadian Sociology: The Effects of a Politics of Gender and a Politics of Knowledge* (2001), she attempts to reverse the politics of erasure that she argues effectively allowed the historical contributions of female sociologists in Canada to be written out of the literature. Eichler undertakes the project by conducting interviews with 10 of the leading female sociologists born before 1930. Through the interviews, Eichler utilizes a life-history approach, allowing the women to tell their own stories about being female sociologists during a period of rapid growth within the university system in general, and sociology departments in particular, as well as in a period when feminist issues first entered the sociological discourse.

One important finding from Eichler's investigation into these women's lives is the fact that they never had problems finding jobs in academe (2001: 393). The expanding university system, as well as the emerging recognition of feminist issues, allowed these women to begin full-time careers with little effort. Although they all faced sexism in some form during their careers, they were able to initiate significant institutional change by their mere presence on campus (e.g., pay equity measures, sexual harassment policies). Their ability to be a critical social presence within the academic community was an important factor in advancing feminist issues on university campuses and in the larger society as the feminist movement gained momentum in Canada.

That impetus led to the establishment of the Royal Commission on the Status of Women in 1967 to "inquire into and report upon the status of women in Canada, and to recommend what steps might be taken by the Federal Government to ensure for women equal opportunities with men in all aspects of

Canadian society" (Cross, 2000). The final report was released in 1970 with 167 recommendations and "became the blueprint for mainstream feminist activism" (Womenspace, 2002). The feminist movement inspired women to reflect differently on their social surroundings and reinforced the need to question social convention. The influence on early female sociology pioneers was equally important, as it encouraged them to critique their own intellectual foundations generally and sociology specifically. As Dorothy Smith notes about this time, "Because we were free to take up issues for women, we didn't feel committed to reproducing the discipline,...it had the effect...of really liberating the discipline in general in Canada, so that you now have an orientation where people feel absolutely comfortable in raising current issues, in addressing what's going on in Canada" (cited in Eichler, 2001: 394). The Royal Commission report opened the debate on women's positions in Canadian society and resulted in the formation of the women's caucus at the Canadian Sociology and Anthropology Association, which still exists today. The feminist movement, and sociology's role within it, is just one example of Canadian sociology's critical foundation and how Canada continues to influence the discipline today.

CONCLUSION

Canadian sociology is defined by its geography, focus on the political economy, the Canadianization movement, and its radical approach to social issues. This brief review should give you some appreciation for the flavour of Canadian sociology and how it represents a unique approach to the discipline and to our understanding of what it means to be Canadian.

NAVIGATING THE CONCEPTS

1. Do you believe that geography influences how academics in a given country see the world? What evidence can you provide to support your answer?

2. Do you think it is still important for Canadian universities and colleges to offer "Canadian sociology" courses even though we participate in a global village?

3. What would your answer be if you were backpacking through Europe and an Italian asked you, "What is Canada like?" Are the things you would mention consistent with the defining features of Canadian sociology?

NOTES

1. The University of Chicago established the first American department of sociology in 1892 and McGill University established the first Canadian one in 1924.

2. The American postsecondary system serves more than 14 800 000 students and the Canadian system around 827 000 (NCES, 2002; Statistics Canada, 1999). In 1999 more than 2400 departments of sociology existed in the United States (ASA, 2002). Canada had around 45 university departments of sociology—including joint sociology/anthropology departments—(McMaster, 2002) and approximately 150 colleges, the majority of which offered at least introductory sociology (ACCC, 2002).

REFERENCES

ACCC (Association of Canadian Community Colleges). 2002. Membership list. [Online]. Available: **http://www.accc.ca/english/colleges/ membership_list.cfm**. Accessed October 27, 2002.

ASA (American Sociological Association). 2002. Departmental listings for 1999. [Online]. Available: **http://www.asanet.org/pubs/dod.html.** Accessed October 27, 2002.

Brym, R., and C. Saint-Pierre. 1997. Canadian sociology. *Contemporary Sociology,* 26(5): 543–46.

Clement, W. 2001. Canadian political economy's legacy for sociology. *Canadian Journal of Sociology,* 26(3): 405–20.

Connor, D. M., and E. Curtis. 1970. *Sociology and anthropology in Canada: Some characteristics of the disciplines and their current university programs.* Montreal: Canadian Sociology and Anthropology Association.

Countries of the World. 2002. Country statistics at a glance. [Online]. Available: **http:// www.infoplease .com/ipa/A0762380.html.** Accessed July 17, 2002.

Cross, P. 2000. Report of the Royal Commission on the Status of Women: Where are we after thirty years? [Online]. Available: **http://www.owjn.org/issues/ equality/thirty.htm.** Accessed January 31, 2003.

Eichler, M. 2001. Women pioneers in Canadian sociology: The effects of a politics of gender and a politics of knowledge. *Canadian Journal of Sociology,* 26(3): 375–403.

Hedley, R. A., and R. T. Warburton. 1973. The role of national courses in the teaching and development of sociology: The Canadian case. *Sociological Review,* 21(2): 299–319.

Hiller, H. H. 2001. Legacy for a new millennium: Canadian sociology in the twentieth century as seen through its publications. *Canadian Journal of Sociology,* 26(3): 257–63.

Hiller, H. H., and L. Di Luzio. 2001. Text and context: Another "chapter" in the evolution of sociology in Canada. *Canadian Journal of Sociology,* 26(3): 487–512.

Innis, H. A. 1954. *The cod fisheries: The history of an international economy.* University of Toronto Press (original work published 1940).

———. 1970. *The fur trade in Canada.* Toronto: University of Toronto Press (original work published 1930).

Langlois, S. 2000. A productive decade in the tradition of Canadian sociology. *Canadian Journal of Sociology,* 25(3): 391–97.

McKay, I. 1998. Changing the subject(s) of the "History of Canadian sociology": The case of Colin McKay and Spencerian Marxism, 1890–1940." *Canadian Journal of Sociology,* 23(4): 389–426.

McMaster University. 2002. Sociology institutions— departments. [Online]. Available: **http://www .mcmaster.ca/socscidocs/w3virtsoclib/cansoc .htm.** Accessed October 27, 2002.

NCES (National Center for Education Statistics). 2002. Digest of education statistics, 2001—Chapter 3: Postsecondary education. [Online]. Available: **http://nces.ed.gov//pubs2002/digest2001/ch3 .asp#1.** Accessed January 31, 2003.

Southcott, C. 1999. The study of regional inequality in Quebec and English Canada: A comparative analysis of perspectives. *Canadian Journal of Sociology,* 24(4): 457–84.

Statistics Canada. 1999. University enrolment, full-time and part-time, by sex. [Online]. Available: **http:// www.statcan.ca/english/Pgdb/educ03a.htm.** Accessed October 27, 2002.

Womenspace. 2002. Since the Royal Commission on the Status of Women. [Online]. Available: **http:// herstory.womenspace.ca/RCSW.html.** Accessed October 23, 2002.

PART 2

Social Interaction

Sociologists appreciate that much of our understanding about society is the result of our interactions with each other.

Chapter 4

Disclaimer Mannerisms of Students: How to Avoid Being Labelled as Cheaters

Daniel Albas and Cheryl Albas

Source: Albas, Daniel, and Albas, Cheryl. (1993). Disclaimer mannerisms of students: How to avoid being labelled as cheaters. *Canadian Review of Sociology and Anthropology*, 30(4), 451–67. Reprinted by permission of the Canadian Sociology and Anthropology Association.

In this article, Daniel Albas and Cheryl Albas review the tremendous lengths that students will go to when they want to demonstrate that they are not cheaters. The authors' research highlights the pressure students face during exams and the way students employ various "disclaimer mannerisms" to cope.

Wherever there are rules there will be temptations for people to break them. Consequently, there is always the possibility of people being labelled deviant whether or not they do break the rules. University examinations are rule-riddled events shrouded in a "suspicion awareness context" where suspecting invigilators are on guard against possible cheaters. Students, aware of this, must avoid all taint of suspicion and the dire consequences of being labelled a cheater. These avoidance strategies consist of impression management in the form of disclaimers. It is the purpose of this article to describe the bizarre and seemingly paranoid length students writing exams go to in: the control of their eyes, deployment of books and notes, and choice of space to avoid the stigma of being labelled a cheater. The emphasis is primarily on the innocent noncheaters but there is brief treatment also of the guilty.

INTRODUCTION

Wherever there are rules, there will be temptations to break them, and the possibility of being labelled deviant by those who made the rules or have a vested interest in their observance. The assumption is that these power figures will institute a monitoring regime and sanctions to achieve compliance and control. In such a situation there are four theoretical possibilities (Becker, 1963): A. an actor might break a rule and be labelled; B. an actor might break a rule but escape detection and labelling; C. an actor might break no rule but be wrongfully labelled; D. an actor might break no rule and not be labelled. This article focuses mainly on category "C". There is only brief comment on categories "A" and "B".... Because of the painful results of labelling, which are usually dramatically impressed on all actors, they will make strenuous efforts to avoid being labelled, whether or not they break the rules. Our focus, then, is on the avoidance that goes on before any labelling occurs as opposed to previous works, particularly by Becker, which focus on the victimized deviants after they have been labelled. Accordingly, the present emphasis as with that of Goffman (1971; 1963a; 1963b; 1959), Lemert (1981), and Matza (1964), is on actors before they are labelled. In addition, we assume actors are aware of the existence of suspicion and are active in its avoidance. We also treat briefly but do not elaborate upon students who actually cheat, are sometimes detected, but continue to try to avoid being labelled. The method of avoidance we shall demonstrate is largely impression management. Such behaviour applies in all suspicion-awareness situations[1] like shop-lifting in department stores and smuggling at customs stations.

In the case with which we are concerned here, students are painfully aware that their identities in the eyes of invigilators are those of potential cheaters. The focus in this paper is on the highly fraught suspicion awareness context of an examination room. The rules of the exam room constitute a "veritable filigree of trip wires" (Goffman, 1971: 106) and the presence of functionaries who, in the eyes of the students, are there principally for catching cheaters and labelling them clearly creates a labelling liable situation. The impression management carried on by the students consists largely of disclaimers. In the usual sense disclaimers are the verbal explanations given by actors before the act of behaviour that might appear to be proscribed and liable to result in labelling. However, in our present study, the disclaimers are largely mannerisms rather than verbalizations (i.e. nonverbal "symbolic gestures" that invite, persuade, and cajole others to respond in one way rather than another). We have chosen this symbolic focus for study here, in part to redress an imbalance in the emphasis on those aspects of the vocabulary of motives (Mills, 1981) which have hitherto stressed the "discursive" (Stone and Farberman, 1981) and largely neglected the nonverbal....

METHOD

This article is part of a larger study of student life and exams conducted over the past 17 years at a large provincial university in Western Canada

(Albas and Albas, 1984). The data come from over 300 individuals who comprise four "generations" of university students. The data originate from three principal sources:

1. Examination logs—These are written accounts by students in which they describe in detail how exams influence their daily lives and noted aspects of exam-related events which they perceived as problematic. More specifically, students wrote about what caused them particular difficulty, anxiety, or trouble and how they coped with it....

2. Interviews—These were conducted by us mostly at the examination site where we mingled with students before and after exams, and in classrooms after test papers were returned. We attempted to get from students their spontaneous explanations of behaviour and practices about which we had questions but which had not yet been verified....

3. Comprehensive observations—To complete the triangulation process, information derived from logs and interviews was combined with careful observations of strategies guided by categories that seemed theoretically and semantically apt (e.g., concealment, revelation, or selective revelation)....

DATA

It is possible to categorize the strategies employed by students in seeking to avoid the label of cheating into two major categories of "Actions Avoided" and "Actions Taken". Actions Avoided are in turn mainly counters to imputed signs of cheating and can be further subcategorized as (a) control of eyes, (b) control of books, notes, formulae and any materials that could be considered "cribs," and (c) morality of place. Actions Taken are all exaggerated shows of (a) picayune overconformity with regulations, (b) the expression (or repression) of "creature releases," and (c) shows of innocence by: default, diligence, affability, declarations, pointless questions.

With the schema that follows we propose to describe the activities the students tell us about and we observe that they carry on to give the impression of complete innocence:

Actions Avoided

1. Control of eyes

The well-understood rule in the examination room is that there should be no looking at other people's papers or exchanging glances with others that might be interpreted as unfair communication. In effect students are expected not to have "roving eyes." On the other hand, it is not humanly possible for students to focus their eyes on their own answer sheet unwaveringly for two or three hours. Accordingly it is necessary to rest and relax from time to time and to remove their eyes from the papers in front of them in order to gather their thoughts. At such times great care is necessary in selecting where to look when they look away from their own papers. A favourite strategy is to keep their eyes fixed on the invigilators. The theory is that if the invigilators see students looking at them, they could not be looking at anybody or anything else. Sometimes this strategy is taken too far and may even backfire so that what is intended as an open, innocent looking into the eyes of another (the invigilator) becomes and is interpreted as a breach of convention—civil inattention (Goffman, 1963a). It may become incriminating if invigilators interpret these long-held glances as an attempt to find an opportunity to cheat when they look away.

Another strategy is to stare at the ceiling where, as one student says, "There is no earthly possibility of deriving unfair help." (There might be the possibility of fair heav-

enly help though, if thoughts accompany the eyes!) Other students say they stare at the back of the head of the person immediately in front or a little above. Quite often they state they go off into brief reveries and suddenly wake up to find themselves staring into the eyes of an invigilator. This contingency is coped with differently by different people. One young woman reports that she smiles ingenuously at the invigilator and moves her eyebrows up and down a few times because as she says, "no cheater would be comfortable enough to do a goofy thing like that." One young male student indicates: "I've given the invigilators a sort of 'help me, I'm stuck' look, hoping it would make them feel sorry for me and so cancel out any thoughts they may have had that I might be cheating." One interesting case observed was of a female student who, in her reverie, was staring at her hands. She looked up to see the invigilator looking at her. She described her reaction and strategy in this way: Using him as a mirror (reflexive role-taking, Turner, 1955: 321) she intuited that he could interpret her to be reading notes written on her palms. She tried to negate that reading by holding up her hands in front of him, palms forward. She found that the invigilator, who at that time had no suspicious thoughts whatsoever, was hard-pressed to understand her actions and showed his puzzlement. He thought that she perhaps wanted to ask a question. She left her seat, went to the front of the room where the invigilator was standing and proclaimed to him explicitly that she was not cheating by showing him the fronts and palms of her hands!

In addition to resting the eyes, it is necessary from time to time for students writing an examination to scratch and stretch and turn their heads from side to side "to get the kinks out." This is a time when many say they feel particularly vulnerable to suspicion. In order to avoid suspicion some report that they cover their eyes with their hands as they stretch and affect to rub them. One student reports that he put his face down on his paper and rolled his head from side to side "where I couldn't possibly be seeing anything, not even my own writing."

Students report that if they drop a pencil or some other object and have to stoop to pick it up they keep their eyes on the invigilator rather than on the object they are trying to pick up in much the same way as touch typists keep their eyes on the copy rather than on the keys.

Some males come into the examination room wearing baseball caps, in order, they claim to conceal unwashed, greasy or unkempt hair made so by the rigours of study preparation. However, to avoid the possible stigma of reading crib notes from under the peak of the cap, they turn it around so that the peak extends over the back of their necks where any invigilator will know that they do not have eyes. On the other hand, some women who have long bangs which can almost cover their eyes (like horse blinders, especially when their heads are lowered) dramatize the fact that they do not copy from others because they could not possibly see through the blinds.

2. Control of notes, books, etc.

Examination rules are explicit that students should not have on their persons any "unauthorized books, tables, notes, or other extraneous material"... "Books or tables authorized for use ... must not contain any additional notes, formulae or other extraneous material." Some instructors allow students writing tests to bring such material into the examination room and even to their desks provided that they do not refer to them during the examination. One may wonder why on earth students would want to put themselves unnecessarily in the vulnerable position of being able to be suspected of

using these materials. That so many do can only be explained by the fact that having these course materials with them when they write provides such students with a "security blanket" (Albas and Albas, 1988a). Perhaps, even more, there is a magical influence imparted by the closeness of their course materials. One woman reported that she kept hers under her feet as a kind of foot stool and was convinced that inspiration from them came up to her through her legs (Albas and Albas, 1989).

Under such circumstances the management of these materials has to be elaborate and intensive in order to convince invigilators that they are not being used illicitly. One man states that he piles these materials on the floor beside his desk with the ones pertaining to the course and might be of any use at the bottom, then on top go the books for other courses, calculators, and other obviously harmless appurtenances. Many students say that before entering an examination room, they "frisk" themselves to ensure that they have not inadvertently forgotten scraps of paper in their pockets which might have notes or formulae written on them. A student stated that once when he opened his wallet to produce his ID card (a recent regulation to prevent "ghost writing") he was embarrassed by various receipts falling out, which of course were innocent but a possible source of suspicion.

Perhaps the most dramatic action reported by a student to counter the imputation of cheating was when the person beside him passed him a note addressed to him asking for help! He indicates: "I was terrified of being caught because my marks reflected a need to cheat. Furthermore, the other student had addressed me by name and signed his as well." Not wanting to pass the note back and not wishing to keep it on his person he resolved his dilemma as follows: "My solution was to eat the note. Fortunately it was a short note written on a small piece of paper!"

3. Morality of Place

Glassner and Corzine (1978) make the point that physical locations become inured with social identities and are important to sociological analysis. Lofland (1973) also stresses the importance of physical location "as a shorthand for imputing social identities to individuals" (Glassner and Corzine, 1978: 83). Students writing exams seem implicitly aware of this connection. One reports: "Since trouble makers (cheaters included) tend to cluster at the back of the room, I stay away from there." Accordingly, it is true to say, as a basic generality, that in choosing their seats in the examination room students "try to avoid the limelight." In other words, they endeavour not to be conspicuous. However, there are some exceptions. For example, some students sit directly in front of the invigilator so that they can be ostentatiously innocent. One invigilator complains of being particularly offended by a student in one of these "conspicuous" seats who cheated—the offence experienced was greater than if the student had chosen an inconspicuous seat at the back or somewhere in the middle. In effect, the student cheated not merely by copying or some other such infringement but he also breached the morality of place by violating the mutual expectations of "the game" in that he cheated in a sacrosanct area rather than in a more sporting locale where the invigilator would routinely patrol, and the odds would be even. However, since students are aware that the inconspicuous seats are suspect, many explicitly avoid them. Others say that they avoid seats beside the well-known high achievers because they may be suspected of trying to copy from them. Also avoided are seats next to known cheaters, students say they do this to escape possible guilt by association. A favoured posi-

tion in the examination room is the aisle seat where it is possible to angle one's body away from the person sitting in the adjoining seat and obviously impossible to see the paper of the person across the aisle. Sitting beside friends is also avoided. If they find themselves so placed they sit with their bodies angled away from each other.

Actions Taken

1. Exaggerated Shows of Picayune Overconformity with Regulations

The cover page of the examination answer booklet lists a number of regulations some of which have been referred to previously. In addition, there are unwritten rules and regulations many of them conveyed dramaturgically in the staging of the examination (Albas and Albas, 1988b). The "trip wires" are numerous—both explicit and implicit. In response students dramatically overconform to these regulations so as to avoid all possible suspicion. The kinds of things they do sometimes approach the bizarre. For example, one male student who had grown a beard since his ID picture was taken says that he strove to recapture on his face the expression he had in the picture so that even with the beard he would be recognizable to the invigilator as the same person. A woman who did not remember her student number which she was required to write at the top of the answer sheet, instead of opening her purse and getting the number from her ID card, waited until she was handing in her paper and with ostentatious innocence got out the ID card and wrote the student number as the invigilator looked on. Her action visibly annoyed him because she slowed down the "traffic" of students handing in their papers and leaving the room. A number of students report that they always hand in their papers before going back to their desk and packing up their effects. This way there can be no possible chance they might sneak a last minute look at notes before the exam paper is turned in. They also say that they pack their equipment while standing up to signal blatantly that they are not doing anything untoward.

These overdrawn precautions by students to escape the suspicion of unfair copying are matched by their efforts to avoid being copied from by exaggerated hunching over their papers, covering them with their hands and, in the case of one person, covering it with a handkerchief. A peculiar example of this ostentatious concealment technique occurs in science laboratory exams in which the room is partially darkened and the questions are flashed on a screen. Because of the darkness and thus increased opportunity for cheating there are usually more invigilators who are also more diligent than in other situations. Accordingly, in order to show that no copying is going on, students turn their answer sheets over as they answer each question. The effect is a periodic, rhythmic "swish" of papers after each question has been answered.

If students have to go into their purses, pencil cases, or bookbags they do so with exaggerated movements designed purposefully to attract attention. They then demonstrate the innocence of the action with the final flourished waving of a [K]leenex like a flag to demonstrate there is no writing on it. One student whose pen ran out of ink shook it violently for a sufficient time to attract the attention of everyone close by and then with two fingers only, delicately extracted a new pen from his jacket pocket.

Students usually attempt to keep a minimum number of irrelevant items like glasses cases, extra pencils, etc. on their desks on the theory that what is not there cannot possibly incriminate them. In contrast to the students mentioned earlier who wear long bangs to "guard their eyes from temptation," others come to the exam with their hair combed

tightly back from their faces so that the rectitude of their eyes can be fully observed: "I wear the sides of my hair pulled back so my eyes are more visible."

One student reports that if, after resting her eyes perhaps in the direction of another paper—she becomes aware of being observed by an invigilator, she delays writing anything for a reasonable interval so as to neutralize any possible suspicion that she might be transferring something she saw on the other paper to her own. This happens particularly in tests using IBM sheets which are machine graded.

2. Expression or Repression of Creature Releases

Goffman (1963b) conceptualizes "creature releases" as "fleeting acts that slip through one's self control and momentarily assert one's animal nature," such things as yawning, sneezing, stretching a cramped limb, or relieving the bladder. These acts are either exaggeratedly expressed in order to make clear beyond all doubt that they are genuine and not meant to mask some guilty activity or they are repressed quite frequently to an excruciating extent in order to avoid the possibility of being falsely accused. Examples of exaggerated expressions include spectacular, wide-mouthed yawning, expansive stretching and vigorous rubbing of the eyes....

Some examples of the repression of creature releases are as follows. One woman... knew that since there were no female exam invigilators there would be no one to accompany her to the washroom. Even though she would have been trusted to go alone if she expressed the need desperately enough, she decided not to risk this but rather with great discomfort that brought tears to her eyes, she "held on" to the bitter end. Another student who suffers from asthma and is required from time to time to use an inhaler would not risk taking it from his knapsack during the examination but instead elected to wheeze his way to the end of his examination. Still another student describes how she had a bad cold, a dripping nose and sneezing spasms but was caught without a supply of Kleenex. Even though the student sitting beside her put some Kleenex within her reach, she delayed accepting it "for a long time."

3. Exaggerated Shows of Innocence

Innocence is blatantly declared by a number of techniques:

(i) By default. Many students come to the exam in clothing devoid of pockets or sleeves (at least long ones) and often women do not wear skirts but opt to dress in pants. By so doing there is no possibility of being suspected of concealing notes in any of these styles of dress. Another case of innocence by default is that of a woman who had finished writing her exam, had already packed up her equipment and was ready to leave the room but wished to wait for her friend who was still writing. In order to make it abundantly clear that she was indeed finished and not trying to copy from anyone else she did three things: she turned her paper face down on the desk, put the cap on her pen with a sweeping flourish and an audible "click," and then she fixed her gaze on some distant object beyond the window.

(ii) By diligence. An emergent norm among the collectivity of exam writers is that any pause or lack of activity is damning. Thus, if they are stumped for a time over the answer to some question, while they think about it they put on a show of diligence in which they may move their lips exaggeratedly as they read the question or they underline and circle words on the question paper while others turn to diligent doodling. In general, they

assume a posture of great seriousness and frowning industry. One says: "When I take a break from writing, I crease my brow as if in deep thought. This lets the professor know that I'm thinking deeply."

(iii) By affability. Students say that when they have any interaction at all with the invigilator during the exam, for example, when ID cards are being checked, the register is being signed, or even when patrolling is going on, they often affect exaggerated affability. Students say, for example, "I always smile and make a joke." "I try to convey as soft, open and honest impression as I possibly can." "I try to be my most charming." They seem to be saying that no self-respecting, decent invigilator could suspect such open friendliness....

(iv) By verbal declarations. Quite often students realize that they have been caught off guard—quite innocently doing something such as looking at a neighbour's watch or being in the midst of a group of other students who are cheating and particularly if, for some reason, they have been asked by an invigilator to change seats. Such people tell us they make a point, upon leaving the exam room, of letting the invigilator know in no uncertain terms that they were not cheating. Some students say they put this in written notes they leave with the invigilator. They say further that by so doing they neutralize any possible suspicion that they are "sneaking off." Sometimes these declarations are posed as pointless questions. For example, students might invite an invigilator to their seat to explain some obviously clear wording in the question, or to ask whether it would be possible to have the room temperature adjusted, or perhaps, to ask how much time is left. One student says: "It lets the professor know I wasn't cheating. If I were, I would not be able to invite her to come near, look her in the eyes and exchange words with her."

DISCUSSION

It seems clear from the presentation above that the examination room is an area highly fraught with suspicion because of the multitude of rules students must follow and the many temptations which exist to break them and thus the possibilities of being labelled. We noted also that the university's staging of examinations introduces numerous additional guilt threatening situations such as the presence of invigilators and their patrolling activities. We found in these and parallel circumstances elsewhere that in the examination room a great deal of impression management goes on in the form of acted out disclaimers intended to ward off labelling. The descriptions provided might strike the reader as exaggerated or, if not an exaggeration on our part, then an overdramatization on the part of the students in their accounts. Indeed, at first glance, it might seem so. However, if we look more closely at the circumstances surrounding these disclaimer displays, exaggerated as they are, they become sociologically explainable. First there does seem to be some paranoia (a term used by many students to describe their state of mind). But are all students paranoid? If not all [,] which ones and why? We shall now try to answer these questions.

Becker (1963) forcefully established the fact that "deviance" is not merely objectively definable as "breach of the norms" but also involves a subjective component open to numerous interpretations in turn resting upon "social constructions of the act." These social constructions and interpretations of student behaviour by invigilators frequently lead to situations that students perceive as false accusations. Furthermore, whether or not these accusations are actually made overt, students imagine that they are made in the invigilator's minds. Thus it becomes more understandable that students might tend to be paranoid.

However, what is also clear is that the paranoid displays do vary to a certain extent depending on the status of the student, the difficulty and significance of the test in question and the "staging" of the test. What follows is an elaboration of these variables and their relation to the degree of paranoid behaviour expressed by students.

Status of Student

A student's status is a function of a complex combination of circumstances and attributes. First, in relation to the powerful professor invigilators, students are in a low-powered, subordinate position. Students tell us that the tone of voice invigilators use tends to infuse more or less awe. The ones who make official and loud announcements, particularly if these announcements include the dire penalties for cheating (which some invigilators feel constrained to do) sets off the drama on an ominous note. Students say also that invigilators who patrol constantly during the examination disturb them most, particularly when they are nearby. Such patterns are consistent with Lofland's (1976: 54–55) observation that "Acute strategic consciousness seems to be the consciousness of underdogs ... they become highly sensitive to the impression their actions are making on the overdog." Argyle and Williams (1969) consistently found that subordinates in role relationships (i.e. interviewee versus interviewer, adolescent versus older person, etc.) feel more self-conscious and demonstrate a greater concern with self presentation. Weems and Wolowitz (1969: 191) indicate that "self-perceived power deficit is a demonstrably prominent factor in the dynamics of ... paranoids." Lemert (1981) also makes the same point....

Second, what we are calling the paranoid aspect of disclaimer displays is generally a function of a student's competence and year in program. Very able students evince less paranoia. Their main anxiety is to have a minimum of interruption or interference until they have completed their answers to the questions. They are seemingly largely unaware of being suspected of cheating and in any case would hardly care because they are so secure and conscious of their ability to prove their competence and demonstrate their innocence if necessary. The mediocre and weak students on the other hand are generally aware of deep down temptations in themselves to cheat. They often imagine that invigilators can telepathically determine these urges ... and so they compulsively watch their ps and qs to avoid betraying these temptations. We also found that as students progress within the academic program from first to last year, their exam behaviour seems to become less paranoid. The explanation for this fact might be that in the higher years they feel somewhat closer in status to invigilators, particularly if the latter are graduate students. Another explanation might be that over the years, through practice, they have become so expert in the performance of disclaimers that they are able to be more poised.

A third dimension of status is ethnicity. We found that visible minority students (e.g., First Nations People, Asians) evince more paranoid-seeming displays than do average, white, middle-class students. This is quite in accord with what Glassner and Corzine (1978) lead us to expect by their discussion of "categorical deviance." They imply that people who do labelling (i.e. power figures) group individuals into categories to which they attach different tendencies to deviance. This, of course, puts "minority" students in a pejorative position in the scale of expectations and they know it.

Fourth, students who wear bristling beards, long "pony tails," tattoos, or present a gen-erally scruffy appearance (much as these appearances provide them with self-satisfactions and status within their own peer groups) are at greater "risk" to be labelled (and they know it) in the "straight" (their assessment) environment of the examination room. Once again we have the corroboration of Glassner and Corzine for this assertion.

Difficulty and Significance of Test

Students classify tests and examinations on a continuum from "a piece of cake" to "a real killer." On another scale these tests vary from "class tests" conducted in the rooms in which the courses are taught to "final examinations" conducted in an auditorium or gymnasium. Our findings suggest that the more difficult the test and the more significant it is, the more paranoid-seeming are the displays. These relationships seem explicable as identity protection. The more one's identity is on the line, the higher the identity risk and the more elaborate the display.

Staging

By staging is meant the dramaturgy surrounding the conduct of the examination. It involves rituals such as admission of students to the exam room on the stroke of the hour, the requirement that they sit in designated seats with plyboard dividers between writing areas, and an army of invigilators making announcements, handing out exam papers (face down), patrolling, etc. This type of elaboration occurs for significant final examinations rather than for class tests. However, even for class tests there are certain formalities and restrictions above the everyday level of class conduct that must be observed. We found that the more elaborate the staging the more paranoid seeming the disclaimers.

The exaggerated disclaimer behaviour to avoid labelling we have described for the classroom is common to a wide range of situations in social life. In spite of being so widespread and, for some people, so intense, a large number of such people are completely unaware of its existence. For example, many professors who have themselves been through the exam-writing trauma will have forgotten and are surprised at the seeming paranoia of their students. They find the acted out disclaimers puzzling and even unintelligible. This is what some writers have referred to as the privilege of insensitivity enjoyed by people in power (Thomas et al., 1972; Rose, 1969). Furthermore, many honest people in department stores, who would never think of shoplifting tell us in interviews of the ends to which they go, for example, keeping their hands out of their pockets, not taking shopping bags into stores, avoiding the area of an unattended counter, not leaving the store in too great a hurry, etc. This is clearly paranoid-like behaviour but it is also understandable given the presence of store detectives and television scanners....

In sum, in this paper we have concentrated on category "C" of the typology—people who have broken no rule but strive by impression management to avoid being wrongfully labelled. There are, however, students in both categories "A" and "B" of the typology, namely those who cheat, are caught and labelled and those who cheat but manage to escape detection and labelling. Even students in this latter category who are sometimes detected manage to argue and turn the stigma away from themselves.

NAVIGATING THE CONCEPTS

1. In your opinion, why does it appear that some of the students' behaviours indicate that they believe they are guilty until proven innocent?

2. From a sociological perspective, discuss why some students choose to cheat while others do not.

3. Can this research into students' "disclaimer mannerisms" apply to any other area of social life? That is, are there other situations where people feel they need to establish their innocence because some may be tempted to cheat? Discuss.

NOTES

1. Glazer and Strauss (1981) define awareness context as the total amount of knowledge we have of the identity (friend, enemy, spy, etc.) of the other and/or our own identity in the eyes of the other. They list four possible awareness contexts: 1/ Closed awareness context—we are unaware of another's identity and/or of our own identity in the eyes of another; 2/ Suspicion awareness context—we are aware that our identity in the eyes of the other is under suspicion or the other's identity is suspected by us; 3/ Pretence-awareness context—we are aware of each other's identity, but pretend not to be; 4/ Open awareness context—we are both aware of each other's identity and make it known.

REFERENCES

Albas, C., and D. Albas. 1988a. Emotion work and emotion rules: The case of exams. *Qualitative Sociology*, 11(4): 259–74.

Albas, D., and C. Albas. 1984. *Student life and exams: Stresses and coping strategies*. Dubuque, Ind.: Kendall/Hunt.

———. 1988b. The institutional staging of an examination. *Canadian Journal of Higher Education*, 18(1): 65–73.

———. 1989. Modern magic: The case of exams. *Sociological Quarterly*, 30(4): 603–13.

Argyle, M., and M. Williams. 1969. Observer or observed? A reversible perspective in person perception. *Sociometry*, 32: 396–412.

Becker, H. 1963. *The outsiders*. New York: Free Press of Glencoe.

Glassner, B., and J. Corzine. 1978. Can labeling theory be saved? *Symbolic Interaction*, 1(2): 74–89.

Goffman, E. 1959. *The presentation of self in everyday life*. Garden City, N.J.: Doubleday/Anchor.

———. 1963a. *Behavior in public places*. New York: Free Press of Glencoe.

———. 1963b. *Stigma: Notes on the management of spoiled identity*. Englewood Cliffs, N.J.: Prentice-Hall.

———. 1971. *Relations in public: Microstudies in the public order*. New York: Basic Books.

Lemert, E. 1981. Paranoia and the dynamics of exclusion. In *Social psychology through symbolic interaction*, 2nd ed., eds. G. Stone, and H. Farberman, 415–28. Toronto: John Wiley.

Lofland, J. 1976. *Doing social life*. New York: Wiley–Interscience.

Lofland, L. 1973. *A world of strangers: Order and action in public urban space*. New York: Basic Books.

Matza, D. 1964. *Delinquency and drift*. New York: Wiley.

Mills, C.W. 1981. Situated actions and vocabularies of motive. In *Social psychology through symbolic interaction*, 2nd ed., eds. G. Stone, and H. Farberman, 325–33. Toronto: John Wiley.

Rose, J. 1969. The role of the other in self evaluation. *Sociological Quarterly*, 10: 470–79.

Stone, G., and H. Farberman. 1981. Introduction. In *Social psychology through symbolic interaction*, 2nd ed., eds. G. Stone, and H. Farberman, 1–20. Toronto: John Wiley.

Thomas, D., D. Franks, and J. Calancino. 1972. Role-taking and power in social psychology. *American Sociological Review*, 37(October): 605–15.

Turner, R. 1955. Role-taking, role standpoint and reference group behavior. *American Journal of Sociology*, 61: 316–28.

Weems, L., and H. Wolowitz. 1969. The relevance of power themes among males, negro and white paranoid and non-paranoid schizophrenics. *International Journal of Social Psychiatry*, 15: 189–96.

Chapter 5

The Oldest Profession: Shopping

Candace Fertile

Source: Fertile, Candace. (1999). The Oldest Profession: Shopping. In Lynne Van Luven and Priscilla L. Walton (Eds.), *Pop Can: Popular Culture in Canada* (pp. 77–81). Scarborough: Prentice Hall Allyn and Bacon Canada. Reprinted with permission by Pearson Education Canada Inc.

In this brief inquiry into the attraction of shopping, Candace Fertile describes her lifelong love affair with what she calls the oldest profession. Fertile's humorous description of the pleasure she feels when shopping is a revealing commentary on our society's culture of consumption.

My shopping career began in earnest when I was seven. My currency was time and deceit. My boutiques were the garbage cans in the alley behind our apartment house in Edmonton.

I could not believe that people threw out such wonderful stuff. What a deal—something for nothing. Perhaps like the first-time gambler who wins and is forever hooked on that adrenaline rush, my love of shopping began with that first magical exposure, on a day when I was wandering home from school, taking my usual route through back alleys. To my extreme delight, I saw peeking out of a galvanized-steel garbage pail what looked like a blue three-ring binder. Acquisition grabbed my seven-year-old soul, and to this day it hasn't let go, fuelled no doubt by relentless advertising and the creation of more and more stuff that announces to the world who we are. Or perhaps who we want to be.

In that alley, my paper-loving self honed in on that blue binder like a cat streaking up from the basement at the sound of a can opener, and I started to understand the power of objects. As a second-grader, I was (unjustly, 1 thought) required to use despised scribblers. The covers were barely more substantial than the rather nasty paper within them. The booklets had three staples in the middle holding the whole ugly mess together. I hated these scribblers, and I hated their name. And I particularly hated the fact that the teacher would stalk around the room, checking to see if we were properly holding our pencils (another affront—I longed to use a pen). Periodically she would sneak up and grab our yellow HBs to make sure that we were not gripping them too tightly. Her actions made me clutch my pencil as if it were keeping my heart pumping. And the choke-hold I had on my pencil meant that I frequently made holes in the flimsy paper of the scribbler. With grim regularity the teacher and I would get into a tug-of-war over my pencil.

It was after such a dismal war (I always had to lose) that the bright blue plastic corner of the binder caught my eye. I debated for some time about whether or not I was allowed to look in the can, or if taking something from a garbage can was stealing. I should mention: not only was I polite, but I was also Catholic. I knew God was watching my every move, and should I be so vile as to commit a mortal sin, lightning bolts would descend and incinerate my evil little soul, so that all that would be transported to Hell would be something the size of a barbecue briquette. The possibility of owning a binder seemed worth the risk.

I inched closer, then looked up and down the alley to make sure no one was watching me. I carefully removed the lid, which was already precariously perched to one side, and laid it on the ground. A perfect, blue, three-ring binder glowed at me. I was in Heaven. I picked it up and with disbelief discovered an unopened packet of three-hole paper inside. The narrow blue (not even the more babyish wide) lines on the stark white paper with the margins marked with a thin pink line were everything my crummy scribbler wasn't. This paper and binder were for grownups, not little kids.

I could hardly wait to write in my new binder. With a pen. I felt instantly grown-up, more important, more substantial, the tug-of-war over my pencil forgotten. I had gained a new status. And this emotional boost into the stratosphere was accomplished by the simplest of means: I had acquired a new object. And it was free. No drug would ever reproduce the rush I felt as my concept of myself and the world tilted.

On subsequent shopping expeditions down the back alleys I never found anything as great as the binder and paper, but sometimes I found stuff for my little brother. At two, he would play with just about anything. I enjoyed his delight, and finding free stuff meant saving my allowance. I now suspect my kid-sized version of dumpster-diving sparked my career as a bargain shopper.

Once I found a scarf—a sophisticated, almost sheer, leopard-spotted scarf. It spoke of glamour, beauty, and fashion, with just an edge of wildness. It was a scarf worn by elegant and capable women on television. It was perfect for my mother, who set off for work each morning with her matching high heels and handbag.

Maybe the scarf wasn't even supposed to have been thrown out, but there it was, dangling from a garbage can a few blocks away from home. (In the space of a few weeks, I had increased my territory substantially.) My mother would love this scarf, I thought, but I had no idea how I would explain the acquisition of such a treasure. I didn't have that kind of money. I had finally revealed the binder to her, as it was too difficult trying to write in it without being found out. Even that was hard, as I'd had to commit what I hoped was a venial sin by lying that a friend's older sister had given me the stuff. I knew that wouldn't work again with a scarf. And I still felt a bit singed around the edges from the lie. For a week I had imagined everyone thought I smelled like a campfire. And while I knew what the wrath of God entailed, I was absolutely sure that the wrath of my mother was worse.

I decided to come clean. I took the scarf home, and when my mother got home from work, I presented it to her. She was astonished, and then asked where I got it. I told her. To my bafflement, she burst into gales of laughter, nearly hiccupping herself into a coma while trying to catch her breath.

When she regained control, she announced that my garbage-looting days were over. Nice girls didn't do such things. And there could be dangerous things in the garbage. Like what, I wanted to know, but she wouldn't tell me. These events happened decades ago—I'm sure my mother was worried I'd cut myself on a tin can or broken bottle, not get jabbed by some hypodermic needle. Garbage was safer then, but not safe enough for my mother's daughter to play in it.

But what sticks indelibly in my mind is that my mother carefully washed and ironed the scarf and wore it faithfully, even proudly, a splash of jungle against her ever-so-fashionable green wool coat with the fur around the sleeves. She would fling one end over her shoulder as she headed out the door in the morning, as if to announce her formidable presence in the universe.

Scavenging no longer an option, I had to find another way to satisfy the desire for acquisition now flowing through my veins. Little did I know that I was turning into a good little twentieth-century consumer. According to Lauren Langman, an academic who studies human development:

In the contemporary world, the signifying and celebrating edifice of consumer culture has become the shopping mall which exists in [a] pseudo-democratic twilight zone between reality and a commercially produced fantasy world of commodified goods, images, and leisure activities that gratify transformed desire and provide packaged self-images to a distinctive form of subjectivity. (40)

Langman's thesis certainly helps to explain not only the label consciousness of shoppers but also the desire of many shoppers to become apparent walking billboards for name-brand products. How much difference, if any, is there between my girlish desire for white go-go boots and the current stampede to wear T-shirts emblazoned with "Roots" or "Nike"?

I prefer to think the difference is significant. I could be wrong, in which case, Langman's argument is unassailable. But another academic offers me some hope. In an article in *Vogue* titled "The Professor Wore Prada," Elaine Showalter, professor of English at Princeton and recently president of the Modern Language Association, comments on her love of fashion and shopping. She does so in a humorous way, defending her intellectualism, femininity, and feminism. As she says, "For years I have been trying to make the life of the mind coexist with the day at the mall, and to sneak the *femme* back into feminist" (80). Showalter delineates the various ways female academics (herself included) have dressed in an effort to be taken seriously, and ends her essay by saying, "if you want to deconstruct my feminist criticism, go right ahead. But you'd better not sneer at my angel backpack or

step on my blue suede shoes. I've paid my dues dressing 'feminist,' and now I'm going to wear what I like" (92). Showalter's essay is full of the pleasure one can gain from shopping, both the activity of looking and actual purchase. Throughout history and likely before, human beings have been drawn to objects of beauty (although certainly the concepts of beauty change).

The acquisition of objects, beautiful or otherwise, is usually an economic transaction. As a child prevented from plundering garbage bins, I needed a new way to get the stuff I wanted. So from time and deceit as currency, I turned to the more usual one: money. Getting that required work. My first job was ironing for my mother. I had seen a T-shirt in Sears, and my mother refused to buy it for me because, as she said, "You don't need it." It's no wonder that nowadays when I buy yet another object I don't need I think of King Lear's "Oh, reason not the need." The other object that captured my fancy was a particular lava lamp. I loved that lava lamp, but it was out of the realm of financial possibility. And my mother was right about the T-shirt. I didn't need it. I wore a uniform to school, and I had sufficient play clothes. Incessant pestering of my mother resulted in the ironing agreement. I ironed like a demon, encouraging my beleaguered mother to change clothes frequently so I could have something to iron. Eventually I saved enough to buy the T-shirt, and I wore it to shreds. It was the first thing I bought for myself with my own money, and I remember it in every detail. Still. It had short white sleeves, a white back, and a front in four coloured squares of red, yellow, blue, and green. If I had had white go-go boots to match, life would have achieved its pinnacle. (Elaine Showalter, by the way, wore white go-go boots to her Ph.D. defence.)

Since those very early days, my shopping has expanded in terms of money, objects, and range. Like many middle-class Canadians, I have more material goods than some small nations, and I am constantly acquiring more. What is interesting is that none of us needs all these things, but lemming-like we hurl ourselves at the nearest mall, which has acquired the status of a cathedral for some. Or else we seek out independent and unique shops in downtowns and other shopping areas. We go to outlets and discount centres. We are the consumer society of which much has been written. Thorstein Veblen's *The Theory of the Leisure Class* (1934) [originally published 1899], Christopher Lasch's *The Culture of Narcissism* (1979), and Hilary Radner's *Shopping Around: Feminine Culture and the Pursuit of Pleasure* (1995) are just three of the many works written to explore humans' need to shop even when we are way beyond buying what is necessary for our survival. Veblen's term "conspicuous consumption" indicates that the purchase of many unnecessary items is a performance. It's interesting to imagine what the performance means. If we examine advertising, which certainly fuels consumer desire, we see that Langman's view of buying an identity is accurate. To wear a certain brand (a "Roots" or "Nike" T-shirt is infinitely more desirable to certain groups than, say, a "K-Mart" T-shirt) or to drive a certain car or to drink a certain beer is presumably a statement of who we are. Or is it?

In his essay "The Individual, Consumption Cultures and the Fate of Community," Rob Shields attends to the performative aspect of purchasing and gives consumers some credit: "Many consumers are now ironic, knowing shoppers, conscious of the inequalities of exchange and the arbitrary nature of exchange value. As social actors, they attempt to consume the symbolic values of objects and the mall environment while avoiding the inequalities of exchange" (100). Shields's essay notes that public spaces have changed and that the mall serves as a gathering place. Thus, the activity of shopping (whether or not a purchase is made) plays a significant social

role. Shields argues: "It is necessary to recognize that consumption itself is partly determined by the non-rational, cultural element of society. Shopping is not just a functional activity. Consumption has become a communal activity, even a form of solidarity" (110). It appears to me that shopping plays a number of roles, and one of these is certainly a communal one, as Shields argues. But it can also be said that in addition to having a connective importance, shopping—and more specifically the purchased goods—can fulfill people's desires both to join a group and to differentiate themselves from one another. For example, clothing choices are laden with meaning, even if the message is inaccurate.

Shoppers, as Shields notes, are becoming more sophisticated and particular, if the growth in thrift stores is any indication. A CBC newscast in July 1998 noted that the thrift store business is so popular that charities depending on donations have to be much more competitive. We are still conspicuously consuming, but we want a bargain. Certain sections of the population have always needed to shop for sale goods, but the practice is now losing any stigma it might have had. In fact, getting a bargain, or a "steal," marks one as a consummate shopper. Getting a deal has become a selling point for much commercial activity. I'd like to mention sales, for example. Anyone in western Canada familiar with Woodward's $1.49 Day will remember the thrust and parry of grabbing for the goodies on this once-a-month sale extravaganza. The deals were often extraordinary, and people didn't want to miss this opportunity. Encountering sharp elbows was common. In contrast, the former frenzy of Bay Day has abated now that the sale lasts for ages and has lost any special air. No need to dive in a scrum for the merchandise. No, it's all there in stacks, and then we stand in line to pay. Infrequent sales events such as Boxing Day sales create line-ups hours before the stores open. The sale must appear to be an unusual event or it garners little excitement. I once worked at Harrods, and the annual sale was marked by the sound of crashing crockery as maniacal shoppers stormed the aisles.

But what are we doing when we shop, and why do I refer to it as the oldest profession? The answer is simple. Well, sort of. In *Shopping Around: Feminine Culture and the Pursuit of Pleasure,* Hilary Radner argues the following: "Feminine culture emphasizes a process of investment and return, of negotiation, in which the given articulation of pleasure is always measured against its costs, the inevitable price of an invitation that is never extended freely, never absolutely, the terms of which change from day to day, from place to place" (178). While the terms and values change, it is surely the case that a shopper considers the relative costs (whether in time, effort, or money) and the benefits of the object gained. And these judgments will differ from person to person even within the same socio-economic group.

Shopping is our contemporary form of hunting and gathering. Men may have hunted, and women may have gathered, but both processes resulted in maintaining life. And if the effort expended exceeded what was gained—the result was death. Such an obvious relationship between acquisition (shopping in a sense) and survival is still evident in the world today. But in rich countries like Canada, hunting and gathering is largely done at the mall, and our survival is not in question. In "Dressed to Kill," Don Gillmor makes fun of men at a clothing sale, and he uses the metaphor of the hunt:

The big game is on the suit rack, though. Some of the men simply drape a dozen business suits over one arm and then try to find a little room in which to sort and sniff them, like lions defending their kill. But to bring down a three-button, blue wool crepe 42R Donna Karan (reg. $2,295, now $395) in open country requires keen eyesight, stealth, and a burst of cheetah-like speed.... [Men] are taking home cashmere and silk and cotton that feels like whipped butter. They have hunted well and they are filled with the self-knowledge that comes with risk and death and loss and dramatic savings. (75)

Whether the hunting is done in an exclusive boutique or a thrift store, it's the thrill of the chase that drives shoppers. It could be the lure of low prices, or exclusive merchandise, or the media-created buzz about something completely useless like Cabbage Patch Dolls or Beanie Babies that gets everyone out there, roaming, foraging, stalking, pouncing, occasionally even wrestling another shopper for the item.

Then we bag our prize and take it back to our cave, er, home. I bet those cavepeople never stopped and said to each other, "Listen, honey, I think we have too many acorns or dried fish or fur blankets." I think they were out there scooping up whatever they thought might come in handy for survival.

And so while many of us shop for a variety of reasons, including pleasure, but rarely need (even grocery stores are full of stuff no one needs to survive; in fact, some of that junk probably shortens lives), perhaps somewhere at the heart of the endeavour is a genetic link to our past, when tracking and locating food was essential for survival. Now different needs drive our shopping expeditions. And survival is perceived in ways beyond the merely physical.

NAVIGATING THE CONCEPTS

1. When, and from where, do you think we develop the understanding that possessing objects is pleasurable?

2. Do you believe that the consumer culture is global? Why, or why not?

3. When young people meet "at the mall," is it just a place to gather or an indication that to have fun they need to be in a location where they can spend money? Discuss.

REFERENCES

Gillmor, D. 1998. Dressed to kill: What really happens when men go hunting for deep discounts. *Saturday Night*, 113(5): 75.

Langman, L. 1992. Neon cages: Shopping for subjectivity." In *Lifestyle shopping: The subject of consumption*, ed. R. Shields, 40–82. London: Routledge.

Radner, H. 1995. *Shopping around: Feminine culture and the pursuit of pleasure*. New York: Routledge.

Shields, R. 1992. The individual, consumption cultures and the fate of community. In *Lifestyle shopping: The subject of consumption*, ed. R. Shields, 99–113. London: Routledge.

Showalter, E. 1997. The professor wore Prada. *Vogue* (December): 80, 86, 92.

Chapter 6

The Body Beautiful: Adolescent Girls and Images of Beauty

Beverly J. Matthews

Source: Matthews, Beverly J. (2000). The Body Beautiful: Adolescent Girls and Images of Beauty. In Lori G. Beaman (Ed.), *New Perspectives on Deviance: The Construction of Deviance in Everyday Life* (pp. 208–19). Scarborough: Prentice-Hall.

Beverly J. Matthews investigates the social world of adolescent girls and the role social forces play in defining their physical selves. Her interviews suggest that young women's self-perception is the result of complex interactions between diverse social influences.

INTRODUCTION

The tyranny of appearance norms have long been recognized in the lives of women (see Brownmiller, 1984; Greer, 1970; or Freedman, 1986, for example). Both academic literature and the popular media have examined factors which underlie the intense pressure women experience to adhere to a cultural ideal and the price they pay for either attempting to comply or failing to do so (see Chernin, 1981; Shute, 1992; Hesse-Biber, 1996; Bordo, 1993). While we are aware of the problem among older teenagers and adult women, recent studies indicate that even girls in early adolescence are prone to eating problems and a preoccupation with food (Pipher, 1996; Brumberg, 1997). Some of the literature in this area focuses on media images and unhealthy portrayals of beauty and the ways in which women are influenced by such portrayals (Wolf, 1991). While this has been a fruitful line of inquiry, it is incomplete. It implies that women uncritically, or helplessly, follow a cultural ideal, simply because it is prescribed by society. The findings of this research study into the social

world of adolescent girls reveal that straining to conform to the "ideal look" is not always an end in itself, that it is often a purposeful act designed to achieve social goals.

Young women are surrounded by images which define attractiveness as a very particular, thin, "perfect" ideal. While many strive to achieve this goal, they do not all do so out of blind conformity, or simply because they have negative images of themselves. The problem is more complex: many girls use appearance as a means for achieving social status and power; they conform to avoid the costs associated with deviating from the ideal. They experience the gender system in a unique way, because of their stage in life, which compounds the pressures all women experience around appearance; however, these girls are not all misguided individuals passively following a societal definition of beauty. Just like older women, adolescents are working to negotiate and achieve their individual goals within a micro and macro gender structure. They are actively finding their location within the peer arena and their relationships with food and appearance

3 — levels

play a key role in this endeavor. In this research, in-depth interviews with adolescent women reveal much about the adolescent world and the importance of appearance norms within it.

EXAMINING THE MULTILEVEL GENDER SYSTEM AND THE SOCIAL WORLD OF ADOLESCENT GIRLS

When studying the social world it is essential to recognize the interplay between the individual and the social context. Although women have the freedom to make their own choices, these choices are constrained by the socially created structures which surround them. Sociologists have long recognized the existence of social structures and have worked to explain their relation to individuals: "social structures create social persons who (re)create social structures who create social persons who (re)create...ad infinitum" (Stryker, 1980: 53). They also recognize that such structures operate on two levels. "[W]e inhabit the *micro-world* of our immediate experience with others in face-to-face relations. Beyond that, with varying degrees of significance and continuity, we inhabit a *macro-world* consisting of much larger structures.... Both worlds are essential to our experience of society" (Berger & Berger, 1975: 8). Sociologists and feminists have studied the creation of the social person and the role that gender plays in that development. They have also examined the gendered dimensions of social structures and their impact upon members of the society (see Risman & Schwartz, 1989; Smith, 1987; Bem, 1993).

Through my research into gender and social behaviour (Matthews & Beaujot, 1997; Matthews, 1997), it has become clear that the gender system can be more fully understood by acknowledging that it operates on several levels at one time. And that analyses are more complete when three levels are integrated into the explanatory framework. This tri-level model of the gender system includes the individual gender role orientation, a micro structure, and a macro structure. On the most basic level, men and women have individual gender role orientations, which they have developed through socialization and interaction over the course of their lives. These orientations consist of their beliefs about the appropriate roles for women and men and serve as guidelines for choices regarding presentation of self, relationships, and activities, as well as attitudes and values. However, these gender role orientations alone do not determine behaviour. Women's choices about how to behave, and how to present themselves, are also influenced by the micro level gender structure, where they encounter others in daily interaction and negotiate their roles. Conforming to expectations is an integral part of interaction; people play roles in order to facilitate communication and joint action. They are also influenced by the macro level gender structure: the societal context which provides a landscape within which people act out their choices. It is my contention that the combination of the three levels and the way in which they interact, sometimes complementary and sometimes contradictory, can advance our understanding of the gender system and of young women's actions concerning weight and appearance.

For women making decisions about weight, food, and dieting, it is apparent that all three levels of the gender system influence their choices and behaviour. The macro structure, which has evolved over time, emphasizes the importance of appearance for women. While women's accomplishments are many, they continue to be judged by their appearance. It provides media images of "perfect bodies" and advertising which constantly criticizes and undermines women with appearance "flaws" (i.e., extra pounds, "problem" skin, gray hair). On the micro level, appearance is also salient. Because slenderness is the norm, there is some pressure in daily interaction to achieve it. Friends and family often encourage, and occasionally coerce, women into dieting and following the cultural ideal. Choosing not to diet, not following the ideal, seems to imply either slovenliness—"she's really let herself go"—or a personal statement about her unwillingness to conform. It is rarely accepted as a woman choosing to be comfortable with herself as she is. Thus interaction with others is influenced by their interpretation of her appearance. At the individual level, women's understanding of themselves is filtered through the existing social structures. Women know that they may be afforded more attention and respect if they follow the ideal;[1] they may also have internalized the societal standards throughout their lives. Thus, not "measuring up" to the ideal may cause personal anguish.

Women's decisions to diet are bound up with several levels of gender and must be considered in this light. The three levels of gender may be complementary or contradictory. That is, while people all live in a social world that appears to appreciate and promote only one body type, individual micro structures or individual gender role orientations may be in agreement or at odds with this standard. Women may be surrounded by people who disregard the cultural ideal and thus feel less pressure to conform in their interactions. They may have developed a critical stance to the societal ideal and experience no internal misgivings about weight and appearance. Or they may experience pressure on all three levels to follow the ideal. Clearly, in order to understand women's relationships to food and diet it is insufficient to focus on only one level. Women's social contexts and their individual gender role orientations are unique and must be considered as such.

Adolescence compounds the imperatives of the gender system. While all people feel the effects of the gender systems in which they operate, adolescents face unique challenges; adolescence is (1) a time of identity construction and (2) a time to find one's own location in the social world. They must navigate their ways through the layers of gender, making their choices and moderating their behaviours based on the context in which they live. And because individuals in this age group do not necessarily have a strong gender role orientation guiding their choices and actions, they are more vulnerable to the influences of the micro and macro gender structures. Also, because they have moved into a new "adolescent world," they can no longer rely on the "borrowed identity" from their childhood or the social status of their families. They must construct a unique self and establish their own position within the social world. This new self will largely be based on measures of status determined by peer groups and the broader youth culture.

Scholars and clinicians have developed a body of literature which discusses adolescent experience in great detail. We can trace study in this area back to Erikson's theory of stages. He argued that adolescence is a time of identity construction (Erikson, 1956). Until adolescence, identity is acquired through the family; individuals are socialized to see themselves much as the family sees them. In childhood, attitudes, values, and definitions are accepted uncritically. During adolescence, the earlier "borrowed" identity is questioned. Individuals ask themselves whether they agree with what they have been told, what they have learned. While reconstructing themselves, adolescents rely less on families (who played an important role in defining their childhood selves) and, in an effort to become independent and autonomous, turn towards their peers and societal standards. Part of this identity construction is, of course, the gender role orientation. Not just "who am I?" but "who am I as a woman?" "What does this involve?" "How should I act? think?" By the time these girls become adults, most have developed a sense of who they are as women. Therefore, when they are confronted with external stressors—for example, pressure from conflicts among individual, micro, and macro levels of the gender system—they have an internal sense of self that provides direction, which is lacking during early adolescence.

During adolescence, peers play a critical role. They are all experiencing similar changes, though at varying paces. By observing each other, they gain a sense of what is considered desirable and appropriate. While they observe, they are painfully aware that they are also being observed. The "imaginary audience" hypothesis suggests that adolescents are so sensitive to the evaluation/judgement of others that they perceive an audience, and behave accordingly, even when they are not being observed (Elkind & Bowen, 1979). As each adolescent is looking at others she is gathering the "raw resources" to shape her "self." Seltzer calls this the "comparative act" (Seltzer, 1989). Through the evaluation and critique and assessment of peers as well as imitation and experimentation, an adolescent gains the materials necessary to construct her "self." The knowledge that one is both judging and being judged makes adolescents highly conscious of their social desirability. Seltzer describes the adolescent world as the "peer arena," the micro structure where identity is constructed.

A further aspect of adolescence is finding one's location; that is, answering the question "where do I fit in?" This clearly is associated with the "social desirability" mentioned above. Just as the adult society is stratified—around class, race, and gender, for example—and one gains social power through position based on resources, the adolescent world is also hierarchical and also involves social power. The young person must find his or her place in this social structure. The social class from which the adolescent has come is still prevalent, but it is not sufficient to define who has power in the peer arena, because it is based on the parent's resources and not on the adolescent's own characteristics. So the hierarchy among adolescents is based largely on personal resources. Because a significant part of constructing the self at this point is coming to understand gender role orientation and sexuality, the adolescent hierarchy is based in large part on one's presentation of manhood or womanhood. That is to say, the more "manly" men, displaying evidence of the strength, courage, and competence stereotypically expected of males, are considered more desirable than others. And among women, appearance and desirability are key attributes.

The powerful effect of the peer arena determines where any individual will fit in the social world. And in this arena, status is linked to appearance. Do you look the part? Or, as important, are you "playing" the part by dieting and making appearance a key part of your conversations and social world? Drawing messages from the larger macro gender structure, peers set the rules for "fitting in." And the unstable aspect of individual adolescents' own sense of self and their incomplete individual gender role orientation makes withstanding the pressure to conform difficult. By later adolescence, the tendency to conform is reduced (Berndt, 1979); individuals are more sure of themselves, have established their identities and gender role orientations, and may be, therefore, less vulnerable to the pressures of the micro and macro structures.

THIS STUDY

We undertook a qualitative research project in the summer of 1997 in Southern Alberta entitled "Growing Up Female." Through 25 depth interviews and focus groups with 6 girls, we explored adolescents' own perceptions of the challenges they face and how they navigate through the peer arena. The analysis was based on the principles of grounded theory (Glaser & Strauss, 1967; Strauss, 1987). That is, rather than trying to verify a specific hypothesis, we attempted to see their world as adolescents see it and discover how the three levels of the sex/gender system interact in their lives. From listening to the girls, reviewing the tapes, and examining transcripts, patterns emerged. The patterns were then explored more fully in subsequent interviews. The goal was not to quantify, but rather to get a sense of the importance of conforming to appearance norms within the adolescent social hierarchy.

The study began with a "typical" sample of young women chosen to represent different ages, social classes, and family arrangements. We quickly came to recognize that one's location in the hierarchy—insider, outsider, popular, outcast, etc.—was a critical variable and that the sample needed to reflect this diversity as well. (The girls' location in the hierarchy was also seen to influence them in terms of vulnerability to outside pressure and suggestion, but not in the ways one might predict.) The girls interviewed were from junior high, high school (one of whom attended an all girl's high school), post-secondary institutions, and "drop outs" (many of whom had moved to alternative schools).

The importance of qualitative studies is that they can answer the question "why?" While quantitative studies can measure patterns to determine how many suffer from eating disorders and/or depression, and can assess the correlation [among] class, race, family and behaviour numerically, one must look deeper to understand the underlying causal connection between these behaviours and the social factors in the girls' lives. One must try to understand their social world as they define and live it. It is vital for the researchers to avoid directing the discussions so as not to artificially focus on "constraints." Questions about what boys do to them or what society does to them denies the agency of the young women. Instead, this study asked the girls what they

did to get along in their world. What are the rules in their world? Where did the rules come from?

Once we had collected information from all of the respondents, we identified patterns and came to understand how fully social hierarchy, and therefore social power, influenced their lives and how salient appearance is within that hierarchy. The best way to convey these findings is through case studies. In the following section, I will present the cases of women located in each of the various positions in the adolescent hierarchy, allowing each to speak about where they fit and how they came to hold that position. (Obviously, names have been changed but other details are unaltered.)

FINDINGS

Not surprisingly, the study indicates that for adolescent girls, appearance is salient and notions about what is a desirable appearance are influenced by cultural norms: the macro structure provides powerful images and pressures. However, the girls made it clear that they were not all victims blindly following a goal set by the larger society without thought. And not all were dissatisfied with their appearances—not even all of those who spent a considerable amount of time and energy complaining about themselves and dieting. As they explained, appearance equals status. "Life would be easier if you looked like that [like the women on *Melrose Place*] because people give you an easier time if you are pretty. If more guys like you, the girls give you an easier time,...I don't think it should be that way, but I think society puts a lot of importance on your looks and size." And dieting and "fat" talk are also linked to status. The girls say they hate their bodies, or themselves, but when they discuss it more fully they often acknowledge that these statements are a means of fitting in.[2] They see that being part of the group means "obsessing" about their bodies, and group membership leads to success and social power. Those who fit the appearance criteria belong to the elite group, have power, know they have it, and enjoy wielding it. They reinforce their own position by deliberately making others feel inadequate. In fact, the power that they gain from their elite status is the power to exclude others. Their actions enhance their own positions while making appearance more salient for all girls (that is, making the micro structure extremely appearance-based).

The findings indicate that the most difficult time for young women was during junior high school, sooner than most people would like to believe is the case. Why should twelve-year-olds be caught up in issues about body and appearance? Are they trying to attract boys or men? Not really. They perceive other girls as both their audience and their harshest critics. Therefore, their preoccupation with weight and body is not about being desirable to the boys so much as gaining acceptance within the hierarchy. Boys can certainly exacerbate the pressure through name-calling and harassment, but this is only one part of the larger issue: finding your place in the social world is based on playing a role and looking the part. Even girls who attended "all girl schools" were subject to appearance pressures.

By later adolescence, women have already begun to develop a stronger sense of self and [have] grown less vulnerable to the group's definition of who they are. By the end of high school, most girls had worked through much of their confusion and vulnerability. While they continued to talk about dieting and eating, about shape and size, this was much less about really planning to change their physical appearance than about "playing the game." Those who wanted to fit into the social hierarchy recognized that playing by these rules was necessary. However, by this stage, many girls had found their own groups of friends and set their own goals and challenges; they felt freer [to] express their own gender

role orientations rather than following the group's definition of "woman."[3]

But in early adolescence, in junior high, most girls are just beginning the process of becoming independent and autonomous. There is a shift from living with the self-image that your parents and family defined for you to finding your "own" self with the assistance of peers. The peers' opinions count for a great deal because they form the social world in which this new self must establish herself. This is for most girls the period of most intense pressure to be autonomous and independent, greatest confusion about self, and therefore greatest vulnerability. And in this setting, young adolescent girls are becoming themselves, adults, and "women."

As indicated, most of the girls had worked through and beyond this understanding that their self worth and status as women was tied to appearance by the time they reached the end of high school. But some girls did not get past this stage as easily as others. They continued to measure themselves by their appearance.

The Elite Group

The first group of those who had trouble moving beyond the adolescent definitions of desirability is made up of girls who were popular in junior high and high school; they were at the top of the social hierarchy. They seemed to be the winners who enjoyed the power that accompanied their status. They basked in the attention of all: other girls, boys, and most teachers. Two of the respondents talked about their experiences at the top of this hierarchy.

Jillian said that she is so good at being part of the group that she has no very clear sense of who she is. While in high school she knew exactly where she belonged. "I was definitely one of the popular ones." She said bluntly, "I consider myself to be pretty, that might have something to do with it [her popularity]. All my friends were popular." In fact, she revelled in the attention she received. She was teased by the boys about her looks ("I have big boobs") but found this flattering rather than intimidating or threatening. Being a part of the elite group was not a problem while in the insulated world of the high school, but she feels completely lost since leaving school. She found that the attributes that had given her power were no longer as valuable and she had no sense of direction. Jillian had allowed herself to be defined by the micro structure of her peer group and did not develop her own identity. She adopted the norms of the group without truly developing her own gender role orientation. Now that she has moved into a new environment, and without the guidance of her own individual gender role orientation, she feels aimless. "Where I stand now I'm not going anywhere. I'm not moving forward, I'm not moving backward, I'm just not going anywhere."

Reva was also very popular in high school, but [she] recognized even at the time that this popularity had no solid foundation. She tried to hang on to status and popularity via appearance but was constantly concerned about it. "I was insecure but I don't know if other people knew it." She was unsure of her "self" and her true desirability. She recognized that popularity in high school was all about "material things, the way things look, everything on the outside." And she knew that she and her friends maintained their position by belittling others: "I think we were back stabbers and snobby, pretty snobby." But at the time this seemed reasonable. Having a boyfriend was an affirmation of Reva's status and her desirability. When she and her boyfriend broke up, she believed that she need only lose weight to regain her social position. "Actually, there were a couple of us that wanted to like, starve ourselves, try to lose weight so we just wouldn't eat." As a result, she developed an eating disorder. Eventually, she went into counselling and slowly has come to recognize the damage that her bulimia caused. But at the time, being thin made sense and gaining even a little bit of weight "really stressed me out."

Being in the elite group is no guarantee of success or well-being. While it worked for some in the short-term because they really did attain power—the power to exclude others—it did not bring long-term contentment. Upon graduation, the micro structure which had given girls power and a valued position was disbanded, leaving them directionless. Even within high school, all was not well. While this group appeared to dictate what was the appropriate appearance around the school, this was often a reflection of media images. "Popular" respondents mentioned TV shows and magazines that influenced their "style." And maintaining their social position involved a constant effort to keep up with the cultural ideal. For some this seemed easy, but for others like Reva, it was both difficult and undermining.

The "Wannabes"

While this seems like a pejorative term, it's how these girls describe themselves. They believe they will be in the most popular group if they just make a few changes; as a result, they spend their adolescent years struggling to reach the top of the pyramid. Kim is a member of this group. She says she understands the hierarchy and knows how it works: "The pressure increases as you move towards the popular group. You always have to prove yourself—based on how you look." She also knows that she is very close to the top and believes she could get there if she could just play the game right. And despite acknowledging that being popular doesn't always allow you to be a good person—"Popular people are jerks, they don't care about others, are very competitive, and treat people badly"—this doesn't stop her from wanting to be one of them. She works hard to win favour, to accept the rules. She believes that she could be popular if she was just a bit thinner. People in her group tend to diet for real, thinking they are just ten pounds away from having social power. She said the whole group began smoking on the same day when one person found out that it suppressed appetite. "We always talked about weight and how to lose it—drink Slimfast, take Dexatrim." Expending so much energy on reaching the top of the social hierarchy means that Kim spends little time trying to find her own direction or "self." She just knows she isn't happy. She feels "insecure, always beating myself up" and says "trying to fit in is limiting." She does not have a strong sense of self and therefore accepts the peer arena as the ultimate arbiter. The unquestioning acceptance of the peer arena and of the validity of the social hierarchy leaves people in this group, like those in the group "above" them on the popularity scale, vulnerable to a gender system which focuses on appearance. Their gender role orientation reflects this desire to achieve the ideal appearance: being a woman means looking the part.

Life in the Middle

The girls on the next level "down" on the hierarchical scale are the least vulnerable. While girls in this group still cope with pressure in the peer arena, they know they will never be at the top. As a result, they tend to examine it more critically, asking whether increased popularity is worth achieving. The answer is usually no. These girls form their own rules, have outside interests, and define "self" by a standard other than that of the hierarchy. One result of this alternate definition of self is that appearance is less salient than ability.

The individuals in this group often have outside interests—music, sports, religion, or the guiding movement, for example—that seem to help them find a self worth regardless

of their status at school. And at school they either are not picked on or don't let it bother them because they know that it isn't real. They construct their "self" based on what they are, not on what someone tells them they should be. Jana is never going to be at the top of the social hierarchy; she knows it and doesn't care. Her parents are of different races and she perceives that being biracial makes her "different." But it isn't a problem for her, she says, she just has to find her own way. When listening to Jana, she convinces you that this makes her stronger. She sees other "kids who try their hardest to be like another person and follow what they do" but distinguishes herself. She says unequivocally, "I am who I am." Racial slurs don't bother her, she makes a joke of it. When her best friend goes on and on about being fat, Jana believes "she does it just for attention." She isn't affected by media images either: "I'm not saying they're not beautiful but I'm saying that you don't know what's under all that make-up, that's four hours of make-up put on. I could look like that too." In essence, Jana isn't caught up in the gender system because she is not trying to prove herself in the peer arena. She has a strong sense of self and does not accept the salience of appearance. However, she also notes that "I've never gotten fat so it has never been an issue for me." She can be truly comfortable with herself even when others in her world are striving to attain an ideal.

Una is also in this middle group. She is involved in both music and sports and spends much of her time with these activities. She says, "there's no pressure in my group. We don't have to spend time on make-up and hair." They don't want to be skinny partly because "the coach encourages us to stay fit." "I just don't have the time or the money to keep up." But she does acknowledge that it was harder to "be yourself" in junior high: "People were starting to form groups and you were left out if you didn't follow the group." But her close circle of friends didn't value the "popular" behaviours and didn't try to look the part.

Freedom from the tyranny of the gender system—which offers an almost impossible beauty standard—seems much more attainable for these young women. Because they do not have an opportunity to join the elite group, and because they have other qualities which make them strong, they are less vulnerable to its dictates. Not being part of the "in" crowd enables them to critique the hierarchy and its norms. In essence, these girls have developed gender role orientations which conflict with the macro structure and most of them have found a group of peers who also reject the salience of appearance.

On The Fringe

The next group—the "lowest" on the scale I have identified—is that of individuals who define themselves as "outsiders." They believe they are excluded because of their size and shape (though some of them have other characteristics which also contribute to their exclusion). These girls don't have the ability to break out of the outsider role into which they have been cast. For adolescents in this group, not fitting in really hurts; they feel rejected, ridiculed, isolated. Because they are so far from the norm—often very overweight or dealing with severe acne—they feel that they are suffering at the hands of their peers.

Some do come to hate themselves because they are treated so cruelly. Rachel describes one hurtful experience[:] "I was trying to walk through the crowd when one guy said 'R, you don't belong in this crowd.' There was another girl who told me to f— off. I was watching them I guess. I was pretty shy too. But I think *it* made me shy[.]" The "it" she refers to is being excluding for not looking the "right" way. She feels very alone, even though there are several other girls on the "outside." She now "rejects the image thing" because she

knows she doesn't fit ("I'm big boned like my dad") but she tried really hard in junior high. She really hated herself, even though she believed she was good on the inside, because of the way she was treated, because her body was devalued. In fact, Rachel feels pressure from her family to try harder to fit in—her mom would like her to change her appearance but she says she "just gave up trying."

Terry was also on the outside because of her weight. She had a couple of close friends "but the rest just left me out." Unlike Rachel, though, she "successfully" lost weight and reaped the rewards of following the group standard. She wanted to be small no matter what and simply stopped eating. At first everyone was pleased. She got more attention at school. People noticed her and talked to her. Initially, Terry liked being popular. "I felt better for a while but then came to realize that my life still sucked. Even when I was skinny I wasn't happy." She came to hate being popular because she could see more clearly than most how artificial the distinction was. Terry believes being skinny actually made her feel worse because the "popular Terry" wasn't the "real Terry." Her peers only saw her outside and still didn't recognize her true worth. Her family and few close friends became worried and did not support her dieting. And "I got tired of measuring every mouthful, having everyone watching and measuring every mouthful, so I started eating again." She gained the weight back and is now more comfortable with herself. "A whole new world opened up when I left school." Both Terry and Rachel understood how the social hierarchy worked. They knew how to gain power by following the mandate of the peer group. But they both chose not to. They lost status within the micro structure but grew more comfortable with themselves.

Karla was in a similar situation and it was terribly damaging. She started out in the popular group but "I found you had to stoop quite low to become popular. You had to be willing to be rude to all the other people." She wanted to be friendly to everyone and eventually the popular crowd turned their backs on her. They began to harass her and single her out; most of the insults were based on her appearance. "After a while, when so many people tell you something, you know you start to believe it's true, like you get it from enough people it starts to seem true, so I got enough people telling me I was ugly enough times, it kind of makes you believe it." Eventually she quit school because it became unbearable. She'd like to go back but "it's hard to get started up again if you live in the same place and you stay in the same place because everyone knows your past.... I can't start over again because the people who knew me, knew me as a geek, a freak." She feels better about herself now but doesn't want to face that kind of pressure again.

Examining the fringe group in terms of the three levels of gender, the "hell" for these girls was the micro gender structure of the peer arena; however, the values of the microsystem seemed to be reinforced—though not caused—by the larger macro structure. Our society is far more conscious of racism and sexism than of "lookism," especially as it is manifested in the adolescent world. Rachel and Karla internalized the negative messages directed at them by their peers. And they both came to hate themselves. Fortunately, they also both were able to overcome those feelings and recognize that their value was determined neither by their appearance nor by the critics in the peer arena.

IMPLICATIONS

Why is appearance so salient for adolescent girls? This study reinforces the understanding that at this period in her life, a girl has few measuring sticks and no long list of personal accomplishments. She must seek some means of reassuring herself that she is becoming an adult, a woman, an individual separate from her earlier, family-defined self. The larger macro gender structure of fashion magazines and advertisement sends messages that appearance is an important feature of power and desirability. This notion is adopted by adolescent girls in part because it is a field over which many feel they have some control (however illusory such a perception might be). They think that they can change their bodies, their clothing, their hairstyles. And they recognize that a specific kind of beauty is valued by the society at large. Thus appearance becomes a standard. This means that appearance actually does serve as a means of attaining social acceptability and power within the peer arena. As the study revealed, becoming a woman has less to do with the role one might play and more to do with the body. An interesting—perhaps startling—paradox emerged when we asked the respondents to define "woman." On the one hand, being a woman, they said, does not constrain career choices. They believe women can become anything they want. As available "sexual" roles grow, women are not defined by filling a specific role—for example, wife or mother. And as they perceive that more and more options are available in the work world, no particular job defines "woman." On the other hand, something distinguishes women from men. And that something is appearance. It is the girl's body that makes her a woman. Therefore, being a woman means one should be preoccupied with one's body and making one's body fit the part. None of the girls we spoke to was trying to diet to avoid growing up into womanhood; indeed, they were dieting to *achieve* womanhood, which they have come to accept is characterized by a very particular physical stature.

Young women are not all passive recipients of society's messages about the body. They perceive that they are not victims, that they are not trying to achieve certain appearances because men or boys want them to. Instead, they see themselves as actively involved in struggles with other women. Their female peers are the harshest critics. Among these critics, appearance brings social power, even if it is only the power to exclude others. They want the right body in order to attain social power and to prove themselves as women. Having a "boyfriend" is important in part because it sends a message to the peer arena that one has successfully achieved the requisite look. This becomes part of the measuring stick.

When the three levels of the gender system—the individual, micro, and macro levels—all agree that appearance is salient, the girl who experiences this will strive to attain the beauty standard. She believes that achieving this look will bring her social acceptance and membership into the elite group. If she fails to measure up to the standard, she faces the painful realization that she will be devalued by those with power in the peer arena. However, if she also learns that the imperatives of the peer arena are not absolute, and she is able to develop her own gender role orientation, then appearance loses its salience, and the elite group loses its power over her. If the three levels do not all agree, if girls have developed gender role orientations which do not incorporate the societal beauty ideal, or they belong to micro structures (as adolescents, perhaps a group of friends, sports team, or social club apart from the school-based peer arena) which value ability rather than appearance, then they are less subject to the appearance standards.

While adolescent girls face an exaggerated version of the gender system, all women are subject to the same forces. We must find our way within a societal landscape that valorizes beauty often above ability. And frequently we must do so in micro structures (in the work place and in our homes) which adopt this standard and devalue our actions. Like these adolescent girls, we remain strong if we develop gender role orientations which do not centre around appearance, and if we foster relationships and micro structures which value women for their strength and skill rather than their outward appearance. The results of this study are suggestive—not yet detailed enough or broad enough to be conclusive—but give us some insight into girls' own perceptions of their world and perhaps into the roots of gender role uncertainty that continues for some women into adulthood.

NAVIGATING THE CONCEPTS

1. With reference to the article, describe the social forces that may explain why adolescent girls respond differently to their physical selves than adolescent boys.

2. Do you believe that the importance of physical attractiveness is increasing or decreasing in our society? What evidence can you provide to support your answer?

3. Although Matthews' research explores the social lives of adolescent girls, does her analysis help you describe the students in your sociology class? For example, can you define another set of social groups (such as the "Elites" and "Wannabes") that would describe the men and women in your class?

NOTES

1. Obviously, this is a generalization. An important point of this argument is that individual women—especially adult women—move in microstructures and have developed "selves" that allow them to function effectively in a way inconsistent with the "body beautiful" standards...society.

2. This is not to say that...[none of the] girls...experience[d] genuine pain and self-hatred—their situations will be explored more fully in subsequent sections. It does mean that many girls are not as negative about themselves as it might appear from listening to their conversations among their peers.

3. It is possible that for university women, living in dormitories, food, eating, and weight once again become salient as a new social hierarchy must be

established. While this was not investigated in this study, we are currently interviewing women in residences to see if the pattern re-emerges.

REFERENCES

Bem, S. 1993. *The lenses of gender.* New Haven: Yale University Press.

Berger, P., and B. Berger. 1975. *Sociology: A biographical approach.* New York: Basic Books.

Berndt, T. 1979. Developmental changes in conformity to peers and parents. *Developmental Psychology,* 15: 606–16.

Bordo, S. 1993. *Unbearable weight: Feminism, western culture and the body.* Los Angeles: University of California Press.

Brownmiller, S. 1984. *Femininity.* New York: Linden Press.

Brumberg, J. 1997. *The body project: An intimate history of American girls.* New York: Random House.

Chernin, K. 1981. *The obsession: Reflections on the tyranny of slenderness.* New York: Harper and Row.

Elkind, D., and Bowen. 1979. Imaginary audience behaviour in children and adults. *Developmental Psychology,* 15: 33–44.

Erikson, E. 1956. The problem of ego identity. *Journal of the American Psychoanalytic Association,* 4: 56–121.

Freedman, R. 1986. *Beauty bound.* Lexington, Mass.: D.C. Heath and Company.

Glaser, B., and A. Strauss. 1967. *Am I thin enough yet?: The cult of thinness and the commercialization of identity.* New York: Oxford University Press.

Greer, G. 1970. *The female eunuch.* London: MacGibbon & Kee.

Hesse-Biber, S. 1996. *Am I thin enough yet? The cult of thinness and the commercialization of identity.* New York: Oxford University Press.

Matthews, B. 1997. *The gender system and fertility: An examination of the hidden links.* Population Studies Centre: Working Paper.

Matthews, B., and R. Beaujot. 1997. Gender orientations and fertility strategies. *Canadian Review of Sociology and Anthropology,* 34(4): 415–28.

Pipher, M. 1996. *Reviving Ophelia: Saving the selves of adolescent girls.* New York: Ballantine Books.

Risman, B., and P. Schwartz. 1989. *Gender in intimate relationships: A microstructural approach.* Belmont: Wadsworth Publishing Co.

Seltzer, V. 1989. *The psychosocial worlds of the adolescent: Public and private.* New York: John Wiley and Sons.

Shute, J. 1992. *Life size.* New York: Avon Books.

Smith, D. 1987. *The everyday world as problematic: A feminist sociology.* Toronto: University of Toronto Press.

Strauss, A. 1987. *Qualitative analysis for social scientists.* New York: Cambridge University Press.

Stryker, S. 1980. *Symbolic interactionism: A social structural version.* Menlo Park: Benjamin Cummings Publishing.

Wolf, N. 1991. *The beauty myth.* New York: Morrow Books.

Chapter 7

"Even If I Don't Know What I'm Doing I Can Make It Look Like I Know What I Am Doing": Becoming a Doctor in the 1990s

Brenda L. Beagan

Source: Beagan, Brenda L. (2001). "Even if I don't know what I'm doing I can make it look like I know what I'm doing": Becoming a doctor in the 1990s. *The Canadian Review of Sociology and Anthropology,* 38(3), 275–92. Reprinted by permission of the Canadian Sociology and Anthropology Association.

Brenda L. Beagan's article explores the training of medical students at Canadian universities. It helps us begin to appreciate the unique manner in which doctors are trained and the steps they go through before they can incorporate their new physician identities.

For most medical students, a remarkable and important transformation occurs from the time they enter medical school to the time they leave.... They become immersed in the culture, environment and lifestyle of the school. They slowly lose their initial identity and become redefined by the new situation. Medical students have to look for something to hang on to. And that something is provided: their new identity as 'doctor.'

— Shapiro (1987· 27)

When students enter medical school they are lay people with some science background. When they leave four years later they have become physicians; they have acquired specialized knowledge and taken on a new identity of medical professional. What happens in those four years? What processes of socialization go into the making of a doctor?

Most of what we know about how students come to identify as future-physicians derives from research conducted when students were almost exclusively male, white, middle- or upper-class, young and single—for example, the classics *Boys in White* (Becker, Geer, Strauss, & Hughes, 1961) and *Student Physician* (Merton, Reader, & Kendall, 1957). When women and students of colour were present in this research it was in token numbers. Even when women and non-traditional students were present, as in Sinclair's (1997) recent ethnography, their impact on processes of professional identity formation and the potentially distinct impact of professional socialization on these students have been largely unanalysed. What does becoming a doctor look like in a medical school of the late 1990s, where many students are female, are of diverse racial and cultural backgrounds, are working-class, gay and/or parents?

This study draws on survey and interview data from students and faculty at one Canadian medical school to examine the processes of professional identity formation and how they are experienced by diverse undergraduate medical students in the late 1990s. As the results will show, the processes are remarkably unchanged from the processes documented 40 years ago.

RESEARCH METHODS AND PARTICIPANTS

The research employed three complementary research strategies: A survey of a third-year class (123 students) at one medical school, interviews with 25 students from that class, and interviews with 23 faculty members from the same school.[1] Third-year students were chosen because in a traditional medical curriculum the third year is a key point for students, an important transition as they move out of the classroom to spend the majority of their time working with patients—patients who may or may not call them "doctor," treat them as doctors, and reflect them back to themselves as doctors (cf. Coombs, 1978; Haas & Shaffir, 1987)....

Survey respondents also identified faculty members who they believed were "especially interested in medical education." Twenty-three faculty interviews were conducted. All interviews took 60–90 minutes following a semi-structured interview guide, and were tape-recorded and transcribed. The interview transcripts were coded inductively using broad categories such as "pressures toward conformity," and "conflicts experienced," and using codes such as "language of medicine" derived from the literature. Initial broad codes were later subdivided into narrower codes.

...[T]he students who completed the survey were evenly divided by gender and were heterogeneous in "race"/ethnicity, as well as in self-identified social class background.[2] Twenty students (28%) self-identified as members of "minority groups," all identifying racial or cultural groups. The students interviewed were slightly less heterogeneous in "race"/ethnicity and first language, and were somewhat more likely to be in committed relationships. The purposive sample of faculty members and administrators was predominately male, English-speaking and of European origin—reflective of the school's faculty more generally.

FIRST EXPERIENCES BECOME COMMONPLACE

When identifying how they came to think of themselves as medical students, participants described a process whereby what feels artificial and unnatural initially comes to feel natural simply through repetition. For many students, a series of "first times" were transformative moments.

Denise:[3] I think there are sort of seminal experiences. The first cut in anatomy, the first time you see a patient die, first time you see a treatment that was really aggressive and didn't work.... First few procedures that I conducted myself, first time I realized that I really did have somebody's life in my hands.... It seems like a whole lot of first times. The first time you take a history, the first time you actually hear the murmur. There are a lot of "Ah-ha!" sort of experiences.

Part of the novelty is the experience of being entitled—even required—to violate conventional social norms, touching patients' bodies, inquiring about bodily functions, probing emotional states: "You have to master a sense that you're invading somebody, and to feel like it's all right to do that, to invade their personal space...."

CONSTRUCTING A PROFESSIONAL APPEARANCE

Students are quite explicitly socialized to adopt a professional appearance: "When people started to relax the dress code a letter was sent to everybody's mailbox, commenting that we were not to show up in jeans, and a tie is appropriate for men." Most students, however, do not require such reminders; they have internalized the requisite standards.

Dressing neatly and appropriately is important to convey respect to patients, other medical staff, and the profession. It probably also helps in patients taking students seriously (survey comment).

Asked whether or not they ever worry about their appearance or dress at the hospital, 41% of the survey respondents said they do not, while 59% said they do.

There were no statistically significant differences by gender, class background or "minority" status, yet gendered patterns emerged when students detailed their concerns in an open-ended question. Most of the men satisfied their concerns about professional appearance with a shave and a collared shirt, perhaps adding a tie: "I do make sure that I am dressed appropriately when I see patients i.e. well-groomed, collared shirt (but no tie)." Women, on the other hand, struggled with the complex messages conveyed by their clothing, trying to look well-dressed yet not convey sexual messages. For women, "dressed up" normally means feminine while a professional image is intended to convey competence. Striking a balance at the intersection can be difficult: "Is it professional enough? Competent looking?... I do not want to appear 'sexy' on the job." As one student noted, while both men and women sometimes violate standards of professional dress, men's violations tend to involve being too informal; women's may involve dressing too provocatively, thereby sexualizing a doctor-patient encounter.

CHANGES IN LANGUAGE, THINKING AND COMMUNICATION SKILLS

Acquiring a huge vocabulary of new words and old words with new meanings—what one student called "medical-ese"—is one of the central tasks facing medical students, and one of the major bases for examining them (Sinclair, 1997). Students were well aware of adopting the formal language of medicine.

Dawna: All of a sudden all I can think of is this lingo that people won't understand. My brother told me the other day, "Sometimes I just don't understand what you are talking about anymore." I don't realize it! I'll use technical terms that I didn't think that other people wouldn't know.

The language of medicine is the basis for constructing a new social reality. Even as it allows communication, language constructs "zones of meaning that are linguistically circumscribed" (Berger & Luckmann, 1966: 39). Medical language encapsulates and constructs a worldview wherein reducing a person to body parts, tissues, organs and systems becomes normal, natural, "the only reasonable way to think" (Good & Good, 1993: 98–9). Students described this as learning to pare away "extraneous" information about a patient's life to focus on what is clinically relevant.

Becky: I see how it happens.... The first day of medicine we're just people. We relate by asking everything about a person, just like you'd have a conversation with anybody. And then that sort of changes and you become focussed on the disease...because right now there's just too much. It's overwhelming I'm hoping that as I learn more and become more comfortable with what I know and I can apply it without having to consciously go through every step in my mind, that I'll be able to focus on the *person* again.

In part through the language of medicine students learn a scientific gaze that reduces patients to bodies, allowing them to concentrate on what is medically important— disease, procedures, and techniques (Haas & Shaffir, 1987).

Not surprisingly, students may simultaneously lose the communication abilities they had upon entering medical school.

Dr. W.: Their ability to talk to people becomes corrupted by the educational process. They learn the language of medicine but they give up some of the knowledge that they brought in.... The knowledge of how to listen to somebody, how to be humble, how to hear somebody else's words.... It gets overtaken by the agenda of medical interviewing.

Another faculty member noted that students' communication skills improved significantly during their first term of first year, but "by the end of fourth year they were worse than they had been before medical school."

LEARNING THE HIERARCHY

Key to becoming a medical student is learning to negotiate the complex hierarchy within medicine, with students positioned at the bottom. A few faculty saw this hierarchy as a fine and important tradition facilitating students' learning.

Dr. U.: You're always taught by the person above you. Third-year medical students taught by the fourth-year student.... Fourth-year student depends on the resident to go over his stuff. Resident depends on maybe the senior or the chief resident or the staff person. So they all get this hierarchy which is wonderful for learning because the attendings can't deal with everybody.

Students, and most faculty, were far less accepting of this traditional hierarchy—particularly of students' place in it.

Both faculty and students pointed out the compliance the hierarchical structure inculcates in students, discouraging them from questioning those above them.

Dr. G.: If they don't appear compliant and so on they will get evaluated poorly. And if you get evaluated poorly then you might not get a good residency position. There's that sort of thing over their shoulders all of the time...the fear.

For students being a "good medical student" means not challenging clinicians.

Valerie: If I ever saw something blatantly sexist or racist or wrong I hope that I would say something. But you get so caught up in basically clamming up, shutting up, and just taking it.... Is it going to ruin my career, am I going to end up known as the fink, am I going to not get the [residency] spot that I want because I told?

Though virtually every student described seeing things on the wards that they disagreed with, as long as there was no direct harm to a patient they stayed silent and simply filed away the incident in their collection of "things not to do when I am a doctor."

Other researchers have noted that medical students develop an approach geared to getting along with faculty, pleasing them whatever their demands (Becker et al., 1961: 281; Bloom, 1973: 20; Sinclair, 1997: 29). Some students, however, had *internalized* the norm of not criticizing clinicians, adopting an unspoken "code of silence" not just to appease faculty, but as part of being a good physician. In particular, one should never critique a colleague in front of patients.

Mark: As students we all critique the professors and our attendings.... But I don't think we'd ever do that in front of a patient. It's never been told to us not to. But most of us wouldn't do that. Even if a patient describes something their doctor has prescribed to them or a treatment they've recommended which you know is totally wrong, maybe even harmful, I think most of us, unless it was really harmful, would tend to ignore it and just accept, "This is the doctor and his patient. What happens between them is okay."

These students had developed a sense of alliance with other members of the profession rather than with lay people and patients—a key to professional socialization. Several faculty referred to good medical students as "good team players' (cf. Sinclair, 1997), invoking a notion of belonging.

Dr. M.: That sense of belonging, I think, is a sense of belonging to the profession.... You're part of the process of health care.... I mean, you haven't a lot of the responsibility, but at least you're connected with the team.

For some students, too, the desire to present a united front for patients was expressed as being a good team player: "You have to go along with some things...in front of the patient. For teams it wouldn't be good to have the ranks arguing amongst themselves about the best approach for patient care." To remain good team players, many students, residents and physicians learn to say nothing even when they see colleagues and superiors violating the ethics and standards of the profession; such violations are disregarded as matters of personal style (Light, 1988).

RELATIONSHIP TO PATIENTS

As students are learning their place in the hierarchy within medicine, they are simultaneously learning an appropriate relationship to patients. Within the medical hierarchy students feel powerless at the bottom. Yet in relation to patients even students hold a certain amount of power. In the interviews there were widely diverging views on the degree of professional authority physicians and student-physicians should display.

Some faculty drew a very clear connection between professionalism and the "emotional distancing" Fox documented in medicine in 1957, describing students developing a "hard shell" as a "way of dealing with feelings" to prevent over-identifying with patients. Emotional involvement and over-identification are seen as dangerous; students must strike a balance between empathy and objectivity, learning to overcome or master their emotions (Conrad, 1988; Haas & Shaffir, 1987): "I only become of use if I can create some distance so that I can function."

Dr. E.: Within the professional job that you have to do, one can be very nice to patients but there's a distancing that says you're not their friend, you're their doctor.

In contrast, several faculty members rejected the "emotional distancing" approach to medicine in favour of one based in egalitarian connection.

Dr. V.: I reject that way of dealing with it.... When I'm seeing a patient I have to try to get into understanding what's bothering them. And in fact it's a harder job, I mean I need to understand well enough so I can help them to understand. 'Cause the process of healing is self-understanding.

These faculty members talked about recognizing and levelling power or sharing power. They saw professional distancing as the loss of humanitarianism, the adoption of a position of superiority, aloofness, emphasizing that clinicians need to know their patients as something more than a diagnosis. Women were slightly over-represented among those expressing the egalitarian perspective, but several male clinicians also advocated this position.

PLAYING A ROLE GRADUALLY BECOMES REAL

Along with emotional distancing, Fox (1957) identified "training for uncertainty" as key to medical socialization, including the uncertainty arising from not knowing everything, and not knowing enough. Alongside gathering the knowledge and experience that gradually reduces feelings of uncertainty, students also grow to simply tolerate high levels of uncertainty. At the same time they face routine expectations of certainty—from patients who expect them "to know it all" and faculty who often expect them to know far more than they do and who evaluate the students' competence (Haas & Shaffir, 1987). Students quickly learn it is risky to display lack of certainty; impression management becomes a central feature of clinical learning (Conrad, 1988). Haas and Shaffir (1987: 110) conclude that the process of professionalization involves *above all* the successful adoption of a cloak of competence such that audiences are convinced of the legitimacy of claims to competence.

Robert Coombs argues that medical professional socialization is partly a matter of *playing* the role of doctor, complete with the props of white coat, stethoscope, name tag, and clipboard (1978: 222). The symbols mark medical students off as distinct from lay people and other hospital staff, differentiating between We and They. Students spoke of "taking on a role" that initially made them feel like "total frauds," "impostors."

Erin: It was really role-playing. You were doing all these examinations on these patients which were not going to go into their charts, were not going to ever be read by anybody who was treating the people so it really was just practice. Just play-acting.

They affirmed the importance of the props to successful accomplishment of their role play—even as it enhanced the feeling of artifice: "During third year when we got to put the little white coat on and carry some instruments around the hospital, have a name tag…it definitely felt like role-playing."

Despite feeling fraudulent, the role play allows students to meet a crucial objective: demonstrating to faculty, clinical instructors, nurses and patients that they know something. They quickly learn to at least look competent.

Nancy: Even if I don't know what I'm doing I can make it look like I know what I'm doing…. It was my acting in high school…. I get the trust of the patient….

RESPONSES FROM OTHERS

The more students are treated by others as if they really were doctors the more they feel like doctors (cf. Coombs, 1978). In particular, the response from other hospital personnel and patients can help confirm the student's emerging medical professional identity.

Rina: The more the staff treats you as someone who actually belongs there, that definitely adds to your feeling like you do belong there…. It's like, "Wow! This nurse is paging me and wants to know my opinion on why this patient has no urine output?!"

For many students patients were the single most important source of confirmation for their emerging identity as physicians. With doctors and nurses, students feel they can easily be caught out for what they don't know; with patients they feel fairly certain they can pull off a convincing performance, and they often realize they *do* know more than the average person.

One response from others that has tremendous impact is simply being called doctor by others (Konner, 1987; Shapiro, 1987). Survey results show 68% (*n* = 48) of students had been called doctor at least occasionally by people other than family or friends. All but two fully recalled the first time they were called doctor and how they felt about it. *Not* being called doctor—especially when your peers *are*—can be equally significant. In previous accounts, being white and being male have greatly improved a medical student's chances of being taken for a doctor (Dickstein, 1993; Gamble, 1990; Kirk, 1994; Lenhart, 1993). In this study, although social class background, minority status and first language made no difference, significantly more men than women were *regularly* called doctor and significantly more women had *never* been called doctor.[4]

These data suggest a lingering societal assumption that the doctor is a man. According to the interviews, women medical students and physicians are still often mistaken for nurses. Two of the male students suggested the dominant assumption that a doctor is a man facilitates their establishing rapport with patients and may ease their relationships with those above them in the medical hierarchy: "I've often felt because I fit like a stereotypical white male, that patients might see me as a bit more trustworthy. A bit more what they'd like to see. Who they want to see." Goffman notes that the part of a social performance intended to impress others, which he calls the "front," and which includes clothing, gender, appearance and manner, is predetermined: "When an actor takes on an established social role, usually he finds that a particular front has already been established for it" (1959: 27). In this case it appears that the role doctor, or medical student, still carries an attached assumption of maleness.

SECONDARY SOCIALIZATION: SUBSUMING THE FORMER SELF?

The fact that roles carry with them established expectations heightens the potential for clashes with the identity characteristics of new incumbents. Education processes, inevitably processes of secondary socialization, must always contend with individuals' already formed and persistent selves, selves established through primary socialization. As Berger and Luckmann (1966: 129) note, "Whatever new contents are now to be internalized must somehow be superimposed upon this already present reality."

In his study of how medical students put together identities as spouses, parents, and so on with their developing identities as physicians, Broadhead (1983) stresses the need for individuals to "articulate" their various identities to one another, sorting out convergences and divergences of attitudes, assumptions, activities and perspectives that accompany different subject positions.

In this research, most students indicated that medicine had largely taken over the rest of their lives, diminishing their performance of other responsibilities. While 55% of survey respondents thought they were doing a good job of being a medical student, many thought they were doing a poor to very poor job of being a spouse (26%) or family member (37%);

46% gave themselves failing grades as friends. Fewer than a quarter of respondents thought they were doing a good job of being an informed citizen (18%) or member of their religion, if they had one (17%).

What emerged from most interviews and from the survey was a picture of medical school dominating all other aspects of daily life. Overwhelmingly, students talked about sacrifice.

Lew: You just sacrifice so much. I don't know about people who don't have children, but I value my family more than anything, and, and I cannot—I didn't know you had to sacrifice that much.

Many students had given things up, at least temporarily: musical instruments, art, writing, sports activities, volunteer activities. Some students spoke of putting themselves on hold, taking on new medical-student identities by subsuming former identities.

This sacrifice of self-identity can be quite serious. Several faculty and students suggested students from non-Western, non-Caucasian cultural backgrounds need to assimilate: "Students from other cultures leave behind a lot of their culture in order to succeed. There's a trade-off." Similarly, faculty and students suggested gay and lesbian students frequently become more "closeted" as they proceed through undergraduate training. One clinician said of a lesbian fourth-year student, "Now all of a sudden her hair's cut very business-like and the clothes are different.... She's fitting into medicine. Medicine isn't becoming a component of her, she's becoming a component of the machine." Some faculty suggested women in medicine may need to relinquish their identity as women in order to fit in as physicians.

Dr. Q.: The women who are in those positions are white men. You just have to look at the way they dress. They're wearing power suits often with ties, you know, they're really trying to fit the image. [One of the women here] recently retired and in the elevator in the hospital they talked about her as one of the boys. So that's the perception of the men is that this is not a woman, this is one of the boys.

Women, they argued, become more-or-less men during medical training, "almost hyper-masculine in their interactions," "much more like men in terms of thought processes and interactions with people."

In addition to letting go of gender identity, sexual identity and cultural identity, some students described losing connections to their families and old friends after entering medical school. Often this was due to time constraints and diverging interests, but for some there was also a growing social distance as they moved into a new social status and education level. Lance was disconnecting from his working-class family:

Lance: My family actually were very unsupportive [when I got into medicine]. They didn't even know what I was doing. And there's still this huge gap between them and myself because they don't want to understand what's going on in my world, and their world seems quite simple, simplistic to me.... I see that gap getting larger over time.

Relationships with family, friends from outside of medicine, and anyone else who cannot relate to what students are doing every day are put "on the back burner." Intimate relationships are frequent casualties of medical school.

Thus some students do not or cannot integrate their medical student identities with their former sense of self; rather they let go of parts of themselves, bury them, abandon them, or put them aside, at least for a while. Another option for students who experience incongruities between their medical-student identities and other aspects of themselves is to segregate their lives. Because human beings have the ability to reflect on our own actions, it becomes possible to experience a segment of the self as distinct, to "detach a part of the self and its concomitant reality as relevant only to the role-specific situation in question" (Berger & Luckmann, 1966: 131). In this research 31%

of survey respondents felt they are one person at school and another with friends and family. Perhaps as a consequence, many students maintain quite separate groups of friends, within medicine and outside medicine. Indeed, some faculty stressed the importance of maintaining strong outside connections to make it through medical school without losing part of yourself.[5]

DIFFERENCE AS A BASIS FOR RESISTANCE

Elsewhere I have argued that intentional and unintentional homogenizing influences in medical education neutralize the impact of social differences students bring into medicine (Beagan, 2000). Students come to believe that the social class, "race," ethnicity, gender and sexual orientation of a physician is not—and should not be relevant during physician-patient interactions. Nonetheless, at the same time those social differences can provide a basis for critique of and resistance to aspects of medical professional socialization. A study of medical residents found that those most able to resist socialization pressures minimized contact and interaction with others in medicine; maintained outside relationships that supported an alternative orientation to the program; and entered their programs with a "relatively strong and well-defined orientation" (Shapiro & Jones, 1979: 243). Complete resocialization requires "an intense concentration of all significant interaction within the [new social] group" (Berger & Luckmann, 1966: 145); it is also facilitated by minimal contradictions between the previous social world and the new world.

In this research, age played a clear role in students' ability to resist some aspects of professional socialization. Older students usually had careers before medicine, which helped put medical school in a different perspective. Often medicine was one of a range of possible things they could be doing with their lives—important, but not worth sacrificing for: "There are other things that are more important to me than this, so if at any point this conflicted too much with those things, I would give it up." One student suggested that being older entering medicine meant she had her goals and self-identity more clearly established. Most older students were in committed relationships with non-medical partners and had clear priorities about maintaining non-medical activities and connections, rather than abandoning them under the onslaught of medical school demands.

Robin: I resolved that I wouldn't let my close friends go by the wayside.... My partner is important to me, and I wouldn't always make him take a back seat to what I was doing.... It was like an ultimatum. If this program won't allow me to do those things, which I thought were reasonable things, then I just wasn't willing to do it.

These outside commitments helped them minimize interactions with their new social group.

The strongest basis for resisting professional socialization, however, came from having a working-class or impoverished family background. Most of the working-class students said they are not seen as particularly praiseworthy within their families—if anything they are somewhat suspect. They expressed a sustained anti-elitism that keeps them from fully identifying with other medical professionals. Janis, for example, insisted that she is not "one of Them," that she came from the other side of the tracks and still belongs there, that she could never fit in at medical school, could never be "a proper med student." She feels very uncomfortable with social functions at school and sees herself as utterly different from her classmates and preceptors: "Let's just say I don't share Dr. Smith's interest in yachting in the Caribbean, you know what I mean? (laughing)."

Lance, who spent his summers working on fishing boats to pay for medical school, described most of his classmates as "the pampered elite." He resists the required dress code because it epitomizes elitism.

Lance: A lot of people, the first thing they did when we started seeing patients was throw on a nice pair of shoes and grab the tie and button up. I've never worn a tie. And I never will.... To me, it symbolizes everything that sets the doctor and the patient apart. It's like...'I'm somewhat better than everyone else'.... It gets in the way of good communication. I think you want a level of respect there, but you don't want that B.S. that goes with it.

Although the number of working class students was small, the data showed quite clearly that they tended to be among the least compliant with the processes of secondary socialization encountered in medical school.

Lance: I think I'm very much different from my classmates...more outspoken, definitely.... Other people tend to say the right thing because they're a little afraid of the consequences. I don't care.... It comes from my background, you know, fishing. I've seen these tough, hard guys, think they're pretty something, but they're puking their guts out being seasick. It kind of reduces to the common denominator.

CONCLUSION

What is perhaps most remarkable about these findings is how little has changed since the publication of *Boys in White* (Becker et al., 1961) and *Student Physician* (Merton et al., 1957), despite the passage of 40 years and the influx of a very different student population. The basic processes of socializing new members into the profession of medicine remain remarkably similar, as students encounter new social norms, a new language, new thought processes, and a new world view that will eventually enable them to become full-fledged members of "the team" taking the expected role in the medical hierarchy.

Yet, with the differences in the 1990s student population, there are also some important differences in experiences. The role of medical student continues to carry with it certain expectations of its occupant. At a time when medical students were almost exclusively white, heterosexually identified, upper- or middle-class men, the identity may have "fit" more easily than it does for students who are women, who are from minority racial groups, who identify as gay or lesbian or working-class. If role-playing competence and being reflected back to yourself as "doctor" are as central to medical socialization as Haas and Shaffir (1987) suggest, what does it mean that women students are less likely than their male peers to be called doctor? This research has indicated the presence of a lingering societal assumption that Doctor = Man. Women students struggle to construct a professional appearance that male students find a straightforward accomplishment. Women search for ways to be in relationship with their patients that are unmarked by gender. Despite the fact that they make up half of all medical students in Canada, women's experiences of medical school remain different. In this research, almost half (6 of 14) of the women students interviewed indicated that they do not identify themselves as medical students in casual social settings outside school lest they be seen as putting on airs; none of the male students indicated this. It remains for future research to determine whether gender differences in the "fit" of the physician role make a difference to medical practice.

Interestingly, it is commonly assumed that the source of change in medical education will be the next generation of physicians—in other words, the current crop of medical students and residents (cf. Sinclair, 1997: 323–24). Over and over again I heard the refrain, "Surely the new generation of doctors will do things differently." This was the response to the hierarchy that stifles questioning or dissent through fear; to the inhumane hours expected of student interns and residents; to the need to show deference to superiors; to the need to

pretend competence and confidence; to the need to sacrifice family, friends and outside interests to succeed in medicine. Yet, there have been many new generations of doctors in the past 40 years...with remarkably little change. Why should we expect change now? Students, residents and junior physicians have very little power in the hierarchy to bring about change. Moreover, if they have been well socialized, why would we expect them to facilitate change? As one physician suggested, those who fit in well in medical school, who thrive on the competition and succeed, those are the students who return as physicians to join the faculty of the medical school. The ones who did not fit in, the ones who hated medical school, the ones who barely made it through—they are unlikely to be involved enough in medical education to bring about change.

Medical training has not always been good for patients (see Beagan, 2000). Nor has it been particularly good for medical students in many ways. Yet efforts at change on a structural level seem to have made little overall difference. In fact medical schools have a history of revision and reform without change (Bloom, 1988). Sinclair suggests moves toward entire new educational processes, such as the move to problem-based learning in medical schools throughout North America, simply "realign existing elements in the traditional training" (1997: 325). Furthermore, additions of new and very different components of the curriculum— such as classes on social and cultural aspects of health and illness, communication courses, and courses critiquing the social relations of the medical profession—are often seriously undermined in clinical teaching (Sinclair, 1997). Again, further empirical research should investigate the impact of such curriculum changes on professional socialization.

Finally, this research shows that the same sources of differentiation that mark some students as not quite fitting in also serve as sources of resistance against medical socialization. Older students, gay students who refuse to be closeted, and students who come from poverty or from working-class backgrounds, may be more likely than others to "do medical student" differently. Whether that translates into "doing doctor" differently is a matter for further empirical research. Future research needs to examine how these "different" students, these resisting students, experience residency and professional practice, whether and how they remain in medical practice.

NAVIGATING THE CONCEPTS

1. As a young sociologist, why do you think that the traditional hierarchy in medical schools (i.e., faculty at the top, students at the bottom) is seen by many as a good thing?

2. Which groups of students were most likely to be able to resist the professional socialization? Why would this be the case?

3. Look ahead to Chapter 8. Are there any similarities between the training of medical doctors in Canada and the "rites of passage" as described in Donna Winslow's article on the Canadian Airborne Regiment?

NOTES

1. In order to gain access to the research site, it was agreed that the medical school would remain unnamed. The school in question was in a large Canadian city with a racially and ethnically diverse population. It followed a traditional undergraduate curriculum.

2. At this medical school classes have been 40%–50% female for about 15 years (Association of Canadian Medical Colleges, 1996: 16); the class studied here was 48% female. Using subjective assessment of club photos, over the past 15 years about 30% of each class would be considered "visible minority" students, mainly of Asian and South Asian heritage.

3. All names are pseudonyms.

4. Never been called doctor, 14% of women, 0% of men; occasionally or regularly, 57% of women, 78% of men (Cramer's V = 0.32).

5. All of the gay/lesbian faculty and students described themselves as leading highly segregated lives during medical school.

REFERENCES

Association of Canadian Medical Colleges. 1996. *Canadian medical education statistics,* Vol. 18.

Beagan, B. L. 2000. Neutralizing differences: Producing neutral doctors for (almost) neutral patients. *Social Science & Medicine,* 51(8): 1253–65.

Becker, H. S., B. Geer, A. L. Strauss, and E. C. Hughes. 1961. *Boys in white: Student culture in medical school.* Chicago: University of Chicago Press.

Berger, P. L., and T. Luckmann. 1966. *The social construction of reality: A treatise in the sociology of knowledge.* New York: Doubleday and Co.

Bloom, S. W. 1973. *Power and dissent in the medical school.* New York: The Free Press.

———. 1988. Structure and ideology in medical education: An analysis of resistance to change. *Journal of Health and Social Behavior,* 29: 294–306.

Broadhead, R. 1983. *The private lives and professional identities of medical students.* New Brunswick, N.J.: Transaction.

Conrad, E. 1988. Learning to doctor: Reflections on recent accounts of the medical school years. *Journal of Health and Social Behavior,* 29: 323–32.

Cooley, C. H. 1964. *Human nature and the social order.* New York: Schocken.

Coombs, R. H. 1978. *Mastering medicine.* New York: Free Press.

Dickstein, L. J. 1993. Gender bias in medical education: Twenty vignettes and recommended responses. *Journal of the American Medical Women's Association,* 48(5): 152–62.

Fox, R. C. 1957. Training for uncertainty. In *The student-physician: Introduction studies in the sociology of medical education,* eds. R. K. Merton, G. G. Reader, and E. L. Kendall, 207–44. Cambridge, Mass.: Harvard University Press.

Gamble, V. N. 1990. On becoming a physician: A dream not deferred. In *The black women's health book: Speaking for ourselves,* ed. E. C. White, 52–64. Seattle: Seal Press.

Goffman, E. 1959. *The presentation of self in everyday life.* New York: Doubleday.

Good, B. J., and M. J. DelVecchio Good. 1993. "Learning medicine." The constructing of medical knowledge at Harvard medical school. In *Knowledge, power, and practice: The anthropology of medicine and everyday life,* eds. S. Lindbaum, and M. Lock, 81–107. Berkeley: University of California Press.

Haas, J., and W. Shaffir. 1987. *Becoming doctors: The adoption of a cloak of competence.* Greenwich, Conn.: JAI Press.

Kirk, J. 1994. A feminist analysis of women in medical schools. In *Health, illness, and health care in Canada,* 2nd ed., eds. B. S. Bolaria, and H. D. Dickenson, 158–82. Toronto: Harcourt Brace.

Konner, M. 1987. *Becoming a doctor: A journey of initiation in medical school.* New York: Viking.

Lenhart, S. 1993. Gender discrimination: A health and career development problem for women physicians. *Journal of the American Medical Women's Association,* 48(5): 155–59.

Light, D. W. 1988. Toward a new sociology of medical education. *Journal of Health and Social Behavior,* 29: 307–22.

Mead, G. H. 1934. *Mind, self, and society: From the standpoint of a social behaviorist.* Chicago: University of Chicago Press.

Merton, R. K., G. G. Reader, and P. L. Kendall 1957. *The student physician: Introductory studies in the sociology of medical education.* Cambridge, Mass.: Harvard University Press.

Shapiro, E. C., and A. B. Jones. 1979. Women physicians and the exercise of power and authority in health care. In *Becoming a physician: Development of values and attitudes in medicine,* eds. E. Shapiro, and L. Lowenstein, 237–45. Cambridge: Bellinger.

Shapiro, M. 1987. *Getting doctored: Critical reflections on becoming a physician.* Toronto: Between the Lines.

Sinclair, S. 1997. *Making doctors: An institutional apprenticeship.* New York: Berg.

Chapter 8

Rites of Passage and Group Bonding in the Canadian Airborne

Donna Winslow

Source: Winslow, Donna. (1999). Rites of passage and group bonding in the Canadian Airborne. *Armed Forces and Society,* 25(3):429–57. Copyright © 1999 by Transaction Publishers. Reprinted by permission of the publisher. Minor editorial changes for the sake of clarity have been made with the publisher's permission.

Donna Winslow reviews the often disturbing "rites of passage" that developed in the Canadian Airborne Regiment (CAR) to foster group bonding and confirm member allegiance. In this article you will find analytical techniques that were developed for the study of traditional societies. Winslow uses the techniques to investigate the role of indoctrination courses and initiation rites in the CAR, and in doing so she reveals the fascinating world of Canada's military culture and its extraordinary resocialization techniques.

In January 1995, the Canadian public was shocked by videotaped scenes of humiliating and, at times, disgusting initiation rites in One Commando of the Canadian Airborne Regiment (CAR). It may seem incomprehensible to an outsider that the initiates actually participated voluntarily in these rites. Yet, the importance of the ritual is, in part, a reflection of the nature of unit requirements at this stage. Initiates are strangers to each other and to the Airborne, and the bonding of the initiation pulls them together in a very short period of time. The impact of this extreme form of initiation was noted as early as the 1950s, when Aronson and Mills[1] remarked that an initiate who endures severe hazing is likely to find membership in a group all the more appealing, because in these rituals soldiers prove their readiness to participate in the group regardless of personal cost and thus gain peer group acceptance. As one soldier put it: "I am proud to have done it, it proves to myself and others that as a member of the Canadian Airborne Regiment, I will face and overpass any challenge or tasking given to me."

This article speaks directly to the issue of primary group bonding and non-conventional methods for promoting unit cohesion. Conventional army training intensifies the power of group pressure within its ranks by teaching recruits the need for teamwork. Teamwork or cohesion is one of the ways in which the army can marshal the capabilities of each individual member for the pursuit of a common goal. In the words of one Canadian soldier:

You have a bond. You have a bond that's so thick that it is unbelievable!... It's the pull, it's the team, the work as a team, the team spirit! I don't think that ever leaves a guy. That is exactly what basic training is supposed to do. It's supposed to weed out those who aren't willing to work that way.... And that's the whole motivation, that when somebody says we want you to do something then you'll do it. You'll do it because of the team, for the team, with the team and because the team has the same focus.[2]

In the Airborne, group bonding is particularly intense because the men must depend upon each other each time they jump. A member of the team will make sure that they exit the aircraft in a secure spot and another member of the team will perform the safety check on their equipment. In fact, some authors have likened the jump experience itself to a rite of passage,[3] and the discussion below shows how the Canadian Airborne Regiment's initiation rites parody the exercises of the Airborne Indoctrination Course (Airborne basic training) and the trust necessary for the parachute jump experience. Thus both formal and informal experience promote the dependence of the individual on the group.[4]

The discussion begins with a brief description of the Canadian Airborne Regiment, formal initiation into the regiment—the Airborne Indoctrination Course, and informal initiation rites. One Commando's initiation rites are presented in detail using models developed in anthropology to describe rites of passage in traditional societies, which occur in three stages. The first occurs when the initiates' former identity is stripped away, and they are set apart and made like one another. They are also leveled into a homogeneous group in an effort to suppress individuality, thus encouraging an investment in the group. Initiates then enter the liminal phase of the rite where events become parodies and inversions of real life, and group bonding is reinforced as the initiates undergo similar processes of testing and humiliation. In the final stage, initiates are reincorporated into the group as members of the regiment. After this discussion of One Commando's rites we look at hazing and rites of passage in the other two commando units of the Canadian Airborne Regiment, and conclude with a discussion of the use of extreme initiation in primary group bonding.

Research for this paper was carried out in 1995–1997 during preparation of a study of Airborne culture for the Commission of Inquiry into the Deployment of Canadian Forces to Somalia.[5] Its interpretations and analysis were based on over fifty in-depth interviews, in addition to several focus groups held with military personnel from a variety of ranks and with some of their families. Interviewees were selected randomly, through snowball word of mouth, and interviews were conducted almost exclusively with former Airborne soldiers and military personnel who were deployed to Somalia, although several were carried out with people who had been involved with the Airborne but not deployed to Somalia. The names and identity of my interviewees have been disguised so that they are all referred to in this text as "Canadian Airborne soldier."[6] I have also drawn upon testimony to the Commission of Inquiry itself. The soldiers and officers who testified are identified in the public transcripts and therefore here as well. I also viewed the footage of three videotapes taken during the initiation rites, which were entered in the public record of the Commission of Inquiry, and military police reports of investigations of these videos.

PARATROOPS IN CANADA

The Canadian Airborne Regiment was formed in 1968.[7] The aim was to create a light highly mobile miniformation capable of small unit or light formation operations in virtually any climate or geographic region in the world. It was to specialize in northern operations and maintain a high state of readiness for peacekeeping commitments. From 1968 to 1977, the 900-man CAR was based in Edmonton. According to the regiment's last commanding officer:

The Regiment's trademark for tough, fast-paced and challenging training was firmly established in the initial years. An array of exercises was conducted embracing Canada's West Coast, a variety of locations in the Canadian Arctic, Alaska, and Jamaica as well as schools in unarmed combat, mountaineering and skiing.[8]

In the early 1970s, due to pressure for equal representation, the Airborne acquired a francophone commando unit; thus, the CAR constituted men and officers sent from each of the three Canadian army regiments. The Canadian army has regimental divisions reflecting geographic and linguistic divisions in Canada; for example, western anglophone (PPCLI, Princess Patricia's Canadian Light Infantry), central and eastern anglophone (the RCR, The Royal Canadian Regiment), and central francophone ([R22eR] Royal 22e Régiment, known as the "Van Doos" in English). These territorial divisions define areas of recruitment, training, and residence for regimental members.

In the 1970s all members of the Airborne, even the Van Doos, worked and mingled together in western Canada in a base near the large urban area of Edmonton. The 1970 October crisis was the first test of the Canadian Airborne Regiment in operation and the unit performed a number of internal security missions in Montreal. At that same time CAR was a UN standby unit. They mobilized in thirty-six hours to go to the Middle East but were not sent. However, in 1974 One Commando was sent on a rotation to Cyprus and, after the Turkish invasion, the rest of the unit joined One Commando on tour. This earned the unit two Stars of Courage and six Medals of Bravery, but the price was over thirty casualties and two deaths. In 1976 CAR was again deployed to Montreal, this time as security for the Olympic Games.

In 1977 the unit was moved to a more remote base in Ontario, Canadian Forces Base Petawawa, near the Quebec border. According to Kenward,[9] the last commanding officer of the Airborne regiment, this was a watershed event, during which significant structural changes occurred, including a reduction in strength and loss of independent formation status. Our interviewees also felt there had been a significant change: "When the Airborne moved to Petawawa it really hurt their pride. A lot of people said that they wouldn't go to Petawawa" (Canadian Airborne soldier). Further change was imposed with the creation of three separate exclusive rifle commandos, around the three parent regiments, the RCR, PPCLI, and R22eR. One Airborne Headquarters and Signal Squadron and One Airborne Service Commando were also created....

As a consequence the Airborne reflected the linguistic and geographic divisions in the Canadian army—Two Commando (western anglophone and PPCLI), Three Commando (central and eastern anglophone and RCR), and One Commando (central francophone and R22eR, the "Van Doos"). Soldiers and officers were encouraged to rotate in and out of the unit in order to gain jump and command experience. Some of our interviewees felt that the purpose of having the three commandos was to enable regiments to track their own people and thus control promotion and performance evaluations....

The result of this administrative change was that commando units no longer mixed with each other on a regular basis, living on base in separate barracks and not mingling with each other socially. Particularly, the francophone and anglophones remained separate. Each began to develop its own particular subculture; that is, its own way of doing things and an associated identity. One Commando from the R22eR was French and sported the fleur de lys flag of the Province of Quebec in their barracks. Two Commando, drawn from the PPCLI, began to adopt the rebel flag, and Three Commando from the RCR became known as quiet professionals with the motto of "never pass a fault." What is important for our research is the separateness of the commandos, with little teamwork occurring outside each specific group. Thus each commando began to develop its own practices for indoctrinating new members into the group.

In 1981 and 1986 CAR did two more tours in Cyprus. In 1991 the regiment prepared for a UN deployment in Western Sahara but did not go. A year later the regiment was again downsized to a battalion structure of 665. The commanding officer went from being a full colonel to a lieutenant colonel and the officers commanding—majors—were reduced to company commanders under the authority of the CO:

The command structure of the Canadian Airborne Regiment changed in the summer of 1992. It went from being commanded by a full Colonel, with the powers of a commanding officer, to being downgraded to a subunit commanded by a Lieutenant Colonel. Each of the Commandos, in the summer of 1992, was commanded by a Commanding Officer, a Lieutenant Colonel. In the summer of 1992 they became Officers Commanding. They were Majors and had no powers of punishment. There is a difference between being a Lieutenant Colonel, Commanding Officer or being an Officer Commanding as a Major.[10]

This represented a considerable loss in power and prestige for the unit.

I suspect that the downsizing affected the Airborne. They downsized it by reducing the number of commanding personnel. So does it have an effect? Sure, anytime you take away a position of status and power, the influence you have and the prestige that you carry are similarly reduced. It has to be. And that's because we have an organization built on visible hierarchy. (Canadian Airborne soldier)

Immediately after downsizing began, the CAR went on its last mission to Somalia.[11] Following incidents during the Somalia mission where Somali citizens lost their lives and the release to the media of shocking videos—one filmed in Somalia containing racist behavior among members of Two

Commando and another of initiation/hazing rites in One Commando[12]—the CAR was disbanded in January 1995.

What is important to note from the above discussion is that, by the 1980s, the Airborne was a constituted regiment, made up of members drawn from the three other army regiments in Canada. Although Airborne soldiers were "three time volunteers" (volunteering to be in the military, the army, and then the Airborne) the regiment still needed to meld the men into a fighting unit quickly. In this way the initiation rites served to create bonds among a group of men whose primary loyalties had previously been to their parent regiment, not the Airborne regiment, nor its commando units.

AIRBORNE RITUALS

Culture is a social force that controls patterns of organizational behavior. It shapes members' cognition and perceptions of meanings and realities. It provides affective energy for mobilization and identifies who belongs to the group and who does not.[13] As in the other army regiments, the Airborne had its own distinctive subculture, in which abstract ideals of brotherhood and harmony, love and union, sacrifice and cooperation, loyalty and discipline, were translated and formulated into concrete aspects of style. They were manifested through a variety of symbols and symbolic patterns, and created a definitive and specific pattern of work and life.[14] A soldier or officer joined the Airborne regiment by first applying to take a jump course. After training, the soldier or officer received his jump wings and returned to his parent regiment. He then applied to join the Airborne regiment and, in one of the next posting seasons, his parent regiment sent him to the Airborne. It is important to note that postings in the Airborne were intended to last only a couple of years, but in practice many men, particularly noncommissioned members, requested to stay on in the

Airborne. Thus, in practice, officers tended to rotate in and out of the regiment while the men stayed on.

New members learned Airborne history during the Airborne Indoctrination Course (AIC, one of the regiment's socialization mechanisms). Soldiers were taught a sense of duty and debt to the past, to those that had fought and died in previous wars.

When you hear about Airborne, it's the pride that strikes you. It goes back to World War II, Normandy and all that. They land and they're already upon the enemy and fighting. You never know what's going to happen. It's really something when you get to thinking about it, just jumping out of a plane, you know you've been there. (Canadian Airborne soldier)

The AIC was run either by the regiment or the commandos. When the AIC was run by the regiment, it was a method for ensuring that all newly arriving members were trained to one common standard. Once the commandos began organizing their own AIC, there was some variety in the way the course was run. The AIC was essentially a review of military and parachute skills (weapons handling, shooting, first aid, demolition, unarmed combat, rappelling, etc.). Because of the emphasis on physical fitness in the Airborne, the AIC had fitness tests (swimming, running) and drills that met a higher standard than that of regular army units. The AIC was an opportunity for a soldier and an officer to show that he could be a member of the group—trustworthy....

At the end of the AIC, there would be a ceremony where new members would receive their Airborne coin—an important symbol of group membership. If someone dropped out of the AIC because of an injury, he did not receive his Airborne coin.

In the 1970s, they created a kind of coin with the Airborne Regiment crest on one side. And anytime you were going to some place, anywhere in the world; somebody could challenge you to prove you were in the Airborne you had to show your coin. If you weren't Airborne, you didn't even know the coin

existed. It was a pact, a secret code. If you were in danger you could show the coin and people would help you. It was like a secret code we had for the Airborne. (Canadian Airborne soldier)

For the remainder of his life, an Airborne soldier is subject to being challenged—"coined"—by anyone else who has passed the Airborne Indoctrination Course. If he does not immediately display the coin, which he should be proudly carrying at all times, then he is obligated to buy a round of drinks for all the Airborne members who are there. Thus every member carries his coin with him at all times.

All new members of the regiment (regardless of rank) would be "cammed" on their first jump with the regiment. I was told that camming began in the 1980s, a tradition picked up from the Americans, which entailed covering the person's face, head, and hands (all exposed body parts) with camouflage crayon. The other members of the group carried out the crayoning. It was somewhat painful, although not intolerable; however, it was somewhat annoying since the camouflage crayon was hard to wash off afterward. The camming would take place just before the jump when fellow jumpers who had already passed through the experience would grab the initiate(s). The "war paint" would be worn throughout the jump and could afterward be removed....

Booze and Buddies

We will see below that overconsumption of alcohol was an important part of Airborne initiation rites. It is also important to note that alcohol consumption was generally encouraged in the Airborne.[15] "Oh yeah, the maroon berets are show-offs: 'I'm a real man. A man's man. I wear my wings and my maroon beret.' When you get older things change. But in the beginning it's fights all the time, women, drugs. Lots of booze. Initiations. You drink and drink" (Canadian Airborne soldier).

Alcohol was very present in the initiations seen in the One Commando videos. Drinking is an important aspect of masculine identity. It can also be an important part of group bonding. As Ingraham has noted in his study of life in an American army barracks, "Soldiering and alcohol have been almost synonymous since the invention of armies."[16] Drinking in the Airborne took the form of sanctioned events that are "beer calls," when an officer would invite the men for a drink. In this case alcohol was used to mark a regimental event or to mark the end of a workweek....

Sometimes unsanctioned drinking binges would begin with sanctioned drinking and continue on in the men's quarters after the sanctioned event. In this case, someone would have to drive into town to purchase the cases of beer and bring them back to the base. At other times, the men would continue their drinking on the base in the noncommissioned members' club or in town at the favorite local watering hole. Drinking was at times purely recreational, that is, friends going for a drink. At other times it was affirmational, that is, the focal activity was alcohol consumption itself.[17] This might mean a bunch of men getting "hammered" on base or it might take the form of bar hopping. This form of heavy drinking carried with it the danger of reckless driving and bar fights. In 1985, the Hewson Report[18] on discipline problems in the Airborne regiment found twice the number of assault cases among the Canadian Airborne Regiment than in any other unit and noted that drinking was high in Petawawa. Our interviewees agreed: "I think alcohol is a big problem, a big issue within Canadian Forces Base Petawawa. Drinking and driving were a serious problem on the base" (Canadian Airborne soldier).

The 1993 Military Board of Inquiry into the Airborne's comportment in Somalia suggested a relationship between heavy use of alcohol and incidents of insubordination by members of Two Commando. Private Grant testified to the Military Board of Inquiry those soldiers in Two Commando lost control due to the consumption of alcohol....

In some cases alcohol was used ceremonially to mark an event. These ceremonies brought together a larger group of men than recreational and affirmational drinking, which was an activity restricted to a small group of friends or a clique.[19]...

In the initiation rites described below, the consumption of alcohol is an integral part of the ceremony.

INITIATION RITES

Much has been made of One Commando initiation rites in the Canadian media. Very briefly, the videos were of initiation rites, not hazing. Hazing is technically continual abuse over an initial entry period into an organization, such as the first year of cadet school or the few first weeks or months of membership in a college fraternity. Hazing has a long tradition in military academies. The U.S. Secretary of War[20] Board of Inquiry into hazing at West Point in 1908 noted that the practice had been going on since the 1860s.

Interestingly, a study by Aronson and Mills[21] showed that the more severe the rite of initiation, the greater the bonding to the group. It is not surprising that members of One Commando were unwilling to talk about their initiation to authorities. For example, Corporal Robin, a black initiate, was reluctant to tell Somalia inquiry commissioners anything that might incriminate or cast a bad light on other members of One Commando. Similarly, he testified that he was willing to put up with having "KKK" written on his back in order to be accepted by the group.[22] As Jones[23] points out, severe initiation to a group promotes increased loyalty and devotion to the group.

Hazing and initiation occur around the world and in countless organizations, from medical student groups to football teams to military academies. Many interviewees were

quick to say that the One Commando ceremonies were not so bad and, besides,
"everyone else does it too."...

Soccer team parties at university are a lot worse than
what's on those videos. I don't see what the big problem is. It's pretty bad when the Canadian government has so little spine that we lose a whole
regiment 'cause of a few stupid parties. (Canadian
Airborne soldier)

U.S. forces are known for hazing and
initiation rites such as the infamous Neptune
ceremony during which sailors ("pollywogs")
first crossing the equator are initiated by
veterans known as "seafarers." The pollywogs
dress up, sometimes in drag, eat inedible food,
perform silly or demeaning tasks, and crawl on
the deck covered in repulsive substances.[24]
American Marines perform blood-wing ceremonies where pins are pounded into the
pectoral muscles of the initiates.[25] They also
capture recruits and tie them up with duct tape
and put boot black on their testicles. Army
soldiers posted overseas drink disgusting
concoctions. As suggested, there are countless
stories and many tragic deaths associated with
initiations.[26]

One Commando Initiation

One initiation rite, which we are going to
examine in detail, took place in August 1992 at
Canadian Forces Base Petawawa. We are also
aware of other initiation rites and viewed the
videotape of one that occurred in 1994.
Although soldiers reported to military police
investigators that initiations were a regular
occurrence in One Commando, no one seemed
to be able to recall when the practice started.
The videos and descriptions of these rites show
that they follow the same pattern as the August
1992 rite with small variations. For example, in
addition to the regular games, the initiates in
1994 had to run large metal spikes across a
board, in the process receiving what appears to
be a sizeable electric shock. The closer the

soldier got to one end of the board, the greater
the electric shock. All One Commando
initiations occurred in an isolated patio area
behind One Commando's barracks....

Initiates were thus physically separated from
other members of the Airborne, which is the
first step in an initiation rite. The actual
initiation lasted several hours, although only
one hour is on tape. The new members—
troopers and corporals—of One Commando
were initiated by the corporals and master
corporals (called godfathers) who were initiates
in the previous year's ceremony and who now
directed the activities for the new initiates. The
rituals were activities of the junior ranks, and
no senior NCOs or officers were present during
the entire ceremony. Sometimes officers and
senior NCOs were present at the beginning of
the rite but left shortly after consuming a beer
or two. Thus the "men" were left to themselves.

In August of 1992, about fifteen to twenty
initiates were told by the older members that
there would be a "get-together" at the end of
the day. The initiates each contributed
approximately $20 to buy beer for the party.

What follows is a brief account of the
August 1992 video of One Commando
initiation:

- Approximately fifteen men (initiates) are
lined up by the One Commando barrack
block in Petawawa. They are passing a piece
of bread to each other, on which they vomit
and urinate prior to placing it in their mouths
and chewing;

- Three initiates are doing push-ups on a piece
of cardboard with feces splattered on it, while
one initiate is pushed down chest first onto
the cardboard by an initiator;

- A black initiate, with "I love KKK" written on
his back, is in the push-up position with
other initiates. An initiator also urinates on
the black initiate's back;

- The black initiate is tied to a tree and one initiator says, "This is the real nature of a black."

Later white powder is thrown on the black initiate and beer is poured down his shorts;

- An initiate is shown on all fours;

- The black initiate is on all fours, with a dog leash wrapped around his shoulders, being led around by an initiator who is holding the leash;

- An initiate fakes sodomy of the black initiate while the black initiate simultaneously fakes fellatio with another initiate;

- Two initiates are close dancing on a picnic table—one is naked with his pants down around his ankles;

- One initiate, with a mop wig on his head and a gun tape dress, kisses another male believed to be his initiator or "godfather";

- During the entire time initiates are encouraged to binge-drink beer and participate in "games" such as turning around a stick, carrying water, push-ups, and jumping from a table blindfolded.

The video of the One Commando ritual establishes clearly these as rites of initiation with the associated three classic phases of separation, liminal inversion, and reintegration. The separation phase is the moment when all initiates are "leveled," i.e., made alike: their hair is shaved, they are all in the same maroon Airborne T-shirt. (No initiators are dressed this way.) As the initiates become progressively dirtier, their initiators remain immaculately clean, so that the initiates are separate and yet the same. It is the initiators, called "godfathers," who direct the activities during the rite.

After separation occurs, initiates in rites of passage are often ritually "killed." In the Airborne case this did not happen as it often does in other cultures' rites; rather, participants were dead drunk and if not falling down from drinking, they were doing so from dizziness after turning around and around on a stick. They were also encouraged to vomit by their initiators—a ritual poisoning and purge,

accomplished primarily by the passing of a wad of bread from initiate to initiate. But between initiates the "boulette" is vomited and urinated on, thus turning it into a method for provoking vomiting in the initiate who must next chew it. Eliade describes similar events in Mayombe, Africa, where initiates' heads are shaven, and they drink a narcotic potion and are spun around until they fall to the ground.[27]...

The ritual killing is followed by a series of acts designed to humiliate and further reduce the collective of initiates. As Newer[28] has noted, the unpleasantness and ordeals of these rites of passage do not constitute negative sanctions (sadism or punishment), but are a test of loyalty and self-control, which are highly valued characteristics in a combat soldier. One interviewee stated:

I can't say that I am proud to see myself on national television, but I can say that I am proud to have done it, to prove to myself and to others that as a member of the Airborne Regiment I will face and overpass any challenges or taskings given to me. (Canadian Airborne soldier) ...

It is interesting to note that the soldier who would obviously stand out and not be like the others—the black initiate—was singled out for special treatment. This is consistent with other reports of similar initiations where there is extreme pressure to "level" all participants. While the black initiate was doused in flour, some of his white associates were rolled in mud. Again the inversion and parody of this liminal period are highlighted—black becomes white and white becomes black.

It's the pride of belonging to a group, like in schools and universities, a rite of passage, but no one makes you do it. No one gets beaten or shaken up. What happens is that they'll pick on some personal characteristic. Like if you're black, they'll paint you white, but being black is not the problem. (Canadian Airborne soldier)

During this liminal phase, the initiates are "betwixt and between," no longer new members to the Airborne but not yet part of the group. Van Gennep,[29] in his comparative work on rites of passage, remarked that in this gap between ordered worlds, almost anything can happen. It is extremely interesting that such a homophobic society as the Airborne would do things that are often associated with homosexuality, i.e., involving urine and feces. This parody of homosexuality is further emphasized by soldiers dancing erotically with each other, men in drag, and mock sodomy. Here we see a parody of the military's emphasis on masculinity, particularly in an all-male society such as the Airborne. Thus the initiation rite touches upon homosexual impulses that surely are evoked in such an all-male climate.[30] Furthermore, Turner[31] tells us that in the interim of liminality, the possibility exists not only of standing aside from one's social position but from all social positions and formulating a potentially unlimited series of alternative social arrangements. By mocking homoerotic behavior, initiates are formulating what is normally considered a totally unacceptable social arrangement for the Airborne....

El Guindi has noted that, during the liminal period in the initiation ritual, neophytes are not yet classified; this is often expressed in symbols modeled on the process of gestation, so that neophytes are likened to or treated as newborn infants.[32] In the Airborne, initiates' heads are shaved, and some eventually end up wearing little or no clothes like newborns. They cannot feed themselves and are fed beer and alcohol like babies—only instead of being fed from the bottle, Airborne initiates are fed from plastic guns.

There is also an abdication of personal responsibility to the initiators, who are like family (godfathers). The initiates do what the initiators ask, trusting them with their personal safety like children. For example, initiates stand blindfolded on a table. The table is raised and shaken by four initiators. The initiate then jumps off, believing he is quite some distance from the ground (when actually he is only one or two inches). In this way the young initiates practice and reenact in parody the abdication of responsibility to superiors that takes place in the military. In the Airborne, soldiers will be asked to do the bidding of their superiors without question even when it puts their personal safety at risk. They will be asked to leap from airplanes, trusting in their superiors to let them out of the plane at a safe altitude and to drop them in the right drop zone. This trust is reinforced by initiators' statements, such as "We take care of you; nowhere else will people take care of you the way we do." Corporal Robin, the black initiate, testified to the Somalia Commission of Inquiry that he was cared for by his initiators; for example, he said that glass was taken away so he would not be hurt when he walked on the ground like a dog, and ropes were loosened so as not to bind his hands too tightly to a tree.[33]

It may seem incomprehensible to an outsider that the initiates actually participated voluntarily in all this. The importance of the ritual is in part a reflection of the nature of the unit at this stage. Initiates are strangers to each other and to the Airborne, and the bonding of the initiation pulls them together in a very short period of time. Perhaps the initiations were more severe in One Commando because of its marginal position as a French unit in a predominantly English base such as Petawawa, but, whatever the reasons, recruits emerge from the ordeal as new beings: members of One Commando. The passage is consummated. In essence, participants have been reborn as Airborne....

Hazing

New men were also subjected to a kind of "cold shoulder treatment" during the first six months of their stay in Two Commando. According to Private Grant, the NCOs and officers had nothing to do with this form of hazing. It was something the troops did to "welcome" a newcomer.

See, when you come to the Commando, you're not a new guy, you are a fucking new guy, that's how you are treated for six months. No one talks to you, no one is your friend, you do what you are told and you carry on. You're told to do this, by whoever, you do it. Now, if people want to get in, what they generally do, in any circumstance, they try their best to please. (Testimony of Private Grant to the BOI Vol V: 864–889)...

Private Bass testified to the Board of Inquiry that a few guys from Three Commando would get drunk and burst into an FNG's room (fucking new guy) and wave guns around to scare the hell out of him. Three Commando seemed to have other forms of bonding. For example, in Rwanda, following Somalia, members of Three Commando had to be hospitalized for cutting their wrists too deep in a blood-brother ritual.

A platoon, I believe, from the Three Commando was sent to Rwanda to provide security. It was a defensive security platoon, which is essentially guarding a certain perimeter. They were not deployed as a unit, just a platoon, 30 men under a captain. And two events took place. First one is one of the members of that platoon committed suicide while, I believe on Christmas night, of all times. I believe there was drinking involved, while I'm not sure. But anyway he was a member of that platoon. Also there was a shooting incident, in that members of the platoon, while guarding a nunnery, were drinking and decided to shoot off their weapons into the air. I think it's at that event too, that they decided to do a blood brother ceremony. Where, if you like some one very much, he becomes your blood brother, kind of an Indian ceremony where you slash your wrists and mix your blood. Now you have to put things in context. You have to remember all the horror of Rwanda, general lawlessness, who's right, who's wrong. Difficult living conditions because a lot of things did not work or were shocking, that kind of stuff. But again the disturbing part is the presence of alcohol. (Canadian Airborne soldier)

Rampage Initiation Rites

On the evening of October 2, military pyrotechnics were exploded illegally at a party at the junior ranks' mess at Canadian Forces Base Petawawa. In the early morning of October 3, a vehicle was set on fire; it belonged to the Two Commando duty officer who had reportedly called the Military Police following the disturbances at the mess. Later that night, various members of Two Commando (and perhaps others) held another party, this time in nearby Algonquin Park, at which they set off more pyrotechnics and ammunition.

It could be postulated that the weekend of the pyrotechnics display in October 1992, when soldiers set off thunderflashes, smoke grenades, and a flare on the base in Petawawa and then went on to party with stolen thunderflashes and personal weapons in Algonquin Park, was a form of rampage initiation rite. Alves[34] describes rampage initiation rites as a form of "improv" initiation rites where antisocial behavior is used to express one's marginal condition. Alves described how individuals prove their daring to each other in street gangs in Los Angeles by committing crime and recounting heroic tales of their daring to their comrades afterward. Thus the Airborne who participated in these events could reinforce their "rebel" identity. It is important to remember that members of Two Commando called themselves the "rebels" and openly displayed the rebel/confederate flag in their quarters. This group had a reputation of challenging authority to the extent of being accused of burning an officer's car. Also, the pyrotechnics and other events such as car burning took place on a weekend of extensive binge drinking.

CONCLUSIONS

The Canadian Airborne considered themselves to be Canada's combat elite. As early as 1945 Grinker and Spiegel noted that the combat personality becomes more mature in self-discipline, self-sacrifice, and cooperation, but from another standpoint the combat personality becomes more dependent. "For what he has given up, he receives constant care and affection from his group as long as he plays his part properly."[35] In the Airborne, pressure was on to be part of the group but the rewards were great.

Most regiments are tight, but the Airborne was more so. Even disbanded they were a family. They really took care of you. They were out for their men. (Canadian Airborne soldier)

We were very tight knit. You always have to cover your buddy; your buddy covers you. You have to look after each other no matter what. Even if you are partying downtown, if he gets out of line or gets in trouble it's your job to get him out. (Canadian Airborne soldier)...

Soldiers who were not able to meld into the Airborne group identity were excluded. Corporal Purnelle testified that when he joined One Commando in 1990, he had not participated in the initiation and suffered some ostracism as a result.[36] To the ordinary civilian ostracism may not seem such a horrible fate. "So, if you get kicked out of one group, you can just join another," may be the reaction. But remember that a member of the military is not free just to join another group.[37] Coming from civilian society that elevates the individual, initiates are in a world where the value of the group is supreme.[38]... Ambrose[39] tells us that the result of these shared experiences is a "closeness unknown to all outsiders. Comrades are closer than friends are, closer than brothers. Their relationship is different from that of lovers. Their trust in, and knowledge of, each other is total."

According to McCoy,[40] "bonding" occurs as a lasting form of group identity brought about through an experience of shared suffering. Studies of male group behavior, whether the Wehrmacht in WWII[41] or West Point cadets in the 1960s, have emphasized the importance of "bonding" or "binding" as a defining aspect of military organizations. Thus, initiation rituals give an outward and visible form to an inward and conceptual process.

It is important to note that although group loyalty and bonding is important during battle, small group bonding can foster and maintain inappropriate norms. According to Janowitz,[42] primary groups that are highly cohesive can impede the goals of military organization because they are informal networks. Group bonding can pose a threat to legitimate authority or undermine discipline when the group becomes more important than anything else, including the army.

A strong group can also foster and maintain inappropriate norms. In addition, by assuring anonymity through norms of group, it can facilitate acts of subversion and defiance, since the group will "circle the wagon" to protect individual members from military or civilian authority.[43] For example, prior to deployment to Somalia, Airborne soldiers would not "give up" the comrades who had been responsible for the burning of an officer's car. Investigations only encountered a wall of silence concerning a serious breach of discipline. Small group loyalty thus became more important than good order and discipline. Similarly, members of One Commando had difficulty "remembering" details concerning the events of the initiation ceremony. In another example, even when Corporal Robin reviewed the video, he still did not want to hurt the good name of the Airborne regiment and was reluctant to criticize.[44] Severe initiation ceremonies such as those carried out by the Canadian Airborne Regiment promote increased loyalty and devotion to the group. But this group bonding is a double-edged sword: what can be functional unit bonding for war can quickly become dysfunctional in an army at peace.

NAVIGATING THE CONCEPTS

1. Can you think of any other groups in Canada that employ "rites of passage" to demonstrate a member's initiation and acceptance into the

group? If so, what are the groups and why would they need to use them? If not, why do you believe the military is alone in using these techniques?

2. Why do you think that "humiliation" played such a key role in the resocialization of soldiers?

3. Are there any parallels between the rites of passage in the Canadian Airborne Regiment and the training students receive while attending college or university? Why, or why not?

NOTES

Author's Note: *I wish to thank the members of the Commission of Inquiry into the Department of Canadian Forces to Somalia for their assistance with and support for this research.*

1. E. Aronson, and J. Mills, "The Effect of Severity of Initiation on Liking for a Group," *Journal of Abnormal and Social Psychology* 59 (1959): 177–81.

2. Canadian soldier quoted in Harrison, D., and L. Laliberté, *No Life Like It: Military Wives in Canada* (Toronto: James Lorimer, 1994), 28.

3. See G. Aran, "Parachuting," *American Journal of Sociology* 80 (1974): 124–52; W. C. Cockerham, "Selective Socialization: Airborne Training as Status Passage," *Journal of Political and Military Sociology* 1 (1973): 215–29.

4. W. Arkin and L. R. Dobrofsky, "Military Socialization and Masculinity," *Journal of Social Issues* 34 (1978): 163.

5. See Donna Winslow, "The Canadian Airborne in Somalia: A Socio-Cultural Inquiry." Study prepared for the Commission of Inquiry into the Deployment of Canadian Forces to Somalia. Ottawa: Public Works and Government Services, 1977.

6. I have chosen not to identify any officers since the initiation rites concerned only noncommissioned members, that is, corporals being initiated by master corporals who had gone through the initiation rite the previous year. The few officers who were present at the beginning of the initiation rites could be easily identified if we were to refer to them as "officer."

7. Canada's paratrooping history actually began in 1942, with the formation of the First Canadian Parachute Battalion, which became part of the British Sixth Airborne Division and fought with it in Northwest Europe during WWII. At the same time a joint Canadian-U.S. unit, the First Special Service Force, or Devil's Brigade, was formed. This unit fought mainly in Italy and Southern France. Disbanded in 1944, the paratroopers from the First Canadian Special Service Battalion became reinforcements for the First Canadian Parachute Battalion, which, in turn, was disbanded at the end of the war. Paratrooping was revived in the Canadian Forces (CF) in 1949 with the formation of the Mobile Strike Force. It consisted of battalions from three Canadian army regiments: The Royal Canadian Regiment (RCR), Princess Patricia's Canadian Light Infantry (PPCLI), and the Royal 22e Régiment (R22eR; Van Doos) plus support elements. This brigade was tasked with Canadian defence, particularly in the north. In 1958, the Mobile Strike Force was drastically reduced, but 10 years later, in 1968, it was revitalized and the Canadian Airborne Regiment (CAR) was born.

8. Col. P. G. Kenward, "The Way We Were: Canadian Airborne Regiment 1968–1995," mimeograph at Petawawa, Ontario, 1995, 1.

9. Ibid., 2.

10. General Boyle, meeting with Judge Advocate General, Ottawa, 20 April 1995. Note that at the time General Boyle gave this presentation, he was a member of the General Staff. He subsequently went on to be the Chief of the Defence Staff.

11. When it was deployed to Somalia the unit had to be augmented with additional personnel (such as medics and engineers), so it became the Canadian Airborne Battle Group. The Commanding Officer of the Battle Group was the Commanding Officer of the Airborne Regiment.

12. The decision to disband the Canadian Airborne Regiment was taken on 23 January 1995, more than 19 months after the return of the troops from Somalia. The decision to disband followed the showing on television of two videos, one depicting a commando unit hazing ritual and the other filmed during the regiment's tour of duty in Somalia. In his press release, the Minister of Defence wrote:

"[T]he incidents in Somalia last fall, which were subsequently investigated by the Chief of Defence Staff, and in combination with these two videos, demand action. I recognize that many changes in personnel and procedures in the Airborne have been made over the past year and that the people now serving are by and large dedicated professionals, however, I believe the problems of the regiment are systemic." Speaking notes for the Honorable David Collenette, P.C., MP, Minister of National Defence. Press Conference, 23 January 1995, 10–11.

13. J. S. Ott, *The Organizational Culture Perspective* (Chicago: Dorsey Press, 1995), 27.

14. L. Parmar, *Society, Culture and Military System* (Jaipur: Rawat Publications, 1994), 152.

15. The role of alcohol in other Airborne units has been described by Ambrose, S. E., *Band of Brothers: E Company, 506th Regiment, 101st Airborne: From Normandy to Hitler's Eagle's Nest* (New York: Simon & Schuster, 1992), 19.

16. L. H. Ingraham, *Boys in the Barracks. Observations on American Military Life* (Philadelphia: Institute for the Study of Human Issues, 1985), 91.

17. Ibid., 1985, 113.

18. C. W. Hewson, "Mobile Command Study: A Report on Disciplinary Infractions and Antisocial Behavior Within FMC with Particular Reference to the Special Service Force and the Canadian Airborne Regiment (Hewson Report)," Ottawa: Department of National Defence, September 1985. Annex H, 20.

19. See Ingraham, "Boys in the Barracks," 119.

20. United States War Department (1909), "Hazing at the United States Military Academy: Letter From the Secretary of War, Transmitting a Response to the Inquiry of the House in Relation to Hazing at the United States Military Academy" (Washington, D.C.: G.P.O., 1909), 63.

21. E. Aronson and J. Mills, "The Effect of Severity of Initiation on Liking for a Group," *Journal of Abnormal and Social Psychology 59* (1959): 157–58.

22. Perhaps the best example of how difficult it can be for those in authority to get to the bottom of what goes on in hazing is the case of Douglas MacArthur. When he was a "plebe" at West Point at the turn of the [twentieth] century, MacArthur found himself in a hazing controversy and was commanded to testify at a congressional court of inquiry following the death of a cadet in a hazing incident. MacArthur "steadfastly refused to name the upperclassmen who had hazed him, yet he tried to appease the select committee by giving them the names of several men who had already quit West Point for one reason or another." See H. Nuwer, *Broken Pledges:*

The Deadly Rite of Hazing (Atlanta, GA: Longstreet Press, 1990) for details.

23. F. E. Jones, "The Socialisation of the Infantry Recruit," in *Canadian Society: Sociological Perspectives*, ed. B. R. Blishen et al. (Toronto: Macmillan of Canada, 1968), 167.

24. H. Nuwer, *Broken Pledges: The Deadly Rite of Hazing* (Atlanta, GA: Longstreet Press, 1990), 201–02.

25. This tradition was also practiced by German paratroopers, who recognized different levels: bronze wings, novice; silver, advanced; gold, expert. The highlight of the German wings ceremony was "blood wings"—the sergeant major pinning the wings through the soldier's tunic into flesh. See Peter Worthington and Kyle Brown, *Scapegoat. How the Army Betrayed Kyle Brown* (Toronto: Seal Books, 1997), 51.

26. See A. W. McCoy, "Same Banana: Hazing and Honor at the Philippine Military Academy," *The Journal of Asian Studies 54* (1995): 689–726; United States General Accounting Office, "DOD Service Academics: More Changes Needed to Eliminate Hazing." Report to Congressional Requesters, Washington, D.C.: The General Accounting Office.

27. Mircea Eliade, *Rites and Symbols of Initiation: The Mysteries of Birth and Rebirth* New York: Harper Torchbooks, 1965), 76.

28. Nuwer *Broken Pledges,* 116.

29. Arnold Van Gennep, *Rites of Passage* (Paris: E. Nourry, 1909).

30. R. Lopez-Reyes, *Power and Immortality: Essays on Strategy, War Psychology, and War Control* (New York: Exposition Press, 1971), 189.

31. Victor Turner, *Dramas, Fields and Metaphors: Symbolic Action in Human Society* (New York: Cornell University Press, 1974), 14.

32. Fadwa El Guindi, *Religion in Culture* (Dubuque, IA: WMC Brown Co., 1977), 40.

33. Testimony of Corporal Christopher Robin to the Commission of Inquiry into the Activities of the Canadian Airborne Battle Group in Somalia. *Transcripts*, Vol. 6.

34. J. Alves, "Transgressions and Transformations: Initiation Rites Among Urban Portuguese Boys," *American Anthropologist 95* (1993): 897.

35. R. R. Grinker and J.W. Spiegel, *Men Under Stress* (Philadelphia: Blakiston, 1945), 123.

36. Corporal Prunelle, Testimony to the Commission of Inquiry into the Activities of the Canadian Airborne Battle Group in Somalia. *Transcripts*, Vol. 35, 6822–23.

37. M. S. Peck, *People of the Lie: The Hope for Healing Human Evil* (New York: Simon & Schuster, 1983), 219.

38. T. E. Ricks, "Separation Anxiety: 'New' Marines Illustrate Growing Gap Between Military and Society," *Wall Street Journal,* 27 July 1995, A1, A4, 4.

39. Ambrose, *Band of Brothers,* 20.

40. See A. W. McCoy, "Same Banana: Hazing and Honor at the Philippine Military Academy," *The Journal of Asian Studies* 54 (1995): 695.

41. Edward Shils and Morris Janowitz, "Cohesion and Disintegration in the Wehrmacht in World War II," *Public Opinion Quarterly* 12 (1948): 280–315.

42. M. Janowitz, *Sociology and the Military Establishment* (Beverly Hills, CA: Sage Publications, 1974), 9.

43. See Lt. Col. K. W. J. Wenek, "Behavioural and Psychological Dimensions of Recent Peacekeeping Missions," *Forum: Journal of the Conference of Defence Associations Institute 8* (December 1993): 20.

44. Testimony of Corporal Robin to the Commission of Inquiry into the Activities of the Canadian Airborne Battle Group in Somalia. *Transcripts,* Vol. 6, 1075.

PART 3

Social Diversity

Sociologists recognize that the fabric of contemporary society is created by weaving together diverse individuals and groups.

Chapter 9

Exploring Deviance in Canada
Linda Deutschmann

Source: Printed with the author's permission (2003). Linda Deutschmann is also the author of *Deviance and Social Control* (2002).

Linda Deutschmann reviews many of the key concepts and principles of deviance in Canada. Her analysis begins by defining deviance and explaining how sociological theory can be applied to help us understand why people commit deviant acts. She concludes her review by exploring how the deviance process can be used as a powerful mechanism of social control.

DEFINING DEVIANCE

Deviance is not just a whole lot of sex, drugs, and violence; wrongdoing by bad people; or the ramblings of people who have forgotten to take their medication. When we look at deviance in Canada, we find a wide array of behaviours that seem to have little in common with each other.

Those called deviant include nasty individuals such as serial killer Paul Bernardo[1] (Burnside & Cairns, 1995) and sadistic pedophile Karl Toft[2] (Sorenson, 2002). They include people such as John Colapinto ("a boy raised as a girl") who struggle to find a place in a society that has only two mainstream gender categories and little tolerance for anyone just a bit different (Colapinto, 2001; Bloom, 2002; Preves, 2003). They also include temporary and accidental deviants such as the Iranian law professor who, on his way to Canada to learn English, told the Air Canada flight attendant to be careful stowing his bag because it might explode (i.e., burst open). His use of English, in the era of post-September 11 sensitivities, resulted in a month in custody and a criminal conviction on mischief charges (MacAfee, 2003). The deviant category includes many other people who find themselves on the outside of social groups because they are seen as unacceptable for some reason. You can argue that each of these people has in some way violated a social norm (or been accused of this) whether they meant to do so or not, and this may be what they all have in common.

Deviance is a violation of a social norm, but not just any violation of a norm. In the course of a regular day, each of us is likely to find situations in which conforming fully to one set of social norms forces us to violate other norms. As we try to balance school and work, family and friends, getting ahead and "having a life," few of us can live up to the expectations of all our social roles all the time. People who violate a few of the rules, and not too often, think of themselves as normal, and usually are thought of by others as normal. What, then, is deviance? What makes a practice or a person or a set of ideas "deviant"?

Whenever we find deviance, whether in Canada or elsewhere, we find that there are *observers*, people who see (or claim to see) some kind of *behaviour or appearance or belief* that violates *normative standards* (norms or rules) regarded as significant (i.e., standards that are worth defending at this time and in this situation). The breaking of rules is not enough, all by itself, to produce consensus that behaviour is deviant. Many rules are used selectively—they are invoked when someone feels such rules are "needed," not every time someone breaks them. If you start looking out for this, you can probably come up with many examples of behaviour that is okay in one situation (e.g., at a rock concert or a hockey rink) but not okay in another (e.g., at a church service), or times when behaviour that has been tolerated for a while will be treated to a "crackdown" and suddenly become the spark for serious regulations.

Notice how this definition places as much emphasis on the *observers* as it does on the behaviour or appearance or belief that is observed. There have been times when the observers have been wrong about, or even lied about, what they have observed. During the witchcraft craze in early Europe, accusers testified about seeing neighbours flying on broomsticks or calling up hailstorms, and in some villages every woman was burned as a witch because of this testimony (Larner, 1980; Levack, 1992). Even in modern times, it is not uncommon to find that people called deviant are victims of rumours or "bad press" put out by those who do not like them. This definition also places importance on the normative standards that are invoked by the observers. The standards will be those shared by the surrounding culture; otherwise the observers would not be able to get people to agree that deviance has occurred.

Consider the following list:

Deviant Category	Normative Standard
Heretic	Religious belief
Traitor	Loyalty
Homosexual	Traditional male gender role
Obese/Anorexic	Medical weight standards
Delinquent	Laws applicable to youth
Trespasser	Privacy, property rights
Dirty, smelly	Cleanliness

Are some of these standards more defensible (commonly shared) than others? Could an "observer" get people to label someone deviant because the observed person was doing something that violated this normative standard? Are some of these standards changing? In this exercise, *you* are acting as the observer.

SEEING DEVIANCE THROUGH THE LENSES OF THEORY

Each of the perspectives of sociology helps us to understand deviance. The definition that we have been using owes a great deal to the *symbolic interaction* perspective, so we will begin with that perspective.

Symbolic Interaction

Making use of this perspective, we can see that even when we notice an important rule has been broken, we may or may not be willing to take action. If we like the person who has committed the perceived offence, we may be reluctant to start the process of stigmatization or labelling that is known as *deviantizing*. We may try to "normalize" what has happened by ignoring, covering up, or excusing the person— for example, by suggesting that the real problem is stress or overwork. If we do not like the offender, or we are very committed to defending the rule, we may choose to make the most of the offence. It always takes a bit of work (awareness, attention, emotional effort, talk...) to produce the reality of deviance. Some people from the ranks of the observers, or those who listen to the observers, have to care enough to make a big deal about what they see, or what has been reported to them. When they undertake this enterprising work, we call them labellers or *moral entrepreneurs*.[3] The result of their work is a new rule or a newly enforced rule, and often a new deviant or a new class of deviants.

A small-scale moral entrepreneur may be the person in your circle of friends who maintains the group standards by way of enthusiastic telephone gossip. This can lead to the exclusion of nonconforming members, or may just mean that they get a lot of teasing or criticism. A larger-scale moral entrepreneur can be the leader of a group that actively seeks to ban Harry Potter books from a school library,[4] or to keep gay couples from attending the school prom, or to cover up naked public statues. Some large-scale moral entrepreneurs become leaders or spokespersons for social movements that target particular kinds of behaviour and people. Examples of this have been temperance crusaders, who campaigned against alcohol, and eugenics leaders, who argued for such causes as the sterilization of anyone "unfit" to reproduce and the tightening of immigration rules (McLaren, 1990). Canada has had no violent equivalent to Carrie Nation, the hatchet-wielding American anti-alcohol crusader who was arrested more than 30 times for destroying saloons in the early 1900s. Canadian temperance activist Nellie McClung was called "Calamity Nell," but this had to do with her fiery language, and not with violence (Hallett & Davis, 1993).

Moral entrepreneurs often have to work hard to make others agree that certain behaviour is evil and that people who practise such behaviour are morally tainted and deviant. Some moral entrepreneurs have become so wrapped up in their cause that they and their followers have been willing to go to terrible lengths to make it succeed. History is full of the stories of persecutions of so-called deviant populations and the untruths that were told to justify these actions. In the late 1930s and 1940s, the German National Socialists (Nazis) made deviants out of Jewish people by accusing them of undermining the German nation, stigmatizing them by forcing them to wear the Star of David symbol, and eventually entering into a systematic plan for their extermination. Judge Emily Murphy (pen name "Janey Canuck") was a Canadian moral entrepreneur who was an anti-marijuana and anti-Chinese-immigration activist. Her book *The Black Candle* (1922) is full of passages linking marijuana with the destruction of the "white race" in Canada and with allegations that homicide and insanity follow upon even minor use of marijuana[5] (Murphy, 1922). Along with the U.S. materials that this book was largely based on, *The Black Candle* had an effect on Canada's immigration and drug laws (Blackwell & Erickson, 1988).

Sometimes it is useful to distinguish between the moral entrepreneurs (the people who work to bring about moral rules) and the rule enforcers (the police, the school authorities, or the company management). Rule enforcers may sometimes be required to enforce rules that they do not support, or they may act to enforce rules in ways that were not originally intended. Political authorities sometimes make rules for schools that school authorities do not appreciate. When this happens, the rules may be subverted in many ways. Rule enforcers may decide that the enforcement of rules in a particular situation is simply not wise. Thus police at rock concerts rarely wade into the thickest part of the crowd to arrest drug sellers and users. On the other hand, sometimes the conflict between the rule makers and rule enforcers results in a clear resolution. Metropolitan Toronto Police Constable David Packer was forced to resign or be dismissed in the 1980s when he refused to stand guard at the Morgentaler abortion clinic in Toronto (Packer, 1988). Packer apparently had the choice of being deviant within the police organization by refusing to obey its rules, or being deviant within the anti-abortion milieu that he and his wife shared. He resigned from the police force.

Usually those who are labelled deviant face some level of punishment and some degree of social exclusion or banishment. While they may not be taken to an actual courtroom, they are treated to judgment in the eyes of those around them and punished by being stigmatized and possibly shunned. Their presence is treated as contaminating or polluting and "decent" people (the insiders) avoid them. When this happens at school, the deviant may be excluded from desirable friendship groups. The consequences of such exclusion can be cumulative. Youths lacking the protection of respectable friends may be vulnerable to bullying. Their performance in the classroom may suffer. Their response to these ramifications may make the situation even worse. Unless reversed, this *deviance amplification* process may continue until the individual gradually comes to have fewer respectable choices, comes to think of his or her identity as more and more deviant, and becomes more and more committed to deviant lines of action. The final result may be a school dropout, a school shooting, or a suicide.

The daycare scandals of the 1980s and early 1990s also provide a good example of how symbolic interaction theory can help us to understand deviance processes. Beginning in the 1980s, there were many "satanic" daycare scandals. Most of these occurred in the so-called Bible-belt areas of the United States, but some took place in Canada and England (Victor, 1993). They were fuelled by a climate of anxiety over child care and beliefs about children's testimony that have since been shown to be incorrect[6] (Ofshe & Watter, 1994; Butler, Fukurai, et al., 2001). One of these scandals occurred in 1992 in Martensville, Saskatchewan. Nine people, five of them police officers, were accused of sexual and satanic crimes against young children[7] (Harris, 1998). This case started with a mother's concern over her daughter's diaper rash, and escalated through the hyper-awareness of a police-woman who had received training about satanic cults, a police chief who believed her, and the activities of several overenthusiastic but improperly trained child therapists. The stories of terrible deeds that were elicited by parents and therapists eventually collapsed in the complete absence of relevant physical evidence, but not before many people were accused of Satanist practices and pedophilia, and not before many children were subjected to "therapy" that was traumatic. This case shows how accusations of deviance can snowball in a community, creating conditions whereby people convince themselves that, if so many other people believe that an accusation is true, it must be true. In the process, many lives are ruined.

Not all deviance is falsely attributed, of course, but the process of deviantizing is the same whether the incident has really occurred or is falsely attributed. When deviance takes the form of a serious violation of the Criminal Code—such as bank robbery—the individual may be stigmatized with the label "criminal" and put in prison. He or she will then be excluded from (almost) all forms of civil society for a designated period of time. There will be an awkward point when it comes time to release and reintegrate such an offender, who is still symbolically labelled a criminal but now is about to rejoin free society. When there is a proposal to put in a halfway house so that the offender can gradually rejoin the community in a supervised way, neighbours will often band together in a NIMBY (Not In My Back Yard) movement to keep criminal people "like this" from living in their neighbourhood (Deutschmann, 2002: 345–46). These movements respond to ex-offenders in the same language of fear and rejection as other NIMBY movements respond to dangerous toxic waste (Walsh, Warland, et al., 1993). Symbolic interaction analysis helps us to see the ways in which the social process of criminalization makes offender reintegration a perilous undertaking. Even a falsely accused offender may find it difficult to find a satisfying legitimate career when returning to society from prison, all because the stigma of criminality persists long beyond the sentence of imprisonment and creates a spoiled identity (Goffman, 1959).

People threatened with being labelled as deviant (stigmatization) sometimes fight back. We see this now in the case of homosexuals, marijuana users, and stigmatized minorities. When this happens, interesting *stigma contests* can take place. A stigma contest evolves when those people who denounce and exclude find that the tables have been turned, and that they have become the accused deviants. The prudish book-banners, busybody meddlers, and racist Archie Bunkers can become figures of fun or condemnation. German-born former Canadian resident Ernst Zundel, for example, has become infamous for his writings and speeches on Holocaust denial, and for neo-Nazi and anti-Semitic activities. These have caused him to be deported from the United States, denied Canadian citizenship, and threatened with deportation from Canada to face trial in Germany. This is part of the pattern whereby those who attempt to label and exclude others are sometimes labelled and excluded themselves.

Some of those who have been labelled deviant do not really mind their outsider status: they may enjoy notoriety and not want to fit in with the mainstream dominant groups. They disdain safe, careful, hard-working and sensible "squares" and relish the fear that they can evoke in the hearts of those who follow the rules and abhor violence and extreme adventure. They seek the respect of a different sort of people. While just 1 percent of bikers pride themselves on being outlaws, the other 99 percent are said to be decent, law-abiding people[8] (Harris, 1985; Lavigne, 2000). This disdain for the square and the safe is shared by many elements within youth subcultures, varying from the style rebel punks and goths to the "weekend warriors" to the "street elite" gang youths of the urban downtown scene. Symbolic interaction helps us to understand the identity construction that underlies the symbols that are displayed by all of these groups. They wear the symbols to show that they belong outside the respectable world and to show that they disdain the people who would exclude them. Erving Goffman calls such symbols "identifiers," since they help to tell the observer a great deal about the person wearing them (Goffman, 1959).

Structural Functionalism

The structural functional theoretical perspective in sociology emphasizes a very different aspect of the reality of deviance.

Functionalists argue that deviance can be beneficial for the maintenance of a social system, even if the people in the system do not recognize its beneficial effects. That is, deviance can have *latent functions*. Societies that are under some kind of threat will tend to "find" a lot of deviants, because this aids societal *boundary maintenance*. Moral outrage against deviants dramatizes the rules and reasserts the old boundary or establishes a new one. For example, Kai Erikson has written about how, in the Puritan New England colony of Salem in the 1690s, accusations of witchcraft arose amid uncertainty and disorder related to political problems, relations with the native Indians, changes in the social structure, and illness due to a fungus growing on the crops (Erikson, 1966). There were 19 hangings and one pressing to death by heavy stones before the outbreak came to an end. During the same period, the very stable colonies of New France saw no outbreak of persecution despite the presence of witchcraft beliefs there (Morison, 1955).

Functionalists argue that each successful system has, or finds, just enough deviance to mark and maintain its borders. Deviance can be adjusted up and down simply by adjusting the official level of sensitivity to it (Krauthammer, 1993; Moynihan, 1993). If we have too many deviants, we ignore many of them. If we do not have enough deviants, we can (and do) invent them, as has happened with witches, the "communists" falsely accused in the McCarthy scandals of the 1950s, and other innocent-but-accused scapegoats in the present (Deutschmann, 2002: Chapters 3 and 8).

Functionalists have identified many other latent functions of deviance in addition to boundary maintenance. Deviance is often a way of inducing tension relief in groups under stress, and the punishment of deviants serves a function by demonstrating the value of conformity and by drawing the conformists together in their shared values of conformity. Sometimes the deviant serves as both tension relief and demonstration of the value of conformity, as when the class clown does something really extreme and ends up in the principal's office, and the rest of the class then settles down to work. Deviance is sometimes the way in which new and better ways of doing things are discovered and eventually brought into the mainstream, and sometimes the way in which bureaucratic red tape is subverted for a good cause.

There are also dysfunctions of deviance. Alcoholic airline pilots do not improve airline service. Pedophiles do nothing good for families or for the children they molest. Corrupt politicians do little to improve our desire to participate in politics, and fraudulent corporate behaviour, especially when unpunished, is not good for the economy. These behaviours tend to tear systems apart, and create a society with substantial areas of anomie.

Anomie means, literally, "without law." In Emile Durkheim's writing, anomie refers to a state of normlessness or deregulation, a state of society not having meaningful rules and values (Durkheim, 1951). Anomie is found when society becomes less regulated; it often appears because of rapid social change through modernization and urbanization (Mestrovic, 1985), although it can also develop as an aftermath of war or disaster. Inner-city areas where there is high population turnover and little stability of family and work life tend to be characterized by high rates of suicide, mental illness, drug abuse, and delinquency. These forms of deviance can be seen as symptoms of Durkheim's version of anomie.

American sociologist Robert Merton developed the concept of anomie further by adding the idea of social strain (Merton, 1938). He saw anomie as a condition of strain between the things we are socialized to want (cultural goals) and the amount of access we have to them (institutionalized means). While most of us are socialized to want, for example, a home, car, a meaningful job, children, and many consumer goods, not all of us are well placed to get these things in the approved ways. Not all of us are positioned well enough to succeed in the right schools or to get rich by getting the right job or marrying into the right family. Merton argued that people adapt to this kind of anomie in five main ways. First, some people are *conformists*. They are usually well enough placed to achieve the goals with the means they have been given. Other people may accept the goals, but decide that the acceptable means either take too long or are too difficult; they become *innovators*. (Innovation includes what most of us would call cheating.) Innovation is most likely to be used by people who are structurally blocked from being able to achieve the goals that are held out as valid for everyone in the "American Dream." Canadian track star Ben Johnson, who was stripped of his gold medal at the 1988 Olympics in Seoul after a positive drug test and whose running career faltered after he was cut off from steroids, is an example of an innovator (Francis & Coplon, 1990; Issajenko, 1990). A third group adapts to structural strain of anomie by becoming *ritualists*. These people give up on the goals but continue to go through the means in an empty way. This might mean staying in school forever, without having any personal or practical goal in mind, or becoming the kind of bureaucrat who compulsively engages in setting up useless paper-pushing systems. Merton has two categories for people who adapt to anomie by rejecting both the goals and the means. The first of these, and Merton's fourth adaptation to anomie, is the *retreatist* category. Retreatists are the social dropouts. The drug-using street people on Vancouver's Lower East Side may be an example of this category. Many of these people have replaced society's goals with the goal of obtaining drugs, and even survival takes second place to this. The second category of rejection, and Merton's fifth adaptation, is the *rebel* category. Rebels reject both the goals and the means, but they continue to engage in society, trying to change the system that does not work for them. Rebels may be seen as deviants by those who are trying to maintain the status quo, but they are often the heroes of the next generation.

Conflict

The conflict perspective is also useful in understanding deviance. Conflict theorists, like functionalists, are interested in the structural level of society. They analyze conflicts by looking at group interests rather than by looking at individual needs, emotions, or personalities. (If this distinction is not kept in mind, you may find it difficult to see that the conflict and symbolic interaction perspectives are very distinct from each other.) Marxist and neo-Marxist theorists analyze class interests, especially economically based class interests, as the most important elements of conflict. Other conflict theorists may look at such interests as those of ethnicity, culture, gender, or age.

Conflict theory looks at how the most powerful groups in society use their power to establish conditions that enhance their own interests and act to keep others from getting into positions that could change these conditions. The kind of power that is important here is the power to make the rules that everyone has to live under. This includes, of course, rules such as the Criminal Code of Canada, but also the rules of companies and schools, and the everyday norms of life that make some cultural groups more comfortable than others. People who are in government and on committees and generally in charge of things get to make the rules; they control how the rules are enforced, and they control how rule breakers are treated. For a very long time, the most comfortable combination of groups in Canada have been the people labelled as White Anglo-Saxon Protestant (WASP) capitalists, and this is shown in the kinds of rules that Canadians, at least those living outside of Quebec, live under. (One aspect of conflict theory is that it tends to point to uncomfortable truths.)

Conflict theorists see it as no accident that Canada's Criminal Code tends to outlaw the things that employers think employees should not do, and things that working-class people are more likely to be caught doing rather than things that rich people are likely to be caught doing. You can attend criminal court in any Canadian city and observe the social class of those caught in the net of the criminal law. You will notice that there are relatively few wealthy defendants before the courts.

In Canada, workplace dangers and shoddy products are much more likely to shorten your life or injure you than are serial killers or street crime, and yet the people responsible are rarely, if ever, identified and called criminal or even deviant (Naylor, 2002). In 1992 the Westray mine explosion killed 26 miners in Nova Scotia. The inquiry that followed revealed that flagrant breaches of health and safety standards had not been attended to or prosecuted. Although the RCMP laid two charges under the Criminal Code, these were dropped. Thus, although 26 human beings died, no one was held criminally responsible (Richard, 1999; Glasbeek, 2002). We fear the criminal in the street. We are oblivious to the much greater threats to our wealth and our health that are hidden from us.[9] While the criminal courts are particularly striking places for conflict analysis, the conflict perspective can help you to understand that there are many other settings—such as schools, clubs, and workplaces—in which deviantization takes place.

While Marx himself thought that criminals were part of the "lumpenproletariat" and thus of no use to capitalist society or to the revolution, some of his followers argued that, since the capitalist inequalities and unjust laws make outlaws of the poor and outsiders, criminals were not really bad people. Criminals were simply people who refused to be exploited. In this view, bank robbers are just expressing their opposition to the exploitation of employers and the evils of the banking system, and are really an advance guard of the revolution, perhaps even heroes of a sort. Marxist historian Eric Hobsbawm, for example, sees early bandits as "social bandits" and part of the pre-industrial class structure of early society (Hobsbawm, 2000). This view is now called *left idealism.* Left idealists have been largely displaced by *left realists*, who recognize that criminal deviants such as murderers, robbers, and parents who beat their children "really" do a lot of harm. Thus, while most conflict theorists regard prisons and other repressive institutions as weapons of the dominant classes to control those they dominate, they recognize that some offenders "really" must be controlled at least until something revolutionary can be done to remove the structural inequalities that produce these damaged and dangerous people (Taylor, Walton, et al., 1973; Quinney, 2000).

DEVIANCE AS PART OF SOCIAL CONTROL

Social control includes all those ways, obvious and not so obvious, by which we are encouraged or coerced, tricked, or bribed into particular patterns of behaviour, or, failing that, put away in jails or asylums where decent people do not have to put up with us. All societies that survive have social controls to ensure that their members do the things that are needful for social life to continue, and all societies respond with processes that isolate or banish or execute members who are identified as impossible nonconformists or scapegoats. Deviance occurs everywhere. Thus we can assert that deviance is universal.

Although universal, deviance is not the same in every society. The food, sexual, and burial practices of foreign cultures may be shocking to outsiders. In Japan, many restaurant delicacies are insect-based. In some cultures, burial customs include the eating of body parts (Conklin, 2001). Within a country as large as Canada, there are many cultural groups. What is normal and accepted in one may be deviant in another. For example, the community of Bountiful in British Columbia is settled by the Fundamentalist Church of Jesus Christ of Latter Day Saints (no relation to mainstream Mormons). The leader of Bountiful, Winston Blackmore, has 26 wives and 80 children.[10] What is a normal family in Bountiful is probably not a normal family where you live. One way of expressing this variation is to say that deviance is *relative* to a particular culture and place.

What is very normal and even required in one time and place may be deviant in another. The practices of our own ancestors would shock us if we could return to them today. Women, children, employees, and servants were regularly treated in ways that we would now consider criminal abuse. Until the late 1880s, cannibalism among stranded sailors was "the custom of the sea" and not considered illegal (Hanson, 2000). On the other hand, people who were deviant ·in their own time may become heroes or saints in a later period. Metis leader Louis Riel was executed as a traitor in 1885, but has since been recognized by some as a father of Confederation[11] (Winsor, 1989). Other examples of people scorned as deviants long ago but now venerated would include Jesus of Nazareth, who was crucified, and Socrates, who was forced to take poison for corrupting the morals of youth by teaching them to argue rationally about conventions of the day (Proietto & Portrer, 1966). As the dominant values change, so do our notions about what, and who, is deviant.

Deviance is relative because deviance depends on the normative standards that the observers are able to invoke when they say that what they observe is deviant, respectable, or even admirable. The same behaviour may be regarded as admirable by some people and deviant by others. Consider the case of great-grandmother Betty Krawczyk, who has been jailed for criminal contempt of court in connection with her role in peaceful protest against logging in old-growth B.C. forest (Krawczyk, 1997). Canadian courts usually use prison sentences to communicate extreme disapproval. But Krawczyk is treated as a heroine in the environmentalist community and is proud of protecting the environment for her great-grandchildren.[12]

There are variations in the level of tolerance for behaviour that might be considered deviant. Summer holidays and major sports events typically allow greater tolerance for differences in clothing styles and public behaviour than do funerals and state functions. Tolerance for social control is also variable. Sometimes we become angry when enforcement of rules is too heavy-handed. In the aftermath of the events of September 11, 2001, Canadians' tolerance for public surveillance and many similar kinds of social control increased dramatically.

SUMMARY

In this chapter we have discussed the sociological definition of deviance as a *negative designation* produced by *observers* and attributed to *persons, behaviour, ideas,* or *characteristics* that violate *normative standards* that are held to apply in a particular time and situation. We have shown how the symbolic interactionist, functionalist, and conflict perspectives help in differing ways to illustrate the role of deviance in our lives and in society. And finally, we have shown that the naming of deviance is an important part of powerful mechanisms of social control that are both universal (found in all societies) and specific (relative to specific cultures, times, and places).

NAVIGATING THE CONCEPTS

1. Deutschmann argues that the definitions of what is deviant vary across time and space. Give three examples of activities or behaviours that were considered deviant in the past but are now accepted, or are now deviant when they had not been before. What factors do you think led to these changing definitions?

2. Briefly consider Deutschmann's review of the theoretical explanations for deviance. Which theory do you consider to be the best explanation? Why?

3. Select a person or group from your community that has been labelled deviant. Can your local example be explained as the result of social control? If yes, how; if not, what alternative explanation can you offer? Provide examples from your community as well as Deutschmann's presentation to support your position.

NOTES

1. Bernardo and his wife Karla kidnapped and killed schoolgirls in the St. Catharines area of Ontario in the early 1990s.

2. Toft was a guard at Kingsclear Training School in New Brunswick. Some 233 compensation claims have been settled since his plea-bargained conviction on just 34 charges.

3. Actually, you probably call them busybodies or meddlers, but Howard Becker, a symbolic interaction theorist and jazz musician, invented the term moral entrepreneur to describe people who made it their business to enforce morals and who often gained something by it. Moral entrepreneurs sometimes become the heads of organizations devoted to dealing with the social problem that they have identified. You can find a summary of Becker's ideas at **http://www.criminology.fsu.edu/crimtheory/becker.htm.**

4. J. K. Rowling's Harry Potter novels were the books most subject to censorship attempts in 1999 and 2000. This was because of their focus on wizardry and magic, according to Kranich, 2000.

5. A brief section from this book is scanned at **http://cannabislink.ca/papers/menace.htm.**

6. To summarize a complex literature, children do not make up complex sexual-assault stories on their own, but improperly trained therapists can lead them to do so, and the process can plant false memories that are damaging in the same ways that the memories would be if the assaults had actually occurred.

7. The CBC's *Fifth Estate* produced a documentary about this called "Hell to Pay," which was broadcast on February 12, 2003. The relevant Web site, which includes documents and resources on the subject, is **http://www.cbc.ca/fifth/martin** (accessed December 31, 2003).

8. The reference to 1 percent traces its origins back to 1947, when an annual biker racing and climbing event at Hollister, California, turned into a drunken rampage. Successive events were also taken over this way. The American Motorcycle Association repeatedly tried to put a distance between itself and the renegade element by stressing that 99 percent of bikers were decent, law-abiding, and civilized. The outlaw biker groups proudly took on the "1%" symbol and wore it on their jackets as part of their so-called identifying patch. Many bikers also wear it as a tattoo (see Lavigne, 1987; Garson, 2003; Veno & Gannon, 2003).

9. Two recent Canadian books can help you to understand the way in which upper-level deviants can make their actions "invisible." See Glasbeek, 2002; Naylor, 2002.

10. More information was available on the CBC *Fifth Estate* Web site, as updated February 2003 at **http://www.cbc.ca/fifth/polygamy.** The government of British Columbia provides a school to this community despite public criticism that the community is immoral.

11. The Louis Riel Institute, created by an act of the Manitoba Legislature in 1995, is responsible for promoting awareness of the history, culture, and values of the Metis people in Manitoba.

12. Information on the environmentalist side of this issue may be found at **http://media.wildernesscommittee.org/.**

REFERENCES

Blackwell, J. C., and P. G. Erickson. 1988. *Illicit drugs in Canada: A risky business.* Toronto: Nelson Canada.

Bloom, A. 2002. *Normal: Transsexual CEOs, crossdressing cops, and hermaphrodites with attitude.* New York: Random House.

Burnside, S., and A. Cairns. 1995. *Deadly innocence: The true story of Paul Bernardo, Karla Homolka and the schoolgirl murders.* New York: Time Warner.

Butler, E. W., H. Fukurai, et al. 2001. *Anatomy of the McMartin child molestation case.* Lanham, Md.: University Press of America.

Colapinto, J. 2001. *As nature made him: The boy who was raised as a girl.* Toronto: Perennial (HarperCollins).

Conklin, B. A. 2001. *Consuming grief: Compassionate cannibalism in Amazonian society.* Austin, Tex.: University of Texas Press.

Deutschmann, L. 2002. *Deviance and social control.* Scarborough, Ont.: Nelson Thompson Learning.

Durkheim, E. 1951. *Suicide.* New York: Free Press (original work published 1897).

Erikson, K. T. 1966. *Wayward puritans: A study in the sociology of deviance.* New York: John Wiley.

Francis, C., and J. Coplon. 1990. *Speed trap.* Toronto: Lester and Orpen Dennys.

Garson, P. 2003. *Born to be wild: A history of the American biker and bikes 1947–2002.* New York: Simon and Schuster.

Glasbeek, H. 2002. *Wealth by stealth: Corporate crime, corporate law, and the perversion of democracy.* Toronto: Between the Lines.

Goffman, E. 1959. *The presentation of self in everyday life.* Garden City, N.Y.: Doubleday.

Hallett, M., and M. Davis. 1993. *Firing the heather.* Saskatoon: Fifth House.

Hanson, N. 2000. *The custom of the sea.* New York: John Wiley.

Harris, F. 1998. *Martensville: Truth or justice?* Toronto: Dundurn Press.

Harris, M. 1985. *Bikers: Birth of a modern day outlaw.* London: Faber and Faber.

Hobsbawm, E. 2000. *Bandits.* New York: New Press.

Issajenko, A., as told to M. O'Malley and K. O'Reilly. 1990. *Running risks.* Toronto: Macmillan.

Kranich, N. 2000. Develop yourself: Expose your mind to a banned book. Speech available online through American Library Association. **http://www.ala.org.** Accessed in 2003.

Krauthammer, C. 1993. *Defining deviance up.* New *Republic* (November): 20–25.

Krawczyk, B. S. 1997. *Clayoquot: The sound of my heart.* Victoria: Orca Book Publishers.

Larner, C. 1980. *Crimen exceptum? The crime of witchcraft in Europe.* In *Crime and the law: The social history of crime in Western Europe since 1500,* eds. V. A. C. Gatrell, B. Lenman, and G. Parker. London: Europa, 49–75.

Lavigne, Y. 1987. *Hell's Angels: Taking care of business.* Toronto: Ballantine Books.

———. 2000. *Hells Angels at war: The alarming story behind the headlines.* Toronto: HarperCollins.

Levack, B. P., ed. 1992. *Witchcraft, women and society,* vol. 10 of Articles on witchcraft, magic and demonology. New York: Garland.

MacAfee, M. 2003. Iranian law professor convicted of mischief in Air Canada case. Man told attendant his briefcase might explode if pushed under the seat. *Halifax Herald* (January 23).

McLaren, A. 1990. *Our own master race: Eugenics in Canada, 1885–1945.* Toronto: McClelland and Stewart.

Merton, R. K. 1938. Social structure and anomie. *American Sociological Review* 3: 672–82.

Mestrovic, S. G. 1985. Durkheim's concept of anomie as derèglement. *Social Problems* 33(2): 81–99.

Morison, S. E. 1955. *The Parkman reader: From the works of Francis Parkman.* Boston: Little, Brown.

Moynihan, D. P. 1993. Defining deviancy down. *American Scholar* 62(1): 17–20.

Murphy, E. F. 1922. *The black candle.* Toronto: Thomas Allen.

Naylor, R. T. 2002. *Wages of crime: Black markets, illegal finance, and the underworld economy.* Montreal: McGill-Queen's University Press.

Ofshe, R., and E. Watter, 1994. *Making monsters: False memories, psychotherapy, and sexual hysteria.* New York: Scribner's.

Packer, A. 1988. *A matter of conscience.* Nazareth Homestead, Constable, N.Y.: Our Lady's Book Service.

Preves, S. E. 2003. *Intersex and identity: The contested self.* Rutgers, N.J.: Rutgers University Press.

Proietto, R., and J. N. Portrer. 1966. Socrates: A sociological understanding of the production of an outcast. *Economy and Society* 25(1): 1–35.

Quinney, R. 2000. *Bearing witness to crime and social justice.* Albany, N.Y.: State University of New York Press.

Richard, Justice K. Peter. 1999. *The Westray mine explosion—aftermath.* In Papers from the 1999 Congress on Medical-Legal Aspects of Work Injuries.

Sorenson, K. 2002. View from parliament. **http://www. crowfoot.ca/mpcolumns.htm.** Accessed September 2003.

Taylor, I., P. Walton, et al. 1973. *The new criminology: For a social theory of deviance.* London: Routledge/Keegan Paul.

Veno, A., and E. Gannon. 2003. *The brotherhoods: Inside the outlaw motorcycle clubs.* Sydney: Allen and Unwin.

Victor, J. S. 1993. *Satanic panic: The creation of a contemporary legend.* Chicago: Open Court.

Walsh, E. J., R. Warland, et al. 1993. Backyards, NIMBYs and incinerator sitings: Implications for social movement theory. *Social Problems* 40(1): 25–38.

Winsor, H. 1989. Tories urged to recognize Riel as a father of Confederation. *Globe and Mail* (August 18).

Chapter 10

Streets, Strangers, and Solidarity

T. M. Nielsen

Source: Reprinted with permission of the author (2003).

T. M. Nielsen offers many important and engaging insights into the social experiences found in lesbian subculture. By navigating her way through the landscape of lesbian interaction in public places, Nielsen is able to reveal how lesbians build nonintimate solidarity through highly sensitive and accurate *gaydar*.

In New York City, my girlfriend and I were walking, holding hands, down a busy East Village sidewalk. We passed a couple of lesbians. All four of us exchanged quick (knowing) glances and subtle nods. The more femme looking one held my gaze for a prolonged moment and smiled. I remarked, jokingly, to my partner that she must have liked me. A few seconds after we passed each other, we all turned our heads to look back at each other. Being caught in the act of obvious recognition was both exhilarating and a bit embarrassing. My partner called out, "Hey, she's mine." We all laughed and then kept on our way. This passing exchange, so seemingly inconsequential that most people on the street did not notice it, created a surge of validation for four lesbians on a New York City sidewalk. In a world surrounded by heterosexual norms, complete strangers shared a moment of "queer pride."

(Fieldnotes)

As unexceptional as this incident may appear, the interactions within it are sociologically significant. The essential role of strangers in building social solidarity in cities has been greatly underestimated. Urban public places have traditionally been viewed as populated by antisocial types who care little about the fellow human beings with whom they share space.

Such an anti-urban attitude is based on a profound misunderstanding of the way urbanites operate. Studious observation of interaction between strangers reveals that, far from being interactional wastelands, public places are sites of rich and dynamic social life (Lofland, 1990). It is difficult to grasp the meaning of fleeting engagements between strangers, such as the one described above, not only because they are short lived, but also because they are so routine that they are often engaged in unconsciously. Marginalized people are necessarily more conscious of their actions than members of dominant groups. I have drawn on this heightened consciousness to illustrate the ways lesbians build nonintimate solidarity, thereby stressing the significance of stranger interaction in the urban public realm.

As an insider in the lesbian subculture, I was able to use a unique empirical method to study the interactional patterns of this group. I actively engaged in participant observation of lesbians in public places in a number of North American cities. After detecting other lesbians on the streets and sharing acknowledgment rituals with them, I stopped them to talk about what had occurred between us and asked them to take part in a survey that I had designed to encourage lesbians to think about their public realm experiences. The empirical materials for this article came from my fieldnotes on these unusual encounters, informal interviews, and completed questionnaires from 38 participants.[1]

SEXUAL IDENTITY AND URBAN SPACES

For gay people, the urban public realm is both challenging and rewarding (Gardner, 1994). In heterosexually dominated urban spaces, gay people often experience the magnified vulnerability and sense of isolation that accompany a stigmatized identity. However, like members of other minorities, when gay people connect, they are more likely to experience moments of heightened civility than people whose identities are in sync with the dominant reality.

Lesbians often possess an enhanced awareness of the presence of other gay people in public places. Interactionally, it is possible to turn this awareness to their advantage. However, lesbians must always be vigilant about the risks that accompany being "out" in a homophobic society.[2] These risks range from breaches in civility, such as staring and harassment, to more serious attacks, such as physical assault. Interesting subcultural rituals have developed over time, as lesbians negotiate the dual processes of building solidarity by recognizing and responding to each other, while dealing with issues of trust and risk. Strategies used by lesbians revolve around the interrelated concepts of *recognition, acknowledgment,* and *encounters.* Signals of recognition (gaydar) and acknowledgment (lesbian interaction rituals) that pass between lesbians often lead to prolonged and more spontaneous engagement (encounters). These interactional episodes, often strategically subtle, have profound effects on the lesbian subculture.

READING STRANGERS' IDENTITIES

The public realm is the world of strangers. City life would not be possible if strangers did not categorize each other so as to define situations and to know how to act toward each other. Habitually drawing on stereotypes or typifications to categorize strangers is a ubiquitous urban phenomenon.[3] Because much of this "ordering of the urban populace" (Lofland, 1973) is automatic and relatively unproblematic, many people are unaware of the influence that these everyday categorization processes have on subsequent social actions and interactions.

Lesbians, however, can take little for granted with respect to their sexual identities. Because a lesbian identity is largely indiscernible, most strangers will assume the "default sexuality" (heterosexuality) unless a lesbian identity is clearly presented to the public world. Although most urbanites tend to have a sophisticated grasp of the diverse identities of the strangers they encounter, based, for example, on age, race, class, and occupation, many are unaware of the signals and cues that represent a lesbian identity.

It would be a mistake to assume that public realm invisibility is an objective for lesbians. The ability to "pass" as straight can be desirable for lesbians who are not out or who feel vulnerable about their sexual orientation. However, it is also common for lesbians to claim that they are troubled by the omnipresent assumption of heterosexuality and therefore to challenge it by designing their presentation of self (Goffman, 1959) towards lesbian visibility. As indicated by this Vancouver lesbian's struggle to explain her presentation of self, impression management is never simple.

I always prefer that people identify me as lesbian— to experience interaction in any other way makes me feel that I am being "accepted" based on an incorrect assumption of heterosexuality. For years I presented myself as a stereotypical dyke, accentuating every possible visual and spatial cue to ensure that I would be recognized by all members of the public. Interestingly, though, I now identify as a more femme lesbian and it rarely occurs to me that I may appear straight. Although I wear make up and have grown my hair to a considerable length, I generally take up a great deal of energy or space in many public settings. I have an open stance, very strong (I hesitate to say masculine) gait and sit most frequently with my legs apart. I also perceive my shoes to be a give-away. I always wear "comfortable" (read: masculine or male-identified) shoes.

The desire to be visible to other lesbians has resulted in an elaborate impression management system in the lesbian subculture. The signalling and receiving behaviour that takes place between gay people in the public realm has been playfully named "gaydar" by the gay/lesbian subculture. Many heterosexuals express disbelief when gay people say they can, in the words of one survey participant, *"spot the queers a mile away."*[4] Those who do think they can detect lesbians often rely on superficial stereotypes. However, lesbians are aware that reading a lesbian identity requires a more finely tuned grasp of coding signals than the presence of masculine traits on a female body. Lesbians are a diverse subculture. If lesbians relied on simplistic readings to detect other lesbians, they would overlook the majority of lesbians in public places. A survey participant discusses the complexity of the New York City subculture.

In New York, there are so many types of lesbians that gaydar is quite complicated. There are the women who wear baggy pants and oversized shirts. Then you have the ones who dress alternatively and have many piercings and tattoos. Then I also see the business/professional types. Then you have the athletic types.... Come to think of it, lesbians are just as diverse as heterosexuals.

Although gaydar is unique to the gay subculture, this concept illustrates the ten-tative and contingent nature of stranger interaction in general. In attempting to make sense of situations, urbanites continually test their conceptions of strangers.[5] Through expressions given and given off (Goffman, 1959), lesbians signify their identities to an audience (i.e., lesbian strangers). The presence of "surface signs" may make a lesbian take a second look at a stranger for more "subtle signs" to confirm a gaydar reading. Surface signs are those more obvious cues signifying a lesbian identity that even some outsiders can discern (e.g., very short hair, a butch appearance or public displays of affection between women). Subtle signs include those cues whose meanings are clear mainly to insiders (e.g., strong stance, lesbian insignia, or prolonged eye contact).

Strangers assess each other's roles and identities using cues based on appearance (e.g., clothing, hairstyles, and jewellery), behaviour (e.g., actions, facial expressions, and body language) and space (e.g., where they are located in the city).[6] A lesbian from New York City made the following humorous observation about appearential cues.

Sometimes I need a set of cues for my gaydar to go off. Short hair, of course, makes me think twice, especially if it is spiky, slicked back, anything butch. In NYC it can get tricky because straight women have co-opted many dyke looks. If a woman has long hair but has piercings in places other than her ears or tattoos I might think she's a dyke. The other things that make me think "hmmm" are clunky black shoes or boots, those damn rainbows, shirts that say "dyke" are pretty easy, baggy jeans hanging off someone's hips, thick black leather belts, torn clothing that looks like it was found under a rock and anything that is considered, by the outside world, as belonging to men.

Although strangers often gain first impressions from appearance cues, appearances can be deceiving. Thus, deeper cues must often be used. A Winnipeg lesbian stressed the importance of assessing behavioural cues.

I think there is more than just clothes and hair—it is a combination that includes body language. A straight woman can wear masculine attire but I have my doubts that she is gay because the *cues are broader.* For example, I have a co-worker who I am sure is a lesbian (it turns out she has a female "roommate" and they seem more involved than sharing house bills). This woman will wear stereotypical feminine clothing but her "sporty" gait makes me think she'd be more comfortable in a ball field. She seems a bit more masculine in voice, manner and body movement. To me this is a common giveaway. Straight women rarely express their body language in that way (and when they do I usually think they are bisexual or closeted).

Like all urbanites, lesbians also assess spatial cues in making lesbian identity placements. As gay/lesbian spaces become more popular as hangouts, these cues can be misleading. As a New Yorker points out:

I am more likely to assume that someone is queer if she is in a lesbian space (i.e., bar, bookstore, pride march) but in the East Village of Manhattan, I do recognize that there are many queer-friendly exceptions even within those spaces.

With the exception of very clear cues such public displays of affection (PDAs) between women, most signals of a lesbian identity are ambiguous. Perhaps for this reason, many lesbians find themselves looking beyond appearential, behavioural, and spatial cues for an attitudinal variable. A lesbian from Toronto put it this way:

I believe there are a thousand hidden cues that we give to one another that we then interpret as a feeling. But there is a feeling I get when I discover another lesbian. I am having a hard time narrowing it down.... It's a look, a feeling, a vibe that they send you that says, I see you, I recognize you. Now I don't believe in ESP so I think it must be a form of non-verbal communication, but it's hard to put my finger on exactly what it is.

All urbanites interpret signals from strangers that are so subtle that describing them is very difficult. These cues are often picked up subconsciously. Because lesbians are motivated to recognize other lesbians, they find it easier to verbalize the nature of these intangible cues. Lesbians often say that their radar picks up a "dyke energy" or "lesbian vibe." A Winnipeg lesbian expressed it this way:

"I identify women as lesbian (I admit it) based on hair, clothes, and mannerisms but also their 'essence.' Lesbians have an indescribable trait that just screams 'I'm a lesbian!'"

A critical reader might ask why lesbians are so concerned about recognizing other lesbians in public places. Although it might be tempting to dismiss gaydar as a frivolous notion, the emotional responses elicited by sighting other lesbians captures the significance of gaydar for the lesbian community. Consider these comments from survey respondents from Minneapolis, Toronto, and New York, respectively.

I feel affirmed, energized and empowered and proud of myself and the lesbians I encounter. It makes me feel that I'm not alone in the world and that I am okay.

I look for lesbians everywhere. Especially at straight functions. It's kind of a game and it makes the experience less lonely. I get thrilled to see lesbians and will work to connect with them in some manner. There is definitely a feeling I get when I discover another lesbian. It's so damn exciting!

Seeing a queer person in a crowd of strangers is like seeing a friend, even if we don't connect, I feel comforted and less alone.

If lesbians engage their "dyke spotting" abilities and invest these sightings with a heightened importance, can we conclude that the process of gaydar ends with recognition and the fleeting "warm and fuzzy" feelings that accompany spotting a "friend" in a crowd of hostile strangers?

ACKNOWLEDGING STRANGERS

The assessment of strangers' identities is, in fact, simply one step in a dynamic interactional process. Symbolic interactionists suggest that all social action stems from these initial categorizations. However, a strong urban norm dictates that strangers appear to pay little heed to each other. Goffman's (1963) concept of "civil inattention" describes the urban interaction ritual in which trust and mutual respect are routinely secured in instances of co-presence between strangers. In a quick scanning of a stranger's eyes, we assess the other's identity and in an equally quick "dimming of the lights" (looking away) we convey respect for the sacredness of the other's self.

Using gaydar can lead to situations of heightened civility where gay strangers momentarily eschew the norms of civil inattention that structure the urban world as they become more attentive to each other based on shared marginalized sexual identity. This "reciprocal responsiveness" (Couch, 1989) takes varied forms. The smallest exchanges between lesbian strangers involve ritualistic mutual acknowledgement. I refer to these actions as "acknowledgement rituals" to capture their habitual nature.

Returning to the scenario described at the beginning of the article, we find that once the four lesbians had read each other's identities, a number of actions followed. These rituals would not likely have been shared among heterosexual strangers. Six lesbian interaction rituals took place on the New York City sidewalk: prolonged eye contact, nodding, smiling, subtle checking out, brief words, and low-level flirting. These rituals have developed historically in lesbian subcultures as ways to show that recognition has occurred and to take that recognition further by displaying solidarity. A Winnipeg lesbian described a number of these rituals.

It is all in the eyes! Initially eye contact and then a subtle smile. If possible, then a longer look to figure out why I think she is or isn't. If I am with another queer person, then we play the "Is She or Isn't She?" game. If it is at all appropriate in the setting, I will engage in low-level flirting. Some lesbians of course carefully avoid any acknowledgment but those who have at least some comfort with who they are make eye contact, smile knowingly, nod hello.

Rituals of acknowledgement in public places are not unique to lesbians. Strangers often find occasion to nod or smile at each other and even to exchange brief greetings. It is the motivation behind the increased interactional civility between lesbians that is unique. In a world where lesbian identity can be problematic, strangers send signals of identity validation to each other through mutual acknowledgment in the form of small gestures filled with amplified meaning. Certain characteristics of these rituals make them specific to the subculture as in the "Is She or Isn't She?" game described above. The persistent use of folk terms such as "the knowing smile," "the butch nod," or "the subtle check out" to describe the ways lesbians respond to each other suggests their ubiquity in the lesbian subculture.

The interactions described in the opening scenario could not have taken place without the most basic of rituals: eye contact. Mutual eye contact is "perhaps the most direct and purest reciprocity which exists anywhere" (Simmel, 1970: 301). In the simplest gestures the most profound messages are sent. It is for this reason that the eye is said to be the window to the soul.

Civil inattention is often altered when lesbians are co-present. Lesbians repeatedly state that they can detect another lesbian by the intensity of the eye contact she makes. Despite the apparent simplicity and brevity of this ritual, its message is profound and its effects in guiding social action enormous. Folk terms for this slightly longer eye contact include "the knowing look," "the prolonged glance," or "the lingering gaze." In a very short time, lasting only a second or two, lesbians convey in "the look" that a secret knowledge is shared. As a Toronto resident put it, "If you catch a woman looking at you (twice or in a cautious but lingering way—apart from the 'through you' stares of public transit) then it is a signal that you are being checked out and read as queer or whatever."

Due to its secretive nature, lesbians often describe intense or prolonged eye contact as exciting. A Winnipeg lesbian observes:

Making eye contact with dykes conjures up feeling of pleasure, delight, a sense of power that we know something about each other that maybe other people on the street don't recognize—or if they recognize it they are not part of it.

Eye contact is both a behavioural cue of recognition and an action of acknowledgment. One way that lesbians determine the accuracy of a gaydar reading is by assessing the quality and length of eye contact they receive from a stranger. In the scenario below, described by a Toronto lesbian, eye contact is the only cue available. It is such a powerful cue, however, that it is enough to solidify a gaydar reading.

My first experience recognizing a lesbian came about when I was 16 years old. A new teacher had come to our school. She dressed femmy, had a good figure and long blond hair. I was in the empty hall going through my locker when she came out of her classroom. It was just she and me in the hallway. I looked up at her and our eyes locked. And I knew, and I knew that she knew. I was almost knocked over with the surprise of it all. I started to laugh and she started to laugh and we just stood there in the hallway smiling and laughing and seeing each other. The bell rang and the hallway filled with students. So what was it? It wasn't her look or anything she wore. It wasn't situational, the high-school hallway. It was the way she looked at me. Like she knew who I was. Like we shared something. It was also wild to know this thing that I was sure no one else in the school knew. That she was willing to let herself be recognized by recognizing me. That was my first real experience with recognizing a lesbian stranger: it was strange and joyful. Later when I told my gay friends about the experience, I couldn't really explain how I knew, but I was and still am 100% certain. I knew because she told me [in the way she looked at me].

Few lesbians, I suspect, would read this story without emotion. This moment, described so lucidly, captures the essence of what gaydar means to many lesbians. Neither of the lesbians in the scenario was "out," in the full meaning of the term, and yet they shared a brief moment of solidarity that placed them outside the heterosexual norm.

Prolonged or intense eye contact seals an identity placement made through assessment of cues. Further rituals (e.g., smiling, nodding, or exchanging greetings) follow eye contact. If the situation is conducive, more spontaneous actions, such as low-level flirting, may take place.[7] These rituals of recognition and acknowledgement temporarily imbue public places with lesbian meaning. Hence, they can ease the difficulties that lesbians experience in negotiating a heterosexist society. Are engagements between lesbian strangers always so subtle and ritualistic?

ENCOUNTERS

Anti-urbanites view the idea of stranger interaction as an oxymoron (Lofland, 1990). The following quote sums up an attitude toward the public realm that continues to influence both the sociological imagination (Mills, 1959) and commonsense beliefs about urbanite interaction:

On the street, in the subway, on the bus [the city dweller] comes in contact with hundreds of people. But these brief incidental associations are based neither on sharing of common values nor on a cooperation for a common purpose. They are formal in the most complete sense of the term in that they are empty of content. (Spykman, 1926: 58)

Is this pessimistic conjecture a reality? Not so, according to urban ethnographers.[8] On the contrary, a moral order underlies the apparent chaos and impersonality of city streets. This "interaction order" (Goffman, 1983) is sustained differently from the morality found in primary groups. Strangers on city streets do not display the kinds of close interaction found in smaller settings; that would be impossible. Yet civil intentions can be detected between strangers, affirming the existence of a collective urban civility.

Being openly gay in public places carries a degree of risk. Despite this fact, or perhaps because of it, gay people may find more opportunities than heterosexuals to engage in encounters. Heightened civility between lesbian strangers, then, moves beyond politeness and a collective effort to sustain an orderly society. Such actions also send messages of solidarity. Once the transitory actions of mutual acknowledgement take place, openings in the norms of silence between strangers may be created where lesbians make contacts that are spontaneous and enduring in nature. These encounters range from small gestures of helping behaviour to more sustained interactions, such as making friends or romantic connections.

Lesbians often state that they are more willing to help a stranger if they perceive her to be gay. They may look for reasons to assist a woman they have tagged as lesbian in order to connect. Two lesbians, from Minneapolis and Vancouver, respectively, illustrate this point.

I always try to be extra nice to the dykes who checkout at my register (give them free stuff, talk more, flirt, etc.). There is a lot of negativity and homophobia out there, so I smile and make eye contact a lot. Sometimes I try to start conversation if it is reasonable.

I decided in my mind which of the staff at a bookstore I shopped at in Vancouver were lesbians based on which ones were more overtly friendly to me when I was buying or browsing through lesbian-themed books. When I worked in retail and lesbians (or women I assumed or suspected were lesbians) came into the store, I was much more friendly to them than to general customers.

Always aware of safety issues, lesbians are often subtle in their interactions with lesbian strangers. Although the events described below by a New Yorker do not typify normal subway riding behaviour, the incident is unexceptional. Though no words are exchanged, the meaning of the nonverbal communication is clear.

My girlfriend and I were riding the subway home, and it was fairly late. A very interesting couple sat across from us holding hands. The younger of the two was an androgynous, butchy dyke, and her girlfriend was much older and clearly femme. My girlfriend was holding my hand and we all very subtly, casually glanced at each other. They were getting off the subway at the same stop as us, and when the subway doors opened, the butchy dyke stood at the opening *holding the door* until her girlfriend, *my* girlfriend and *myself* had safely exited. The funny thing is, we would have made it through the door just fine on our own, I mean we'd definitely done it many times before...*but*, it was simply the *beauty*, and *respect* and *recognition* and *pride* of the gesture that really struck me. The subway is definitely one of the scariest places to be out, because you are surrounded by some of the scariest people in New York ya know? It was just so beautiful how this woman *without* words made such as huge statement to me and my girl, by showing concern and recognizing us.

The exchange among the four subway riders can be interpreted as a silent honouring of the boldness of being "out" in one of the cities "scariest places." In a marginalized subculture, signals of solidarity are political in nature, even when not intended as political statements. Through displays of solidarity, the subculture is strengthened and heterosexual hegemony is challenged.

Political and safety issues aside, strangers connect for the pure pleasure of engaging with fellow human beings (Lofland, 1990). Nonintimate social interaction, although qualitatively different from intimate social interaction, can be deeply satisfying. In fact, these encounters have certain advantages, not the least of which are that differences are not immediately threatening and group dynamics do not come into play. Jane Jacobs has referred to "sidewalk terms" to capture the nature of these types of social engagements. In public places, it is possible to connect with people

without unwelcome entanglements, without boredom, necessity for excuses, explanations, fears of giving offence, embarrassments respecting impositions or commitments and all such paraphernalia of obligations which accompany less limited relationships. It is possible to be on excellent sidewalk terms with people who are very different from oneself (Jacobs, 1961: 62).

Sidewalk connections are made easily among lesbians because they share a symbolic culture that facilitates the breaking down of boundaries. A New Yorker recalls an encounter with a stranger that transformed her bus riding experience. Take notice of the way the interaction unfolded. The mutual reading of identity cues (assisted by subtle actions) was followed by acknowledgement, which led to an encounter.

I was on a city bus. It was extremely crowded with people pushing and shoving their way home. A woman sat down next to me and, although we did not initially acknowledge one another, I read her as a dyke right away. She was middle-aged, with a short haircut and style that I read as 70s feminist lesbian. I realize that I did something I often do when I see others I perceive as queer. I picked up my backpack so that the rainbow beads on the zipper were visible. Whether or not any conversation takes place, I feel a sense of connection with others when I know they've recognized a common sign. I got out my book and began reading. I noticed the woman next to me peering over at the page. Normally I'd be irritated by this, but I was interested to connect with this woman I perceived to be "family" in this straight crowd. I acknowledged her glance by looking back in a friendly way. She mentioned her surprise to see the book and said she [had known] the author long ago. We spoke about the book and about where one might buy the book and she mentioned that she hosts a poetry night at Bluestockings [a lesbian bookstore collective] once a month. We got off the bus at the same stop and went our separate ways...but, speaking with her even just briefly created a sense of connection to the community in me that stayed with me the whole day.

The fact that this episode took place in an ordinary public place is important. The creation of "free territories" in the city is a resistance tactic of marginalized people (Lyman & Scott, 1970). Lesbian territories are spaces where lesbians can interact, free from heterosexual constraints. In more restrictive times, lesbians and gays forged urban spaces in underground places such as bars (Nestle, 1997). With the advent of the gay rights movement, many lesbian spaces, such as coffee shops, bookstores, and urban neighbourhoods with large numbers of lesbians living in them, have become available (Valentine, 1995). Recently, however, the gay community, refusing to be ghettoized, has emphasized the right to be "out" in heterosexually dominated public places.

Considering the historical restriction of lesbian interaction to specified spaces, it is no surprise that interacting as lesbians in nongay public places is exciting. This strategy of being visible in public has become progressively, politically significant.

"Such visibility reacts against the confined space of the 'closet,' which has been perhaps the most compelling metaphor for visibility and identity within gay and lesbian narratives. The closet symbolizes the space of denial, darkness, confinement. To come out depends on emerging from the spatial structures of the closet and into the public, onto the street. Therefore, the process of attaining an authentic gay identity relies on the movement from one space to another—from the closet to the street" (Polchin, 1997: 386).

As lesbians struggle to express themselves freely in public places, the connection between lesbian visibility and street level solidarity continues to grow in importance. Each time lesbians engage with each other in public places, they strengthen the subculture and challenge the right of heterosexuals to dominate those spaces. These interactions infuse a lesbian reality into a society that would otherwise render lesbians invisible. The significance of gaydar and the interactions that follow, then, cannot be underestimated nor dismissed as the trivial imaginings of an elitist subculture. They are parts of the dynamic identity and community building processes that occur on city streets. As Giddens (1984) has argued, it is through the collective actions of individual social actors that structures of society are created and recreated. Indeed Goffman (1967: 91) expressed it best when he observed: "The gestures which we sometimes call empty are perhaps in fact the fullest things of all."

NAVIGATING THE CONCEPTS

1. Nielsen argues that lesbians are motivated to recognize and respond to each other in the public realm. Why is seeing other lesbians in public important for the lesbian subculture? Does this insight apply to other minority groups?

2. Nielsen suggests that lesbians often find interactions with other lesbians in a non-gay public place exciting. As a budding sociologist, how would you explain such a reaction?

3. With reference to the article, explore the quotation, "The gestures which we sometimes call empty are perhaps in fact the fullest things of all."

NOTES

1. This article is drawn from my Ph.D. dissertation. For details of the methodology, theoretical outcomes, and in-depth quotations from participants see Nielsen (2002), "Streets Strangers and Solidarity: A Study of Lesbian Interaction in the Public Realm." Unpublished dissertation. The University of Manitoba.

2. The word "out" is used by gays and lesbians to refer to being open (i.e., "out of the closet") about their sexual identity.

3. Outright condemnation of stereotyped thinking is unrealistic. Although it is tempting to relegate stereotyping to the rigid attitudes of prejudiced people, in reality all people must employ stereotypes to organize the kaleidoscopic flow of events around them. A more realistic approach is to confront the dual reality of these "enabling conventions" (Goffman, 1971) as both distorters of reality and doorways to social engagement.

4. Note that as part of the "gay pride" movement, gays and lesbians have re-appropriated pejorative labels such as queer, dyke, fag, and homo. By adopting these labels for their own use, the subculture has reduced their power to stigmatize.

5. Turner's (1990) concept of "role making" describes the way that social actors impose meanings on situations through the process of testing the inferences they make about others in social situations.

6. For a detailed analysis of the ways that strangers use these different types of cues (appearential, behavioural, and spatial) in making sense of the chaotic "world of strangers" see Lofland (1973).

7. For an explanation of why low-level flirting takes on ritualistic qualities in the lesbian subculture as both a gaydar cue and a recognition strategy, see Nielsen (2002). The dissertation outlines the details of these rituals and the situational variables that affect whether they take place (i.e., safety, spatial concerns, racial variables, and outness levels).

8. Urban ethnographers have steadily chipped away at the pervasive belief in the emptiness of urban interaction. See Lofland (1998) for an overview of these ethnographic studies.

REFERENCES

Couch, C. 1989. *Social processes and relationships*. New York: General Hall.

Giddens, A. 1984. *The constitution of society: Outline of the theory of structuration*. Cambridge: Polity Press.

Gardner, C. B. 1994. A family among strangers: Kinship claims among gay men in public places. In *The community of the streets*, eds. L. Lofland, and S. Cahill, 95–120. London: JAI Press Inc.

Goffman, E. 1959. *The presentation of self in everyday life*. New York: Anchor.

———. 1963. *Behavior in public places*. New York: Free Press of Glencoe.

———. 1967. *Interaction ritual*. New York: Pantheon Books.

———. 1971. *Relations in public*. New York: Basic Books.

———. 1983. The interaction order. *American Sociological Review,* 48: 1–17.

Jacobs, J. 1961. *The death and life of great American cities*. New York: Vintage Books.

Lofland, L. 1973. *A world of strangers: Order and action in urban public space*. New York: Basic Books.

———. 1990. Social interaction: Continuities and complexities in the study of nonintimate sociality. In *Sociological perspectives on social psychology,* eds. K. Cook, G. Fine, and J. House, 176–201. Boston: Allyn and Bacon.

———. 1998. *The public realm: Exploring the city's quintessential social territory*. New York: Basic Books.

Lyman, S., and M. Scott. 1970. Territoriality: A neglected sociological dimension. In *Social psychology through symbolic interactionism,* eds. G. Stone, and H. Faberman, 214–26. Massachusetts: Xerox College Publishing.

Mills, C. W. 1959. *The sociological imagination*. London: Oxford University Press.

Nestle, J. 1997. Restriction and reclamation: Lesbian bars and beaches in the 1950s. In *Queers in space: Communities, public places, resistance,* eds. G. Ingram, A. Bouthilette, and Y. Retter, 61–8. Seattle: Bay Press.

Nielsen, T. 2002. Streets, strangers and solidarity: A study of lesbian interaction in the public realm. Unpublished dissertation. Winnipeg: University of Manitoba.

Polchin, J. 1997. Having something to wear: The landscape of identity on Christopher Street. In *Queers in space: Communities, public places, resistance,* eds. G. Ingram, A. Bouthilette, and Y. Retter, 381–90. Seattle: Bay Press.

Simmel, G. 1970. On visual interaction. In *Social psychology through symbolic interactionism,* eds. G. Stone, and H. Farberman, 300–02. Massachusetts: Xerox College Publishing.

Spykman, N. 1926. A social philosophy of the city. In *The urban community: Selected papers from the proceedings of the American Sociological Society,* ed. E. Burgess. Chicago: University of Chicago Press.

Turner, R. 1990. Role-taking: Process versus conformity. In *Life as theatre: A dramaturgical sourcebook,* eds. D. Brissett, and C. Edgley, 85–100. New York: Aldine de Gruyter.

Valentine, G. 1995. Out and about: Geographies of lesbian landscapes. *International Journal of Urban and Regional Research,* 19: 96–112.

Chapter 11

The Rebels: A Brotherhood of Outlaw Bikers

Daniel R. Wolf

Source: Wolf, Daniel R. (1991). *The Rebels: A Brotherhood of Outlaw Bikers*. Toronto: University of Toronto Press. (Reprint pp. 3–21.) Reprinted with permission of the publisher.

Daniel R. Wolf gained entry into the outlaw biker gang the Rebels while using a classic social research strategy, fieldwork. He reviews his experiences.

ENTERING THE WORLD OF THE OUTLAW

All the world likes an outlaw. For some damn reason they remember 'em.

(Jesse James)

A midnight run shatters the night air. Thirty Harley-Davidson motorcycles stretch out for a quarter-mile, thundering down the highway. The pack moves in tight formation, advancing as a column of staggered twos. Veteran riders make sure there are fifteen yards between themselves and the bikes they are riding behind, three yards and a 45-degree angle between themselves and the bikes they are riding beside. Thirty men ride in boots and jeans, leathers and cut-off denim jackets, beards and long hair, tattoos and earrings, buck knives and chain belts. Each rider follows the grimacing skull on the back patch of the rider in front of him. Some ride with their ol' ladies, "jamming in the wind" with a laid-back coolness bordering on arrogance, a combination of speed, grace, and power. The lead biker snaps his wrist to full throttle and the supercharged V-twin engines heat up and pound out the challenge. Each biker is locked into the tunnel vision of his own world. He feels the heavy metal vibrations in every joint of his body, but he can no longer hear the rumble of his own machine, just a collective roar. Headlamps slice open just enough darkness to let the sculptured metal of extended front ends slide through. Cool blackness clips over high-rise handlebars, whips their faces, then quickly swallows the red glare of tail-lights. A grey blur of pavement that represents instant oblivion passes six inches beneath the soles of their boots. At a hundred miles an hour the inflections of the road surface disappear, eye sockets are pushed back, and tears flow. Riders hurtle down the highway, in total control of their own destinies, wrapped in the freedom of high sensation. They are the Rebels: Caveman, Blues, Tiny, Wee Albert, Gerry, Slim, Tramp, Danny, Onion, Jim Raunch, Ken, Voodoo, Larry, Killer, Whimpy, Clayton, Steve, Indian, Armand, Crash, Big Mike, Smooth Ed, Yesnoski, Snake, Dale the Butcher, Saint, and Terrible Tom.

Outlaw motorcycle clubs originated on the American west coast following the Second World War. With names such as the Booze Fighters and their parent club the 13 Rebels, the Galloping Gooses, Satan's Sinners, and the Winos, they rapidly spread across the United States and into Canada in the early 1950s; Canada's first outlaw club was the Canadian Lancers in Toronto, Ontario. Today, outlaw motorcycle clubs are an international social phenomenon. As of 1990 the outlaw club subculture had spread into eleven other countries, including the European nations of Great Britain, West Germany, France, Switzerland, Austria, Belgium, Denmark, and the Netherlands in the mid-sixties and early seventies, and then into Australia, New Zealand, and Brazil in the mid-seventies and early eighties.

What is or is not considered deviant by society, and how society reacts to that deviance, always involves the process of social definition. Technically, the label "outlaw motorcycle club" designates a club that is not registered with the American Motorcycle Association (AMA) or the Canadian Motorcycle Association (CMA), which are the respective governing bodies for the sport of motorcycling in the United States and Canada. The AMA and CMA are themselves affiliated with the Fédération Internationale Motorcycliste (FIM), the international coordinating body for motorcycling whose headquarters are located in Paris, France. A motorcycle club that is registered with the AMA or CMA obtains a club charter from those parent bodies that allows the club and its members to participate in or sponsor sanctioned motorcycle events— mainly racing competitions. AMA or CMA registration further aligns the club with the legal and judicial elements of the host society; some clubs will go one step further and incorporate themselves as "registered societies" with the local state or provincial authorities. Non-registered clubs are labelled "outlaw" and considered as the 1 per cent deviant fringe that continues to tarnish the public image of both motorcycles and motorcyclists. For its part, the outlaw-biker community graciously accepted the AMA's "one percenter" label as a means of identifying a "righteous outlaw." Today, many outlaw club members wear 1% badges as a supplement to their club colours; or, as Sonny Barger, president of the Hell's Angels, first did in the sixties, they make a very personal and uncompromising statement on where they stand on the issue of being an outlaw by having the 1% logo tattooed on their shoulders.

Historically, the initial and most dramatic definition of outlaw clubs occurred in response to the world's first motorcycle riot in the rural town of Hollister, California, on 4 July 1947. Approximately five hundred non-affiliated bikers disrupted an AMA-sponsored Gypsy Tour and competition events involving 2500 affiliated bikers by drinking and racing in the streets of the host town of Hollister. The ineffective efforts of a numerically insufficient seven-man police force, in conjunction with the sometimes provocative vigilante tactics of indignant local residents, caused the motorcyclists to coalesce as a mob. At the height of the riot, bikers rode their motorcycles into bars and restaurants and through traffic lights, tossed bottles out of upper-floor windows, and got rid of the beer they had been drinking in the streets (indecent exposure). The unruly behaviour lasted for approximately thirty-six hours, from July 4th to 5th; the world's first motorcycle riot ended with the departure of many of the partyers on the evening of the first day and the arrival on the second of an auxiliary police force of thirty-two officers.

The national exposure that was given the Hollister incident by *Life* magazine and others resulted in the stigmatization of an image: the motorcyclist as deviant. *Life's* account started a mass-media chain reaction that saw the Hollister incident grow considerably in its sensationalistic portrayal, and, as a result, the image of the motorcyclist as deviant become more defined and immutable. In 1949, Frank Rooney wrote a short narrative entitled "Cyclist Raid," based on *Life's* one-hundred-and-fifteen-word documentary, in 1951, "Cyclist Raid" was published in *Harper's* magazine. The *Harper's* serial was read by Stanley Kramer, a Hollywood producer, who immortalized the "motorcycle riot" in the movie *The Wild One,* released in 1953. The anti-hero image of the motorcyclist was cast in the person of Marion Brando, while Lee Marvin personified the motorcyclist as villain. Interestingly enough, the striped shirt that Lee Marvin wore in the movie was later bought by a member of the Hell's Angels Motorcycle Club (MC)—a symbolic indication of events to come. The movie was to titillate the North American media with its "factual" account of a "menacing element of modern youth":

A little bit of the surface of contemporary American life is scratched in Stanley Kramer's "The Wild One"...and underneath is opened an ugly, debauched and frightening view of a small, but particularly significant and menacing element of modern youth....

The subject of its examination is a swarm of youthful motorcyclists who ride through the country in wolf-pack fashion and terrorize the people of one small town.... These "wild ones" resent discipline and show an aggressive contempt for common decency and the police. Reckless and vandalistic, they live for sensations, nothing more—save perhaps the supreme sensation of defying the normal world. (Crowther, *New York Times*, 31 December 1953)

Audiences who like their facts dished up with realism, no matter how painful, might pay attention to "The Wild One"—a picture that is factual.... It displays a group of hoodlums, motorcyclists who ride around the country with a contempt for the law and a fondness for annoying people, who take over a small town...a slice of contemporary Americana at its worst. (Hartung, *Commonweal*, 3 February 1954)

The above "factual" accounts were based on viewing a Stanley Kramer movie production whose script was written by John Paxton; Paxton's script was based on Kramer's reading of Frank Rooney's serialized story in *Harper's* magazine; Rooney's short story was in turn based on his reading of *Life's* one-hundred-and-fifteen-word report—complete with photo —which itself was originally construed by adding four major distortions to a brief press-wire release.

By contemporary standards the amount of property damage and civic duress incurred in Hollister was minimal. In actuality there were only thirty-eight arrests (out of approximately three or four thousand bikers), fighting was mostly confined to the bikers, and no one was killed, maimed, or even gang-kissed. "Wino Willie" Forkner is a biker who has ridden Harleys since he was a teenager in the 1930s. He had returned from the Second World War after fighting the Japanese as a waist gunner and engineer for the American Seventh Air Force. He attended the Hollister incident as a charter member of the Booze Fighters MC:

The worst thing that happened was that a bunch of guys wanted to break Red Daldren out of jail. I was in a bar and somebody came in and said there were about 500 bikers ready to break him out, and I thought, "Shit, that's all we need, something like that." So I ran down to where the crowd was assembling and told 'em, "Hell, old Red's drunk and he needs a good night's sleep. Leave him stay—he'll be out in the morning." Then I turned around and went back to the bar, and damned if the cops didn't come and nail me for inciting a riot [the charges were dropped]...but no big bad things happened. There were a few broken windows that we paid for. ("Wino Willie" Forkner, interview in *Easyriders*, September 1986: 107)

However, as *Life* was to point out twenty-five years after the Hollister riot, the significance of the media chain reaction was its very real consequences: "The *Wild One* became a milestone in movie history, launching the cult of gang violence in films. It also helped create an image of motorcycling that non-violent bike riders have been trying to live down for a quarter of a century now" (*Life*, September 1972: 32). After the Hollister incident and, more to the point, after the movie, the AMA issued its now famous statement about 1 per cent of the motorcycling public, specifically clubs like the Booze Fighters, being a deviant criminal fringe element.

There is a tendency to view the Hollister motorcycle riot and its subsequent national media coverage as the genesis of the "outlaw biker"—it was the birth of an image. In effect, the outlaw biker image that was created served as a frame of reference for many young and restless rebels who copied the celluloid vision in search of both a thrill and a cause. Historically, outlaw motorcycle clubs have operated in the shadows of several different media stereotypes, all of which have been variations on the theme of "social menace." In the 1950s bikers were depicted as social rebels and deviants; in the sixties and seventies the clubs were seen as subcultures of violence and drugs. The contemporary image adds a spectre of organized crime. In 1984 the Criminal Intelligence Service of Canada (CISC) declared that outlaw motorcycle gangs had become as much of an organized-crime threat to Canada as the traditional Mafia. According to the CISC report, outlaw clubs "are involved in practically all major crime activities from murder to white-collar crime." At the annual meeting of Canadian police chiefs in 1985, outlaw motorcycle clubs were again acknowledged as the number-one concern in the area of organized crime; media headlines carried the claim: "Bikers more powerful than Mafia" (Canadian Press release, *Edmonton Journal*, 15 August 1985: A12). How law-enforcement agencies have come to view outlaw motorcycle clubs is summarized in the following profile contained in an application for a search warrant made out by a member of the City of Calgary police department's Special Strike Force:

Outlaw Motorcycle Gangs have over the years evolved into highly sophisticated "organized crime" bodies, involved in drug manufactured/ distribution/trafficking, prostitution, "gun running," fencing of stolen property and strong arm debt collection.

Law enforcement agencies across Canada have recognized that outlaw motorcycle gangs as "organized crime" bodies pose the single most serious threat to the country.

An outlaw motorcycle gang is "Any group of motorcycle enthusiasts who have voluntarily made a

commitment to band together and abide by their organization's rigorous rules enforced by violence, who engage in activities that bring them and their club into serious conflict with society and the law."

It is their involvement as a group in criminal activities and antisocial behaviour which sets them apart from other organized groups. (Detective Brendan Alexander Kapuscinski, City of Calgary police force, "Application for Warrant to Search and Seize," 1988: 2)

"If the Cops are the Good Guys," writes the representative of an American federal law-enforcement training centre, "then it's hard to imagine a more archetypal Bad Guy than the outlaw motorcyclist!" (Ayoob, 1982: 26). North Americans typically react with an interesting mixture of apprehension and fascination to the fearsome images of aggression, revolt, anarchy, and criminal abandon that are used to portray outlaw-biker gangs.

Ironically, the appeal of outlaw clubs to their members is very different from what the public understands. Outlaw bikers view themselves as nothing less than frontier heroes, living out the "freedom ethic" that they feel the rest of society has largely abandoned. They acknowledge that they are antisocial, but only to the extent that they seek to gain their own unique experiences and express their individuality through their motorcycles. Their "hogs" become personal charms against the regimented world of the "citizen." They view their club as collective leverage that they can use against an establishment that threatens to crush those who find conventional society inhibiting and destructive of individual character. In an interesting twist of stereotypes the citizen becomes the bad guy, or at least weak, and the outlaw becomes the hero. Bikers make much of the point that the differential treatment—harassment—accorded outlaw clubs by law-enforcement agencies runs counter to the basic principles of self-determination. They protest that a truly democratic society should be able to tolerate diversity and accommodate an awareness that drifting away from society's conventions is very different from opting out of society's laws. Somewhere between the convenient stereotype of "criminal deviants" used by the police and the stylized self-conscious image outlaws have of themselves as "frontier heroes" lies the story of real people.

The Rebels Motorcycle Club is an outlaw club. It began in 1969 as a small club of motorcycle enthusiasts who rode their Harley-Davidsons on the streets of Edmonton, Alberta, a mid-sized Canadian city with a population of approximately 700,000 people. Today (1990), the Rebels MC is a federation of four clubs—located in the provinces of Alberta and Saskatchewan—that maintains informal social and political ties with the Hells Angels MC. Becoming a Rebel means being part of a tightly knit voluntary association that operates as a secret society within an organizational framework that includes a political structure, a financial base, a geographical territory, a chain of command, a constitution, an elaborate set of rules, and internal mechanisms for enforcing justice and compliance from within.

At its best a veteran club will operate with the internal discipline and precision of a paramilitary organization, which is completely necessary if it hopes to beat the odds and survive. These men close their world to the outside, turning to each other for help and guidance. They protect themselves with a rigid code of silence that cloaks their world in secrecy. Thus, despite the fact that outlaw motorcycle clubs are found in every major urban centre in Canada and the United States—there are approximately 900 clubs—*the subculture had remained ethnographically unexplored.*

As a doctoral graduate student in anthropology at the University of Alberta, Edmonton, I wanted to study the "Harley tribe." It was my intent to obtain an insider's perspective on the emotions and the mechanics that underlie the outlaw bikers' creation of a subcultural alternative. My interest in

outlaw motorcycle clubs was not entirely theoretical; it was also a personal challenge. Brought up on the streets of a lower-class neighbourhood, I saw my best friend—with whom I broke into abandoned buildings as a kid—sent to prison for grand theft auto, and then shot down in an attempted armed robbery. Rather than be crushed like that, I worked in meat-packing plants and factories for thirteen hours a day and put myself through university. I also bought myself a British-made Norton motorcycle. My Norton Commando became a "magic carpet ride" of thrills and excitement that I rode with lean women who were equally hungry to get their share. But it was more than that. I rode my motorcycle in anger; for me it became a show of contempt and a way of defying the privileged middle class that had put me down and had kept my parents "in their place." I felt that the Establishment had done me no favours and that I owed it even less. At that time I saw outlaw bikers as a reflection of my own dark side. I made them the embodiment of my own youthful rebellion and resentment. In retrospect, I believe that it was this aspect of my non-academic background—the fact that I had learned to ride and beat the streets—that made it possible for me to contemplate such a study, and eventually to ride with the Rebels.

At the time of beginning my fieldwork I had been riding British-made motorcycles for three years and had talked briefly to members of the King's Crew MC in Calgary. But this was not enough to comprehend the outlaw-biker community or to study it. My impression of outlaw bikers was narrow and incomplete and, in that sense, almost as misleading as the stereotype held by most "citizens." I was physically close to the scene, but far removed from a balanced understanding; that understanding would only come from "being there."

I customized my Norton, donned some biker clothing, and set off to do some fieldwork. My first attempts at contacting an outlaw club were near disasters. In Calgary, I met several members of the King's Crew MC in a motorcycle shop and expressed an interest in "hanging around." But I lacked patience and pushed the situation by asking too many questions. A deviant society, especially one that walks on the wild side of illegal activities, will have its own information network for checking out strangers. I found out quickly that outsiders, even bikers, do not rush into a club, and that anyone who doesn't show the proper restraint will be shut out. That was mistake number one. Days later, I carelessly got into an argument with a club "striker," a probationary member, that led to blows in a bar-room skirmish. He flattened my nose and began choking me. Unable to get air down my throat and breathing only blood through my nostrils, I managed a body punch that luckily found his solar plexus and loosened his grip. I then grabbed one of his hands and pulled back on the thumb till l heard the joint break. Mistake number two. It was time to move on. I packed my sleeping-bag on my Norton and headed west for Vancouver with some vague and ridiculous notion of meeting up with the Satan's Angels, now a chapter of the Hell's Angels.

Riding into Burnaby (Greater Vancouver) I discovered that an outlaw biker has to learn a whole new set of rules for dealing with the law. I had decided to modify my public identity in order to facilitate participant observation of a deviant group; I could not expect any favours from legal authorities and I would have to learn how to cope with what might be termed differential treatment—bikers use the term "harassment"—on the part of police officers. I saw the flashing red light in my rear-view mirror moments before l heard the siren. I had been looking for the Admiral Hotel, a bar where the Satan's Angels hung out. I started to gear down when I noticed that the RCMP (Royal Canadian Mounted Police) cruiser was only three feet from my rear tire. I continued to slow down and hoped that he knew what he was doing. I pulled into the parking lot behind the Admiral bar, got off my bike, and turned around to approach the officer. As I reached for my wallet he immediately ordered me to turn around and put my hands behind my head. I froze in what was probably 90 per cent uncertainty and 10 per cent defiance. When I didn't move he unlatched the holster that held his pistol; he gripped the weapon and then reached inside his car and grabbed the radio mike to call for a backup. Within moments a second cruiser was on the scene. He lined me up with the car's headlights, turned on the high beams, and then began the standard shakedown. Upon request I produced my operator's licence, vehicle registration, and insurance, and was then asked where I was from, what club I rode with, if I had a criminal record, and if I had ever been in trouble with the law before. As I answered the questions, wondering what kind of trouble I was in now, a third cruiser pulled up, turned on its bright lights, and two more officers joined in. At that time some of my identification read "Daniel" and some read "Danny," which prompted a series of questions about aliases and a radio check about outstanding arrest warrants and vehicle registration. When this failed to produce any evidence against me, I was asked if I was carrying any weapons or drugs. The answer to both questions was "no" and the whole situation began to seem absurd. I was being put on stage under the spotlights of three police cruisers in a back alley drama directed by five RCMP officers. Meanwhile, the Satan's Angels that I'd come to meet were relaxing and having some cool beers in the bar across the alley. I began to laugh at the irony, which was mistake number three. "Put your hands up against that wall!" yelled a constable who was angered by my apparent disdain for he law. One officer searched through the pockets of my leathers and jeans while another rummaged through the leather saddle-bags on my bike. After the bike and body search, I asked the officers if motorcycle clubs were a major problem in their area. I was told they weren't, "but some guys figure they're king shit when you pull them over, and you've got to remember that no matter how tough you are, there's always someone tougher!" I was then asked how long I was staying, and I replied that it depended on my financial situation. I answered straightforwardly and stated that I was carrying credit cards and a little more than three hundred dollars, as the police already knew—having counted it. Only then did one of the officers explain: "When he asked you how long you're staying, what he's saying is that this road leads to Harvey Avenue, which leads to the highway out of town!"

I had sewn a secret pocket into the sleeve of my leather jacket. It contained a letter from the [Social Sciences and Humanities Research Council]...(SSHRC) addressed to the RCMP that identified myself and my research. The officers failed to find it, and I wasn't about to reveal it. My research goal was to find out and experience what happens within the outlaw-biker scene, not be told what happens from the outside. Three days earlier I had talked to a Vancouver city police officer who knew me as a researcher: "I'll save you a whole lot of trouble, maybe even your neck, and explain this whole biker thing to you," he said. "They're all just psychologically unstable. That's all you have to know; otherwise none of it makes any sense."

"Those cops [at the Admiral Hotel] were setting you up," Steve, the Rebels MC sergeant at arms, would explain some months later. "They were just waiting for you to make a stupid move and they've got you by the balls. They could have beaten the shit outta you, and you'd have five cops as witnesses. Well, it would've been tough shit for you!" I learned that one does not play the role of Jesse James when being pulled over by "the man," especially on a "club run," or motorcycle tour, where police can make a shakedown last up to two hours. One learns to avoid all eye contact and restrict all verbal responses to a monosyllabic "no" or "yes." Over the next few years I got lots of practice; that first summer I was pulled over and interrogated fifteen times—on only one of these occasions was I actually charged with an offence, a speeding violation.

While touring through the British Columbia interior I joined up with three members of the Tribesmen MC from Squamish, BC, whom I met at a Penticton hamburger stand. From the Tribesmen I learned that gaining entry into a club would take time. The time factor meant that my best chance of success lay in studying the Rebels in the familiar confines of my own back yard in Edmonton. "You don't make friends with members of a club," cautioned Lance of the Tribesmen. "You let them make friends with you." Lance pointed out that in order to ride with a club I would have to be accepted by all the members, get to know some of the members personally, and at least one member well enough that he would be willing to sponsor me and take responsibility for my actions. A critical suggestion emphatically made by all three Tribesmen was "Get yourself a hog [Harley-Davidson]!"

These first experiences "in the field" made it clear that I couldn't study any club I wanted, at any time that suited me. There was a good reason for this, as I discovered later. Restricting contacts with non-club members was a key to club survival. With time I realized that maintaining strict boundaries is a central theme that underlies all aspects of club life. This fact presented a major ethical dilemma. I could not do a study if I explained my research goal at the outset. However, an "undercover" strategy contravened a fundamental ethical tenet in which I believed, that no research should be carried out without the informants' full awareness. I devised an alternative strategy that satisfied myself, my thesis committee, and the guidelines that the University of Alberta had set down for ethical research. The plan was that initially I would attempt to establish contact with the Rebels as a biker who also happened to be a university—anthropology—student. If I were successful in achieving sufficient rapport and mutual trust with club members, I would officially ask the Rebels MC for permission to conduct a study. The bottom line was that it would be the Rebel club members I rode with who would make the final decision as to whether or not the study would go beyond my personal files.

This strategy was not without risks. Outlaw clubs are aware that they are under constant police surveillance, often by special police units, such as the RCMP's E-squad in Vancouver or the City of Calgary's Strike Force. I learned that the Edmonton Rebels suspected that a biker who had recently attempted to gain entry into their club as a "striker" was an agent of the RCMP. After repeated attempts, the police have long since discovered that infiltrating an outlaw club is a long, arduous, and risky process when it is being done for "professional" reasons. "Infiltration of the gangs is difficult. 'They have an internal discipline that makes it dangerous,' said a police officer. 'It's an area we have trouble infiltrating. The conditions of initiation make it almost impossible....' 'They are scary,' said one police intelligence officer, who asked not to be identified. 'We've had two or three informants killed, found tied to trees up north with bullet holes in them'" (Canadian Press release, *Edmonton Journal,* 29 September 1979).

In the United States the FBI had gone so far as to have several agents start up their own club in order to bypass the striker (probation) period that screens out bogus bikers. The Edmonton police play a wide variety of angles in order to update their information on the Rebels. On one occasion, two plain-clothes officers wore media badges at a biker rally protesting mandatory helmet legislation in order to move freely among the club members and take pictures. If the Rebels discovered my research motive before I was ready to tell them, it would have been difficult to communicate any good intentions, scientific or otherwise.

There existed the distinct possibility that more than just the study would have been terminated prematurely. I lived with that possibility for three years.

I fine-tuned my image before I approached the Rebels. This was going to be my final make-it-or-forget-it attempt. I purchased an old 1955 Harley-Davidson FL, a "panhead," which I customized but later sold in favour of a mechanically more reliable 1972 Electraglide, a "shovelhead." I had grown shoulder-length hair and a heavy beard. I bought a Harley-Davidson leather jacket and vest, wore studded leather wristbands and a shark's-tooth pendant, and sported a cut-off denim jacket with assorted Harley-Davidson pins and patches, all symbolic of the outlaw-biker world-view. While I was still very nervous about approaching the Rebels, I had become more comfortable with myself. My public image expressed what I now felt was my personal character. There was no pretension. As far as I was concerned, I was a genuine biker who was intrigued with the notion of riding with an outlaw club.

I discovered that I was a lot more apprehensive than I thought as I sat at the opposite end of the Kingsway Motor inn and watched the Rebels down their drinks. The loud thunder of heavy-metal rock music would make initiating a delicate introduction difficult if not impossible; and there were no individual faces or features to be made out in the smoky haze, only a series of Rebel skull patches draped over leather jackets in a corner of the bar that outsiders seemed to warily avoid. It was like a scene out of a western movie: hard-faced outlaws in the bar, downing doubles while waiting for the stagecoach to arrive. I decided to go outside and devise an approach strategy, including how I would react if one of the Rebels turned to me and simply said, "Who invited you?" I had thought through five different approaches when Wee Albert of the Rebels MC came out of the bar to do a security check on the "Rebel iron" in the parking lot.

He saw me leaning on my bike and came over to check me out. For some time Wee Albert and I stood in the parking lot and talked about motorcycles, riding in the wind, and the Harley tradition. He showed me some of the more impressive Rebel choppers and detailed the jobs of customizing that members of the club had done to their machines. He then checked out my "hog," gave a grunt of approval, and invited me to come in and join the Rebels at their tables. Drinking at the club bar on a regular basis gave me the opportunity to get to know the Rebels and gave them an opportunity to size me up and check me out on neutral ground. I had made the first of a long sequence of border crossings that all bikers go through if they hope to get close to a club.

Wee Albert became a good buddy of mine, and he sponsored my participation in club runs and at club parties. In addition to my having a Sponsor, my presence had to be voted on by the membership as a whole at their weekly Wednesday meeting, if two of the twenty-five members voted "no," then I wasn't around. The number of close friends that I had in the club increased and I was gradually drawn into the Rebel brotherhood. Measured in terms of social networking, brotherhood meant being part of a high frequency of interpersonal contacts that were activated over a wide range of social situations. Among the activities that I took part in were drinking and carousing in the club bar, assisting members in the chopping (customizing) and repair of motorcycles, loaning and borrowing money, shooting pool and "bullshitting" at the clubhouse, exchanging motorcycle parts along with technical information and gossip at a motorcycle shop owned by two club members, going on a duck hunt and on fishing trips, making casual visits and receiving dinner invitations to members' homes, general partying and riding together, providing emotional support, and, when necessary, standing shoulder-to-shoulder in the face of physical threat. Brotherhood, I came to learn, is the foundation of the outlaw-club community. It establishes among members a sense of moral, emotional, and material interdependence; feelings of commitment arise out of a sense of sharing a common fate. The enduring emotion of brotherhood is comradeship. To a "patch holder" (club member) brotherhood means being there when needed; its most dramatic expression occurs when brothers defend each other from outside threats. I vividly remember sitting with the Rebels in the Kingsway Motor inn bar, trying to sober up quickly while I mentally acted out what I thought would be my best martial-arts moves. I looked down at my hand: I had sprained my thumb the night before while sparring in karate. My right hand was black, blue, swollen, and useless. I watched nervously as sixty-five members of the Canadian Airborne Regiment strutted into the bar. Their walk said that they were looking for us and a brawl. I came to view brotherhood as both a privilege and a tremendous personal responsibility.

I watched my own identity change as the result of experiences I had on my own as a biker and those I shared with club members. These often involved the process of public identification, or labelling, and other reactions by outsiders. I learned that a lone biker on the highway is vulnerable. I was run off the road three times over a four-year period. On one of those occasions I was forced off a mountain road into the side of a cliff and nearly catapulted into oblivion. Another lesson was that an outlaw biker has to be ready for "the heat to come down" at the most unexpected times. For instance, while I was washing my bike at a car wash, the owner phoned the police about a suspicious-looking biker. The police came, searched my bike, and I was arrested and charged with carrying a concealed and illegal weapon—a switch-blade. I felt sure that I would have a criminal record long before, and maybe instead of, a PhD. Fortunately, I discovered that a good lawyer, who is "owed a favour" by the crown prosecutor, can get the charges dropped—in this case, three minutes prior to the start of the trial. I learned that a police officer will follow an outlaw biker for five miles to give him a ticket for doing 35 mph in a 30-mph zone. A biker could be given a ticket for a balding tire or because his custom handlebars were one-half of an inch too high above the motorcycle's seat. I recall being turned down by insurance companies for vehicle coverage, refused admittance to private camp-grounds, and kicked off a public beach by Penticton police who thought we intended to incite a riot. I found that associating with outlaw patch holders could be an invitation to danger. While riding with the club, I and some patch holders were pulled over by a cruiser and warned that members of the Highway Kings MC were out gunning for Rebels with shotguns. None of these situations could have been acted out in a detached manner. My involvement demanded the intensity of a highly emotional reaction. Each encounter was an escalation towards an outlaw-biker identity. My record of personal encounters with citizens and the police, especially those that were threatening, enabled me to understand and articulate the biker's perspective on drifting away from the Establishment and being drawn into the club. Sometimes, as I watched the faces of the Rebels, I could see the hardening of an attitude—"us-against-the-world."

Gradually my status changed from being a "biker" with a familiar face to being a "friend of the club." There were no formal announce-ments. Tiny just yelled across at me one afternoon while we were starting up our bikes, "Hey! 'Coyote!' No way I'm riding beside you. Some farmer is going to shoot our asses off and then say he was shooting at varmints." This was a reference to the coyote skin I had taken to wearing over my helmet. Wee Albert looked at me, grinned, and said "That's it, 'Coyote.' From now on that'll be your club name." Most of the patch holders had club names, such as

Spider or Greaser. These names are reminders of club association. More important, they separate the individual from his past, giving him the opportunity to build a new persona in terms of group-valued traits. Pseudonyms give members an aura; they draw upon a collective power. They are no longer just Rick, Allan, or Bill; they are Blues, Terrible Tom, and Caveman; they are outlaw bikers!

As a "friend of the club" I took part informally in political rhetoric concerning the club's future, such as debates concerning the hot issue of club expansion. This position of trust with the Rebels brought me into contact with other outlaw clubs such as the King's Crew of Calgary, the Spokesmen of Saskatoon, the Bounty Hunters of Victoria, the Gypsy Wheelers of White Rock, and the Warlords of Edmonton. Through these inter-club contacts I became familiar with the political relationships of conflict and alliance that exist among outlaw clubs. Meeting members of different clubs also provided me with the comparative data I needed to isolate those aspects of behaviour and organization that were shared by all clubs, and helped to explain how some clubs were different and why. My long-term association with the Rebels gave me a valuable historical perspective that included insights into the developmental sequence of clubs. I was able to describe how new clubs form, why few emergent clubs beat the odds and survive, and how a chosen few clubs achieved long-term success and expansion while all that remains of other clubs is their colours hanging upside down as trophies on the wall of a rival's clubhouse.

If the Rebels had at any time refused permission for the study, I would have destroyed all the data I had collected and closed the investigation. The fact that I had established myself as a friend of the club was no reason for the members to agree to become scientific units of analysis. Rejection of the study appeared more and more imminent as I grew to sense and share members' distrust of outsiders. I had come to appreciate some of the multifaceted advantages of having a negative public stereotype—however unrealistic. When outsiders look at an outlaw biker, they do not see an individual, all they see is the club patch that he wears on the back of his leathers. The negative image that comes with the Rebel skull patch discourages unnecessary intrusions by outsiders. "That way I'm not bothered," explained Steve of the Rebels, "and I don't have to tell the guy 'Fuck off, cunt!'" The patch becomes part of the biker's threat display: it effectively keeps violence to a minimum by warding off those outsiders who might otherwise choose to test the mettle of the bikers. For the majority of outsiders, the prospect of having to initiate even the briefest of encounters with an outlaw biker brings forth emotions ranging from uneasiness to sheer dread. Ironically, the more I got to know the members and the greater the bonds of trust and brotherhood, the less I expected that they would approve of the study. "The best public relations for us," according to Indian of the Rebels, "is no public relations!" I found it increasingly difficult to live with the fact that the closer I came to my destination of knowing the Rebels, the further distant became my goal of doing an ethnographic study.

One night, during a three-week Rebel run to the west coast, I was sharing a beer with Tiny while sitting on the porch of the Bounty Hunters' clubhouse. We were watching officers of the Victoria police force who were watching us from their cruisers in the street and from a nearby hotel—binoculars between closed curtains. "You know, Coyote," grumbled a 6-foot, 275-pound Tiny in a very personable tone, "I've talked with some of the guys and we think that you should strike [enter probationary membership] for the club. The way I see it, it shouldn't take you more than a year to earn your colours [club patch]." The pressure was now on and building for me to make a move that would bring me even closer to the club. I had made a commitment to myself that

under no circumstances would I attempt to become a full-fledged member without first revealing my desire to do a study on the club. It was time to disengage. It was time for me to sell my study to the Rebels, but I was at a loss as to what to say. I had been a brother through good times and bad, thick and thin; but to distance myself from the Rebels by announcing a study done for outsiders of a way of life I had shared with them against the world seemed nothing short of a betrayal. Entering the field as a biker and maintaining relations of trust and friendship during the course of fieldwork prevented my leaving the field with my notes. I had accomplished what I had hoped to during my fieldwork, but at this point there was no way out. There was no formula for disengagement of the field project. As far as I was concerned, I had lost a three-year gamble.

Weeks of personal frustration and near-depression later, I had an incredible stroke of luck. Wee Albert, who took great pleasure in talking about "what it means to be a Rebel and a brother," approached me and said, "Being an anthropologist you study people, right? Well, have you ever thought of maybe doing a study on the club? Chances are it probably wouldn't carry [club approval], but maybe. I'd like to see it happen." I told Wee Albert that I'd consider it and approach the executive members with the proposal. The door of disengagement was open; Wee Albert had provided me with an honourable way out. Whether or not it would be a successful disengagement—the approval of an ethnography—remained to be seen.

I first talked to Ken and Steve about the prospect of "doing an anthropological study." Ken, president, and Steve, sergeant at arms, were both friends of mine and well-respected club officers, but their most positive response was a shrug of the shoulders and "We'll see." Ken decided to bring up the proposed study at a meeting of the club executive. The officers of the club discussed the proposal among themselves and determined that no harm would be done if they presented it one week later to the general membership at a club meeting. For me it was the longest night of the year as I waited for the decision. The issue was hotly debated, a vote was held, and the study approved. Why? Granting me permission for the study was done as a "personal favour": "You have come into favour with a lot of the members and been nothing but good to the club. All in all you've been a pretty righteous friend of the club. But there was a lot of opposition to your study, especially from guys like T.T. [Terrible Tom] and Blues. The way I see it the vote went the way it did because you were asking us a favour. You didn't come in promising us the moon, you know, money from books and that sort of thing. You promised us nothing so we did it as a personal favour" (Wee Albert). Any offers of economic remuneration on my part would have been interpreted as an insult; the Rebels were doing me a favour. I strongly suspect that any researcher who buys his or her way into a closed society—with promises of money or royalties—will garner information that is at best forced, at worst fabricated. However, I did give the "victims" of the four-and-one-half-hour questionnaire a twenty-six-ounce bottle of Alberta Springs (Old Time Sipping Whisky) and a Harley-Davidson beer mug. "Fair return" for the club as a whole was a bound copy of my thesis, which found a home in the Rebels' clubhouse.

I continued to ride with the Rebels for another year and a half, during which time I carried out formal data-gathering procedures. These included extensive open-ended interviews with a number of Rebel patch holders and ended with the administration of a four-hour-long structured questionnaire to six members. Interestingly enough, Blues, a Rebel who was both a friend and a staunch opponent of the study, was one of the six. "The club is all I have. It means everything to me. It's with me all the time. I feel leery about talking to anybody about it. If I wasn't 100 per cent for

you I wouldn't be here. If you'd been asking these questions three years ago [when I initially made contact with the Rebels MC], well no fucking way. We've been burned before, but never again!" Blues's trust and vote of confidence brought me a tremendous degree of personal satisfaction.

The theoretical framework and methodological approach that I use in [my] book are based on a cognitive definition of culture. Culture is here defined as the rules and categories of meaning and action that are used by individuals to both interpret and generate appropriate behaviour. I therefore view the outlaw-biker subculture as a human experience. It is a system of meaning in which I, as an anthropologist, had to involve myself in order to develop an adequate explanation of what was being observed. That is, in order to understand the biker subculture, or any culture for that matter, one must first try to understand it as it is experienced by the bikers themselves. Only then can one comprehend both the meaning of being an outlaw and how that meaning is constructed and comes to be shared by bikers. Only by first seeing the world through the eyes of the outlaws can we then go on to render intelligible the decisions that they make and the behaviours they engage in. Those meanings, decisions, and behaviours may lead you to applaud outlaw bikers as heroes. Alternatively, they may lead you to condemn them as villains. Labelling them as heroes or villains is a subsequent value judgment that the reader has the option of making. That value judgment is quite separate from first knowing outlaw bikers—my job as an ethnographer.

In order to operationalize this theoretical position of capturing an insider's perspective, I adopted a research methodology that closely resembles that of a symbolic interactionist. That is, within the overall framework of participant observation I emphasize analysis that is proximate—events are described in terms of variables that are close to the immediate situation in which the actors find themselves; processual—events are viewed as an emerging step-by-step reality whose completion requires actors to meet a series of contingencies; and phenomenological—events are explained in a manner that pays serious attention to how the actors experience them (Lofland, 1969: 296–97). By blending the methodological strategy of participant observation with the perspective of symbolic interactionism (Visano, 1989: 3, 29), I hope to replicate for the reader the experienced natural world as it unfolds for the outlaw biker.

NAVIGATING THE CONCEPTS

1. With reference to Wolf's analysis and your own subjective perceptions, would you consider the social organization of a teen "gang" similar to that of a bike gang? Why?

2. Do you think that the image of the biker has changed since the Hollister incident in 1947? If so, what factors would you argue explain the change? If not, why do you feel the image has remained the same for such a long time?

3. Has Wolf's presentation of the Rebels changed how you look at bike gangs? If so, how; if not, why?

REFERENCES

Ayoob, M. 1982. Outlaw bikers. *Police Product News,* 6(5).

Forkner, W. 1986. "Wino" Willie Forkner: All the old romance retold. *Easyriders* 16(159).

Kapuscinski, B. A. 1988. Application for warrant to search and seize. Attorney-General of the Province of Alberta: 2.

Lofland, J. 1969. *Deviance and identity*. Englewood Cliffs. N.J.: Prentice-Hall.

Visano, L. 1989. Researching deviance: An interactionist account. Paper presented at the Canadian Sociology and Anthropology Association annual conference, Quebec City.

Chapter 12

Researching Dealers and Smugglers

Patricia A. Adler

Source: From *Wheeling and Dealing* by Patricia A. Adler © (1985) Columbia University Press. Reprinted with the permission of the publisher.

Patricia A. Adler reviews her research into a group of drug traffickers. Her experiences demonstrate the many challenges, both personal and professional, that sociologists face as they investigate potentially dangerous subcultures. The lessons Adler learned translate easily into social scientific research and show how the lines between scholarly interest and real life often overlap.

I strongly believe that investigative field research (Douglas, 1976), with emphasis on direct personal observation, interaction, and experience, is the only way to acquire accurate knowledge about deviant behavior. Investigative techniques are especially necessary for studying groups such as drug dealers and smugglers because the highly illegal nature of their occupation makes them secretive, deceitful, mistrustful, and paranoid. To insulate themselves from the straight world, they construct multiple false fronts, offer lies and misinformation, and withdraw into their group. In fact, detailed, scientific information about upper-level drug dealers and smugglers is lacking precisely because of the difficulty sociological researchers have had in penetrating into their midst. As a result, the only way I could possibly get close enough to these individuals to discover what they were doing and to understand their world from their perspectives (Blumer, 1969) was to take a membership role in the setting. While my different values and goals precluded my becoming converted to complete membership in the subculture, and my fears prevented my ever becoming "actively" involved in their trafficking activities, I was able to assume a "peripheral" membership role (Adler & Adler, 1987). I became a member of the dealers' and smugglers' social world and participated in their daily activities on that basis. In this chapter, I discuss how I gained access to this group, established research relations with members, and how personally involved I became in their activities.

GETTING IN

When I moved to Southwest County [California] in the summer of 1974, I had no idea that I would soon be swept up in a subculture of vast drug trafficking and unending partying, mixed with occasional cloak-and-dagger subterfuge. I had moved to California with my husband, Peter, to attend graduate school in sociology. We rented a condominium townhouse near the beach and started taking classes in the fall. We had always felt that socializing exclusively with academicians left us nowhere to escape from our work, so we tried to meet people in the nearby community. One of the first friends we made was our closest neighbor, a fellow in his late twenties with a tall, hulking frame and gentle expression. Dave, as he introduced himself, was always dressed rather casually, if not sloppily, in T-shirts and jeans. He spent most of his time hanging out or walking on the beach with a variety of friends who visited his house, and taking care of his two young boys, who lived alternately with him and his estranged wife. He also went out of town a lot. We started spending much of our free time over at his house, talking, playing board games late into the night, and smoking marijuana together. We were glad to find someone from whom we could buy marijuana in this new place, since we did not know too many people. He also began treating us to a fairly regular supply of cocaine, which was a thrill because this was a drug we could rarely afford on our student budgets. We noticed right away, however, that there was something unusual about his use and knowledge of drugs: while he always had a plentiful supply and was fairly expert about marijuana and cocaine, when we tried to buy a small bag of marijuana from him he had little idea of the going price. This incongruity piqued our curiosity and raised suspicion. We wondered if he might be dealing in larger quantities. Keeping our suspicions to ourselves, we began observing Dave's activities a little more closely. Most of his friends were in their late twenties and early thirties and, judging by their lifestyles and automobiles, rather wealthy. They came and left his house at all hours, occasionally extending their parties through the night and the next day into the following night. Yet throughout this time we never saw Dave or any of his friends engage in any activity that resembled a legitimate job. In most places this might have evoked community suspicion, but few of the people we encountered in Southwest County seemed to hold traditionally structured jobs. Dave, in fact, had no visible means of financial support. When we asked him what he did for a living, he said something vague about being a real estate speculator, and we let it go at

that. We never voiced our suspicions directly since he chose not to broach the subject with us.

We did discuss the subject with our mentor, Jack Douglas, however. He was excited by the prospect that we might be living among a group of big dealers, and urged us to follow our instincts and develop leads into the group. He knew that the local area was rife with drug trafficking, since he had begun a life history case study of two drug dealers with another graduate student several years previously. That earlier study was aborted when the graduate student quit school, but Jack still had many hours of taped interviews he had conducted with them, as well as an interview that he had done with an undergraduate student who had known the two dealers independently, to serve as a cross-check on their accounts. He therefore encouraged us to become friendlier with Dave and his friends. We decided that if anything did develop out of our observations of Dave, it might make a nice paper for a field methods class or independent study.

Our interests and background made us well suited to study drug dealing. First, we had already done research in the field of drugs. As undergraduates at Washington University we had participated in a nationally funded project on urban heroin use (see Cummins et al., 1972). Our role in the study involved using fieldwork techniques to investigate the extent of heroin use and distribution in St. Louis. In talking with heroin users, dealers, and rehabilitation personnel, we acquired a base of knowledge about the drug world and the subculture of drug trafficking. Second, we had a generally open view toward soft drug use, considering moderate consumption of marijuana and cocaine to be generally nondeviant. This outlook was partially etched by our 1960s-formed attitudes, as we had first been introduced to drug use in an environment of communal friendship, sharing, and counterculture ideology. It also partially reflected the widespread acceptance accorded to marijuana and cocaine use in the surrounding local culture. Third, our age (mid-twenties at the start of the study) and general appearance gave us compatibility with most of the people we were observing.

We thus watched Dave and continued to develop our friendship with him. We also watched his friends and got to know a few of his more regular visitors. We continued to build friendly relations by doing, quite naturally, what Becker (1963), Polsky (1969), and Douglas (1972) had advocated for the early stages of field research: we gave them a chance to know us and form judgments about our trustworthiness by jointly pursuing those interests and activities which we had in common.

Then one day something happened which forced a breakthrough in the research. Dave had two guys visiting him from out of town and, after snorting quite a bit of cocaine, they turned their conversation to a trip they had just made from Mexico, where they piloted a load of marijuana back across the border in a small plane. Dave made a few efforts to shift the conversation to another subject, telling them to "button their lips," but they apparently thought that he was joking. They thought that anybody as close to Dave as we seemed to be undoubtedly knew the nature of his business. They made further allusions to his involvement in the operation and discussed the outcome of the sale. We could feel the wave of tension and awkwardness from Dave when this conversation began, as he looked toward us to see if we understood the implications of what was being said, but then he just shrugged it off as done. Later, after the two guys left, he discussed with us what happened. He admitted to us that he was a member of a smuggling crew and a major marijuana dealer on the side. He said that he knew he could trust us, but that it was his practice to say as little as possible to outsiders about his activities. This inadvertent slip, and Dave's subsequent opening up, were highly significant in forging our entry into Southwest County's drug world. From then on he was open in discussing the nature of his dealing and smuggling activities with us.

He was, it turned out, a member of a smuggling crew that was importing a ton of marijuana weekly and 40 kilos of cocaine every few months. During that first winter and spring, we observed Dave at work and also got to know the other members of his crew, including Ben, the smuggler himself. Ben was also very tall and broad shouldered, but his long black hair, now flecked with gray, bespoke his earlier membership in the hippie subculture. A large physical stature, we observed, was common to most of the male participants involved in this drug community. The women also had a unifying physical trait: they were extremely attractive and stylishly dressed. This included Dave's ex-wife, Jean, with whom he reconciled during the spring. We therefore became friendly with Jean and through her met a number of women ("dope chicks") who hung around the dealers and smugglers. As we continued to gain the friendship of Dave and Jean's associates we were progressively admitted into their inner circle and apprised of each person's dealing or smuggling role.

Once we realized the scope off Ben's and his associates' activities, we saw the enormous research potential in studying them. This scene was different from any analysis of drug trafficking that we had read in the sociological literature because of the amounts they were dealing and the fact that they were importing it themselves. We decided that, if it was at all possible, we would capitalize on this situation, to "opportunistically" (Riemer, 1977) take advantage of our prior expertise and of the knowledge, entrée, and rapport we had already developed with several key people in this setting. We therefore discussed the idea of doing a study of the general subculture with Dave and several of his closest friends (now becoming our friends). We assured them of the anonymity, confidentiality, and innocuousness of our work. They were happy to reciprocate our friendship by being of help to our professional careers. In fact, they basked in the subsequent attention we gave their lives.

We began by turning first Dave, then others, into key informants and collecting their life histories in detail. We conducted a series of taped, depth interviews with an unstructured, open-ended format. We questioned them about such topics as their backgrounds, their recruitment into the occupation, the stages of their dealing careers, their relations with others, their motivations, their lifestyle, and their general impressions about the community as a whole.

We continued to do taped interviews with key informants for the next six years until 1980, when we moved away from the area. After that, we occasionally did follow-up interviews when we returned for vacation visits. These later interviews focused on recording the continuing unfolding of events and included detailed probing into specific conceptual areas, such as dealing networks, types of dealers, secrecy, trust, paranoia, reputation, the law, occupational mobility, and occupational stratification. The number of taped interviews we did with each key informant varied, ranging between 10 and 30 hours of discussion.

Our relationship with Dave and the others thus took on an added dimension—the research relationship. As Douglas (1976), Henslin (1972), and Wax (1952) have noted, research relationships involve some form of mutual exchange. In our case, we offered everything that friendship could entail. We did routine favors for them in the course of our everyday lives, offered them insights and advice about their lives from the perspective of our more respectable position, wrote letters on their behalf to the authorities when they got in trouble, testified as character witnesses at their non-drug-related trials, and loaned them money when they were down and out. When Dave was arrested and brought to trial for

check-kiting, we helped Jean organize his defense and raise the money to pay his fines. We spelled her in taking care of the children so that she could work on his behalf. When he was eventually sent to the state prison we maintained close ties with her and discussed our mutual efforts to buoy Dave up and secure his release. We also visited him in jail. During Dave's incarceration, however, Jean was courted by an old boyfriend and gave up her reconciliation with Dave. This proved to be another significant turning point in our research because, desperate for money, Jean looked up Dave's old dealing connections and went into the business herself. She did not stay with these marijuana dealers and smugglers for long, but soon moved into the cocaine business. Over the next several years her experiences in the world of cocaine dealing brought us into contact with a different group of people. While these people knew Dave and his associates (this was very common in the Southwest County dealing and smuggling community), they did not deal with them directly. We were thus able to gain access to a much wider and more diverse range of subjects than we would have had she not branched out on her own.

Dave's eventual release from prison three months later brought our involvement in the research to an even deeper level. He was broke and had nowhere to go. When he showed up on our doorstep, we took him in. We offered to let him stay with us until he was back on his feet again and could afford a place of his own. He lived with us for seven months, intimately sharing his daily experiences with us. During this time we witnessed, firsthand, his transformation from a scared ex-con who would never break the law again to a hard-working legitimate employee who only dealt to get money for his children's Christmas presents, to a full-time dealer with no pretensions at legitimate work. Both his process of changing attitudes and the community's gradual reacceptance of him proved very revealing.

We socialized with Dave, Jean, and other members of Southwest County's dealing and smuggling community on a near-daily basis, especially during the first four years of the research (before we had a child). We worked in their legitimate businesses, vacationed together, attended their weddings, and cared for their children. Throughout their relationship with us, several participants became co-opted to the researcher's perspective[1] and actively sought out instances of behavior which filled holes in the conceptualizations we were developing. Dave, for one, became so intrigued by our conceptual dilemmas that he undertook a "natural experiment" entirely on his own, offering an unlimited supply of drugs to a lower-level dealer to see if he could work up to higher levels of dealing, and what factors would enhance or impinge upon his upward mobility.

In addition to helping us directly through their own experiences, our key informants aided us in widening our circle of contacts. For instance, they let us know when someone in whom we might be interested was planning on dropping by, vouching for our trustworthiness and reliability as friends who could be included in business conversations. Several times we were even awakened in the night by phone calls informing us that someone had dropped by for a visit, should we want to "casually" drop over too. We rubbed the sleep from our eyes, dressed, and walked or drove over, feeling like sleuths out of a television series. We thus were able to snowball, through the active efforts of our key informants,[2] into an expanded study population. This was supplemented by our own efforts to cast a research net and befriend other dealers, moving from contact to contact slowly and carefully through the domino effect.

THE COVERT ROLE

The highly illegal nature of dealing in illicit drugs and dealers' and smugglers' general level of suspicion made the adoption of an overt research role highly sensitive and problematic. In discussing this issue with our key informants, they all agreed that we should be extremely discreet (for both our sakes and theirs). We carefully approached new individuals before we admitted that we were studying them. With many of these people, then, we took a covert posture in the research setting. As nonparticipants in the business activities which bound members together into the group, it was difficult to become fully accepted as peers. We therefore tried to establish some sort of peripheral, social membership in the general crowd, where we could be accepted as "wise" (Goffman, 1963) individuals and granted a courtesy membership. This seemed an attainable goal, since we had begun our involvement by forming such relationships with our key informants. By being introduced to others in this wise rather than overt role, we were able to interact with people who would otherwise have shied away from us. Adopting a courtesy membership caused us to bear a courtesy stigma,[3] however, and we suffered since we, at times, had to disguise the nature of our research from both lay outsiders and academicians.

In our overt posture we showed interest in dealers' and smugglers' activities, encouraged them to talk about themselves (within limits, so as to avoid acting like narcs), and ran home to write field notes. This role offered us the advantage of gaining access to unapproachable people while avoiding researcher effects, but it prevented us from asking some necessary, probing questions and from tape recording conversations.[4] We therefore sought, at all times, to build toward a conversion to the overt role. We did this by working to develop their trust.

DEVELOPING TRUST

Like achieving entrée, the process of developing trust with members of unorganized deviant groups can be slow and difficult. In the absence of a formal structure separating members from outsiders, each individual must form his or her own judgment about whether new persons can be admitted to their confidence. No gatekeeper existed to smooth our path to being trusted, although our key informants acted in this role whenever they could by providing introductions and references. In addition, the unorganized nature of this group meant that we met people at different times and were constantly at different levels in our developing relationships with them. We were thus trusted more by some people than by others, in part because of their greater familiarity with us. But as Douglas (1976) has noted, just because someone knew us or even liked us did not automatically guarantee that they would trust us.

We actively tried to cultivate the trust of our respondents by tying them to us with favors. Small things, like offering the use of our phone, were followed with bigger favors, like offering the use of our car, and finally really meaningful favors, like offering the use of our home. Here we often trod a thin line, trying to ensure our personal safety while putting ourselves in enough of a risk position, along with our research subjects, so that they would trust us. While we were able to build a "web of trust" (Douglas, 1976) with some members, we found that trust, in large part, was not a simple status to attain in the drug world. Johnson (1975) has pointed out that trust is not a one-time phenomenon, but an ongoing developmental process. From my experiences in this research I would add that it cannot be simply assumed to be a one-way process either, for it can be diminished, withdrawn, reinstated to varying degrees, and re-questioned at any point. Carey (1972) and Douglas (1972) have remarked on this waxing and waning process, but it was especially pronounced for us because our subjects used large amounts of cocaine over an extended period of time. This tended to make them alternately warm and cold to us. We thus lived through a series of ups and downs with the people we were trying to cultivate as research informants.

THE OVERT ROLE

After this initial covert phase, we began to feel that some new people trusted us. We tried to intuitively feel when the time was right to approach them and go overt. We used two means of approaching people to inform them that we were involved in a study of dealing and smuggling: direct and indirect. In some cases our key informants approached their friends or connections and, after vouching for our absolute trustworthiness, convinced these associates to talk to us. In other instances, we approached people directly, asking for their help with our project. We worked our way through a progression with these secondary contacts, first discussing the dealing scene overtly and later moving to taped life history interviews. Some people reacted well to us, but others responded skittishly, making appointments to do taped interviews only to break them as the day drew near, and going through fluctuating stages of being honest with us or putting up fronts about their dealing activities. This varied, for some, with their degree of active involvement in the business. During the times when they had quit dealing, they would tell us about their present and past activities, but when they became actively involved again, they would hide it from us.

This progression of covert to overt roles generated a number of tactical difficulties. The first was the problem of *coming on too fast* and blowing it. Early in the research we had a dealer's old lady (we thought) all set up for the direct approach. We knew many dealers in common and had discussed many things tangential to dealing with her without actually mentioning the subject. When we asked her to do a taped interview of her bohemian lifestyle, she agreed without hesitation. When the interview began, though, and she found out why we were interested in her, she balked, gave us a lot of incoherent jumble, and ended the session as quickly as possible. Even though she lived only three houses away we never saw her again. We tried to move more slowly after that.

A second problem involved simultaneously *juggling our overt and covert roles* with different people. This created the danger of getting our cover blown with people who did not know about our research (Henslin, 1972). It was very confusing to separate the people who knew about our study from those who did not, especially in the minds of our informants. They would make occasional veiled references in front of people, especially when loosened by intoxicants, that made us extremely uncomfortable. We also frequently worried that our snooping would someday be mistaken for police tactics. Fortunately, this never happened.

CROSS-CHECKING

The hidden and conflictual nature of the drug dealing world made me feel the need for extreme certainty about the reliability of my data. I therefore based all my conclusions on independent sources and accounts that we carefully verified. First, we tested information against our own common sense and general knowledge of the scene. We adopted a hard-nosed attitude of suspicion, assuming people were up to more than they would originally admit. We kept our attention especially riveted on "reformed" dealers and smugglers who were living better than they could outwardly afford, and were thereby able to penetrate their public fronts.

Second, we checked out information against a variety of reliable sources. Our own observations of the scene formed a primary reliable source, since we were involved with many of the principals on a daily basis and knew exactly what they were doing. Having Dave live with us was a particular advantage because we could contrast his statements to us with what we could clearly see was happening. Even after he moved out, we knew him so well that we could generally tell when he was lying to us or, more commonly, fooling himself with optimistic dreams. We also observed other dealers' and smugglers' evasions and misperceptions about themselves and their activities. These usually occurred when they broke their own rules by selling to people they did not know, or when they commingled other people's money with their own. We also cross-checked our data against independent, alternative accounts. We were lucky, for this purpose, that Jean got reinvolved in the drug world. By interviewing her, we gained additional insight into Dave's past, his early dealing and smuggling activities, and his ongoing involvement from another person's perspective. Jean (and her connections) also talked to us about Dave's associates, thereby helping us to validate or disprove their statements. We even used this pincer effect to verify information about people we had never directly interviewed. This occurred, for instance, with the tapes that Jack Douglas gave us from his earlier study. After doing our first round of taped interviews with Dave, we discovered that he knew the dealers Jack had interviewed. We were excited by the prospect of finding out what had happened to these people and if their earlier stories checked out. We therefore sent Dave to do some investigative work. Through some mutual friends he got back in touch with them and found out what they had been doing for the past several years.

Finally, wherever possible, we checked out accounts against hard facts: newspaper and magazine reports; arrest records; material possessions; and visible evidence. Throughout the research, we used all these cross-checking measures to evaluate the veracity of new information and to prod our respondents to be more accurate (by abandoning both their lies and their self-deceptions).[5]

After about four years of near-daily participant observation, we began to diminish our
involvement in the research. This occurred
gradually, as first pregnancy and then a child
hindered our ability to follow the scene as
intensely and spontaneously as we had before.
In addition, after having a child, we were less
willing to incur as many risks as we had before;
we no longer felt free to make decisions based
solely on our own welfare. We thus pulled back
from what many have referred to as the
"difficult hours and dangerous situations"
inevitably present in field research on deviants
(see Becker, 1963; Carey, 1972; Douglas, 1972).
We did, however, actively maintain close ties
with research informants (those with whom
we had gone overt), seeing them regularly and
periodically doing follow-up interviews.

PROBLEMS AND ISSUES

Reflecting on the research process, I have
isolated a number of issues which I believe merit
additional discussion. These are rooted in
experiences which have the potential for greater
generic applicability.

The first is the *effect of drugs on the data-
gathering process.* Carey (1972) has elaborated
on some of the problems he encountered when
trying to interview respondents who used
amphetamines, while Wax (1952, 1957) has
mentioned the difficulty of trying to record
field notes while drinking sake. I found that
marijuana and cocaine had nearly opposite
effects from each other. The latter helped the
interview process, while the former hindered
it. Our attempts to interview respondents who
were stoned on marijuana were unproductive
for a number of reasons. The primary obstacle
was the effects of the drug. Often, people
became confused, sleepy, or involved in eating
to varying degrees. This distracted them from
our purpose. At times, people even simulated
overreactions to marijuana to hide behind the
drug's supposed disorienting influence and

thereby avoid divulging information. Cocaine,
in contrast, proved to be a research aid. The
drug's warming and sociable influence opened
people up, diminished their inhibitions, and
generally increased their enthusiasm for both
the interview experience and us.

A second problem I encountered involved
assuming risks while doing research. As I noted
earlier, dangerous situations are often generic
to research on deviant behavior. We were most
afraid of the people we studied. As Carey
(1972), Henslin (1972), and Whyte (1955) have
stated, members of deviant groups can become
hostile toward a researcher if they think that
they are being treated wrongfully. This could
have happened at any time from a simple
occurrence, such as a misunderstanding, or
from something more serious, such as our
covert posture being exposed. Because of the
inordinate amount of drugs they consumed,
drug dealers and smugglers were particularly
volatile, capable of becoming malicious toward
each other or us with little warning. They were
also likely to behave erratically owing to the
great risks they faced from the police and other
dealers. These factors made them moody, and
they vacillated between trusting us and being
suspicious of us.

At various times we also had to protect our
research tapes. We encountered several threats
to our collection of taped interviews from
people who had granted us these interviews.
This made us anxious, since we had taken great
pains to acquire these tapes and felt strongly
about maintaining confidences entrusted to us
by our informants. When threatened, we
became extremely frightened and shifted the
tapes between different hiding places. We even
ventured forth one rainy night with our tapes
packed in a suitcase to meet a person who was
uninvolved in the research at a secret rendez-
vous so that he could guard the tapes for us.

We were fearful, lastly, of the police. We
often worried about local police or drug agents
discovering the nature of our study and
confiscating or subpoenaing our tapes and

field notes. Sociologists have no privileged relationship with their subjects that would enable us legally to withhold evidence from the authorities should they subpoena it.[6] For this reason we studiously avoided any publicity about the research, even holding back on publishing articles in scholarly journals until we were nearly ready to move out of the setting. The closest we came to being publicly exposed as drug researchers came when a former sociology graduate student (turned dealer, we had heard from inside sources) was arrested at the scene of a cocaine deal. His lawyer wanted us to testify about the dangers of doing drug-related research, since he was using his research status as his defense. Fortunately, the crisis was averted when his lawyer succeeded in suppressing evidence and had the case dismissed before the trial was to have begun. Had we been exposed, however, our respondents would have acquired guilt by association through their friendship with us.

Our fear of the police went beyond our concern for protecting our research subjects, however. We risked the danger of arrest ourselves through our own violations of the law. Many sociologists (Becker, 1963; Carey, 1972; Polsky, 1969; Whyte, 1955) have remarked that field researchers studying deviance must inevitably break the law in order to acquire valid participant observation data. This occurs in its most innocuous form from having "guilty knowledge": information about crimes that are committed. Being aware of major dealing and smuggling operations made us an accessory to their commission, since we failed to notify the police. We broke the law, secondly, through our "guilty observations," by being present at the scene of a crime and witnessing its occurrence (see also Carey, 1972). We knew it was possible to get caught in a bust involving others, yet buying and selling was so pervasive that to leave every time it occurred would have been unnatural and highly suspicious. Sometimes drug transactions even occurred in our home, especially

when Dave was living there, but we finally had to put a stop to that because we could not handle the anxiety. Lastly, we broke the law through our "guilty actions," by taking part in illegal behavior ourselves. Although we never dealt drugs (we were too scared to be seriously tempted), we consumed drugs and possessed them in small quantities. Quite frankly, it would have been impossible for a nonuser to have gained access to this group to gather the data presented here. This was the minimum involvement necessary to obtain even the courtesy membership we achieved. Some kind of illegal action was also found to be a necessary or helpful component of the research by Becker (1963), Carey (1972), Johnson (1975), Polsky (1969), and Whyte (1955).

Another methodological issue arose from the *cultural clash between our research subjects and ourselves*. While other sociologists have alluded to these kinds of differences (Humphreys, 1970; Whyte, 1955), few have discussed how the research relationships affected them. Relationships with research subjects are unique because they involve a bond of intimacy between persons who might not ordinarily associate together, or who might otherwise be no more than casual friends. When fieldworkers undertake a major project, they commit themselves to maintaining a long-term relationship with the people they study. However, as researchers try to get depth involvement, they are apt to come across fundamental differences in character, values, and attitudes between their subjects and themselves. In our case, we were most strongly confronted by differences in present versus future orientations, a desire for risk versus security, and feelings of spontaneity versus self-discipline. These differences often caused us great frustration. We repeatedly saw dealers act irrationally, setting themselves up for failure. We wrestled with our desire to point out their patterns of foolhardy behavior and offer advice, feeling competing pulls between our detached, observer role which advised us not to influence the natural setting, and our involved, participant role which called for us to offer friendly help whenever possible.[7]

Each time these differences struck us anew, we gained deeper insights into our core, existential selves. We suspended our own taken-for-granted feelings and were able to reflect on our own culturally formed attitudes, character, and life choices from the perspective of the other. When comparing how we might act in situations faced by our respondents, we realized where our deepest priorities lay. These revelations had the effect of changing our self-conceptions: whereas we, at one time, had thought of ourselves as what Rosenbaum (1981) has called "the hippest of non-addicts" (in this case nondealers), we were suddenly faced with being the straightest members of the crowd. Not only did we not deal, but we had a stable, long-lasting marriage and family life, and needed the security of a reliable monthly paycheck. Self-insights thus emerged as one of the unexpected outcomes of field research with members of a different cultural group.

The final issue I will discuss involved the various *ethical problems* which arose during this research. Many fieldworkers have encountered ethical dilemmas or pangs of guilt during the course of their research experiences (Carey, 1972; Douglas, 1976; Humphreys, 1970; Johnson, 1975; Klockars, 1977, 1979; Rochford, 1985). The researchers' role in the field makes this necessary because they can never fully align themselves with their subjects while maintaining their identity and personal commitment to the scientific community. Ethical dilemmas, then, are directly related to the amount of deception researchers use in gathering the data, and the degree to which they have accepted such acts as necessary and therefore neutralized them.

Throughout the research, we suffered from the burden of intimacies and confidences. Guarding secrets which had been told to us during taped interviews was not always easy or pleasant. Dealers occasionally revealed things about themselves or others that we had to pretend not to know when interacting with their close associates. This sometimes meant that we had to lie or build elaborate stories to cover for some people. Their fronts therefore became our fronts, and we had to weave our own web of deception to guard their performances. This became especially disturbing during the writing of the research report, as I was torn by conflicts between using details to enrich the data and glossing over description to guard confidences.[8]

Using the covert research role generated feelings of guilt, despite the fact that our key informants deemed it necessary, and thereby condoned it. Their own covert experiences were far more deeply entrenched than ours, being a part of their daily existence with non-drug world members. Despite the universal presence of covert behavior throughout the setting, we still felt a sense of betrayal every time we ran home to write research notes on observations we had made under the guise of innocent participants.

We also felt guilty about our efforts to manipulate people. While these were neither massive nor grave manipulations, they involved courting people to procure information about them. Our aggressively friendly postures were based on hidden ulterior motives: we did favors for people with the clear expectation that they could only pay us back with research assistance. Manipulation bothered us in two ways: immediately after it was done, and over the long run. At first, we felt awkward, phony, almost ashamed of ourselves, although we believed our rationalization that the end justified the means. Over the long run, though, our feelings were different. When friendship became intermingled with research goals, we feared that people would later look back on our actions and feel we were exploiting their friendship merely for the sake of our research project.

The last problem we encountered involved our feelings of whoring for data. At times, we felt that we were being exploited by others, that we were putting more into the relationship than they, that they were taking us for granted or using us. We felt that some people used a double standard in their relationship with us: they were allowed to lie to us, borrow money and not repay it, and take advantage of us, but we were at all times expected to behave honorably. This was undoubtedly an outgrowth of our initial research strategy where we did favors for people and expected little in return. But at times this led to our feeling bad. It made us feel like we were selling ourselves, our sincerity, and usually our true friendship, and not getting treated right in return.

CONCLUSIONS

The aggressive research strategy I employed was vital to this study. I could not just walk up to strangers and start hanging out with them as Liebow (1967) did, or be sponsored to a member of this group by a social service or reform organization as Whyte (1955) was, and expect to be accepted, let alone welcomed. Perhaps such a strategy might have worked with a group that had nothing to hide, but I doubt it. Our modern, pluralistic society is so filled with diverse subcultures whose interests compete or conflict with each other that each subculture has a set of knowledge which is reserved exclusively for insiders. In order to serve and prosper, they do not ordinarily show this side to just anyone. To obtain the kind of depth insight and information I needed, I had to become like the members in certain ways. They dealt only with people they knew and trusted, so I had to become known and trusted before I could reveal my true self and my research interests. Confronted with secrecy, danger, hidden alliances, misrepresentations, and unpredictable changes of intent, I had to use a delicate combi-

nation of overt and covert roles. Throughout, my deliberate cultivation of the norm of reciprocal exchange enabled me to trade my friendship for their knowledge, rather than waiting for the highly unlikely event that information would be delivered into my lap. I thus actively built a web of research contacts, used them to obtain highly sensitive data, and carefully checked them out to ensure validity.

Throughout this endeavor I profited greatly from the efforts of my husband, Peter, who served as an equal partner in this team field research project. It would have been impossible for me to examine this social world as an unattached female and not fall prey to sex role stereotyping which excluded women from business dealings. As a couple, our different genders allowed us to relate in different ways to both men and women (see Warren and Rasmussen, 1977). We also protected each other when we entered the homes of dangerous characters, buoyed each other's initiative and courage, and kept the conversation going when one of us faltered. Conceptually, we helped each other keep a detached and analytical eye on the setting, provided multiperspectival insights, and corroborated, clarified, or (most revealingly) contradicted each other's observations and conclusions.

Finally, I feel strongly that to ensure accuracy, research on deviant groups must be conducted in the settings where it naturally occurs. As Polsky (1969: 115-16) has forcefully asserted:

This means—there is no getting away from it—the study of career criminals *au natural,* in the field, the study of such criminals as they normally go about their work and play, the study of "uncaught" criminals and the study of others who in the past have been caught but are not caught at the time you study them.... Obviously we can no longer afford the convenient fiction that in studying criminals in their natural habitat, we would discover nothing really important that could not be discovered from criminals behind bars.

By studying criminals in their natural habitat I was able to see them in the full variability and complexity of their surrounding subculture, rather than within the artificial environment of a prison. I was thus able to learn about otherwise inaccessible dimensions of their lives, observing and analyzing firsthand the nature of their social organization, social stratification, lifestyle, and motivation.

NAVIGATING THE CONCEPTS

1. Do you believe there have been any significant changes in how a social scientist should gain entry into a drug subculture since Adler's original research in the mid-1970s? If yes, what are the changes? If no, why has this approach to research remained stable over time?

2. In your opinion, is it ethical for social scientists to participate in illegal behaviours? What are the potential benefits and costs of conducting such an investigation, for the researcher, the community, and academic scholarship?

3. What definable subcultures are there at your school? With reference to Adler's article, how would you go about gaining entry into one of those groups to conduct research?

NOTES

1. Gold (1958) discouraged this methodological strategy, cautioning against overly close friendship or intimacy with informants, lest they lose their ability to act as informants by becoming too much observers. Whyte (1955), in contrast, recommended the use of informants as research aids, not for helping in conceptualizing the data but for their assistance in locating data which supports, contradicts, or fills in the researcher's analysis of the setting.

2. See also Biernacki & Waldorf, 1981; Douglas, 1976; Henslin, 1972; Hoffman, 1980; McCall, 1980; and West, 1980 for discussions of "snowballing" through key informants.

3. See Kirby & Corzine, 1981; Birenbaum, 1970; and Henslin, 1972 for more detailed discussion of the nature, problems, and strategies for dealing with courtesy stigmas.

4. We never considered secret tapings because, aside from the ethical problems involved, it always struck us as too dangerous.

5. See Douglas (1976) for a more detailed account of these procedures.

6. A recent court decision, where a federal judge ruled that a sociologist did not have to turn over his field notes to a grand jury investigating a suspicious fire at a restaurant where he worked, indicates that this situation may be changing (Fried, 1984).

7. See Henslin, 1972 and Douglas, 1972, 1976 for further discussions of this dilemma and various solutions to it.

8. In some cases I resolved this by altering my descriptions of people and their actions as well as their names so that other members of the dealing and smuggling community would not recognize them. In doing this, however, I had to keep a primary concern for maintaining the sociological integrity of my data so that the generic conclusions I drew from them would be accurate. In places, then, where my attempts to conceal people's identities from people who know them have been inadequate, I hope that I caused them no embarrassment. See also Polsky, 1969; Rainwater & Pittman, 1967; and Humphreys, 1970 for discussions of this problem.

REFERENCES

Adler, P. A., and P. Adler. 1987. *Membership roles in field research.* Beverly Hills, Calif.: Sage.

Becker, H. 1963. *Outsiders.* New York: Free Press.

Biernacki, P., and D. Waldorf. 1981. Snowball sampling. *Sociological Methods and Research,* 10: 141–63.

Birenbaum, A. 1970. On managing a courtesy stigma. *Journal of Health and Social Behavior,* 11: 196–206.

Blumer, H. 1969. *Symbolic interactionism.* Englewood Cliffs, N.J.: Prentice-Hall.

Carey, J. T. 1972. Problems of access and risk in observing drug scenes. In *Research on deviance,* ed. J. D. Douglas, 71–92. New York: Random House.

Cummins, M., et al. 1972. *Report of the Student Task Force on Heroin Use in Metropolitan Saint Louis*. St. Louis, Mo.: Washington University Social Science Institute.

Douglas, J. D. 1972. Observing deviance. In *Research on deviance*, ed. J. D. Douglas, 3–34. New York: Random House.

——. 1976. *Investigative social research*. Beverly Hills, Calif.: Sage.

Fried, J. P. 1984. Judge protects waiter's notes on fire inquiry. *New York Times* (April 8): 47.

Goffman, E. 1963. *Stigma*. Englewood Cliffs, N.J.: Prentice-Hall.

Gold, R. 1958. Roles in sociological field observations. *Social Forces*, 36: 217–23.

Henslin, J. M. 1972. Studying deviance in four settings: Research experiences with cabbies, suicides, drug users and abortionees. In *Research on deviance*, ed. J. D. Douglas, 35–70. New York: Random House.

Hoffman, J. E. 1980. Problems of access in the study of social elites and boards of directors. In *Fieldwork experience*, eds. W. B. Shaffir, R. A. Stebbins, and A. Turowetz, 45–56. New York: St. Martin's.

Humphreys, L. 1970. *Tearoom trade*. Chicago: Aldine.

Johnson, J. M. 1975. *Doing field research*. New York: Free Press.

Kirby, R., and J. Corzine. 1981. The contagion of stigma. *Qualitative Sociology*, 4: 3–20.

Klockars, C. B. 1977. Field ethics for the life history. In *Street ethnography*, ed. R. Weppner, 201–26. Beverly Hills, Calif.: Sage.

——. 1979. Dirty hands and deviant subjects. In *Deviance and decency*, eds. C. B. Klockars and F. W. O'Connor, 261–82. Beverly Hills, Calif.: Sage.

Liebow, E. 1967. *Tally's Corner*. Boston: Little, Brown.

McCall, M. 1980. Who and where are the artists? In *Fieldwork experience*, eds. W. B. Shaffir, R. A. Stebbins, and A. Turowetz, 145–58. New York: St. Martin's.

Polsky, N. 1969. *Hustlers, beats, and others*. New York: Doubleday.

Rainwater, L. R., and D. J. Pittman. 1967. Ethical problems in studying a politically sensitive and deviant community. *Social Problems*, 14: 357–66.

Riemer, J. W. 1977. Varieties of opportunistic research. *Urban Life*, 5: 467–77.

Rochford, E. B. Jr. 1985. *Hare Krishna in America*. New Brunswick, N.J.: Rutgers University Press.

Rosenbaum, M. 1981. *Women on heroin*. New Brunswick, N.J.: Rutgers University Press.

Warren, C. A. B., and P. K. Rasmussen. 1977. Sex and gender in field research. *Urban Life*, 6: 349–69.

Wax, R. 1952. Reciprocity as a field technique. *Human Organization*, 11: 34–37.

——. 1957. Twelve years later: An analysis of a field experience. *American Journal of Sociology*, 63: 133–42.

West, W. G. 1980. Access to adolescent deviants and deviance. In *Fieldwork experience*, eds. W. B. Shaffir, R. A. Stebbins, and A. Turowetz, 31–44. New York: St. Martin's.

Whyte, W. F. 1955. *Street corner society*. Chicago: University of Chicago Press.

PART 4

Social Inequality

Sociologists investigate and challenge any condition where people are treated unequally because of their membership in a minority population.

Chapter 13

Explaining Canada's Ethnic Landscape: A Theoretical Model

Alan B. Anderson and James S. Frideres

Source: From *Perspectives on Ethnicity in Canada: A Reader* by Madeline A. Kalbach and Warren E. Kalbach. © 2000. Reprinted with permission of Nelson, a division of Thomson Learning: www.thomsonrights.com. Fax 800 730 2215.

Alan B. Anderson and James S. Frideres emphasize that Canadian society is facing a "pervasive and profound crisis" in how it deals with the social problems resulting from ethnic inequality. The authors suggest that while ethnicity is not the only challenge to equality, it is one of the most important factors to explain group dynamics in Canada and the rest of the world.

INTRODUCTION

As a society, we are in the midst of a pervasive and profound crisis in Canada, forcing us to deal with a host of social problems, including ethnic inequality, prejudice, racism, systemic discrimination, and ethnic conflict. While this essay focusses on ethnic issues, the reader must understand that the problems related to ethnicity are only part of a large range of social issues facing Canadians. In short, ethnic differentiation co-exists with other aspects of inequality that are beyond the scope of this analysis (see also Berry & Laponce, 1994). A review of intergroup behaviour in Canada and elsewhere in the world provides ample evidence that ethnicity has become the peak of the pyramid and can no longer be accorded a secondary theoretical or practical significance. Anyone who wishes to better understand Canadian society must view ethnicity as one of the most important factors (Wanner, 1999). This situation is not uniquely Canadian. Elsewhere in the world, whether in Africa, South America,

or Europe, ethnicity has become a central element in the way individuals and groups interact (Breton et al., 1990). Conflict, so prevalent in today's society, usually has an ethnic dimension. Thus, it is important that ethnicity be acknowledged as a major factor in group dynamics, not only in Canada, but also throughout the world.

The important issues of our day are matters of human behaviour. Almost all the problems currently facing individuals, organizations, or societies are the result, more or less, of the way people behave toward one another. Humans obtain their principal satisfactions and motivations from their relationships with other people. As the twenty-first century approaches, the diverse attitudes, opinions, motivations, and contextual constructs that underlie social behaviour are only beginning to be understood. As our society becomes more complex, the need to advance this knowledge of human behaviour becomes even greater. A better understanding of ethnic issues provides a basis for predicting and explaining group dynamics, including ethnic conflict (see also Driedger, 1996).

It is obvious to many that Canadians are experiencing a crisis in social relations. The tensions between English and French, whether inside or outside Quebec, are evident, and are made more so by the mass media every day. Television and newspapers depict ethnic conflicts in a variety of contexts, for example, in police, housing, educational, and playground settings. What is even more remarkable is that today's leaders in Canada fail to acknowledge this crisis, a failure that reflects an inability to deal with real social issues or problems. Our leaders are lacking the intellectual and political will to carry out social analysis of human behaviour and to develop policies that could ameliorate the tensions and potential conflicts among ethnic groups. It is in this area that social scientists can add to the study of human behaviour.

In this chapter, we limit our focus to ethnic or race relations in Canada. We discuss how social scientists are able to identify specific historical, contextual, and individual attributes that signal how people of different ethnicities act toward one another, and the consequences of such actions (see also James, 1996).

THE CENTRALITY OF ETHNIC RELATIONS: CANADIAN SOCIETY

Few, if any, countries in the world today can legitimately claim to have a population consisting entirely of a single ethnic group. Most societies are pluralistic, or multi-ethnic, consisting of a variety of ethnic groups, each comprising a different proportion of the total population and controlling its own destiny, to differing degrees (Isajiw, 1999). Canada is no exception; over the past three decades, the pluralistic diversity of our society has become a major practical and policy issue, and one that is hotly debated by nearly all Canadians.

This fact alone makes ethnic relations a prominent area of study within the social sciences, particularly sociology, covering a wide range of topics of relevance in most of the traditional fields of sociological inquiry. Whether you are studying residential patterns, intermarriage patterns, youth conflict, criminal behaviour, or employment equity, issues of ethnicity are in the foreground. Nearly all state activities and institutions, such as religion, education, and bureaucracies, shape the social behaviour of individuals and groups (Li, 1999; Marger, 1996).

THE COMPLEXITY OF CANADIAN SOCIETY

A single model of ethnic relations is impossible to formulate. The difficulty lies in the fact that almost every ethnic group within Canadian society is a minority (where "minority" denotes a lack of power and "majority" indicates power), at least at the national level. Moreover, there are well over a hundred clearly defined ethnic groups (some native born, others of immigrant origin) in Canada, not to mention distinctive subgroups. Cross-cutting these delineations, we find some groups that exhibit "visible minority" attributes, for example, skin pigmentation, that allow for quick identification (real or mistaken) and categorical placement. These ethnic/racial populations range in number from hundreds to millions. Many of them are exclusively urban; others are primarily rural. Virtually all embrace a wide range of opinions among their members as to exactly what constitutes ethnic identity, to what extent this identity should be stressed, and how it might be sustained (Driedger, 1996).

Ethnic relations in Canada are unique, even though some parallels with other countries are evident (Reitz & Breton, 1994). As Canada exists within its own historically formed social/economic/political framework, it must be examined in that context. For example,

Canadian society has chosen, in many forms and manners of expression, to enact a "liberalist" position rather than a conservative perspective. Moreover, in dealing with ethnic relations, Canada has focussed on two aspects: removing institutional barriers in the economic sphere, and developing strategies to help integrate people into Canadian society, for example, language, social skills, and job training programs. In short, Canadians adopt a liberal position which argues that state intervention is required to deal with the sociological and institutional barriers that prevent non-British (and non-white) groups from achieving necessary education and employment.

More than twenty years ago, academic observers of the Canadian social scene suggested that the following characteristics were peculiarly relevant to an understanding of Canadian society:

- A weak sense of national identity accompanied by a strong sense of regional identification. In the case of certain provinces, such as Quebec, regional identification is interlinked with particular ethnic group loyalties.

- A hierarchical social structure which is associated with the existence of class-based inequalities in educational and occupational opportunities.

- An ethnic stratification system based on familial, religious and linguistic allegiances that is intertwined with existing class structure.

- An official ideology that espouses the doctrine of cultural pluralism rather than assimilation. (Pike & Zureik, 1975: viii–ix).

Nothing that has happened over the past quarter century suggests that these attributes of Canadian society have changed. With the introduction of more than 200 000 immigrants from non-traditional countries over the past two decades, Canada has become more culturally diverse, and the mosaic has taken on many different hues. Those ethnic groups who were considered recent immigrants have now become "old," and recent arrivals have the status of "new" members of Canadian society. The third force (non-French, non-British) now makes up a substantial proportion of the Canadian population (nearly 20 percent), and an even greater proportion of the population of large urban areas, for example, over 40 percent of Toronto residents, is made up of immigrants, thus adding to the complexity of ethnic relations. The arrival of visible minorities has further complicated intergroup relations by introducing "race" as an additional factor when trying to explain behaviour.

ETHNIC RELATIONS: UNDERSTANDING AND MAKING PREDICTIONS

Most Canadians find ethnic issues complex and seemingly without resolution. They continually ask questions such as: Why don't "ethnics" integrate into Canadian society? How come "ethnics" seem to want to maintain their ancestral ethnic linkages? Why don't immigrants become more like "regular" Canadians? Canadians look to social scientists for answers. In this chapter, we want to situate the issues and sort out the various positions in the current debate, and give you, the reader, some idea of what is at stake. We want to map the activities, and then give you the means to discover explanations for the role and function of specific actions taken by individuals and ethnic groups. A number of theoretical perspectives have been put forward to explain ethnic relations (Richmond, 1994). One of the oldest theoretical perspectives is the biological model. The central thesis of this perspective is that non-whites are, in some sense, genetically or biologically different from whites. A. Jensen (1969) was one of the first contemporary social scientists in the United States to take such a stand, and the publication of his article in the

Harvard Educational Review gave instant international exposure to his ideas. Hernstein and Murray (1994) expanded and developed Jensen's ideas, but their conclusions were rejected once other scholars undertook methodological and statistical analyses of their data. In Canada, P. Rushton and A. Bogaert (1987), utilizing data bases with suspect validity, continued this line of thinking and argued that Asians were the brightest of "races," followed by whites, and then Blacks and aboriginals. Jensen's initial findings were widely publicized in the media, and it was quickly recognized that he had used flawed methodologies; ultimately, his research was published only in obscure, ideologically biased journals, his work having being discredited by scholars and policy-makers. Nevertheless, it is important for the reader to realize that these contemporary researchers have tried to resurrect biological theories as an explanation of why ethnic or racial groups behave in the way they do and as a means to predict interethnic/interracial relations. Thus, many individuals' aversion to non-whites is an opinion based on "scientific" grounds, and, for them, the oppression of non-whites is simply part of nature.

Cultural theorists, extending this general thesis, argue that the character and content of non-white (read non-British/French origin) cultures inhibit them from successfully competing with other whites in the areas of education, business, and occupation (McRobbie, 1994). The attributes noted as leading to success in these areas, for example, motivation, deferred gratification, work ethic, are missing from non-white ethnic groups. These culturalists and post-modernists note that, while the educational and occupational difference among ethnic groups seemed to be decreasing between the turn of the century and the 1960s, in more recent times, the differences have been increasing (Li, 1999; Lian & Matthews, 1998). These differences are a result, according to the cultural theorists, of the influx of non-white immigrants into

Canadian society. They argue that only when non-whites are able to overcome these deficiencies will they be able to compete equally with whites. We reject such models or explanations of behaviour and note that there is no empirical evidence to support such claims. However, these biological and cultural models have been evident in the literature for many years and seem to have undergone some resurgence of popularity in the recent past. The model we utilize to explain ethnic and race relations reflects the sociological imagination, drawing upon the macro and micro sociological factors that surround all of us each day.

MACRO AND MICRO MODELS

Two perspectives make up the theoretical model we use to explain human behaviour—macro and micro variables. The former focus on the structure of society; the latter focus on the individual. The first of these perspectives is usually associated with Karl Marx; the second, with Sigmund Freud. Macro theorists attempt to explain social behaviour by looking at how the structure of society impinges upon the individual. For example, people living on an Indian reserve will, because of the social conditions and social structure that predominates there, behave in ways almost unthinkable for those living in the Mount Royal area of Montreal. Likewise, individuals living in ethnic enclaves in the city of Toronto behave in ways that individuals living in rural Newfoundland cannot fathom. There are many variations of a macro perspective, some focussing solely on demographic factors or economic issues, and others using a combination of different structural factors to explain human behaviour.

At the other end of the continuum, the micro theorists focus solely on the individual to explain human behaviour. For them, individuals are capable of transcending the structural conditions in which they operate (sometimes referred to as the exercise of "free will"), and thus behaviours can be best explained by looking at the attributes of the individual. For these theorists, the individual personality or sociodemographic attribute of the individual, for example, age or sex, is the key to explaining behaviour.

To our way of thinking, attempts to utilize one or the other perspective produce an infertile theory, incapable of fully understanding or predicting human behaviour. We argue that a social-psychological perspective has to be employed in order to explain and predict human behaviour. We define a social-psychological perspective as one that attempts to explain behaviour as a result of the intersection of society and the individual. Figure 13.1 identifies the principal components of this perspective and how they link.

As is evident from Figure 13.1, we agree with West (1993) when he argues that a full theory of race/ethnic relations has to have three conceptual conditions if adequate explanation and prediction are to occur:

• an understanding of the historical conditions which produced the logic of discrimination and prejudice in Canadian society;

• a micro understanding of how people operate in their day-to-day lives;

• and an understanding of the social structure of society (institutional linkage) and how this relates to ethnic group relations.

This model provides a map of how individuals participate in the institutional network of society on an ongoing basis. It shows that many factors impinge upon the individual or group, restricting or enlarging the behavioural repertoire. Some of these are external to the individual, and others are internal; some are psychological, and others are structural. Adding to the complexity and dynamics of this model is the variable of "context," or situational determinants. All behaviour, to some extent, is situationally determined, and this context must be taken into account if we are to explain behaviour. The context in which behaviour takes place gives logic, consistency, and legitimacy to the behaviour we engage in. The "weight" or importance of these situational determinants will vary and needs to be taken into account when assessing the matrix of possible behaviours that can be exhibited by the individual. In short, individual (micro) and structural (macro) factors need to be identified within a field of context if we are to make predictions and explain social behaviour.

Figure 13.1 Theoretical Model Used for Explaining Ethnic Relations

Historical Context

Macro

Marxist
Demographic
Structural–Functional
Ecological
  - region
  - ethnic group
  - economic order

→ Social–Psychological ←

Micro

Freudian
Frustration–Aggression
Psychoanalytical
Reinforcement
  - personality
  - attitudes
  - sociodemographic
    factors

Behaviour

It is clear that the macro and micro perspectives need to be integrated if ethnic relations in Canadian society are to be explained. Whether one begins with the micro or macro is of little importance, as long as both are taken into consideration in explaining ethnic relations. For example, some researchers argue that individuals operate within a social structure, and thus their individual actions are constrained by these structural conditions; for example, social class imposes certain limits on an individual's behaviour (Bourdieu, 1989: Satzewich, 1992). Thus they prefer to begin with the macro factors, and then move to an analysis of the micro elements. In more practical terms, this means that one must look at both structural variables and individual factors in order to explain social behaviour.

In summary, the micro or psychological approach focusses on personality factors, for example, those behind racial prejudice. It neglects the social context in which these attitudes have developed, are reinforced, and operate. We argue that if one focusses solely on the individual as the major operative force in explaining human behaviour, the very concept of society tends to be destroyed. On the other hand, the macro models tend to ignore the individual and focus on the social system. One problem with these approaches is, for example, their treatment of social change. While there is nothing inherent in sociological approaches that precludes their treatment of social change, previous work using these models tended to ignore change or treated it in a most simplistic fashion.

THE HISTORICAL CONTEXT

The reader is reminded that, to fully understand and predict ethnic relations, we need to accept the principle of historical specificity. This principle forces us to understand the conditions under which non-British (and non-French) groups have been treated over time, and the structural constraints under which these people have to live. Put another way, one cannot adopt an ahistorical approach to studying ethnic relations. One must fully appreciate the history of the relations, whether myth or reality, that impinges upon the views, attitudes, and behaviour of ethnic-group members. The recent events in Yugoslavia and Kosovo reveal animosities that can be traced back to the fourteenth century. Irish–British antagonisms reflect real and imagined atrocities occurring nearly 800 years ago. Thus, the historical collective conscience of the ethnic group is an important contextual factor that will give us fertile ground upon which to build a theoretical explanation of today's behaviour.

The reader must also understand that ethnic relations change over time and context. Aboriginals were once military allies of the British, the French promoted an intermarriage policy with Aboriginal peoples, Eastern European immigrants to Canada were treated as though they were only just a step above farm animals, Blacks and Jews were refused entrance to Canada, and Chinese and Japanese were deported from Canada. As McVey and Kalbach (1995) point out, the population composition of Canada has revealed a chameleon trend over the past century. Thus, ethnic relations have a dynamic that must be fully appreciated, and the reader must understand that, while the relationships among the groups may change, the underlying explanatory model remains the same. Moreover, it is important to remember that the salience of the macro or micro factors may also vary over time. Nevertheless, social-psychological analysis must ferret out the salience and importance of each factor.

CONCEPTUAL MODELS

The goal of theory is to predict and understand. It is important to note that these are separate goals, and achieving one may not mean achieving the other. The student is reminded to keep these differences in mind. You see these differences all the time. For example, when the weather person predicts rain for the day and it does not occur, the audience does not reject further weather predictions. Undaunted, the weather person is able to explain why her or his prediction did not come true. We feel that taking a solely micro approach will allow you to achieve some prediction of behaviour. On the other hand, if you take a macro approach you will be able to achieve some understanding of the relations between and among various ethnic groups. It is only when an integration of the two approaches is utilized that you, the analyst, will be able to achieve both prediction and explanation with sufficient accuracy to warrant the acceptance of social psychology as a valuable discipline for policy-makers, social leaders, and others who have to make decisions that have an impact upon individual and group behaviour.

Our assumptions are simple. We believe, first, that humans are social animals who live and learn in human groups. Second, individuals become human through social interaction with others. Third, while society has an impact upon individual behaviour, individuals have an impact upon the social structure. In short, the relationship between individuals and society is reciprocal. Using these assumptions, we believe that models of ethnic relations can be constructed that will yield a better understanding of how and why ethnic groups act in particular ways. One has to view how an individual behaves in a particular social structure during a specific time and place if a full understanding of human behaviour is to be achieved.

We argue for a sociohistorical theoretical approach. Theorists adopting this approach have developed elaborate models of ethnic-group reactions at the time of contact that have far-reaching effects on the relationships today. Only through the use of such an approach will we be able to integrate the individual, societal factors, and the situational contexts in which the events are occurring (Isajiw, 1999). Such an approach offers the reader a full and informative understanding of social reality.

CONCLUSION

By using a theoretical model that incorporates both the micro and the macro, we hope to integrate different theoretical perspectives. Such a model allows us to incorporate the local community, and the regional, national, and global context, in explaining ethnic relations. In doing so, we can make sense out of the enormous complexity of our country, which is at once unicultural, bicultural, and, at another level, multicultural. The intersection of the different units of analysis provides for a more complete explanation of how such factors as globalized capitalism simultaneously integrate and segment the workforce by ethnicity, and it allows us to situate local cases within the global context.

Using this model allows us to explain why "assimilation" was the preferred manner in which dominant groups dealt with minority groups at the turn of the century. It also leads us to an understanding of how this policy changed over time and has resulted in today's championing of "multiculturalism" (Kymlicka, 1998). Ethnicity as a salient component of an individual's life changes over time, and its impact upon behaviour is equally variable. Ethnic and racial groups are gradually incorporating into Canadian society, and these structural events need to be taken into consideration if an understanding of intergroup behaviour is to be achieved. Nevertheless, all these factors must be part of the "calculus" if adequate and illuminating explanations of ethnic and race relations are to emerge.

Focussing upon the individual and structural factors also allows us to assess both the internal dynamics of an ethnic group and the interaction among two or more ethnic communities in a given locale. The integration of these factors will demystify the ways in which different forms of relationships among ethnic groups are produced and reproduced. This model allows us to assess the meaning, identity, and ideology of ethnic relations, and to show how they have continually been created, contested, and transformed. Finally, such a perspective allows us to assess the way "mediating institutions" shape, structure, and constrain interrelations, often within hierarchies that assert the dominance of established groups. In this way, issues of class and power are brought into the analysis of ethnic relations. In the end, to fully understand ethnic relations in any pluralistic society, we must pursue a historical frame of reference, both a micro and a macro perspective as well as an interdisciplinary approach.

NAVIGATING THE CONCEPTS

1. Given Anderson and Frideres' findings, do you feel the Canadian government is doing enough to support ethnic equality? Discuss.

2. What historical factors have influenced the ethnic makeup of your own community?

3. With reference to the article, discuss and critique the biological model of ethnic relations.

REFERENCES

Berry, J., and J. A. Laponce, eds. 1994. *Ethnicity and culture in Canada: The research landscape.* Toronto: University of Toronto Press.

Bourdieu, P. 1989. Social space and symbolic power. *Sociological Theory,* 7: 14–21.

Breton, R., W. Isajiw, W. Kalbach, and J. Reitz. 1990. *Ethnic identity and equality: Varieties of experience in a Canadian city.* Toronto: University of Toronto Press.

Driedger, L., ed. 1996. *Multi-ethnic Canada: Identities and inequalities.* Toronto: Oxford University Press.

Hernstein, R., and C. Murray. 1994. *The bell curve: Intelligence and class structure in American life.* New York: The Free Press.

Isajiw, W. 1999. *Understanding diversity: Ethnicity and race in the Canadian context.* Toronto: Thompson Educational.

James, C. 1996. *Seeing ourselves: Exploring race, ethnicity and culture.* Toronto: Thompson Educational.

Jensen, A. 1969. How much can we boost IQ and scholastic achievement? *Harvard Educational Review,* 39(3): 1–123.

Kymlicka, W. 1998. *Finding our way: Rethinking ethnocultural relations in Canada.* Toronto: Oxford University Press.

Li, P. 1999. *Race and ethnic relations in Canada,* 2nd ed. Toronto: Oxford University Press.

Lian, J., and D. Matthews. 1998. Does the vertical mosaic still exist? Ethnicity and income in Canada, 1991. *Canadian Review of Sociology and Anthropology,* 35: 461–82.

Marger, M. 1996. *Race and ethnic relations: American and comparative perspectives.* Belmont, Calif.: Wadsworth.

McRobbie, A. 1994. *Postmodernism and popular culture.* New York: Routledge.

McVey, W., and W. Kalbach. 1995. *Canadian population.* Toronto: Nelson Canada.

Pike, R., and E. Zureik, eds. 1975. *Socialization and values in Canadian society.* Toronto: McClelland and Stewart.

Reitz, J., and R. Breton. 1994. *The illusion of difference: Realities of ethnicity in Canada and the United States.* Toronto: C. D. Howe Institute.

Richmond, A. 1994. *Global apartheid: Refugees, racism and the new world order.* Toronto: Oxford University Press.

Rushton, P., and A. Bogaert. 1987. Race differences in sexual behavior: Testing and evolutionary hypotheses. *Journal of Research in Personality,* 21: 529–51.

Satzewich, V., ed. 1992. *Deconstructing a nation: Immigration, multiculturalism and racism in '90's Canada.* Halifax: Fernwood.

Wanner, R. 1999. Prejudice, profit or productivity: Explaining returns to human capital among male immigrants to Canada. *Canadian Ethnic Studies,* 30(3): 24–55.

West. C. 1993. *Keeping faith: Philosophy and race in America.* New York: Routledge.

Chapter 14

Does the Vertical Mosaic Still Exist? Ethnicity and Income in Canada, 1991[*]

Jason Z. Lian and David Ralph Matthews

Source: Lian, Jason Z., and Matthews, David R. (1998). Does the vertical mosaic still exist? Ethnicity and income in Canada, 1991. *The Canadian Review of Sociology and Anthropology*, 35(4), 461–81. Reprinted by permission of the Canadian Sociology and Anthropology Association.

Jason Z. Lian and David Ralph Matthews review John Porter's work on Canada's "vertical mosaic" and explore it from a contemporary perspective by applying various data analyses to see if the mosaic still exists in Canada. The authors find that visible minority status has become the fundamental basis for income inequality in Canada.

This paper updates our knowledge about the relationship between ethnicity and social class in Canada using *The Public Use Microdata File for Individuals* drawn from the 1991 Census of Canada. We provide three levels of analysis. First, we examine the relationship between ethnicity and education by ethnic group. Second, we examine the "return to education" in terms of income for those of various ethnic groups. Third, we use log-linear regression to examine the relationship between ethnicity, education, and income while controlling for the effects of a variety of other social variables. We find that, at most educational levels, Canadians of French ethnicity now earn significantly more than those of British ethnicity when other variables are controlled. With this exception, for those of European ethnic backgrounds there are

now virtually no significant differences in income within educational levels when other social variables are controlled. However, those who belong to visible minorities have significantly lower incomes than other Canadians at all educational levels. Race is now the fundamental basis of income inequality in Canada.

In 1965, John Porter described Canadian society as a "vertical mosaic" stratified along ethnic lines (1965: 60–103). Porter argued that the British and French, as the first ethnic groups to come into Canada, became the "charter groups" and to a considerable extent dictated the circumstances under which other ethnic groups were subsequently permitted to enter. He argued that "entrance status" was generally granted to those of other ethnic

[*]This is a revised version of a paper presented at the Canadian Ethnic Studies Association, Biennial Meeting, Gimli, Manitoba, October 1995. We thank Margaret Denton, John Fox, and Wulong Gu for helpful suggestions and comments.

groups who were willing to accept lower level occupational roles (63–73) and that, as a result, "immigration and ethnic affiliation...have been important factors in the formation of social classes in Canada" (73). Porter used census data from the 1931 to 1961 period to demonstrate that the British dominated the French in all of the most prestigious occupational categories, and that other ethnic groups were generally distributed in a hierarchy below them.

Since then, considerable effort has been expended by researchers to support or refute Porter's thesis and to examine the extent to which ethnic social class mobility has occurred as previous immigrants overcame their "entrance status" and moved up the social class hierarchy. Proponents of the vertical mosaic thesis have argued that differences in occupational status among Canadian ethnic groups remain substantial. Over the past thirty years, they have demonstrated that, for the two charter groups, the occupational status of the British has remained significantly higher than that of the French (Royal Commission, 1969: 34–45; Breton & Roseborough, 1971; Boyd et al., 1981). They have argued that among other groups, Jews and those from the north and west of Europe are generally in favourable positions, South Europeans and visible minorities are generally in disadvantaged positions, and Aboriginal Peoples are at the bottom of the Canadian occupational hierarchy (Reitz, 1980; Porter, 1965; Jabbra & Cosper, 1988; Li, 1988; Lautard & Guppy, 1990). Thus, in 1984, Lautard and Loree could still claim that "occupational inequality is still substantial enough to justify the use of the concept 'vertical mosaic' to characterize this aspect of ethnic relations in Canada" (343).

In contrast, a number of other researchers have argued that the influence of ethnicity in the process of social mobility was and/or is minimal in Canada, and that ethnic affiliation did not operate as a significant block to social mobility as Porter had suggested. Most such works have examined the relationship between ethnicity and occupation, while controlling for a range of other variables. Using such methods, they have argued that the association between ethnicity and occupational status was minimal and declining (Pineo, 1976; Darroch, 1979; Ornstein, 1981) and that the contention of the vertical mosaic thesis that the status of immigrants groups has been rigidly preserved is "patently false" (Tepperman, 1975: 156). Other researchers have suggested that a convergence process in occupational status among ethnic groups in Canada has become more apparent since Porter's original analysis (Reitz, 1980: 150–53), the relationship between ethnic origin and class position has been in flux (Nakhaie, 1951), and that gains by non-charter groups have been significantly greater than those of the charter groups (Boyd et al., 1981; Pineo & Porter, 1985: 382–83). Porter, himself, has argued that the situation he described in 1965 may have been in existence only for a relatively short period in Canadian history (Pineo & Porter, 1985: 390). It is also argued that, to the extent that any ethnic status hierarchy remains, Porter's status hierarchy of ethnic groups has changed dramatically with the British dropping from the top to the middle and the Asians moving to the top with the Jews (Herberg, 1990). As a result, it has been stated recently that ethnicity is no longer a drawback for social mobility in Canada (Isajiw, Sev'er & Driedger, 1993).

In many such works, the relation of education and ethnicity has come under considerable scrutiny. Thus, proponents of the ethnic inequality thesis have argued that the Canadian education system has been a mechanism to reproduce social inequality (Shamai, 1992: 44–5) and that educational opportunity was not equally accessible to all groups (Li, 1988: 77–96). Alternatively, those who have been critical of the ethnic inequality thesis have argued that there is little evidence of ethnic inequality in education in Canada and that a *"contest-achieved"* system of status attainment is operating (Herberg, 1990). Indeed, Porter was himself involved in work which argued that non-charter groups have gained significantly in educational achievement compared to the British (Pineo & Porter, 1985: 384) and that the educational system has worked to help minority Canadians overcome the disadvantages of their background (391).

The general conclusion of this body of work would seem to be that there is a collapsing of the vertical mosaic. However, there is growing evidence (see Li, 1988; Reitz, 1980; Agocs & Boyd, 1993) that Canada has retained what Geschwender and Guppy have called a "colour-coded vertical mosaic" (1995: 2). Such works suggest that, whereas ethnic stratification has lessened among white European groups, differences between racial groups have persisted and that, in effect, Canada's mosaic has been reduced to a division based principally on skin colour (1995: 2).

This paper will examine the evidence for and against ethnic inequality in Canada with respect to income distribution, using *The Public Use Microdata Files for Individuals* (PUMFI) provided by Statistics Canada, which constitutes a 3% sample of the 1991 Census. Such files have been made available since 1971, but the 1991 PUMFI provides both a more extensive list of ethnic groups and a more detailed categorization of other variables that may be employed as controls than were available in previous issues. Thus, the present paper is able to provide more current information on the relationship between ethnicity and income than most previous studies, and also is able to identify ethnicity more precisely and use more stringent control variables in the analysis.

To carry out the analysis we have used those respondents in the PUMFI who were in the "working population," and from this group

have eliminated those respondents for whom data were not available or who had zero or negative earnings.[1] These latter reductions reduce the number of respondents in the working population sample by 4.78%, nearly half of whom had zero or negative earnings in 1990. As a result of these adjustments, the average earnings of the sample increased by approximately 4%, but the ethnic composition changed very little.... Thus, for purposes of the present study which focuses on ethnicity, our sample was not affected significantly.

ETHNICITY AND EDUCATION

In any study of ethnic stratification and mobility, education is seen as a critically important intervening variable between ethnicity and income. A fundamental question in such studies is whether educational achievement is distributed equally among ethnic groups. Earlier we noted the diverging positions on this subject in Canada—some argued that the educational system has functioned to reproduce the existing socio-economic hierarchy in favour of the dominant groups (Li, 1988: 73–7; Shamai, 1992: 53–5), and others argued that the educational system has functioned as a source of upward mobility for Canadian minority groups since the early decades of this century (Herberg, 1990).

It is not possible to test this issue fully using data from a single time period. However, data from the 1991 PUMFI show a considerable variation in education among ethnic groups when compared with the Canadian average and this variation remains even when one separates out the Canadian born from the foreign born. This indicates that, among native-born Canadians, educational achievement is unevenly distributed by ethnicity....

In 1991, approximately 30% of the employed labour force in Canada had less than secondary education, just over 54% had secondary or non-university post-secondary education, and almost 17% had post-secondary education. About two-thirds of the European groups and half of the visible minority groups were close to this Canadian average. However, several Southern European groups (Italians, Greeks, Portuguese), Vietnamese, and Aboriginal Peoples had proportionally more persons with this lower educational level while Arabs, West Asians, Jews and Filipinos were under-represented in the lower educational groups.

At the other extreme, in terms of post-secondary (university) education most European groups were around the national average, Poles were moderately above and Jews were nearly three times [more] likely to have a university degree than were those of European origin *per se*. With the exception of the Black/Caribbean and Aboriginal groups who ranked substantially below the national level, the remaining visible minority groups had high rates of university education. This was particularly the case for those of Arab, West Asian, South Asian, Chinese, Filipino and Other East and Southeast Asian ethnic backgrounds.

To some considerable degree this latter finding is a reflection of Canadian immigration policy since the 1970s, which has favoured those with high levels of education and training. Thus, Arab, West Asian, South Asian, Filipino, and Vietnamese foreign born were generally better educated than their Canadian-born counterparts. This relationship held for most other groups with the notable exception of the Greek, Italian, and Balkan ethnic groups among whom the native born were generally better educated than recent immigrants.

EDUCATION AND INCOME DIFFERENCES AMONG ETHNIC GROUPS

While differences in education by ethnic group, particularly among the Canadian-born, are an indication of possible ethnic discrimination, the more significant indication is whether the "returns for education" are also unequal among ethnic groups. That is, does similar education (at whatever level) generate significantly different incomes among the ethnic groups?...

At the national level, those with secondary education earned about 50% more than those without secondary education and those with university education earned about 150% more than those without secondary education.... However, there are extreme ethnic differences at all three educational levels.

The following analyses are all based on comparisons with the national average for each of the educational categories. Looking first at the two "charter groups," workers of British origin with non-secondary education earned 3% more than the national average for this educational level, those with secondary education earned 7% more, while those with university education earned 8% more. In comparison, workers of French ethnicity with non-secondary education earned 12% more than the national average, those with secondary education earned 1% less and those with university education earned 4% more. Thus, in contrast to Porter's finding that the French were rewarded significantly less than the British for their educational achievement, at the lower educational level they now have a significant edge over the British, and are above the national average in income at the higher educational levels.

Those of Western European ethnic background earned considerably higher incomes than the Canadian average in each of the education categories, the exception being university educated persons of Dutch and German ethnic backgrounds who earned only marginally more. Eastern Europeans also tended to earn more than the Canadian average, with Hungarians and Ukrainians earning substantially more at all levels. Persons of Polish ethnicity with lower as well as middle levels of education earned more than average, but better educated persons of Polish ethnicity earned less.

For those whose Jewish ethnic background was recorded, those with the lowest level of education earned 9% more than the Canadian average income for that level, while those with university education earned 19% more than the Canadian university educated average income. However, those with secondary education earned 4% less than the average Canadians at their educational level.

The pattern for Southern Europeans is mixed. At the lowest educational level, most of these ethnic groups earned above the Canadian average income with those of Italian, Portuguese, Greek, and Balkan origin earning considerably higher than that average. However, at higher educational levels Southern Europeans were generally disadvantaged.

However, it is when we consider visible minorities that the largest discrepancies between education and income are apparent. At the lower education levels all 10 visible minority groups earned less than an average Canadian with similar education, ranging from 5% less for those of Arab ethnicity to 33% less for those of Filipino ethnic background and 42% less for Aboriginal Peoples. Likewise, among those with secondary education, all 10 visible minority groups earned substantially less than the comparable Canadian average. Similarly, amongst those with post-secondary education, while those of Black and Chinese ethnicity earned only somewhat less than the Canadian average, those in the other eight visible minority groups received earning[s] substantially below that level.

The overall conclusion to be drawn from these two tables is that persons of European background generally receive above average income for their educational level with the exception of persons with higher education from some Eastern and Southern European

ethnic groups. Indeed, persons from many such ethnic backgrounds now receive incomes relative to education that are higher than for either of the two "charter groups." *However, for visible minorities a very different picture emerges. For all visible ethnic groups and at all educational levels, the rewards for education are substantially below the Canadian average.*

ETHNICITY AND INCOME DIFFERENCES WITHIN EDUCATIONAL CATEGORIES, TAKING INTO ACCOUNT OTHER VARIABLES

Although the preceding analysis has provided strong indications that the rewards for education vary by ethnic group and particularly that workers of visible minorities receive comparatively less than other workers with similar education, it is possible that these results are not due to ethnicity *per se* but to a range of other factors such as the age composition, marital status, or period of immigration of workers from various ethnic groups. Thus, if one wants to measure directly the effect of ethnicity on earnings within educational categories, it is necessary to take into account the effect of these other earnings-related variables.

To do this, we developed a semi-logarithmic regression model of earnings determination with interaction terms constructed of ethnicity and education, controlling for gender; age and age squared; marital status; province of residence; metropolitan versus non-metropolitan area of residence; geographic mobility in the past five years; period of immigration; knowledge of official languages; occupational level; industrial sector; weeks worked and weeks worked squared; and full versus part-time weeks worked. Controlling for these factors in a semi-logarithmic regression yields an adjusted R square of 0.58007, indicating that 58% of the variations in log earnings have been accounted for by the variables included in the model.

Because of the dominant position of the British in Canadian society both numerically and socio-economically, we have used them as the base line category in the regression for an estimation of the net log earnings of the other ethnic groups at each educational level. While persons of British ethnicity with "no degree, certificate, or diploma" were used as the reference category for all other interactive categories of ethnicity and education in the regression, for easy interpretation, we have converted the partial coefficients for the other ethnic groups as deviations from those of their category of "no degree, certificate, or diploma" for the British. The coefficients derived in this manner have been converted into percentages and displayed in Table 14.1 [page 140].

As an example of how to interpret the table, we would note that the 3.1% in the cell for French with "no degree, certificate, or diploma" indicates that workers of French ethnic origin earned 3.1% more than their British counterparts with comparable education when all the dimensions in our model have been taken into account. Similarly, persons of British origin with "no degree, certificate, or diploma" are used as the base category for their British counterparts at other levels of education. Thus, for example, workers of British origin with "high school graduate certificates" earned 13.2% more than their counterparts of British origin, who had "no degree, certificate, or diploma," when all the other factors in our [regression] were taken into account. As also noted, this difference is significant at the 0.05 level.

Looking first at the two "charter groups," it is obvious that the net economic returns to education for workers of British origin is significant, with each advancing educational category providing progressively higher

returns. It is clear that the economic value of education for persons of British origin in the Canadian labour market is beyond doubt.

However, of more significance is the somewhat surprising finding that, after the other factors are controlled, persons of French origin at *all* educational levels had earnings above that for persons of British origin. Moreover, at the Bachelor's degree level and below, these differences of income between the French and the British are statistically significant. Hence, whatever may have been the situation in the past, it is clear that any suggestion that today the French are discriminated against in terms of the returns they receive for their education, is clearly not the case. Indeed, especially at lower levels, the French are significantly favoured over the British in terms of this relationship.

Among Europeans, whether from the north, east, or south of Europe, most ethnic groups had approximately the same income levels as their British counterparts with similar education. Notable exceptions were the Dutch and Poles who, in several of the upper educational levels earned significantly less, and those of Jewish ethnicity in the lowest educational categories who earned significantly more. The most significant discrepancies occurred, not in relation to any ethnicity, but in terms of certain educational categories. Thus, where respondents held either a "university certificate below the bachelor's level" or a "degree in medicine," persons from continental Europe were quite likely to have incomes significantly below that of the British when other factors were taken into account. The frequency of such discrepancies in these two categories suggests that this may have to do with the evaluation of educational qualification at these levels rather than just ethnicity.

In sharp contrast to the situation for Europeans, adjusted earnings of visible minorities were much lower than for the British at

Table 14.1 Adjusted Earnings[1] of Persons of Different Ethnic Origins[2] as Percentage Differences from Those of Persons of British Origin by Educational Level, Canada, 1990

Ethnic Origin	No Degree, Certificate, or Diploma	High School Graduation Certificate	Trades Certificate	Other Non-University Certificate	University Certificate below Bachelor Level	Bachelor's Degree(s)	University Certificate above Bachelor Level	Masters Degree(s)	Earned Doctorate	Degree in Medicine[3]
				Highest Degree Obtained						
British[4]	3.1**	13.2**	16.8**	21.3**	27.3**	39.6**	47.4**	58.3**	76.6**	141.7**
French	0.5	1.7**	3.0**	5.3**	8.1**	2.3*	2.8	1.2	5.4	4.2
Dutch	3.7*	2.8	1.6	-2.0	-18.4**	-3.9	-3.9	-12.4*	1.9	-40.6**
German		-0.5	-2.1	0.7	3.7	-2.6	-3.4	-7.0	-3.4	-14.7
Other W European	14.0**	5.2	1.0	14.3**	-18.7	0.9	-7.4	2.4	6.1	-24.4
Hungarian	-2.4	-2.1	-1.3	-11.3**	-18.7	-2.0	4.4	11.4	-17.0	8.3
Polish	-3.6	-1.1	1.8	1.1	-19.2**	0.6	-3.0	-14.4**	-6.1	-12.5
Ukrainian	2.7	3.1	2.7	4.0**	-14.4**	5.6*	-2.2	-3.4	-13.8	6.3
Balkan	2.4	-3.6	-2.0	5.3	4.6	-2.1	-5.6	-5.8	-8.6	-3.4
Greek	-6.3**	-6.6**	0.4	-1.7	-32.5**	-9.3	-15.7	-2.4	-25.9	-50.1**
Italian	-0.6	2.7*	-0.0	7.1**	8.3	-1.1	-2.1	3.6	-1.8	-26.4*
Portuguese	11.0*	3.1	4.8	2.8	-22.5*	-4.9	5.3	0.6	–	41.7
Spanish	4.1	-14.4**	0.7	-6.0	-13.1	-14.7	0.5	-20.2	48.5	14.6
Jewish	21.9**	8.0**	3.3	3.1	3.2	4.4	6.7	0.7	6.7	-2.2
Arab	1.4	-6.2*	-12.6**	1.6	-22.7**	-17.8**	-22.3**	-18.1**	1.6	-27.7**
West Asian	-5.4	-10.4**	-5.3	-0.6	-10.7	-7.5	-15.6	-18.2**	-25.7	-30.5*
South Asian	2.9	-3.9*	-8.6**	-4.1	-0.7	-17.7**	-12.8*	-18.9**	-6.8	-15.9*
Chinese	-4.4**	5.3**	-3.3	-5.6**	-6.6	-7.3**	-14.1**	-10.3**	-26.3**	-15.2*
Filipino	-6.4	-2.1	-12.5**	-8.2*	-7.5	-12.4**	-12.5	-20.9*	–	13.0
Vietnamese	0.8	-11.9**	-19.7**	3.2	-19.3*	-12.7*	-39.2**	-6.9	-7.0	-42.7**
Other E & SE Asian	-4.2	-10.2**	-3.7	-6.8	20.2*	-14.6**	-10.1	-12.1	-27.5	-35.1**
Latin American	3.7	-11.7**	-2.3	-29.8**	-7.8	-24.4**	-31.1**	-18.7	-30.4	-40.6
Black	-8.1**	-3.1	-3.3	-10.4**	-3.7	-10.0**	10.6	-12.4	-10.3	-10.2
Aboriginal	-18.8**	-16.0**	-20.0**	-24.7**	-1.9	-8.0	-24.2	-20.2	-49.4	-76.7*
Others	-2.7**	-0.3	-1.7*	-0.9	0.3	-3.7**	-2.5	-6.7**	-2.6	-7.2

Source: *Public Use Microdata File for Individuals*, 1991 Census of Canada.

1. Controlling for gender, age, marital status, province of residence, metropolitan/non-metropolitan area, geographic mobility, period of immigration, knowledge of official languages, occupation, industrial sector, weeks worked, and part-time/full-time weeks worked.
2. The earnings of workers of various ethnic origins are expressed as percentage differences from the earnings of workers of British origin in the same educational category....
3. Including degrees in medicine, dentistry, veterinary medicine, and optometry.
4. The category of "no degree, certificate, or diploma" for the British is the base category for other categories for the British [....]

*Significant at 0.10
**Significant at 0.05

most educational levels. Compared to their British counterparts, out of the 10 educational categories, most visible minority groups earned less than their British counterparts in the majority of categories. Moreover, in many of the educational categories, visible minorities earned *significantly* less than their British counterparts.

Given this obvious evidence of discrimination against all visible minority groups, it is difficult to single out any one or two groups as being more hard done by than others. Perhaps persons of Chinese background might fit this category as they earned less than those of British ethnicity in all 10 educational categories and significantly less than the British in 8 of the 10 educational categories. However, Aboriginal Peoples and West Asians also earned less in 10 categories, and most other visible minority groups earned less in nine of them. While the Arabs might seem better off amongst visible minorities in that they earned lower in only 7 categories, they were significantly less in all 7, a level of earnings discrimination surpassed only by those of Chinese ethnicity.

Whereas one might have thought that increased level of education would lead to lower levels of discrimination, there is little in Table 14.1 to support such a position. From high school to doctorate there is clear evidence of lower earnings amongst visible minorities compared to their British counterparts at the same educational level. Thus, all visible minorities earned less than the British at the high school graduate level, at the level of bachelors degree holder, master's degree holder and, with the exception of Arabs, at the level of doctorate degree holder. Likewise, all visible minorities who held degrees in medicine earned less than their British counterparts, as did all but the Blacks among those who held a university certificate above bachelor's but below master's level. Moreover, in the majority

of cases *these differences were either significant or highly significant. In sum, it is clear from these findings that educational achievement at any level fails to protect persons of visible minority background from being disadvantaged in terms of the income they receive.*

SUMMARY AND DISCUSSION

We began this paper with the question, "Does the 'vertical mosaic' still exist?" It has been our assumption that the most appropriate place to look for evidence to either support or refute the vision of Canadian society as a "vertical mosaic" is through an examination of the relationship between ethnicity and income, first controlling for educational level, and then controlling for other key social variables so that this relationship can be measured more directly and precisely.

Our conclusion is that, by 1991, for the majority of ethnic groups in Canada there is no evidence that the traditionally accepted image of a vertical mosaic still remains. Among the two charter groups, the French now earn more for comparable education than their British counterparts when other factors are controlled. Likewise, many ethnic groups from all parts of Europe who had entered Canada with generally little education and hence occupied lower income positions, have now moved up the educational and income hierarchies and there is very little evidence of discrimination against any such ethnic groups.

On the other hand, there is also clear evidence that visible minorities have not fared well. When education and a range of other social variables are controlled, Aboriginal Peoples still remain mired at the bottom of Canadian society. Almost all Asian groups and most of those of Latin American and Middle Eastern ethnicity were also similarly disadvantaged.

In sum, the evidence indicates that similar educational qualifications carried different economic values in the Canadian labour market for individuals of different "racial" origins. All visible minority groups had below-average earnings in each of the categories, while most of those of European ethnicity had above-average earnings.

It is possible that there are some other variables than "race" which systematically operate to discriminate against people of colour in Canadian society. However, the 1991 *Public Use Microdata File for Individuals* permits more "controls" for other possible variables than has ever previously been possible in such a large data set based on Canadian society. Thus, we have controlled for most of the other competing factors and their interaction effects which might conceivably affect the fundamental relationship between education and income that lies at the centre of our analysis. If there are other factors which might affect this relationship, we cannot easily discern what these might be. More importantly, the large literature on the relationship between education, income, and ethnicity in Canada which we have reviewed provides no clue of any other factor or factors which might have such a significant influence.

Consequently, whereas we began this paper with the question, "Does the vertical mosaic still exist?," we must end it with an even more serious question, namely, "Is Canada a racist society?" Canadians have long prided themselves on their policy of ethnic pluralism in contrast to the "melting pot" of the United States. We have also generally seen ourselves as a more racially tolerant society than the American one. However, our data suggest that there are limits to our tolerance of cultural and racial divisions. While we are apparently willing to accept cultural differences (particularly from a wide range of European cultures) in terms of the income received relative to level of education, we show no such tolerance for those who are racially "visible" from the white majority in Canadian society. All our evidence suggests that, while our traditional "vertical mosaic" of ethnic differences may be disappearing, it has been replaced by a strong "coloured mosaic" of racial differences in terms of income rewards and income benefits. While this does not necessarily mean that we have racial discrimination when it comes to other social benefits such as location of residence, access to public facilities, and the extreme forms of discrimination that have characterized some other societies, our evidence leads us to conclude that there is some considerable level of racial discrimination in Canada in terms of financial rewards for educational achievement. In this respect at least, yes, we are a racist society.

NAVIGATING THE CONCEPTS

1. With reference to the article, what did Porter mean by the term *vertical mosaic*?

2. Canadians pride themselves as being a tolerant people who support multiculturalism. Given the evidence presented by Lian and Matthews, do you feel that Canada qualifies as a racist society? Do you have any examples from your own community that would support your position?

3. From the sociological perspective and with reference to the article, do you believe that people with a post-secondary education are less racist than those without post-secondary education? Discuss.

NOTES

1. The analysis is based on 425,107 cases. The 1991 PUMFI contains 809,654 cases. Respondents who did not work in 1990 (nearly half of whom were under age 15) have been excluded, thereby dropping the sample to 446,478 cases representing the working population of Canada in 1990. A small number of persons were on employment authorizations or Minister's permits or were refugee claimants. As the income of such persons could have been significantly affected by factors atypical of the Canadian labour market, they have been excluded, thereby reducing the sample to 443,161 cases. Also eliminated were a small number of cases with missing information on education, age, marital status, geographic mobility, and period of immigration (i.e., the factors of earning determination used in this study), thereby reducing the sample to 439,959 cases. Finally, to estimate the net effect of ethnicity on earnings with educational categories, we employed linear least-squares regression with logarithms of earnings as the dependent variable..., and this meant persons with zero or negative earnings had to be eliminated. This further reduced the sample to 425,107 persons.

REFERENCES

Agocs, C., and M. Boyd. 1993. The Canadian ethnic mosaic recast for the 1990s. In *Social inequality in Canada: Patterns, problems, policies*, eds. J. Curtis, E. Grabb, and N. Guppy, 330–60. Scarborough, Ont.: Prentice-Hall Canada Inc..

Boyd, M., J. Goyder, F. E. Jones, H. A. McRoberts, P. C. Pineo, and J. Porter. 1981. Status attainment in Canada: Findings of the *Canadian mobility study*. *Canadian Review of Sociology and Anthropology*, 18(5): 657–73.

Breton, R., and H. Roseborough. 1971. Ethnic differences in status. In *Canadian society: Sociological perspectives*, eds. B. R. Blishen, F. E. Jones, K. D. Naegele, and J. Porter, 450–68. Toronto: Macmillan of Canada Ltd.

Darroch, A. G. 1979. Another look at ethnicity, stratification and social mobility in Canada. *Canadian Journal of Sociology*, 4(1): 1–24.

Geschwender, J. A., and N. Guppy. 1995. Ethnicity, educational attainment and earned income among Canadian-born men and women. *Canadian Ethnic Studies*, 27(1): 67–84.

Herberg, E. N. 1990. The ethno-racial socioeconomic hierarchy in Canada: Theory and analysis of the new vertical mosaic. *International Journal of Comparative Sociology*, 31(3–4): 206–20.

Isajiw, W. W., A. Sev'er, and L. Dreidger. 1993. Ethnic identity and social mobility: A test of the "drawback model." *Canadian Journal of Sociology*, 18(2): 177–96.

Jabbra, N. W., and R. L. Cosper. 1988. Ethnicity in Atlantic Canada: A survey. *Canadian Ethnic Studies*, 20(3): 6–27.

Lautard, E. H., and N. Guppy. 1990. The vertical mosaic revisited: Occupational differentials among Canadian ethnic groups. In *Race and ethnic relations in Canada*, ed. P. S. Li, 189–208. Toronto: Oxford University Press.

Lautard, E. H., and D. J. Loree. 1984. Ethnic stratification in Canada, 1931–1971. *Canadian Journal of Sociology*, 9: 333–43.

Li, P. S. 1988. *Ethnic inequality in a class society*. Toronto: Thompson Educational Publishing Inc.

Nakhaie, M. R. 1995. Ownership and management position of Canadian ethnic groups in 1973 and 1989. *Canadian Journal of Sociology*, 20(2): 167–92.

Ornstein, M. D. 1981. The occupational mobility of men in Ontario. *The Canadian Review of Sociology and Anthropology*, 18(2): 181–215.

Pineo, P. C. 1976. Social mobility in Canada: The current picture. *Sociological Focus*, 9(2): 109–23.

Pineo, P. C., and J. Porter. 1985. Ethnic origin and occupational attainment. In *Ascription and achievement: Studies in mobility and status attainment in Canada*, eds. M. Boyd, J. Goyder, F. E. Jones, H. A. McRoberts, P. C. Pineo, and J. Porter, 357–92. Ottawa: Carleton University Press.

Porter, J. 1965. *The vertical mosaic*. Toronto: University of Toronto Press.

Reitz, J. G. 1980. *The survival of ethnic groups*. Toronto: McGraw-Hill Ryerson, Ltd.

Royal Commission on Bilingualism and Biculturalism, Canada. 1969. *Report of the Royal Commission on Bilingualism and Biculturalism,* Vol. 3A. Ottawa: Queen's Printer.

Shamai, S. 1992. Ethnicity and educational achievement in Canada: 1941–1981. *Canadian Ethnic Studies,* 24(1): 41–57.

Statistics Canada. 1993. *Standard occupational classification, 1991.* Ottawa: Ministry of Industry, Science and Technology.

———. 1994. User *documentation for public use microdata file for individuals, 1991 Census.* Catalogue No.: 48-030E. Ottawa: Statistics Canada.

Tepperman, L. 1975. *Social mobility in Canada.* Toronto: McGraw-Hill Ryerson.

Chapter 15

The Changing Colour of Poverty in Canada
Abdolmohammad Kazemipur and Shiva S. Halli

Source: Kazemipur, Abdolmohammad, and Halli, Shiva S. (2001). The changing colour of poverty in Canada. *Canadian Review of Sociology and Anthropology*, 38(2), 217–38.

In this article, Abdolmohammad Kazemipur and Shiva S. Halli investigate how ethnicity and racial colour influence a person's chances of being poor in Canada. In analyzing census data from 1991 and 1996, the authors suggest that recent immigrants to Canada are not doing very well economically and are influenced in part by the minimization of their educational attainment and professional qualifications. Kazemipur and Halli also highlight the issues of racial discrimination and where future research needs to focus. They argue that, left unchecked, the "problem of race" will continue to intensify in Canada.

Using the 1991 and 1996 Canadian census data, the present study addresses the issue of poor or low-income immigrants, a topic largely overlooked in previous immigration research. The authors found that, compared to native-born Canadians, immigrants were consistently overrepresented among the poor, and that this overrepresentation had a clear ethnic and racial colour, with visible minority immigrants experiencing the most severe conditions. For them, the logistic regression models show, the odds of poverty are noticeably higher, even after controlling for all other relevant variables. The poverty rates of different generations of immigrants also show an unexpected pattern, in which those who have migrated during their adolescent years experience unusually severe poverty conditions. A comparison of the situation in 1991 and 1996 shows that human capital endowments are becoming less rewarding for immigrants.

In the last two decades of the 20th century, like many other industrial nations, Canada went through some radical transformations, influenced by two major forces—one economic, the other political. The Canadian economy has been shifting away from a structure based on manufacturing to one dependent on information processing, and from one dependent on domestic resources to one increasingly operating in a global scene. This development has influenced many aspects of Canadian society, but particularly its occupational structure, income distribution, and regional inequality (Marchak, 1991; Rifkin, 1995). In the political arena, a new wave of conservatism, which some have called Neoliberalism (Abu-Laban, 1998) and others New Right (Marchak, 1991), has swept across the country forcing major Canadian social institutions—such as education, health care, occupations, the social safety net and the taxation system—to depart from their postwar paths of development. Despite having dynamics of their own, these two trends—economic and political—have converged in at least one area, eroding the middle class and generating a bipolar structure in the economy, job market, and income distribution (Teeple, 1995). The essence of this development is well captured in a commonly expressed metaphor that the industrial societies are leaving a pyramid shape in favour of an hourglass one (Portes and Rumbaut, 1996).

One area in which the effects of the new economic and political circumstances have been more visible is in immigration policy and the social and economic experiences of immigrants. This has partly to do with the nature of the Neoliberal prescriptions that, according to Abu-Laban (1998: 194), "have a tendency to create discourses of enemies and scapegoats, transforming what were once seen as victims into victimizers (e.g., single mothers, the poor, immigrants and so on are blamed for stealing 'our' welfare, 'our' social and educational services, or 'our' jobs)." In many Western countries, she argues, "such discourses relating to immigrants have resulted in both a tightening of criteria for formal citizenship, and a tightening of immigration controls vis-à-vis certain groups and nationals— typically those from countries of the Third World" (194). The clear implication of this proposition is that, in an era of Neoliberal politics, with its associated fiscal conservatism and priority of deficit reduction, the vulnerable groups such as immigrants are more likely to suffer disproportionately.

The present study tries to shed some light on the validity of the above proposition by empirically examining the experience of poverty by immigrants to Canada, and the factors behind it. The choice of poverty as the topic is justified based on two facts. First, in an era marked by transition from a "pyramid"- to an "hourglass"-shaped social structure, a larger number of people may find themselves at the lower level of social structure and income

scale, as reflected in the constant rise of poverty levels in Canada since the late 1980s. A study of poverty, therefore, will address a social problem that more and more people will be struggling with. Second, in the particular case of immigrants, most of the previous research has treated them as one homogeneous sub-population, masking the enormous diversity that exists among them. The plight of low-income immigrants has gone largely unnoticed in serious academic research, though it has received some attention in the popular media.

The central questions with which we are concerned are: 1) What is the magnitude of poverty among immigrants, compared to non-immigrants? 2) What is the composition of poor immigrants, in terms of ethnic origin, location of residence, period of migration, and age at arrival? 3) What are the causes of poverty among immigrants, and are they different from those of non-immigrants? and finally 4) How has immigrants' experience of poverty and its causative factors changed during the period of the Neoliberal swing in Canadian politics? In what follows, we first introduce an overarching conceptual framework for understanding the causes of poverty among immigrants. This framework has an eclectic nature; it includes conceptual elements taken from various theoretical approaches. This allows for an examination of the relative significance of the different factors emphasized by different perspectives. Then we address the methodological issues and describe the nature of the data used. The article concludes with a presentation of the findings, and the implications for future research.

THE CONCEPTUAL FRAMEWORK

The paucity of research on poverty among immigrants has hindered the development of theories specifically formulated to address this issue. This theoretical shortage is certainly, at least partly, a result of the paucity of research on poverty in Canada. But it has also been reinforced by the long-held view that the problem of poverty among immigrants is not any more serious than among the native-born. Against this background, it is understandable why the poverty of immigrants has never come to the foreground, nor ever been high in the immigration research agenda. To these factors of theoretical significance, one may add a possible third factor of a more practical nature: an unconscious reluctance among researchers to raise an issue that could be easily used against immigrants and in favour of more restrictive immigration policies. The result, whatever the causes, is the current lack of a well-developed theory of immigrant poverty.

The paucity of specific theories of poverty, however, does not mean that we are left in a theoretical vacuum. Indeed, there exists a rich literature on the general economic performance of immigrants that has useful implications for the study of poverty. Examining the validity of John Porter's thesis of the "vertical mosaic," Lautard and Loree (1984), for instance, found that the occupational inequality among ethnic groups in Canada was substantial enough to justify the use of the notion of a "vertical mosaic," and that the differences observed "do not seem to be explainable by the effects of differences in regions and differences in education" (342). In a search for factors that can explain these persisting patterns of inequality, Grant and Oertel (1998: 70) suggest three possibilities: "A slower rate of acquisition of unobservable skills (such as language proficiency and awareness of cultural norms specific to Canada); a higher degree of discrimination with the rising percentage of visible minorities among immigrants; or a change in the structure of employment in Canada in favour of lower-paid service occupations." This proposition, indeed, encompasses three major theoretical approaches employed in the previous research on the economic performance of immigrants: one that emphasizes the individual factors such as assimilation and human capital; another that stresses the economic environment of the host society at the time of immigrants' arrival; and a third that highlights the social environment in the receiving country, along with factors such as discrimination, as predictors of immigrants' performance. Over time, each of these theoretical approaches has branched out into various versions, with slight differences. Below, we introduce the variations of these perspectives in more detail, along with their implications for the issue of concern in this study, that is, poverty.

Assimilation Thesis

The *assimilation thesis* considers poverty of immigrants as a passing phenomenon, due to immediate post-migration difficulties; a problem that eases up with longer stay in the new home. The assimilation theory would hypothesize that over time immigrants produce better economic records, as they become increasingly familiar with their new environments, develop better communication skills, and become more realistic in their expectations. In other words, in their early years after arrival immigrants face the harshest situation. This harshness, however, subsides as time allows for more assimilation to take place. It follows that the situation is even more favourable for the second generation of immigrants, as for them such a process starts from childhood and even from birth. As far as poverty is concerned, the most vulnerable immigrants—that is, those with a high risk of poverty—are to be found among those in their early years of arrival, those with little or no knowledge of the official languages, and those who migrated at an older age.

Entrance Status Thesis

While the early "assimilationists" paid more attention to cultural and ideational processes (see Park & Burgess, 1924; Gordon, 1964), the later ones put more emphasis on economic factors. Porter (1965) suggested "the entrance status thesis," in which immigrants start from the lowest jobs in the market and move their way up the occupational hierarchy, leaving the entrance status jobs for the newly arrived immigrants. In this perspective, immigrants' economic performance is a function of their occupational ranking, itself a function of their duration of stay in the host society and the existence of consecutive waves of immigrants. Those immigrants who are in the early years of their arrival, according to this view, are more likely to have higher poverty rates, but this likelihood diminishes with longer stays and movement to more rewarding jobs.

Human Capital Thesis

This perspective puts more emphasis on human capital endowments of immigrants as determinants of their economic performance. A low-income status, according to this thesis, can result from factors such as low education, low job skills, old age, poor health, and low geographical mobility. A low education, for example, can suppress one's chance of admission into well-paid jobs that demand a highly skilled labour force; old age can be detrimental when successful performance in a job requires mastery of modem technology; low geographical mobility, both nationally and internationally, tends to deprive one of the job opportunities available elsewhere. Borjas (1994), for instance, has attributed the lower level of economic achievement among recent immigrants in the United States to the fact that they have come mostly from developing countries, and with low levels of educational qualifications and occupational skills (Massey et al., 1994).

Discrimination Thesis

Despite the significance of human capital factors, many studies have shown that an explanation merely based on such factors runs the risk of being too static and fairly simplistic. Some have raised the possibility that the lower economic achievement of recent immigrants may be attributed not to their lower level of

human capital endowment but to the diminishing returns for it. Gordon (1995: 530), for example, attributes the lower educational attainments of second generation immigrants to the diminishing returns for their education: "[against] a background of environmental disadvantages, institutional racism, and doubts about the likely rewards for qualifications, educational attainments have been uneven." Basran and Zong (1998), on the other hand, argue that even when the educational attainments are high for immigrants, they are not recognized accordingly. They show that large numbers of immigrants in Canada have occupations inferior, in terms of both prestige and financial gains, to those for which they are trained, due to the fact that their credentials are not recognized appropriately.

The studies cited above clearly imply that the positive impact of human capital factors can be intercepted by other factors such as discrimination, both at interpersonal and institutional levels. Among all possible types of discrimination, one based on race and ethnic characteristics is found to be most common and persistent, as well as more conducive to poverty. This relationship is well captured in an observation by Dunk (1999) that "it is no historical accident...that skin colour and poverty are related."

Empirical studies of the impact of discrimination on the economic performance of immigrants in Canada have yielded mixed results. A report by the Economic Council of Canada (1991), for instance, claimed that there was no substantial discrimination against immigrants, and in particular against visible minorities. This report was later criticized for its flawed statistical and measurement methods, two of which being the use of country of birth instead of ethnic and racial origins, and the smallness of the samples—as low as a dozen for some ethnic groups (Reitz and Breton, 1994). More rigorous treatment of the problem in later research resulted in an opposite finding. In a study to measure the "market value of race," for example, Li (1999: 126) found that "non-white origin creates a penalty for all visible minorities in the labour market." He attributed such a penalty to a range of mechanisms, from refusing to recognize the non-white immigrants' credentials, to their lower likelihood of being hired, higher chances of being screened out in the job application process owing to their language characteristics, accent, and deviation from the language standard of the dominant group. Along this line, Reitz and Breton (1994: 122) found "consistent and substantial net earnings disadvantages" for both adult immigrants and immigrants raised in Canada. The expression of the opposing views in regard to whether immigrants face discrimination in Canada justifies their inclusion in our analysis. However, due to the fact that discrimination does not easily lend itself to direct observation, and that its impact is often confounded by other variables, the findings of this study on discrimination need to be approached cautiously. The variables included in census data are only indirect proxies for discrimination.

Period Effect Thesis

In addition to assimilation, human capital and discrimination, the period in which one migrated can also affect one's economic performance. Commenting on the experiences of recent immigrants to the United States, Gans (1992) remarked:

... the long-term periods of economic growth, the first that began after the Civil War and the second that started after World War II, are not likely to return soon. The first helped to spur the arrival of the new European immigrants and enabled them to find more or less steady jobs so that many of them or their children could escape poverty by the end of the 1920s. The second enabled the descendents of that immigration to move at least into the upper-working and lower-middle classes, and in many cases, firmly into the middle class. Even if periods of long-term economic growth return, they will probably not be equally labour-intensive. No-one expects a revival in physical labour, and even many low-level

service jobs may be computerised, sent abroad, or left undone. Such trends have special meaning for the new immigration and its second generation since, among other things, they could lead to what I have earlier called second-generation decline (181).

In Canada, likewise, the post–World War II decades were especially prosperous, providing newly arrived immigrants with plenty of opportunities. Shorter periods of waiting to get into a first job, the rarity of employment terminations, and the prevalence of full-time occupations enabled immigrants to have an early financial take-off and establish themselves more easily. Such an economic environment, however, is totally nonexistent for those immigrants who have landed in Canada since the mid-1970s. There is, therefore, a higher likelihood for these groups of immigrants to be poorer than their preceding peers.

The theoretical propositions discussed above guide the present study. While some of these propositions are derived from competing theoretical perspectives, as mentioned earlier, we have attempted to include all of them in our conceptual model to verify them empirically. Figure 15.1 [page 150] encapsulates the conceptual synthesis that we use in the present study.

DATA AND METHODOLOGY

The data used in this study consist of the individual Public Use Micro Files (PUMFs) of Canada's 1991 and 1996 censuses....

A word is ... needed on the notion of poverty and the way it is defined. Like most discussions of poverty in Canada during the last 25 years, this study has employed Statistics Canada's "Low Income Cut-Offs (LICOs)," which are calculated for communities and for families of various sizes within those communities. Table 15.1 [page 151] contains the poverty lines for the census year 1996. It is important to note that not all researchers agree upon the legitimacy of using LICOs as poverty status indicators. Whether LICOs should be used as

Figure 15.1 The Conceptual Model of the Causes of Poverty among Immigrants

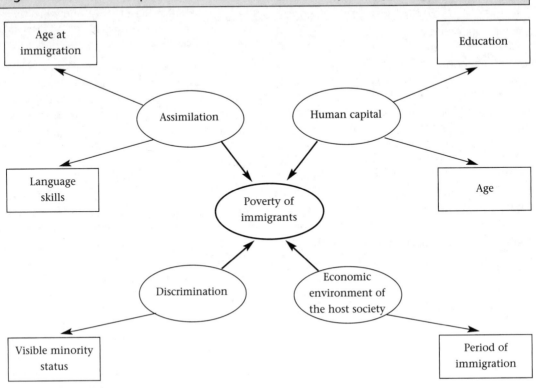

indicators of poverty, or should simply be considered as indicators of low income, is still debated (see, for instance, Sarlo, 1992; 1994; Fellegi, 1997). Such a debate is not new, and is certainly not confined to Canada. It is a part of a larger and yet unsettled debate among academics and policy makers on the measure of poverty (see Ruggles, 1990; Kazemipur and Halli, 2000). An examination of the debate surrounding this issue, however, is beyond the scope of this study. Even if the reader does not consider low-income and poverty as equivalent, the trends and patterns found in this study will still remain pertinent to low-income, if not poor, immigrants.

FINDINGS

Table 15.2 [page 152] shows the magnitude of poverty for immigrants in Canada in 1996. To provide a better view of the possible impacts of location and ethnicity, poverty rates are reported by city and ethnic origin. Poverty rates of non-immigrants are also included, to compare and to isolate the particular effect of immigrant status. The values that are highlighted specify those groups of immigrants who have poverty rates higher than their non-immigrant counterparts of the same ethnic origin and living in the same city. The table is also divided into three sections based on the

Table 15.1 Low-Income Cut-offs for Families and Unattached Individuals (1986-Based), in Dollars, 1996

	Size of Area of Residence				
Family Size	500,000 or More	100,000 to 499,999	30,000 to 99,999	Small Urban Areas	Rural Areas (Farm and Non-Farm)
1	15,819	13,895	13,574	12,374	10,769
2	21,442	18,835	18,399	16,771	14,600
3	27,256	23,941	23,387	21,318	18,556
4	31,383	27,561	26,927	24,547	21,364
5	34,287	30,114	29,419	26,818	23,343
6	37,219	32,686	31,932	29,109	25,337
7 or More	40,029	35,159	34,347	31,311	27,252

Source: Statistics Canada (1998).

geographical origins of the ethnic groups. The top section shows the rates for western and northwestern Europe, the middle section for southern and eastern Europe, and the bottom section for the developing countries.

The first thing to note is the overall magnitude of poverty rates in the three sections of Table 15.2, which reveal a number of consistent patterns. First, a cursory look at the distribution of the cases in the table shown in boldface—that is, the ethnic groups in which immigrants have higher poverty rates than non-immigrants of the same ethnic origin—shows that they occur with much higher frequencies in the middle and bottom sections. To be more specific, considering the three centres of concentration of immigrants, i.e., Montreal, Toronto and Vancouver, out of a total of fifteen groups in this category, seven groups (47%) show higher rates of poverty for immigrants as compared to non-immigrants of the European ethnic origin. The proportion is 26 out of 30 (or 87%) for the middle section, and 18 out of 33 (or 57%) for the bottom section. At face value, this may indicate that immigrants of eastern and southern European

origin are the most disadvantaged groups. This implication, however, is qualified when the magnitude of poverty is taken into consideration. The poverty rates for the eastern and southern European groups vary mostly in the range of 20s and 30s, while those of visible minorities in the bottom section vary in the range of 40s and 50s, with one higher than 60. Also, it should be noted that the poverty rates of the non-immigrants in the bottom section are so noticeably high that being an immigrant hardly aggravates the poverty level. Except for variations in the range of poverty rates, this pattern exists for all three cities.

Second, in addition to the differential rates of poverty for immigrants and non-immigrants, the severity of poverty for certain groups is particularly noticeable. A search for the groups with poverty rates of more than 50% in all CMAs yields an alarming result: one western/northwestern European group, 21 southern/eastern European (particularly Spanish), and 103 visible minorities, four of which show a 100% poverty rate (i.e., West Asian non-immigrants in Quebec City, West Asian immigrants in Sherbrooke–Trois-Rivières,

Table 15.2 Poverty Rates by Ethnic Origin, CMA and Immigration Status, 1996

	Montreal		Toronto		Vancouver		All other CMAs	
	Non-Immigrants	Immigrants	Non-Immigrants	Immigrants	Non-Immigrants	Immigrants	Non-Immigrants	Immigrants
British	26.6	22.7	15.1	14.5	18.4	17.0	17.1	13.3
French	20.5	27.3	16.4	18.6	21.8	28.6	19.7	17.7
Dutch (Netherlands)	13.5	13.2	9.9	12.9	14.9	21.3	12.4	12.5
German	20.7	15.9	12.3	15.9	19.2	17.4	14.5	16.2
Other Western European	19.3	21.3	15.4	14.2	21.9	18.6	12.0	14.2
Hungarian (Magyar)	18.0	27.2	18.8	27.8	28.6	36.6	13.8	19.9
Polish	32.7	37.1	17.7	30.2	23.9	31.1	15.3	22.0
Ukrainian	25.6	29.8	14.5	32.0	20.9	36.6	15.7	20.1
Balkan	26.2	37.1	13.4	25.8	15.0	41.7	16.2	33.2
Greek	28.8	31.7	19.7	21.5	19.5	24.0	19.0	16.3
Italian	19.9	23.2	11.7	17.2	15.3	18.8	11.0	15.3
Portuguese	25.3	24.0	19.5	19.7	15.6	18.3	16.9	14.2
Spanish	53.5	52.8	49.3	43.8	45.2	36.0	67.1	48.6
Jewish	19.7	29.5	8.3	20.5	10.7	13.5	10.4	22.3
Other European	20.3	42.7	14.6	23.4	22.7	27.8	17.5	20.5
African	70.7	62.6	57.8	55.2	36.4	45.5	57.6	65.6
Lebanese	54.9	53.0	38.4	45.6	27.3	30.8	42.4	46.6
Other Arab	47.9	54.6	35.5	46.1	38.5	46.4	44.9	50.1
West Asian	38.8	48.1	45.8	47.3	61.8	50.4	50.8	59.7
South Asian	51.4	54.9	27.6	32.6	20.2	23.9	23.4	25.9
Chinese	37.7	45.9	22.1	33.4	19.5	39.5	19.2	31.5
Filipino	28.8	27.5	18.8	23.3	16.1	22.2	18.4	22.4
Vietnamese	41.1	40.5	47.5	38.7	72.2	52.0	43.3	41.2
Other East/Southeast Asian	56.9	49.8	15.5	36.7	22.4	35.7	28.7	42.2
Latin/Central/South American	69.2	58.7	40.7	35.7	52.0	44.8	49.2	45.3
Caribbean	58.4	53.4	44.7	32.5	25.9	17.6	41.2	32.6
Total	24.0	39.6	16.0	27.7	18.3	29.9	18.2	23.9

Spanish non-immigrants in Hamilton, and Lebanese immigrants in Regina–Saskatoon).

It should be noted, however, that more than 60% of the Spanish reported a Latin American country as their place of birth. This is to say that the most disadvantaged group in the middle section of Table 15.2 is more closely associated with the developing world than with Europe.

The immigrant groups with the highest rates of poverty have another thing in common: the majority of them arrived in Canada since the late 1960s. This commonality can be related to their higher rates of poverty in two ways. First, they arrived after the postwar economic boom in Canada, hence their lower economic performance and higher poverty rates. Second, they are still new immigrants, with a low level of familiarity with Canada, and are still building up their careers. The former possibility alludes to what may be called the "period effect"; the latter to the "assimilation effect." By showing the poverty rates of different cohorts of immigrants, Table 15.3 [page 154] allows an empirical examination of these possibilities.

Table 15.3 reports the poverty rate of immigrants by their period of immigration. The last row of the table contains the overall poverty rates for those who migrated in seven different periods. The poverty rate starts at 21.3% for those who arrived before 1946, and consistently declines in three subsequent categories, reaching its lowest level in the 1960s (14.2%). It then rises noticeably. This trend clearly supports the period effect, as it is perfectly synchronized with the postwar periods of economic boom and bust in Canada. This general confirmation should be qualified, however, with a reminder that the best way to isolate the period effect is through the use of longitudinal data. In the absence of such data, the period effect can be confounded by other variables, thus obscuring the findings.

When it comes to testing the assimilation effect, however, Table 15.3 is more reliable.

One implication of assimilation theory was that immigrants who migrated at an earlier age would show better economic performance, owing to their familiarity with the social environment and market demands in their new homes, access to job-searching social networks, better language skills, less severe cultural conflict, and recognized education. It follows that the poverty rates of immigrants should increase as their age at migration increases. The average poverty rates of immigrants by their age at migration shown in the last two columns of Table 15.3 support this argument, though with some qualification. The poverty rates for all immigrants reported in the first column yields the surprising result that those who migrated at a younger age are as, or more, disadvantaged than their parents, as far as their poverty is concerned. The exclusion of those under 16, with the justification that they are not at the employment age and therefore do not yet earn income, improves the results to some extent. It clearly shows that those who migrated at age 0–4, who can be considered analogous to second-generation immigrants, have the lowest rate of poverty. The poverty rate then rises as the age at migration increases. The only anomaly in this trend is the poverty rate of those who migrated at age 13–19, for whom the poverty rate exceeds those of the age groups immediately before and after them. This anomaly persists regardless of the period of immigration, and it clearly runs in contrast to the expectation derived from the assimilation theory. It therefore demands an explanation. In the absence of any previous study on this issue, one can only speculate about the possible reasons, as potential hypotheses for future research.

Rumbaut (1997) lays a theoretical foundation for treating various generations of immigrants, which may be of use here. To the conventional categories of first and second generations, Rumbaut (1997: 951) adds the intermediary categories of "1.25," "1.5" and

Table 15.3 Poverty Rates of Cohorts of Immigrants, 1996

Age at Immigration	Period of Immigration							Average (All Immigrants)	Average*
	Before 1946*	1946–50*	1951–60*	1961–70*	1971–80*	1981–90*	1991–96*		
0–4	17.1	10.9	10.8	12.7	21.9	23.0		23.9	15.7
5–12	18.3	10.5	10.5	12.7	18.9	34.0	50.0	27.2	19.0
13–19	28.8	13.5	14.6	13.2	18.8	31.7	54.9	26.6	25.9
20–24	27.5	12.8	16.4	10.4	16.6	29.4	44.9	21.6	21.6
25–29	27.6	17.6	15.7	12.9	14.9	29.6	43.1	23.4	23.4
30–34	33.3	18.6	17.4	17.3	15.6	25.6	48.7	26.6	26.6
35–39	37.5	29.9	19.5	19.7	18.8	27.9	53.4	31.7	31.7
40–44	100.0	34.6	28.3	19.1	22.6	28.9	53.5	34.5	34.5
45–49		31.3	27.7	21.7	24.9	29.2	51.0	34.5	34.5
50–54		33.3	38.7	33.7	28.2	30.1	44.4	34.7	34.7
55–59			14.3	30.8	31.3	35.4	43.7	36.9	36.9
60 +				27.3	31.1	36.2	40.5	37.1	37.1
Average	21.3	15.1	15.2	14.2	18.8	30.1	48.3	26.6	24.9

*Only those aged 16 years and older in 1996 included.

"1.75" generations, in reference to those who migrated at ages 13–17 (adolescence and secondary school), 6–12 (after primary socialization and the beginning of elementary school), and 0–5 (preschool), respectively. Using this categorization, it is clear that the age group with an unusually high rate of poverty is the "1.25" generation. Adolescence is often a time of enormous psychological and emotional unrest. Adolescents have to deal with a range of difficulties, from generational conflict to peer pressures. Such pressures are confounded for immigrant adolescents, as they have also to deal with the burdens of learning a new language and functioning in a new cultural environment. Immigrant adolescents are also more likely to experience what Igoa (1995) calls "fragmented formal education" owing to their families' frequent mobility and high instability during the immediate years after arrival. Rumbaut points out that to overcome these difficulties, they need strong support by, and the collaboration of, parents and teachers. In most cases, however, immigrant parents are too busy securing their economic foothold, particularly in the early years of arrival, and have little time to spend with their children. The possibility of discrimination at school also deprives adolescent immigrants of the potential support of their teachers. The "1.25" generation immigrants find themselves alone in the face of these difficulties. Everything is left to their individual capacities and motivation. But, as Gordon (1995: 530) has remarked, the individual motivation for educational attainment and economic success may also be suppressed against "a background of environmental disadvantages, institutional racism, and doubts about the likely rewards for qualifications." The most likely outcome to which such circumstances are conducive is failure.

Another possible explanation of the poor economic performance of the "1.25"' generation immigrants may be their lower level of social capital, as suggested by Portes (1995).

The main thrust of Portes's thesis is that second-generation immigrants become assimilated, but not necessarily into the mainstream culture. Depending on factors such as their neighbourhoods, he argues, they may be assimilated into the underclass:

> [the] overconcentration in the inner cities, which is a direct consequence of the lower economic resources of recent immigrants, has an unexpected consequence, namely to bring the offspring of these immigrants into close contact with downtrodden domestic minorities.... The confrontation with inner-city values places the second generation in a serious dilemma (Portes, 1995: 252).

Although this issue has not been systematically addressed in the Canadian context, the available studies allude to its relevance to Canada as well. In a study of neighbourhood poverty in Canada, Kazemipur and Halli (1997), for instance, have shown the over-concentration of certain ethnic groups, mostly visible minorities, in neighbourhoods with more than 40% poverty rates. In another attempt, Kazemipur and Halli (2000) have found that the visible minority immigrants, who are overrepresented in ghetto neighbourhoods, also tend to show a lower level of intergenerational mobility in terms of education and occupation. Further and more sophisticated research on this issue is seriously hampered by the lack of specific data sets combining the neighbourhood variables and individual characteristics....

CONCLUSION AND IMPLICATIONS

Some have argued that recent immigrants show a lower-than-expected economic performance, and have alluded to their lower "quality" (e.g., education, work experience) as the cause (Borjas, 1994). Our study of the experiences of low-income immigrants in Canada supports the first part of this argument—that is, that recent immigrants have a poorer economic record as compared to the previous cohorts—but it seriously questions the validity of the second part pertaining to the causes of such trends. Rather, we found that the odds of poverty among immigrants increased due to lower levels of returns to "quality" variables such as education, language skills, and type of employment, along with the penalizing effects of factors such as their racial origin and immigrant status....

Such findings, if sustained through more rigorous studies using more comprehensive data, have far-reaching implications for both public policy and future research. Over the past few years, Canadian studies have increasingly highlighted the significance of the lower returns to human capital endowments of immigrants, manifested in things such as the mismatch between their educational qualifications and occupations, or between their professional qualifications before and after migration (Basran and Zong, 1998); the lower returns to the educational investment of those immigrants with credentials earned abroad (Wanner, 1998); and the adoption of self-employment by immigrants as a result of their blocked mobility in salaried jobs typically dependent on education (Li, 2000). The problem is cited too frequently, and its existence and prevalence shown in too many different ways, to be disregarded as a passing phenomenon. It calls for a thorough revision of the procedures currently in effect for evaluation of the foreign credentials of immigrants.

Racial discrimination is another problem that deserves more attention. Although the findings of this study on the effect of racial discrimination are far from definitive (due to the inherent measurement limitations in the data used here), they are consistent with the findings of many previous studies and also with the trends observed in other immigrant-receiving countries. If left unchecked, the problem of race is only going to intensify. As Reitz (1998) has legitimately argued, the current flows of immigrants from Asia, Africa

and Latin America is going to make racial diversity a central feature of all industrial nations, and more so for immigrant-intensive countries such as Canada. Against this background, prevalence of racial discrimination in Canada would imply underutilization of human resources at present, and the potential for social conflicts in the future. None of these is a small enough problem to ignore.

The present study also implies two particular directions for future research, one more of a technical nature, the other conceptual. Despite their richness, the census data do not provide adequate information on language skills. Given the centrality of language acquisition in the later social and economic experiences of immigrants, this inadequacy renders census data of limited use for the study of immigrants. Ironically, there is enough emphasis on measuring language skills in procedures related to immigrants—including the processing of the applications for landed immigrant status, or the decisions regarding the costs of language training of family-class immigrants—but these emphases evaporate in the later data collection practices.

The conceptual problem involves the gender aspect of the issue of poverty examined above. In the recent surge of poverty in Canada, women have suffered more severely compared to men, a notion captured in the use of the term "feminization of poverty" in recent sociological literature (see Duffy and Mandell, 1994; Duffy and Pupo, 1992; Kazemipur and Halli, 2000). So, a study of poverty in the general population without regard to gender runs the risk of masking the peculiar situation of low-income women. For immigrant women, the problem has an additional dimension, as their experiences are different from both native-born women and also immigrant men. At the heart of these differential experiences lies the fact that, according to Pendakur and Pendakur (1998), the heads of prospective immigrant families are likely to be men, screened for occupational suitability and job readiness, and therefore more likely to enter Canada with recognized and rewarded credentials and jobs ready for them. As a result, female immigrants are more susceptible to losing their human capital or not getting its full return. Several studies have persuasively shown that the findings based on the study of male immigrants are not readily generalizable to female immigrants (Satzewich, 1995; Reitz, 1998; Pendakur and Pendakur, 1998), so much so that Ng (1986) has argued that "immigrant women" have come to be constituted as a distinct social category in the Canadian labour market. The findings of this study need to be furthered by including the gender dimension of poverty among immigrants.

NAVIGATING THE CONCEPTS

1. As a budding sociologist, how would you explain the relative lack of research into the economic performance of immigrant populations in Canada?

2. From a social policy perspective, argue the pros and cons of recognizing the professional qualifications of immigrants. What are the possible long-term consequences of each position?

3. Review and discuss how Kazemipur and Halli's results apply to your community. With local examples, can you find evidence to support or refute the unequal treatment of immigrant populations in your town or city?

REFERENCES

Abu-Laban, Y. 1998. Welcome/STAY OUT: The contradictions of Canadian integration and immigration policies at the millennium. *Canadian Ethnic Studies,* 30(3): 190–211.

Basran, G. S., and L. Zong. 1998. Devaluation of foreign credentials as perceived by non-white professional immigrants. *Canadian Ethnic Studies,* 30(3): 6–23.

Borjas, G. J. 1994. The economics of immigration. *Journal of Economic Literature,* 32: 1667–1717.

Duffy, A., and N. Mandel. 1994. Poverty in Canada. In *Society in question,* ed. R. Brym, 96–104. Toronto: Harcourt Brace.

Duffy, A., and N. Pupo. 1992. *Part-time paradox: Connecting gender, work, and family.* Toronto: McClelland and Stewart.

Dunk, T. 1999. Racism, ethnic prejudice, whiteness and the working class. In *Racism and social inequality in Canada,* ed. V. Satzewich, 201–22. Toronto: Thompson Educational Publishing.

Economic Council of Canada. 1991. *New faces in the crowd: Economic and social impacts of immigration.* Ottawa: Minister of Supply and Services.

Fellegi, I. P 1997. On poverty and low income. http://www.statcan.ca/english/concepts/poverty/pauv.htm. Accessed January 27, 1998.

Gans, H. J. 1992. Second-generation decline: Scenarios for the economic and ethnic future of the post-1965 American immigrants. *Ethnic and racial studies,* 15(2): 173–92.

Gordon, I. 1995. The impact of economic change on minorities and migrants in western Europe. In *Poverty, inequality, and the future of social policy,* eds. K. McFate, R. Lawson, and W. Wilson, 521–42. New York: Russell Sage Foundation.

Gordon, M. M. 1964. *Assimilation in American life.* New York: Oxford University Press.

Grant, H. M., and R. R. Oertel. 1998. Diminishing returns to immigration? Interpreting the economic experience of Canadian immigrants. *Canadian Ethnic Studies,* 30(3): 56–76.

Igoa, C. 1995. *The inner world of the immigrant child.* New York: St. Martin's Press.

Kazemipur, A., and S. S. Halli. 1997. Plight of immigrants: The spatial concentration of poverty in Canada. *Canadian Journal of Regional Science,* 20(1–2): 11–28.

———. 2000. *The new poverty in Canada: Ethnic groups and ghetto neighbourhoods.* Toronto: Thompson Educational Publishing.

Lautard, E. H., and D. J. Loree. 1984. Ethnic stratification in Canada, 1931–1971. *Canadian Journal of Sociology,* 9(3): 333–44.

Li, P. 1999. The market value and social value of race. In *Racism and social inequality in Canada,* ed. V. Satzewich, 115–30. Toronto: Thompson Educational Publishing.

———. 2000. Economic returns of immigrants' self-employment. *Canadian Journal of Sociology,* 25(1): 1–34.

Marchak, M. P. 1991. *The integrated circus.* Montreal and Kingston: McGill-Queen's University Press.

Massey, et al., 1994. An evaluation of international migration theory: The North American case. *Population and Development Review,* 20(4): 699–751.

Ng, R. 1986. The social construction of immigrant women in Canada. In *The politics of diversity: Feminism, Marxism and nationalism,* eds. R. Hamilton, and M. Barrett, 269–86. Montreal: Bookcentre.

Park, R. E., and E. W. Burgess. 1924. *Introduction to the science of sociology.* Chicago: University of Chicago Press.

Pendakur, K., and R. Pendakur. 1998. The colour of money: Earnings differentials among ethnic groups in Canada. *Canadian Journal of Economics,* 31(3): 518–48.

Porter, J. 1965. *The vertical mosaic.* Toronto: University of Toronto Press.

Portes, A. 1995. Children of immigrants: Segmented assimilation and its determinants. In *The economic sociology of immigration,* ed. A. Portes. New York: Russell Sage Foundation.

Portes, A., and R. G. Rumbaut. 1996. *Immigrant America: A portrait,* 2nd ed. Berkeley: University of California Press.

Reitz, J. G. 1998. *Warmth of the welcome: The social causes of economic success for immigrants in different nations and cities.* Boulder, Colo.: Westview Press.

Reitz, J. G., and R. Breton. 1994. *The illusion of difference: Realities of ethnicity in Canada and the United States.* Toronto: C. D. Howe Institute.

Rifkin, J. 1995. *The end of work.* New York: G. P. Putnam's Sons.

Ruggles, P. 1990. *Drawing the line: Alternative poverty measures and their implications for public policy.* Washington, D.C.: The Urban Institute Press.

Rumbaut, R. G. 1997. Assimilation and its discontents: Between rhetoric and reality. *International Migration Review,* 31(4): 923–60.

Sarlo, C. A. 1992. *Poverty in Canada.* Vancouver: The Fraser Institute.

———. 1994. *Poverty in Canada,* 2nd ed. Vancouver: The Fraser Institute.

Satzewich, V. 1995. Social stratification: Class and racial inequality. In *Social issues and contradictions in Canadian society,* 2nd ed., ed. B. S. Bolaria, 98–121. Toronto: Harcourt Brace Canada.

Statistics Canada, 1998. Low income cut-offs. Catalogue no. 13-551-X1B.

Teeple, G. 1995. *Globalization and the decline of social reform.* Toronto: Garamond Press.

Wanner, R. A. 1998. Prejudice, profit, or productivity: Explaining returns to human capital among male immigrants to Canada. *Canadian Ethnic Studies,* 30(3): 24–55.

Chapter 16

Aboriginal Identity: The Need for Historical and Contextual Perspectives

Jean-Paul Restoule

Source: Restoule, Jean-Paul. 2000. Aboriginal identity: The need for historical and contextual perspectives. *Canadian Journal of Native Education,* 24(2), 102–12. Abridged with the permission of the Canadian Journal of Native Education, University of Alberta, and University of British Columbia.

Jean-Paul Restoule explores Canadian Aboriginal identities from legal and historical perspectives, as well as from the personal and subjective experiences of Aboriginal peoples themselves. As he focuses on Aboriginal identity formation and the importance of recognizing the dynamic nature of *identifying*, Restoule's personal account reveals important insights into the psyche of Canada's founding peoples.

Employing a perspective that distinguishes between "identity" and "identifying" demonstrates the limitations inherent in typical conceptions of cultural identity. Identifying is situational and historical, shaped by the time and place in which it occurs, whereas identity is thought to transcend history and social situations. Identity is represented in the Indian Act and its definition of "Indian." Métis efforts for recognition as an Aboriginal people in their own right is seen as identifying. The potential harm of identity is demonstrated by the Crown's arguments in the case for Gitksan-Wet'suwet'en Aboriginal title.

I recently attended a conference where a number of us were discussing issues concerning Aboriginal identity. We talked about how our parents had tried to hide any semblance of their Aboriginal identity and how in our experience today it was not only acceptable, but indeed desirable to be Aboriginal. In our experience dreamcatchers were everywhere and Aboriginal plays and events in the city were sold out. "What happened?" we asked each other. Then someone pointed out that where she came from there was not the luxury to talk about identifying as Aboriginal as if it were a choice. Shame about being Aboriginal continued to exist in her community. Most of the people from her community would hide their Aboriginality if possible. For many of them it was not even an option. They were "known" as Aboriginal people. Also, in her experience the issue of drug abuse, AIDS, diabetes, unemployment, spousal abuse, and others were seen as more pressing concerns than identity.

Her words had quite an impact on me. How can some of us talk about the struggle for identity when on a daily basis so many of us struggle just to survive? Is writing about these matters really helping to change anything? I keep coming back to this idea that some of the people in her community would hide their Aboriginality if they could. Understanding what influences our pride or shame in identifying as Aboriginal people is important. How we feel about ourselves contributes to and arises from the issues my colleague felt were more urgent to discuss than identity. I have seen examples where pride in Aboriginal identity is the basis for fighting addiction and where shame in identity is a factor in developing a habit of substance abuse (Restoule, 1999). It is important to explore what identifying as Aboriginal means and what is gained and lost in attempting to erase that identity, as well as what it means to change the referents of what is meant by Aboriginal identity.

IDENTITY AND IDENTIFYING

The term *identity* expressed popularly, as well as in academic circles, implies a fixed nature over a given time period. In psychology, identity is often qualified as, for example, sex-role identity or racial identity (Sutherland, 1989). These qualities are assumed to have some continuity over time for the individual. In Piaget's work, identity refers to a state of awareness that something holds its value despite surface appearances to the contrary (Sutherland, 1989). In logic, identity refers to two words, properties, or statements that are so similar that they can substitute one for the other in an equation without altering the meaning (Sutherland). In sum, identity has been conceived to mean sameness. For social scientists discussing cultural identity, the sameness inherent in the definition of identity refers to the shared norms, traits, and habits of members of a cultural group at one historical moment. Unfortunately, there are educators, lawyers, and policymakers who make the error of assuming Aboriginal identity must hold over several generations.

To talk about Aboriginal identity assumes a sameness and continuity that belies the fluidity and change that Aboriginal people experience and demonstrate. When this assumed permanence of character is run through institutions like the education and court systems "Aboriginal identity" can be constrictive and colonizing. I return to this idea below with a discussion of the case for Gitksan-Wet'suwet'en Aboriginal title. If we change the focus from *identity* to *identifying*, we move from noun to verb and set off a potentially liberating way of conceiving and talking about self-definition. *Identity* implies fixedness; that the "things" that make one Indian remain the same and should be the same as those things associated with Indianness by the Europeans at the time of historical "first" contact. Identity places power in the observer who observes Aboriginal people from the outside and defines them, giving them an identity. *Identifying* shifts control to the self, and motivations come to the fore. This perspective favors a set of referents that are put into action at the historical time one identifies as an Aboriginal person and in the contextual place where one identifies. Identifying is a process of being and becoming what one is in the moment. The power is placed in the self, for the Aboriginal person who emphasizes his or her Indigenous roots at a particular place and time. This allows for the salient components of an Aboriginal identity to be expressed as the actor feels is expedient, allowing for cultural change and adaptation. Identifying is situational and historical, whereas identity is thought to transcend history and social situations.

In this article I use a number of examples to make clearer the distinction between identity and identifying. Dunn's (2001) research on the Métis of the Red River region shows that the tension between identity and identifying existed even in the 1800s. I provide a brief overview of Canadian legislation defining "Indians" as an example of identity as I characterize it above. As a point of contrast, Métis participation in the Constitutional Conferences of the 1980s and the Royal Commission on Aboriginal Peoples (RCAP, 1996) demonstrate identifying.

Employing a perspective that distinguishes between identity and identifying might help us problematize typical conceptions of cultural identity limited in their ability to reflect the situational and contextual identifying that exists in contemporary Aboriginal life. To demonstrate the limitations of an identity perspective, I look at Fitzgerald's (1977) notion of cultural identity as an interplay between color, culture, and class. This conception of cultural identity, I feel, is fairly typical. I refer to work by Valentine (1995) and Pinneault and Patterson (1997) to demonstrate that identity/identifying is indeed contextual and is shaped by the time and place in which it occurs....

LIMITATIONS OF IDENTITY IN ABORIGINAL NORTH AMERICA

Identity is a complicated concept. Cultural identity is often conceived as an interplay between biology, socioeconomic status, and cultural knowledge. Fitzgerald (1977), in his study of Maori students, refers to these three components as color, culture, and class. To Fitzgerald color represents a biological connection to the original peoples. In other words, it is the blood connection, the lineage that can be traced to Aboriginal communities and families. By culture Fitzgerald means knowledge of the traditions, language, and ceremonies or the "markers" of the race. Class stands for socioeconomic position in the greater society. Society is perceived as the greater economic and political entity where many cultures coexist. Each culture participates in the larger society where it is located, although the cultural norms of the group may be distinct from the rest of the society.

Race is often conflated with class, so that a racial group or cultural group is likely to be thought of as occupying a particular class position in relation to the greater society. Power is maintained by barriers that keep racial groups from advancing socioeconomically. Although certain individuals may succeed in

being upwardly mobile, much of the group continues to experience difficulty. As Fitzgerald (1977) observed, "The central tensions between groups do not seem to be essentially cultural but originate in inequalities over power and participation in society. More and more, groups are trying to invent cultures through identity assertions" (p. 221). Identity tends to be more persistent and stable over time, whereas cultures are in a constant state of reinvention. This is because identity often has to do with how the out-group culture views the in-group. Fitzgerald (1977) found that some Maoris he studied validated their right of acceptance in the Maori group by overemphasizing their biological connections and/or class position, especially if they knew little about the culture. I suspect this to be the case among Aboriginal people in Canada. Those who know little about the Aboriginal culture to which they claim a connection probably will emphasize their blood ties to an Aboriginal culture. Claiming to be born "Ojibwe" or "Blackfoot" does not necessarily entail a familiarity with the music, ceremonies, or language. This is a reality of living in a dispersed culture where there have been generations of increased pressure not to exhibit these cultural knowledges.

The interplay of biology, culture, and class cannot maintain its integrity when applied to Aboriginal cultures in North America. Perhaps in the mid-nineteenth century most Aboriginal people could be slotted by class, culture, and biology such that the categories remained relatively stable. Aboriginal persons for the most part were not only able to demonstrate who they were related to (biology), but also could make their way in their culture and were probably lower-class citizens in relation to the class structure of British North America. Today these factors are not necessarily applicable to each Aboriginal person, and it is impossible to predict with any certainty one's placement in each of these categories. For example, today many

Aboriginal people may be slotted into lower socioeconomic categories in relation to Canadian class structure, but individual Aboriginal people are not necessarily reducible to a particular class. Also, many people with Aboriginal cultural knowledge have no ties to their home communities or to an officially recognized community. Conversely, many Aboriginal people with blood ties to Aboriginal communities have little or no Aboriginal cultural knowledge. The instability of these categories is evident when one looks at contemporary Aboriginal people on Turtle Island today.

IDENTIFYING AS SITUATIONAL AND CONTEXTUAL

Fitzgerald's (1977) observation that "cultural identity has relevance only in a situation of cultural homogeneity" (p. 59) appears to be supported by the research of both Valentine (1995) and Pinneault and Patterson (1997). Valentine lived and worked among the Anishinabe of Lynx Lake, Ontario where the community is composed almost entirely of Aboriginal families. As Valentine explains,

In southern Ojibwe communities, where forced contact with the White matrix society has been long standing, Native people tend to define themselves vis-à-vis the "other." Thus, if something is "White" then it is necessarily "not-Indian" and vice versa.... In the north, where there has been relatively little and generally recent contact with Whites, the Native people define themselves internally. In a situation such as that in Lynx Lake, it is moot to ask if one element or another is "White" or even "borrowed." If the people are using it, the item is being used "Natively." The question asked by the people of Lynx Lake is "Will X be useful to us?" not "Will the use of X compromise our Nativeness?" (p. 164)

Here the question of what is Aboriginal is raised only in comparison with cultures outside the community.

Contrast the Lynx Lake community with Pinneault and Patterson's (1997) work in urban schools in the Niagara region of Ontario. Here Pinneault and Patterson counsel youth who struggle with debunking myths and labels or with trying to find where they fit in. Pinneault and Patterson describe the situation thus.

Attempt to put yourself in the following story. You are living in a land which is the first and only foundation of your philosophy, spiritual beliefs, historical patterns, cultural distinction, and ancestral connections. At the same time, you never see a reflection of yourself within the philosophy of others, the educational system, popular culture, or day-to-day events within the community. Stereotyping remains entrenched in most societal situations and you are constantly in a position of needing to defend your rights and position. When you are able to visualize yourself, it is through the interpretation of others who have little understanding of who you are. You are constantly being defined and redefined from an outside system. (p. 27)

Many students in the south are struggling with the creation of safe places to increase self-esteem and build understanding and acceptance of some of the Aboriginal cultural traditions. Obviously identity issues come to the fore when there is sustained contact between culturally different groups, and especially when they are valued differently on the social scale.

Another way to understand the differences between the disparate groups in Niagara and Lynx Lake is to discuss identifying rather than identity. Identifying in Niagara has different meanings and consequences than it does in Lynx Lake. Aboriginal people in Lynx Lake do not identify as "Native" in Lynx Lake because the homogeneous nature of the population makes it redundant to do so. The identity of the people in the distant communities is not different necessarily. Rather the factors that influence an Aboriginal person's choice to identify change from one region to another are different....

LEGISLATIVE DEFINITIONS AS IDENTITY

The Indian Act has been the source of many problems in the history of Aboriginal survival. It has been the legal support for violence enacted against Aboriginal peoples in the form of regulations imposed on personal mobility, language use, and participation in cultural activities. Relevant to this discussion is its peculiar claim of distinction as a rare piece of legislation that sets out in law a definition of a people. This definition has had a profound impact not only in how we are understood by non-Aboriginal people, but also in how we have come to understand ourselves....

In early legislation designed to contain potential violence between Aboriginal people and newcomers, a broad definition of *Indian* was set into law. For example, the 1850 Indian Protection Act defined Indians broadly:

The following classes of persons are and shall be considered as Indians belonging to the Tribe or body of Indians interested in such lands: First—All persons of Indian blood, reputed to belong to the particular Body or Tribe of Indians interested in such lands, and their descendants. Secondly—All persons intermarried with any such Indians and residing amongst them, and the descendants of all such persons. Thirdly—All persons residing among such Indians, whose parents on either side were or are Indians of such Body or Tribe, or entitled to be considered as such: And Fourthly—All persons adopted in infancy by any such Indians, and residing in the Village or upon the lands of such Tribe or Body of Indians, and their descendants.

The only important distinction was between European and Indian. Interestingly enough, early definitions of Indian like this one allowed for men and women of European descent who lived with an Aboriginal community to be considered Indian before the law. What mattered more than blood (although this too was important) was the evidence that one lived as an Indian. One would have to assume this distinction was relatively simple to

make in the nineteenth century. Otherwise the definition would have been drafted differently.

As laws governing Indian lands were consolidated, the definition of an Indian in law was redrafted to exclude more Aboriginal people and to encourage the assimilation of registered Indians into the Canadian body politic (RCAP, 1996). Assimilation is genocide according to the United Nations Genocide Convention, signed by Canada in 1949 and unanimously adopted in Parliament in 1952. Chrisjohn and Young with Maraun (1997) have argued that Canada could be tried in violation of the genocide convention for the operation of residential schools. The Canadian Civil Liberties Union, in debates held before Canada enabled legislation in 1952, recognized the potential for Canada's transfer of Indian children to residential schools to be seen as genocide (Churchill, 1997). Enfranchisement was also a key tool of assimilation or genocide.

Enfranchisement, along with definitions privileging patrilineal descent, reduced the number of Indians eligible for the Register. The children of interracial marriages were counted as Indians only when the father was Indian. Native women who married non-Native men were removed from the Register and often distanced from their communities. Over the years there were many ways Indians could lose their status. Some examples include earning a university degree, requesting the right to vote in a federal election, or requesting removal from the Indian Register for a share of the monies that would have gone to the band on their behalf. Most significantly, Indian women who married non-Indian men were enfranchised involuntarily, and the children of these marriages were ineligible for status. Clearly the goal of the Gradual Enfranchisement Act, and its subsequent absorption into the Indian Act, was assimilation (RCAP, 1996).

The Métis, as an Aboriginal people, found themselves caught in the middle of the changing legal definitions. The numbers of Métis who would have been entitled to receive the benefits of Indian status in 1850 were gradually reduced by arbitrary legislation. Great pains were taken to extinguish Métis claims to Aboriginal title, and they were not accorded any benefits in exchange for the land. This does not mean that only "full-blooded" Indians were entitled to be registered. What mattered was whether it was one's father or mother who was officially recognized as Indian. Often these non-status Indians would align themselves politically with the cultural Métis, who had for the most part been denied any rights as Aboriginal people. This denial occurred despite Métis treaties with Canada in the Manitoba Act and the Dominion Lands Act(s).

BEING AND BECOMING MÉTIS AS AN EXAMPLE OF IDENTIFYING

The Métis provide an interesting example of how colonial definitions are played out and affect self-definitions. Most people believe that Métis means simply "mixed" denoting the mixing of the blood of European and Indian parents in their child. The word has been used to designate various groups with a tie to Aboriginal peoples present on the continent before European settlement. How were the new populations that were a result of the new inter-relationships between Indian and non-Indian characterized or written about in the earliest times? How did Métis, which originally meant simply mixed, come to mean specific kinds of mixes and in specific times and locations?

Dunn (2001), a descendant of the Red River Métis and consultant to the RCAP, has an excellent Web site (**www.otherMétis.net**) that catalogues the many terms and names that have been used to describe the intermixing of European and Aboriginal peoples. It is important to note that there is little evidence of what these groups of people under discussion preferred to be called in the nineteenth century,

and few records of what they called themselves exist. Most of these terms were used by colonial bureaucrats and traders who thought it important enough and necessary to write about this growing and influential population in their particular region.... The diversity of names used indicates at least two important points. First, the groups now known as Métis were seen as a distinct social fact by most of the social groups sharing the same region. Second, the names accorded these groups of "mixed-race" people are ways for people external to the group to make an identity for them. Obviously some terms are meant to be disparaging. Dunn's ancestors were called Half-breed by the government officials of the day. At the same time, Dunn's great-great-grandfather used the term *Natives of the country* when referring to his group. In any case, as Dunn points out, "the external application of terminology does not guarantee that the term accurately communicates the expression of an internal identity" (para. 22). Identity is a process of being and becoming, and nouns cannot adequately be used to describe identity; rather they merely serve to label and fix a group of persons (Peterson & Brown, 1985). The attributes of the group that make it identifiable as distinct from others are constantly changing, and the words that are used to fix the group also change their referents. The use of the word Métis was taken up by these groups of "mixed blood" or "ancestry" and applied in different ways and for different ends.

At the constitutional conferences in the mid-1980s the leader of the Métis National Council (*The Métis Nation,* 1986) stated:

Surely it is more than racial characteristics that makes a people. What about a common history, culture, political consciousness? Our origins, like that of any people when traced back far enough, are mixed, but once we evolved into a distinct aboriginal people, the amount of this much or that much ancestry mattered less than being Métis.

Note that he stressed the acceptance of the community and identification with the community.

This distinction was promoted by the 1996 *Report of the Royal Commission on Aboriginal Peoples,* although it made some concessions for the Congress of Aboriginal Peoples definition of Métis, which is based solely on Aboriginal ancestry (blood). The RCAP (1996) recommendation is as follows:

The Commission recommends that Métis Identity 4.5.2 Every person who (a) identifies himself or herself as Métis and (b) is accepted as such by the nation of Métis people with which that person wishes to be associated, on the basis of criteria and procedures determined by that nation be recognized as a member of that nation for purposes of nation-to-nation negotiations and as Métis for that purpose. (vol. 4: 203)

This definition, although leaving the choice of political affiliation to the individual claimant, is broad enough to include both Métis National Council and Native Council of Canada/Congress of Aboriginal Peoples members.

It should be noted that the Commission's recommendation above is made in respect to the sphere of political rights. The Commission (1996) recognizes that the identification of Aboriginal communities for legal purposes has taken a different approach. Essentially, after some analysis, the Commission laid out three elements that seemed to be acceptable to courts in determining membership in an Aboriginal community:

• some ancestral family connection (not necessarily genetic) with the particular Aboriginal people;

• self-identification of the individual with the particular Aboriginal people; and

• community acceptance of the individual by the particular Aboriginal people. (vol. 4: 297–98)

A fourth element was mentioned as also being of relevance in some cases: "a rational connection, consisting of sufficient objectively determinable points of contact between the individual and the particular Aboriginal people" (vol. 4: 298). Acceptable criteria include residence, family connections, cultural ties, language, and religion (vol. 4: 298).

In many ways it seems as if we have come full circle. Early attempts to legislate who is an Indian were broad and inclusive and allowed for anyone living in an Aboriginal community to qualify as Indian under the law. Definitions became increasingly exclusive, causing inequities and suffering and dissension among Aboriginal peoples. The RCAP (1996) recommended that all Aboriginal peoples be entitled to rights as members of an Aboriginal community. But history has seen individuals with Aboriginal "blood" migrate to urban areas where they may not live in Aboriginal communities that are located in a tight geographical configuration. As sound and fair as it may appear for legal reasoning to recognize only Aboriginal communities and members of those communities, in practice it may again turn out to be a politically expedient way of reducing the numbers of Aboriginal people whom the government must recognize. In the end it really may be up to the individuals in communities of interest to decide what factors of their personality and culture make them distinctly Aboriginal and continue a process of being and becoming that cannot be legislated.

THE IMPACT OF IDENTITY

Once when I was talking to a friend and tenant at a native housing co-op where I worked, I told her that my lack of knowledge on a particular issue was because I was not a politically active person. She replied, "For an Indian, being born is political." I realize now that she meant that from the time we are born, as Indians we are in a particular relationship with the Canadian state by virtue of the treaties, the Indian Register, and the Indian Act. She also meant that because the state had been seeking our disappearance for centuries, each time one more of us is born we are directly in opposition to the goals of the state. Each of us through our birth proved we would not disappear. When we are born, we are defined by the state as a particular kind of Indian. Either we are eligible for the Indian Register and designated a Status Indian, or we are denied the rights that this heritage should lend itself to. There were times when not being registered was an advantage because the strict enforcement of the Indian Act imposed many measures on recognized Indians. The drawback, of course, was that many identifiable Indians were disallowed connections with their extended families and some of the treaty rights their ancestors had negotiated.

Using strictly the legal view of Indianness, in my family's experience, my father was born an Indian, later "earned the right not to be an Indian" through enfranchisement, and many years later was seen as a Status Indian once again. I was not born an Indian and was given Indian Status only after passage of the amended Indian Act of 1985. Receiving that card in the mail made me question a lot of things, and it caused me to look at my family in a new way. I was confused about how we had an identity decided for us. Why was it not a given that we could define for ourselves who we were?

The issue of Aboriginal identity is most often played out in Canadian law. Aboriginal "difference" from others is used to maintain inequities in power when it is convenient for those with power (Macklem, 1993). However, when our difference results in what is seen as privilege, arguments are made that treating Aboriginal people differently is "un-Canadian" because it is in opposition to the stated goal of equality among individuals before the law. There is a constructed image of what Indians

are supposed to be that has to be played into or against in order to make advances in Canadian institutions, especially courts of law (Crosby, 1992; Razack, 1998). If we do not appear Indian enough or do not exhibit enough of the traits that are somewhat expected of Indians, then we will be judged to be no longer different enough from the Euro-Canadian assumption of the mainstream, and thus no longer Aboriginal. We will, in fact, be assumed to have assimilated into the assumed mainstream Canadian norm.

This line of logic has been argued by lawyers for the Crown in the case for Gitksan-Wet'suwet'en Aboriginal title (Crosby, 1992). The Crown argued that because the contemporary Gitksan eat pizza from microwaves and drive cars, they have essentially given up their Aboriginality. Indian rights flow only to those who meet the criteria for authenticity established by the Eurocentric courts (Crosby, 1992). Sustained colonization has caused many Aboriginal people to move away from a subsistence economy to a market economy, often without their choice. Many of the traditional ways of life seen from the Eurocentric position as "authentic Indian ways" have been altered by the imposition of colonial policies and laws, and then these very charges are used against us as arguments that we are no longer Aboriginal people.

The criteria accepted in the legal system, however, are often limited to material "stuff." What makes one Aboriginal is not the clothes one wears or the food one eats, but the values one holds. There is more to Aboriginal cultures than "fluff and feathers" (Doxtator, 1992). Johnston (1995), an Ojibwe ethnologist, recalls the time a young student in an elementary school, having spent five weeks learning about tipis, buskskin, canoes, and so much other stuff, asked him, "Is that all there is?" Johnston wanted people to know that there was more to Anishinabe culture than mere stuff, and this led him to write books like *Ojibway Heritage* (1976), *Ojibway Ceremonies* (1982), and *The*

Manitous (1995). Unfortunately, in museums, movies, and courts of law it is the stuff that is exhibited. We are not Indian unless we prove that we still cling to the stuff that defined us in the eyes of others over 100 years ago. This conception will continue as long as we talk about identity and not identifying.

An interesting exercise is to turn these arguments around and apply them to the Eurocentric arguments for our assimilation. Does the lawyer who said the Gitksan-Wet'suwet'en drive cars realize that Europeans did not drive cars at the point of contact either? Was this lawyer wearing the same clothes his forefathers wore in 1763? Does this lawyer use the number zero? I think the use of zero may be been a case of cultural adoption, not unlike the Aboriginal people who adopt the use of snowmobiles. The culture that made the law is privileged to adapt and change over time, whereas the Aboriginal cultures are denied this same privilege. Although it may not be the stated objective of the law, the result is often the maintenance of inequitable relations of power. Keeping Indians in the place they had at confederation is a goal of the consolidated Indian Act of 1876.

CONCLUSION

The Indian Act had as its goal nothing less than the assimilation of Aboriginal people in Canada (RCAP, 1996). A key strategy in achieving this goal was increasingly to limit who is an Indian by law and to change the status of those who were already on the list through enfranchisement. In this law "Indians" are identical to one another, but "different" from the Canadian power majority. The writers of legislation did not consider our cultures and histories important. Our identity as Indians was invented. Although at times we have used this identity to our own interests, forming coalitions across cultures to seek political gains (such as inclusion in the Constitution Act, 1982), we have also

used these invented identities against one another, allowing these government categories to intrude on our social and cultural affairs (Coates, 1999). In our lives, in our work, in our efforts to educate others, let us identify as Aboriginal people from our inside place, from ourselves, our communities, our traditions. Let us not allow others to decide our identity for us.

ACKNOWLEDGMENTS

I would like to thank the anonymous reviewers of an earlier draft for their comments.

NAVIGATING THE CONCEPTS

1. From a sociological perspective, why would possessing a positive self-identity influence how you lived your life?

2. With reference to the article, are Aboriginal people in Canada treated any differently than any other minority group?

3. In your opinion, do we gain anything by employing historical and contextual perspectives when studying minority groups? Be sure to refer to the article as well as to provide contemporary examples to support your position.

REFERENCES

Chrisjohn, R., & Young, S., with Maraun, M. 1997. *The circle game: Shadows and substance in the Indian residential school experience in Canada.* Penticton, B.C.: Theytus.

Churchill, W. 1997. *A little matter of genocide: Holocaust and denial in the Americas 1492 to the present.* San Francisco, Calif.: City Lights Books.

Coates, K. 1999. Being Aboriginal. In *Futures and identities: Aboriginal peoples in Canada,* ed. M. Behiels, 23–41. Montreal: Association for Canadian Studies.

Crosby, M. 1992. Construction of the imaginary Indian. In *Vancouver anthology: The institutional politics of art,* ed. S. Douglas, 267–91. Burnaby, B.C.: Talonbooks.

Doxtator, D. 1992. *Fluff and feathers: An exhibit of the symbols of Indianness.* Brantford, Ont.: Woodland Cultural Centre.

Dunn, M. 2001, January. Métis identity—A source of rights? Paper presented at Trent University. [Online]. Available: **http://www.otherMétis.net/index.html/ Papers/trent/trent1.html#Terminology**. Retrieved January 4, 2001,

Fitzgerald, T. K. 1977. *Education and identity: A study of the New Zealand Maori graduate.* Wellington: New Zealand Council for Educational Research.

Johnston, B. 1976. *Ojibway heritage.* Toronto: McClelland and Stewart.

———. 1982. *Ojibway ceremonies.* Toronto: McClelland and Stewart.

———. 1995. *The Manitous: The spiritual world of the Ojibway.* Toronto: Key Porter Books.

Macklem, P. 1993. *Ethnonationalism, Aboriginal identities, and the law.* In *Ethnicity and Aboriginality: Case studies in ethnonationalism,* ed. M. D. Levin, 9–28. Toronto: University of Toronto Press.

Peterson, J., & J. S. H. Brown (eds.). 1985. *The new peoples: Being and becoming Métis in North America.* Winnipeg: University of Manitoba Press.

Pinneault, A., & Patterson, C. 1997. Native support circles in urban schools. *Orbit,* 28(1): 27–29.

Razack, S. 1998. *Looking white people in the eye: Gender, race and culture in courtrooms and classrooms.* Toronto: University of Toronto Press.

Restoule, J. P. 1999. Making movies, changing lives. Aboriginal film and identity. In *Futures and identities: Aboriginal peoples in Canada,* ed. M. Behiels, 180–89. Montreal: Association for Canadian Studies.

Royal Commission on Aboriginal Peoples. 1996. *Report of the Royal Commission on Aboriginal Peoples.* Ottawa: Ministry of Supply and Services.

Sutherland, N. S. 1989. *The international dictionary of psychology.* New York: Continuum.

The Métis Nation. 1986. 2(1): Winter.

Valentine, L. P. 1995. *Making it their own: Severn Ojibwe communicative practices.* Toronto: University of Toronto Press.

PART 5

Social Institutions

Sociologists explore how social institutions define and influence our understanding of the world around us.

Chapter 17

Looking Back, Looking Ahead: Canadian Families in Perspective

Beverly J. Matthews

Source: Printed with permission of the author (2003).

Beverly J. Matthews's analysis is an exploration of how Canadian families have changed over time. By investigating numerous resources from Statistics Canada, Matthews demonstrates that families in Canada are constantly changing because of various social and economic factors. The article concludes by asking the reader to ponder how contemporary economic, technological, and cultural factors may lead to even more changes for Canadian families.

Who do you live with? A roommate? Your parents? Your children? A lover? Your cat? Whatever your answer, there is a good chance that it is not the same answer that your grandparents or great-grandparents would have given when they were your age. North American family patterns and household arrangements have changed dramatically since the early 20th century. For example, in 1901, 69 percent of Canadian families consisted of married couples and their children (Vanier, 2000). By 2001, only 44 percent of family households contained two parents and their children (Statistics Canada, 2002f). In 1921 there were only 6.4 divorces for every 100,000 Canadians (Statistics Canada, 2002d), but in the year 2000 there were 231 divorces for every 100,000, or 71,144 divorces (Statistics Canada, 2002c).

These patterns suggest that family life has undergone a profound shift. Many people are concerned that these trends are indicators of serious problems in Canadian families. In fact, a 1994 Angus Reid poll published in *Maclean's* magazine found that 63 percent of Canadians believed that the Canadian family was in a state of crisis (Nemeth, 1994). Family sociologists and demographers measure these trends and analyze their causes and consequences. And, of course, they are of great interest to us, as they influence the family arrangements we experience and the choices available to us. If we look back at trends in Canadian family life and explore some of their underlying causes, we will be better equipped to look ahead and consider the future of families in Canada.

DEFINITIONS

To begin, we must consider what we mean by "family." This seems like a simple undertaking. After all, if you ask people you meet on the street "Who is in your family?" they will all have an answer. However, what you may not realize is that our societal understanding of what constitutes a family has changed over time. If you asked a senior social scientist in your department to find his or her oldest text on families and read out the definition, you would probably hear something like this: Family is

a social group characterized by common residence, economic cooperation, and reproduction. It includes adults of both sexes, at least two of whom maintain a socially approved sexual relationship and one or more children, own or adopted, of the sexually cohabiting adults. (Murdock, 1949: 1)

or

a social arrangement based on marriage and the marriage contract, including the rights and duties of parenthood, common residence for husband, wife and children, and reciprocal economic obligations between husband and wife. (Stephens, 1963: 5)

Do these definitions still hold true today? Are you a member of a family according to Murdock and Stephens? If you live alone, with a roommate (or with your cat), you are not; if you aren't married but live with an intimate partner, you are not. Even if you are married but because of career requirements your spouse and children live in another city, you do not qualify as a family according to Murdock and Stephens. Their definitions are quite narrow and consequently exclude large portions of the population. More recently, our understanding of what constitutes family has expanded substantially: Family is

Any combination of two or more persons who are bound together over time by ties of mutual consent, birth and/or adoption or placement who, together, assume responsibilities for variant combinations of some of the following:

• physical maintenance and care of group members

• addition of new members through procreation or adoption

• socialization of children

• social control of members

• production, consumption, distribution of goods and services

• affective nurturance—love

(Vanier, 2000: v)

This definition is broad enough to encompass all manner of familial arrangements. Virtually everyone reading this chapter will recognize that their family fits this definition. Today, social scientists tend to define family by the relationships between the members, rather than by the identified statuses (e.g., husband, wife) of its members.

For the purposes of this chapter, we are going to rely on Statistics Canada data to examine changes in family patterns, so we will utilize their definition: a family household

refers to a married couple (with or without children of either or both spouses), a couple living common-law (with or without children of either or both partners) or a lone parent of any marital status, with at least one child living in the same dwelling. A couple living common-law may be of opposite or same sex. "Children" in a census family include grandchildren living with their grandparent(s) but with no parents present. (Statistics Canada, 2002a: 1)

You will probably have noticed that this definition does not consider a person living alone to be a member of a family household. Statistics Canada provides many definitions of types of families (e.g., census families, economic families, family households), but the dictionary does not contain an all-encompassing definition of "family" (Statistics Canada, 2002a). Statistics Canada does not specifically preclude people in single-person households from being members of families, but for the purposes of counting and identifying household types, single-person households are considered non-family units. Statistics Canada has a long history of collecting information on family patterns, which enables us to study the evolving patterns of family life.[1]

LOOKING BACK: THE TRENDS

The following graphs, tables, and charts show various trends in family patterns. Unless otherwise stated, the information comes from Statistics Canada census data.

A. Family Households

The membership of family households has changed over time. As you can see in Figure 17.1, the proportion of family households with two married parents and their children is declining. Even when children living with parents in a common-law union (CLU) are included, the decline is evident. The proportion of married couples with no children has remained fairly steady at approximately 30 percent of all family households (ranging between 28.1 percent and 32.5 percent over 70 years). However, if you combine all couples (married and CLU) with no children at home, there has been an increase (36.6 percent in 2001, up from 30.8 percent in 1981). The major

Figure 17.1 Family Households, 1931–2001

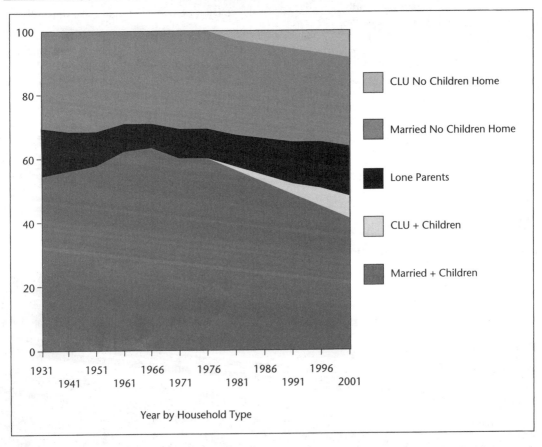

Year by Household Type

Source: Data compiled from **http://www12.statcan.ca/english/census01/products/analytic/companion/fam/timeline.cfm**. Accessed July 15, 2003.

Figure 17.2 Total Fertility Rate, 1921–97

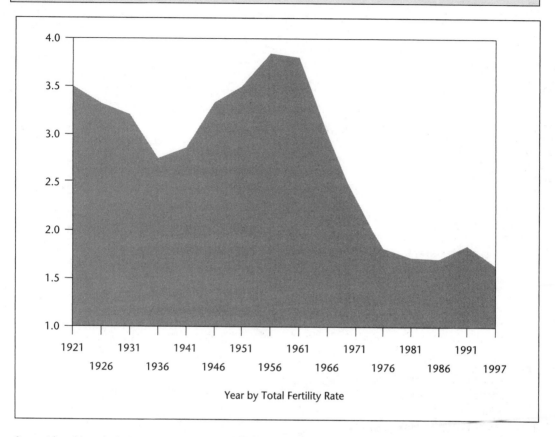

Year by Total Fertility Rate

Source: Adapted from the Statistics Canada publications "Vital statistics compendium", 1996, Catalogue 84-214, November 1999, page 23, from "Health reports", Supplement 14, 1992, Catalogue 82-003, Vol. 4, No. 1, Table 16, and from "Births and deaths", 1997, Catalogue 84-210, September 1999, Table 1.4.

shift, though, has been the increase in lone-parent families.

B. Family Size

Family size changed substantially over the 20th century. The entire Western world experienced a long-term decline in fertility, part of the demographic transition, throughout the 19th century and into the 20th. Canadian fertility rates similarly declined, from 6.8 children per woman in 1851 to 3.53 children in 1921.[2]

Figure 17.2 shows that this rate has changed significantly since then.

The sharp peak indicates the baby boom years, when couples who had delayed childbearing during the Depression and the Second World War began their families, as did younger couples who reached marriageable age during the 1950s. The abrupt decline beginning in the 1960s has been described as the "baby bust" (Romaniuc, 1984). During this time, fewer people were marrying and the number of common-law unions and divorces was increasing, as was the number of single-person households.

In recent years, an increasing proportion of young adults have either returned to or remained in their parents' household [Table 17.1]. This coincides with an increase in levels of education, a tendency to delay marriage, and an increase in partnership dissolution.

Table 17.1	Percentage of Young Adults in the Parental Home, 1961–2001		
Age	1981	1991	2001
Age 20–24	42.1%	51.2%	58.0%
Age 25–29	11.8%	17.8%	23.7%

Source: Data from **http://142.206.72.67/02/02d/02d_graph/02d_graph_002_1e.htm**. Accessed 7/15/2003.

C. Single-Person and Two-Person Households

The number of Canadians living alone has been steadily increasing. By 2001, more than a quarter of all households contained only one resident. Just under 10 percent of all Canadians live by themselves. Living in single-person households are adults from across the age spectrum: some young, some elderly, and some whose unions have ended (either marriages or common-law relationships). Two-person households have also become more common [Table 17.2].

Table 17.2	Percentage of Single- and Two-Person Households, 1981–2001	
Year	1981	2001
Single-Person	20%	25%
Two-Person	29%	33%

Source: Data compiled from **http://www12.statcan.ca/english/census01/products/analytic/companion/fam/canada.cfm**. Accessed July 15, 2003.

Figure 17.3 Common-Law Unions, 1981–2001

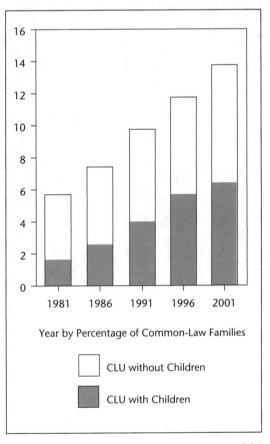

Year by Percentage of Common-Law Families

☐ CLU without Children

■ CLU with Children

Source: Data compiled from **http://www12.statcan.ca/english/census01/products/analytic/companion/fam/timeline.cfm**. Accessed July 15, 2003.

D. Cohabitation

As Figure 17.3 shows, when common-law unions were first counted in the 1981 census, they accounted for less than 6 percent of all family households. In only 20 years, they have grown to account for almost 14 percent of Canadian families. We can also see that the number of CLU families with children has tripled from less than 2 percent to 6.3 percent of families in that time span.

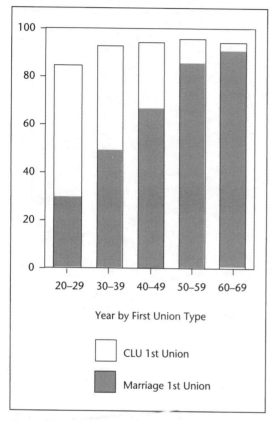

Figure 17.4 Probability of First Union Being CLU or Marriage, 2001

Year by First Union Type

☐ CLU 1st Union

■ Marriage 1st Union

Source: Data compiled from **http://142.206.72.67/02/02d/ 02d_001b_e.htm**. Accessed June 17, 2003.

The link between age and the probability of a person's first union being a CLU is also telling: Figure 17.4 shows an increasing likelihood of this occurring with each generation. People in their 20s right now are more likely to have a first union that is NOT a marriage.

E. Same-Sex Couples

In 2001, the Canadian Census measured same-sex households for the first time (similar questions are asked in the United States and New Zealand). While this new question tells us the current number of such households, it is not possible to effectively assess whether this is a growing trend using census data. It is important to realize that the question was not designed to measure sexual orientation. So the findings do not tell us the number of gay and lesbian Canadians, only how many people self-identified as living in a same-sex union. Of these 34,200 same-sex couples, 19,000 were males and 15,200 were female. Table 17.3 shows the breakdown of types of two-adult-family households.

Table 17.3 Type of Union, 2001

Married	CLU: 2 sexes	CLU: same sex
83.5%	15.9%	0.5%

Source: Data compiled from **http://www.statcan.ca/Daily/English/ 021022/d021022a.htm**. Accessed July 15, 2003.

F. Divorce

The trends in divorce were not uniform over the 20th century. Figure 17.5 [page 176] shows periods when divorce rates increased substantially and then returned to a lower level. Figure 17.6 [page 177] provides a more detailed graph of the 15-year span between 1985 and 1999. These dramatic fluctuations are linked to changes in the divorce laws and the availability of legal aid (Statistics Canada, 2002c).

G. Lone-Parent Families

As previously noted, the number of lone-parent families is increasing [Figure 17.1]. However, this trend has not been uniform. Early in the 20th century, approximately 13.6 percent of family households contained a single parent. This percentage dropped to a low of 8.2 percent in 1966 and has now risen to 15.7 percent [Figure 17.7, page 178].

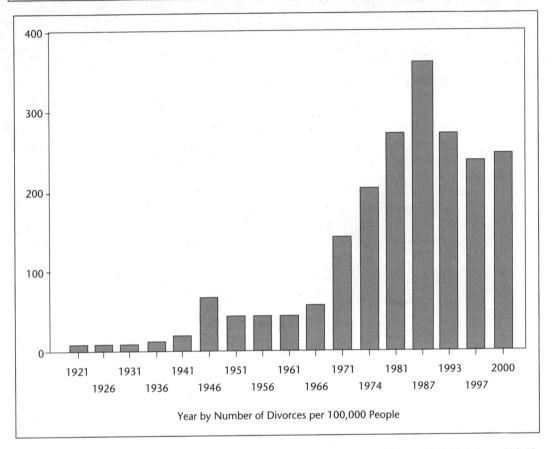

Figure 17.5 Divorce Trend, 1921–2000

Year by Number of Divorces per 100,000 People

Sources: Data compiled from **http://www.statcan.ca/english/freepub/11-516-XIE/sectionb/sectionb.htm** (table B75-81). Accessed July 15, 2003. And from **http://www.statcan.ca/english/Pgdb/famil02.htm**. Accessed July 15, 2003. And from **http://cansim2.statcan.ca/cgi-win/CNSMCGI.EXE** (table 053-0002). Accessed October 21, 2003.

Table 17.4 Percentage of Families by Parental Status, 2001

Parental Status	Percent
Married	70%
CLU	14%
Lone Mothers	13%
Lone Fathers	3%

Source: Data compiled from **http://www.statcan.ca/english/Pgdb/famil54a.htm**. Accessed July 15, 2003.

It is important to note that even though there is not a much larger proportion of lone-parent families now than in the 1930s, the causes of lone parenthood have changed. Earlier in the 20th century, one-parent households were usually the result of the death of one spouse (recall that the divorce rates were very low and life expectancy was shorter than today). Now, children living in lone-parent households typically have a non-residential parent, still alive and living

Figure 17.6 Divorce Trend, 1985–99

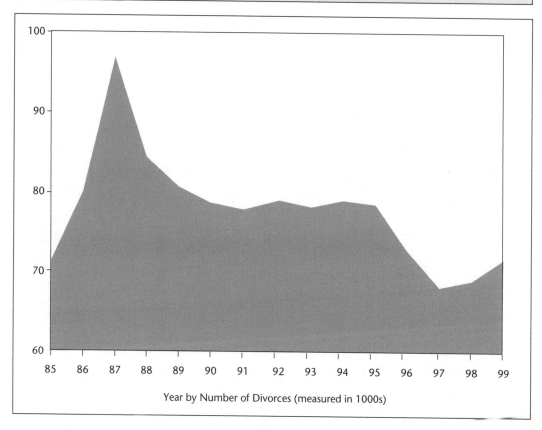

Year by Number of Divorces (measured in 1000s)

Source: Data from **http://cansim2.statcan.ca/cgi-win/CNSMCGI.EXE** (table 053-0002). Accessed October 21, 2003.

elsewhere. "In the 1950s and 1960s, more than 60 percent of lone parents were widowed. This proportion fell to 20 percent in the 1990s, as a result of the growing incidence of divorce, separation and birth outside marriage" (Statistics Canada, 2003). Table 17.4 shows us the pattern of current family arrangements.

H. Step/Blended Families

Just as there were lone-parent families in the past, there were also "stepfamilies." Life

Table 17.5 Step/Blended Families, 2001

Type of Stepfamily	Percent
His Children	10%
Her Children	50%
Blended Family (children in common)	32%
Blended Family (no children in common)	8%

Source: Data from **http://www.statcan.ca/Daily/English/020711/d020711a.htm**. Accessed July 15, 2003.

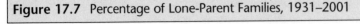

Figure 17.7 Percentage of Lone-Parent Families, 1931–2001

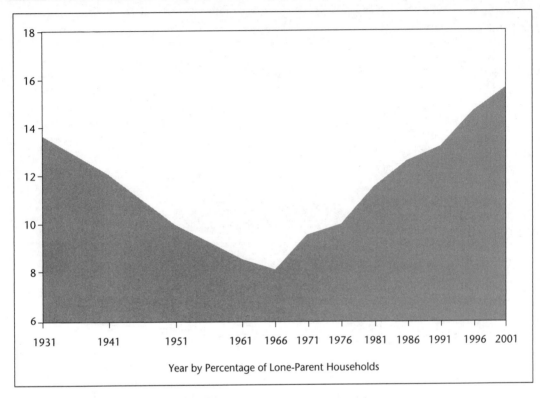

Year by Percentage of Lone-Parent Households

Source: Data compiled from **http://www12.statcan.ca/english/census01/products/analytic/companion/fam/timeline.cfm**. Accessed July 15, 2003.

expectancy was shorter then, so there was an increased likelihood of parents dying before their children had left home. The remaining parent would often remarry, creating a stepfamily.[3] Stepfamilies today are much more likely to have been created by divorce rather than death. In 2001 there were 503,100 stepfamilies, 12 percent of all families with children [Table 17.5]. "The total number of step families is split equally between married and common-law couples, just over 250,000 of each" (Statistics Canada 2002b).

After examining all of these patterns and figures, we can see that profound changes have occurred. Your grandparents were more likely to marry and to have larger families; they were less likely to live alone or in a common-law union; and they were less likely to divorce than you are.

EXPLANATIONS

When you ask people on the street why family patterns have changed so dramatically, they provide a wide range of answers. Explanations I have been given include the following: "People don't try as hard to keep marriages together as they used to"; "The laws around marriage and divorce are too complex, so people prefer just to live together"; "Feminists have undermined family relationships"; "Conflicting job demands pull people apart"; "The stresses associated with the economy mean people have fewer children and marriages are less stable"; and "Society's values have changed so much that people can live any way they want—it's OK to be gay."

In fact, there are elements of truth in many of these responses. But in order to understand the changing patterns more fully, we must consider multiple causes. Keep in mind that entire books have been written to explain these trends,[4] but we will focus on three key factors: economic, technological, and social.

A. Economic Factors

At the beginning of the 20th century, the majority of Canadians lived in rural areas, working on the land. The population in 1901 was approximately 5,400,000, and only 35 percent of these people lived in towns and cities (Beaujot & McQuillan, 1982). It wasn't until 1941 that the number of urban dwellers surpassed the rural population in Canada. In one century, the economy shifted from an emphasis on the resource sector (agriculture, forestry, mining, etc.) to manufacturing, and then later to the service and information sectors. These economic changes influenced family patterns in several ways.

First, when the majority of families were engaged in farming activities there was an obvious need for large families to undertake the necessary work. The labour of men, women, and children was vital to the success of the family farm. Caldwell (1982) developed the idea of "wealth flows." He argues that, as societies grow away from an agricultural base and become more urban, the contribution of children changes:

children begin to cost parents more (including the cost of educating them as demanded by a modernizing society), and the amount of support that parents get from children begins to decline (starting with the income lost because children are in school rather

than working). As the wealth flow reverses and parents begin to spend their income on children, rather than deriving income from them, the economic value of children declines. (Weeks, 1999: 99)

Caldwell's theory was developed to explain the decline in family size in Europe, but it provides insight into the Canadian situation also. In Canada, agriculture and manufacturing developed side by side with the opening up of new territory and the influx of immigrants. The country grew increasingly urban during the 20th century (Beaujot & McQuillan). Urban couples sought to limit family size in part because of the downward flow of wealth that Caldwell described. He notes that if childbearing decisions were based entirely on economic factors, couples would most likely forgo having any children at all (Caldwell, 1982). But, of course, our family formation and childbearing patterns are not solely based on rational, economic decisions: cultural factors also play a profound role (Matthews, 1994).

Second, family patterns changed when the division of labour between husbands and wives was altered by the separation of household and workplace. This reflects the pattern known as the "traditional family," where men worked outside the home for pay and women mainly engaged in unpaid labour in the household. Many people mistakenly believe that the "traditional family" existed throughout history until its predominance waned in the 1960s. In fact, this two-sphere arrangement was relatively short-lived, occurring with urbanization and the transition from agriculture to industrially based economies (Nett, 1988). Its decline began before the Depression years of the 1930s, but it reappeared briefly during the baby boom years of the 1950s (Beaujot, 1991). After the Second World War, the North American economy grew rapidly. "In the mid 1940s one-third of U.S. homes did not have running water and half did not have electric refrigerators, the post war boom brought relative affluence. The median family income rose 42 percent in the 1950s and 38 percent in the 1960s" (Hackstaff, 1999: 32, citing Cherlin, 1992: 35). Prosperity, combined with post-war and post-Depression optimism, influenced family patterns: birth rates rose and divorce rates fell as we saw in Figures 17.2 and 17.5. It was not only the economy that influenced family patterns in the 1950s; the culture and social changes associated with the end of the war also played a significant role (Weiss, 2000).

Third, as the service and information sectors gained economic primacy, the nature of work changed again. Physical strength and endurance became less important than interpersonal communication, computer, and critical thinking skills. Women's perceived physical disadvantage became less salient in this emerging work world, enhancing their career opportunities. The move to the information age further eroded the gender division of labour that identified housework as women's work and paid work as men's work—changing the dynamic within both the household and in the workplace (Hochschild, 1989). Often a higher level of formal education for both women and men is required for career-type jobs, meaning people spend more time in post-secondary education. Marriage and child-bearing are delayed (and common-law union is seen as a viable option) or, in some cases, for-gone completely (e.g., average age at marriage for first-time brides in 1996 was 27 and first-time grooms was 29 (Statistics Canada, 2002e). The opportunities for women to be financially independent may reduce the necessity of marrying or remaining in a marriage that they perceive to be unworkable. Thus, job opportunities potentially decrease marriage and increase separation and divorce. This widely accepted argument is based on the work of Parsons (1949) and Becker (1981).

Parsons believed that stable marriages must involve a gender-specific division of labour. Becker advanced this premise with the notion that mutual dependence of spouses based on gender roles makes marriage a desirable option.

As women have more paid opportunities, their economic dependence in marriage—which Parsons and Becker described—becomes unnecessary. It must be noted that women's so-called economic independence, in and of itself, is not a sufficient explanation for the lowered marriage rates and increased divorce rates. Oppenheimer (1997), in a comprehensive study of this issue, finds little support for this assertion. While it is true that cross-sectional, aggregate analyses show a correlation between women's increasing labour force activity and increasing divorce rates, quite a different pattern emerges when we use time series data and family history data.

Micro-level event history analyses that follow cohorts through their young adulthood generally show that women's educational attainment, employment, and earnings have little or no effect on marriage formation, or, where they do have an effect, find it to be positive. (Oppenheimer, 1997: 449)

Thus it seems that enhanced economic opportunities for women work in concert with other factors to influence family and household patterns.

Finally, the economic prosperity that emerged in North America after the Second World War raised our standard of living substantially. This prosperity has enabled more people to live alone. Many single-person households contain either post-divorce individuals or seniors. "In 2001, 35% of women aged 65 and over lived alone and 16% of men in this age group did so.... For women aged 85 and over, the proportion of seniors living alone grew from 25% in 1981 to 38% in 2001" (Statistics Canada, 2002f: 6). The ability to earn sufficient income to save for retirement is possible in part because of the rise in income in the second half of the 20th century (improved pensions also play an important role; Lindsay, 1999). Even with long-term growth in the economy, though, we have also experienced economic downswings that influence family patterns. One result is the return of adult offspring to the family household or a delay in leaving the parental home when job opportunities are limited. A total of "64% of men aged 20–24 lived with their parents in 2001, while this was the case for 52% of women in the same age group.... According to the 2001 General Social Survey, about 33% of men and 27% of women aged 20–29 returned home at least once after an initial departure" (Statistics Canada, 2002f). Table 17.1 gives an indication of how many young adults live in their parents' homes.

Clearly economic phenomena are linked to family patterns. When we look to the future, then, we should acknowledge that economic realities, like the continued widening of the gap between the rich and poor and short-term economic fluctuations, will influence the choices we make.

B. Technological Factors

Anyone who lived through the decades of the late 20th century knows how much technology has advanced. Computer-based technology has revolutionized production, transportation, communication, health care services, and countless other elements of our social world. Not surprisingly, then, technology has had an impact on family life. Several of these changes are connected to the changing economy. Obviously, it was technological change, in part, that led to a decreasing emphasis on the manufacturing sector and the primacy of service and information-based jobs (as discussed in the previous section).

But technology has also contributed to changes in health care and, thus, in demographic patterns. We live longer now than our ancestors did in large part because of technology. Early declines in mortality rates were linked to the improved standard of living that accompanied modernization and the availability of relatively safe and secure food and water supplies (Davis, 1986). More recently,

technology has allowed us to eradicate many infectious diseases through vaccines and to treat other health concerns with antibiotics and medical therapies. It has led to treatments for cancer and diabetes that may not be "cures" but that extend life nevertheless. The average life expectancy for women in Canada is over 80 years and it is almost 76 years for men (Statistics Canada, 2002f). Another major impact of technology on demographic patterns is through contraception. Of course, various means of contraception have existed through-out history (McLaren & McLaren, 1997) but it wasn't until the 20th century that safe, effective, and relatively unobtrusive contraceptives became available.

The combination of much longer lives and fewer children has revolutionized family arrangements (Davis, 1986). Where our grand-parents, early in the 20th century, would have spent the vast majority of their adult lives childrearing, and most would die before their last child was grown (average life expectancy in 1921 was 60.6 years for women and 58.8 years for men [Chappell et al., 2003]), Canadians now expect to live the majority of their adult lives in activities other than childrearing. Think of it: if you live to be 80, even if you spend 25 years raising your children, you could still have 35 or more adult years in a child-free household.

The chances of living alone after the death of a spouse increased for women over the 20th century as the gap between life expectancies of the two sexes expanded. This difference in life expectancy is often exaggerated by the common practice of women marrying men slightly older than themselves. Although this gap has narrowed slightly since 1980, there is still a preponderance of elderly women. In 2001, there were 2,315 women and 740 men over 99 years old (three times more women than men; Statistics Canada, 2002g).

Some have even argued that the risk of divorce increases as life expectancy is extended: "improved longevity increases the number of years that marriages can survive; however the number of years that marriages are exposed to the risk of divorce correspondingly increases. This change has undoubtedly influenced the recent escalation in divorce and separation rates" (McVey & Kalbach, 1995: 205). But, of course, increased life expectancy alone is not sufficient to explain these changes.

Looking ahead, we have good reason to believe that technological advances will continue to have a marked impact on family life. Medical researchers are developing ever more powerful reproductive technologies either to avert pregnancies or to create them. Cloning and genetic engineering open the door to the creation of human life without conception as we currently understand it. Similarly, improved technologies that promote health and reduce the impact of disease and injury will likely result in even greater numbers of Canadians reaching their 9th and 10th decades of life.

C. Cultural Factors

Looking back over the past century, we have clearly seen that economic patterns and technological advances have had a profound influence on family arrangements. However, the importance of cultural changes in norms and values, as well as the programs and laws, must not be underestimated. There have been many changes in North American culture in the past 100 years and it is well beyond the scope of this chapter to consider them all. However, we will focus on three major changes in values that have influenced our normative expectations about family life, on the one hand, and the laws and programs that support (or undermine) it, on the other hand. These three changes are secularization, individualism, and egalitarianism. In combination, they have a tremendous impact on all our family decisions.

Secularization refers to a long-term decline in people's participation in organized religions, and the reduced significance of religious institutions in their daily lives (Abercrombie, et al., 1988). This pattern varies by country, culture, and region, but it has been noted in most Western societies. Contrary to the expectation of some early sociologists (e.g., Max Weber), religion has not been entirely replaced by science and rationalism, but it certainly has declined. According to the World Values Survey, only 27 percent of Canadians attend weekly church services, and only 51 percent of Canadians responded that God was important in their lives (Nevitte, 1996). Secularization is linked to family patterns because organized religions tend to support certain family arrangements: they frequently sanction marriage and censure divorce (Hackstaff, 1999), encourage childbearing and oppose abortion, support male dominance, and oppose same-sex families. If religion is salient in our lives, we will follow its doctrines, and our family arrangements will reflect its tenets: fewer divorces, fewer common-law and same-sex unions, more children, and fewer blended families.[5] Hackstaff associates religion with a "marriage culture." She argues that the kind of "family values" many religions support have diminished as our society has experienced secularization (1999). Along with secularization, the value shift toward individualism also influences family patterns. Individualism is a belief that one's own needs and goals should take precedence over the needs of others and the larger community. The movement toward individualism has been linked with an increased desire for personal autonomy, privacy, and independence. Hackstaff (1999) argues that we are moving away from the "marriage culture" toward a pattern of greater individualism.

Marriage culture should be understood as a cluster of beliefs, symbols and practices, framed by material conditions that reinforce marriage and deter divorce. It is constituted by three beliefs that reflect a stance toward marriage *and* divorce: marrying is a given, marriage is forever, and divorce is a last resort. (Hackstaff, 1999: 1)

Over time, our ideas have changed and people are less willing to initiate or continue in relationships that they perceive would irrevocably harm their individual needs and goals. This is illustrated in opinion polls and in behaviour (Thornton, 1989; Matthews, 1994). Hackstaff argues that now people are more inclined to believe "marrying is an option; marriage is contingent; and divorce is a gateway" (1999: 2). People are willing to live alone, in CLUs and in same-sex unions, if these arrangements fulfill their needs. They are also willing to end CLUs or marriages, should they find the union unfulfilling. Like Hackstaff, Inglehart (1977, 1990) also discusses value change in Western society. He argues that it's not simply secularization that has led to these patterns, but that increased affluence and security leads people to adopt post-materialist values. These post-materialist values reflect the importance of individual freedom of choice. Lesthaeghe (1983) connects this value shift directly to demographic change, showing the link between increasing individualism and fertility decline.

The final cultural change we will consider is egalitarianism, specifically the move toward gender equality. Throughout the 20th century in North America, we have seen tremendous changes in the experiences of women. Remember, women were not allowed to vote and were considered to be legal "minors" in 1899. Now women's full equality is entrenched in the Canadian Charter of Rights and Freedoms. In Canada it is not legal to exclude women from educational and employment opportunities. Of course, laws and practices aren't entirely compatible—the protection of equal rights doesn't guarantee that women have equal opportunity. But we have certainly seen an improvement over time. The increasing equality of opportunity for women is reflected in the changing division of labour we

discussed in the section on economic factors. This equality challenges the status quo that existed under the "marriage culture" (Hackstaff, 1999) and has been linked to changing roles within families (Hochschild, 1989), to the higher divorce rates (Gold-scheider & Waite, 1991), and to lower fertility (Davis, 1984). This does not mean that all feminists are avoiding family arrangements. In fact, there is evidence that existing sex role attitudes don't predict the occurrence of divorce in the future (Thornton et al., 1983) and some evidence shows that improved opportunities for individual women have "a positive effect on marriage formation" (Oppenheimer, 1997: 449). What it does mean is that the gender revolution has an impact on the opportunities and choices of women and men. When this is combined with other elements of our society (such as secularization, individualism, economic, and technological change), we can see a noticeable change in the family patterns of Canadians.

As our values and behaviours change, so to do the laws, policies, and programs that have an impact on family arrangements. I will offer two examples to illustrate. First, divorce laws and policies are changing. As we saw in Figures 17.5 and 17.6, divorce rates have peaked and dropped dramatically in particular years. In 1968 Canada revolutionized its divorce laws to reduce the adversarial nature of divorce proceedings. It was no longer necessary to prove that one spouse was guilty of a marital offence; instead, divorces were granted if the individuals had lived separately for three years (in the United States, this is known as "no-fault divorce"). Divorce rates climbed immediately after this change, showing that many marriages had already ended in all but the legal sense. The law was changed again in 1985 to reduce the three-year waiting period to only one year; again the divorce rates rose. Divorce rates declined slightly in 1996–97, leading many to hope that marriages were becoming more stable and that the high divorce rate would fall. However, on further study it became apparent that the rates were a reflection of a new policy in Ontario that cut the number of divorces legal aid funded by almost 6,000. Thus, many poor people could no longer get financial assistance to pay for a divorce and the rate dropped (Statistics Canada, 1998). This is just one example of how changing laws and policies influence family arrangements. A second example is the much-improved pension system for Canadian seniors. Pension reform that provided a new benefit, called the Guaranteed Income Supplement, for the poorest people had a profound impact on their standard of living. For instance, between 1971 and 1986 "the income of unattached women aged 65 and over increased by 61 percent and went up 36 percent for men in this age group"(Lindsay & Donald, as quoted in Novak & Campbell, 2001: 158). Instituting a pension structure that raises seniors' incomes increases the likelihood of their living independently—a third of the people living in single-person households are over the age of 65 (Ram, 1990).

It is not possible to look ahead and accurately predict how our values and policies will change. But we can easily see that values, policies, and family patterns are intricately connected and that change is inevitable. A case in point is the discussion that erupted in 2003, in the media and among politicians and citizens, about the right to have legally recognized same-sex marriages. The Charter of Rights and Freedoms is a reflection of Canadian values, and yet its protection of non-heterosexual families became a divisive issue. Some Canadians argued that marriage is sacred and should be reserved for heterosexual couples. Others accepted the premise that in an egalitarian society it is discriminatory to privilege heterosexual unions. (The issue remained unresolved as this chapter went to press).

LOOKING AHEAD

Family patterns have changed dramatically over the past century, as our exploration of the Canadian census data has shown us. Despite changes in the membership and activities of families, though, the "ties of mutual consent" (Vanier, 2000: v) at the heart of all families are likely to endure. We have explored some of the many causes for these trends and now we look to the future. Given what you know, who do you think your grandchildren will live with? Their parents? Their children? Their lovers? Their cats? Or, maybe you won't have any grandchildren at all. Obviously, no one can perfectly predict the future, but you can use the insights you have gained to consider possibilities. How do you think future economic fluctuations and the widening gap between the rich and poor will influence you? What about genetic engineering and increased longevity? Finally, how might the growing emphasis on egalitarianism, individualism, and secularization affect your choices? Your answers to these questions are the key to the future. The decisions you and your generation make about marriage, divorce, cohabitation, and child-rearing will determine the trends for the coming century.

NAVIGATING THE CONCEPTS

1. With reference to the article, what do you feel were the most important changes to the family over the past 100 years? Why?

2. What do you feel will be the most influential factors (economic, technological, cultural) influencing the family over the next 100 years? Why?

3. Describe how families in your grandparents' generation were different from those of today. Which do you feel are better for raising children? Justify your answer.

NOTES

1. Statistics Canada collects census data on all Canadians, every five years. In addition, numerous national surveys are undertaken to assess Canadians' activities and behaviours on a regular basis (e.g., the General Social Survey and the Labour Force Survey). It is required by law that someone from every household responds to a questionnaire, detailing the membership of that household (age, sex, marital status—including common-law and same-sex unions). One in five households must complete a longer questionnaire that asks about a wider range of information (e.g., ethnicity, religion, language, and birthplace; Statistics Canada, 2002e).

2. The expected number of children per woman is calculated using a measure called the Total Fertility Rate. It indicates how many children each woman would have if she followed the same childbearing pattern, throughout her lifetime, that all Canadian women experienced in that particular year.

3. "Stepfamily" refers to a family in which at least one of the children in the household is from a previous relationship of one of the parents. In a "simple" stepfamily, the child(ren) of one of the spouses lives in the household. A "blended" family contains children from both spouses from one or more previous unions or one or more children from the current union and one or more children from previous unions. (Statistics Canada, 2002a)

4. See, for example, Ram, 1990; Goldsheider & Waite, 1991; Beaujot, 1991; Hackstaff, 1999; Beaujot, 2000; Weiss, 2000; Wu, 2000.

5. To illustrate: the doctrines of Roman Catholicism oppose most forms of contraception. At one time, demographers could readily discern distinct trends in the childbearing patterns of Catholic and Protestant families. As the salience of church doctrine diminished, the gap in fertility rates disappeared (Westoff & Ryder, 1977).

REFERENCES

Abercrombie, et al. 1988. *Dictionary of sociology*, 2nd ed. London: Penguin Books.

Beaujot, R. 1991. *Population change in Canada*. Toronto: McClelland and Stewart.

———. 2000. *Earning and caring in Canadian Families*. Peterborough, Ont.: Broadview Press.

Beaujot, R., and K. McQuillan. 1982. *Growth and dualism*. Toronto: Gage Publishing.

Becker, G. 1981. *A treatise on the family*. Cambridge: Harvard University Press.

Caldwell, J. 1982. *Theory of fertility decline*. New York: Academic Press.

Chappell N., et al. 2003. *Aging in contemporary Canada*. Toronto: Prentice Hall.

Cherlin, A. 1992. *Marriage, divorce and remarriage*, revised and enlarged ed. Cambridge: Harvard University Press.

Davis, K. 1984. Wives and work: The sex role revolution and its consequences. *Population and Development Review*, 10(3): 397–417.

———. 1986. Low fertility in evolutionary perspective. In "Below replacement fertility in industrial societies," supplement to *Population and Development Review*, 12: 48–65.

Goldscheider, F., and L. Waite. 1991. *New families, no families?* Berkeley: University of California Press.

Hackstaff, K. 1999. *Marriage in a culture of divorce*. Philadelphia: Temple University Press.

Hochschild, A., with A. Machung. 1989. *The second shift*. New York: Viking.

Inglehart R. 1977. *The silent revolution: Changing values and political styles among western publics*. Princeton: Princeton University Press.

———. 1990. *Culture shift in advanced industrial society*. Princeton: Princeton University Press.

Lesthaeghe, R. 1983. A century of demographic and cultural change in Western Europe: An exploration of the underlying dimensions. In *Population and Development Review*, 9(3): 411–35.

Lindsay, C. 1999. *A portrait of Canadian seniors*, 2nd ed. Ottawa: Statistics Canada.

Lindsay, C., and S. Donald. 1988. Income of Canadian seniors. *Canadian Social Trends* (Autumn): 20–25.

Matthews, B. 1994. The relationship between gender and fertility strategies. Ph.D. dissertation. Sociology Department, University of Western Ontario.

McLaren, A., and A. Tigar McLaren.1997. *Bedroom and the state : The changing practices and politics of contraception and abortion in Canada*, Toronto: Oxford University Press.

McVey, W., and W. Kalbach. 1995. *Canadian population*. Toronto: Nelson Canada.

Murdock, G. 1949. *Social structure*. New York: Macmillan.

Nemeth, M. 1994. The family. *Maclean's* (June14): 30–38.

Nett, E. 1988. *Canadian families: Past and present*. Toronto: Butterworth's.

Nevitte, N. 1996. *The decline of deference*. Peterborough, Ont.: Broadview Press.

Novak M., and L. Campbell. 2001. *Aging and society: A Canadian perspective*, 4th ed. Toronto: Nelson.

Oppenheimer, V. 1997. Women's employment and the gain to marriage: The specialization and trading model. *Annual Review of Sociology*, 23: 431–53.

Parsons, T. 1949. The social structure of family. In *The family: Its function and destiny*, ed. R. Anshem, 173–201. New York: Harper and Brothers.

Ram, B. 1990. *New trends in the family*. Ottawa: Statistics Canada.

Romaniuc, A. 1984. *Fertility in Canada: From baby boom to baby bust*. Ottawa: Statistics Canada.

Statistics Canada, 1998. Marriages and divorces, 1996. *The Daily* (January 29).

———. 2002a. *Census dictionary*. 2001 Census reference material.

———. 2002b. Changing conjugal life in Canada. *The Daily* (July 11).

———. 2002c. Divorces. *The Daily* (December 2).

———. 2002d. *Divorces: Historical statistics of Canada*. Catalogue no. 82-573 GIE.

———. 2002e. *History of the census of Canada*. 2001 Census general information.

———. 2002f. *Profile of Canadian families and households: Diversification continues*. 2001 Census analysis series.

———. 2002g. *Profiles of the Canadian population by age and sex: Canada ages*. 2001 Census analysis series.

———.2003. *The people: Household and family life*. Canada e-book.

Stephens, W. 1963. *The family in cross cultural perspective*. New York: Holt Rinehart and Winston.

Thornton, A. 1989. Changing attitudes towards family issues in the United States. *Journal of Marriage and Family*, 51(4): 873–93.

Thornton, A., et al. 1983. Causes and consequences of sex role attitudes and attitude change. *American Sociological Review*, 48: 211–27.

Vanier Institute for the Family. 2000. *Profiling Canada's families II*.

Weeks, J. 1999. *Population: An introduction to concepts and issues*, 7th ed. Belmont: Wadsworth Publishing.

Weiss, J. 2000. *To have and to hold: Marriage, the baby boom and social change*. Chicago: University of Chicago Press.

Westoff, C., and N. Ryder. 1977. *The contraceptive revolution*. Princeton: Princeton University Press.

Wu, Z. 2000. *Cohabitation: An alternative form of family living*. Don Mills, Ont.: Oxford University Press.

Chapter 18

The Boundaries of Public Education in the Knowledge-Based Economy

Terry Wotherspoon

Source: Printed with permission of the author (2003).

Terry Wotherspoon explores the role of education in contemporary society. His analysis reviews how education and training programs are being transformed and guided by certain economic imperatives that enable some populations while marginalizing others. Wotherspoon's investigation inspires the reader to reconsider what education is and how it can be viewed from various, and often competing, perspectives.

INTRODUCTION

Education, long regarded as a fundamental institutional feature of highly developed societies, has gained a place of higher prominence in contemporary societies. We now have various interrelated terms—including the *new economy,* the *knowledge economy,* the *learning society,* and the *information society*—to characterize the social and economic relationships that are emerging in an environment associated with intense global market competition driven by revolutionary developments in both production and information and communications technologies (ICT). These trends, as the terminology reveals, signify a newfound importance for education. When it is understood within the broader framework of lifelong learning, education is valued for its contributions to human capital formation, which lies at the heart of any strategy to promote economic growth and development. In the process,

education and training are being transformed as they come to be guided increasingly by particular kinds of economic imperatives.

The altered educational landscape holds the possibility of expanding opportunities for segments of the population that previously faced limited chances for social participation and economic advancement, but it also carries the danger that educational requirements and practices could become marginalizing rather than enabling for many segments of the population. Educational processes, when they are extended and modified within and beyond formal schooling, enter a realm in which personal and social relationships are reconstituted as market economic relationships that produce serious personal and family risks for those in positions of competitive disadvantage. This chapter assesses the mixed implications that the knowledge-based economy holds for Canadian education systems and for diverse groups of participants within those systems.

VARIED DIMENSIONS OF EDUCATION SYSTEMS

Sociologists and policy analysts in other fields have long recognized the importance of the connection between schooling and work, although the relationships are understood in diverse ways. Liberal theorists emphasize the social or individual utility of education for economic advancement, while critical theorists highlight the importance of power relations that privilege dominant groups over others, but the two camps agree generally that formal education assumes increasing importance in industrial and post-industrial societies as a way of selecting and orienting people to gain the knowledge, skills, and predispositions that are essential for the performing of socially necessary tasks. Most commentators acknowledge that education, since it provides a crucial opportunity for social and personal development, cannot be reduced to its economic functions. Such diverse groups as youth, parents, governments, business, community organizations, and educators agree strongly on the need for more highly integrated transitions between schooling and work, and education systems are taking several measures to address this issue and to ensure that persons in the labour force have continuous opportunities to upgrade their skills in appropriate forms. Nevertheless, there continues to be considerable debate over the extent to which education is—and should be—aligned with economic priorities (Council of Ministers of Education Canada, 1998: 19; Wotherspoon, 2004).

These debates reflect, to a large extent, the importance of education as an area around which various social groups and interests engage in struggles for strategic positioning. Education offers access to desired knowledge, credentials, and capacities relevant to labour market entry and job performance, but it also has more general social, cultural, and ideological significance as a means by which we come to develop particular understandings about the world and our places within it, along with habits, expectations, and practical capabilities that have other social applications. In the same way that some groups may use educational credentials as a way of controlling access to particular jobs or positions and securing their own competitive advantage relative to others (Collins, 1979), different groups can also attempt to use education, variously, as a vehicle to convert social or cultural resources into economic ones, or to block this conversion process (Bourdieu & Passeron, 1990).

One way in which to make sense of the competing and often contradictory forces that shape education in contemporary societies is through the tension between what Carnoy and Levin (1985) call the capitalist imperative and the democratic imperative. The former refers to the processes by which schooling contributes to the changing labour force requirements to maintain profitable production within capitalist economies. Whereas the capitalist imperative is driven by corporate interests that perpetuate inequality and hierarchy, the democratic imperative is guided by popular demands for participation, expansion of social and economic opportunity, and social justice for all social groups. Carnoy and Levin (1985: 247) argue that, while the balance between these two forces shifts periodically, schools remain a focus for public controversy and conflict "because they have the dual role of preparing workers and citizens."

The historical development of education in Canada reveals these dynamics at work, in part, through changing "boundaries" and mechanisms of inclusion and exclusion (Wotherspoon, 2002). Public education is hypothetically open to all citizens, providing opportunities for social participation that contribute to differing credentials and levels of success that, in turn, become translated into job opportunities and other socio-economic prospects. In practice, however, various processes of exclusion, discrimination, and marginalization have made it more difficult for some groups, relative to others, to advance in and through education. The current emphasis on the changing requirements of education for the knowledge society or new economy provides an opportunity to analyze the educational significance of economic transformations that are grounded in appeals to the apparent compatibility between both social and economic roles and responsibilities.

EDUCATION AND THE KNOWLEDGE ECONOMY

Concepts related to the new economy or knowledge society have appeared with increasing frequency over the past four decades in policy discussions and analysis of changing economic environments. The term *new economy* generally refers to the process that has resulted in the industrial production and distribution of material goods being increasingly altered and replaced by a rapid expansion in productivity made possible by revolutionary advances in information and communications technologies, which have brought with them unprecedented capacities to produce, store, and manipulate data. Knowledge is an essential resource because it enables firms and organizations to develop and implement technological innovations, thereby contributing to enhanced productivity both directly and as a result of adjustments made from monitoring existing procedures. Human capital, in turn, in the form of a highly educated, skilled, innovative, and adaptable workforce (understood as both existing and potential workers), is posed as the motor that drives the production and application of knowledge. In previous incarnations, human capital was conceptualized as an individual attribute that had benefits for society more generally; now it is seen more as an attribute to be harnessed within social and technical relationships that advance the interests of specific firms or organizations.

Globalization is a central characteristic of new economies, both through intensified competition among firms and nations on a global basis and in the accelerated movement of people, goods and services, and data across national boundaries. These trends are accompanied by a central contradiction: the quest for innovation and flexibility is accompanied by demands that there be open markets for goods, services, expertise, technologies, and workers, and conditions that make it difficult for governments to regulate what happens within specific boundaries, yet there is a parallel search for measures to coordinate the development and flow of data, resources, and people.

There is also a political and social dimension to these relationships in the sense that economic and labour market transformations contribute to considerable uncertainty and displacement in people's lives. As jobs, enterprises, or industries are restructured, some of the consequences include periodic job loss; shifts between education and employment for training or retraining; economic insecurity; migration from one locale or nation to another; and the modification of family life to accompany new working arrangements. Governments and community agencies are confronted with pressures to intervene, not only to ensure that labour market demands for the new economy can be fulfilled, but also to devise policy solutions to social displacement. One common response in highly industrialized nations is renewed emphasis on strategies for social cohesion, social integration, and social capital built around notions that social inclusion and participation in economic arrangements, combined with relations of trust and cooperation, are the best safeguard against social unrest and division.

Recent employment trends illustrate the impact these changes are having on the structure of work. The Organisation for Economic Co-operation and Development (2001: 55–56), for instance, reports that between 1992 and 1999, employment in the

United States and European Union nations grew by 3.3 percent for knowledge workers (defined as scientists, engineers, and information and communications technology specialists and technical workers who produced new knowledge), compared to 2.2 percent for service workers, 1.6 percent for management workers, and 0.9 percent for data workers, while employment declined by 0.2 percent among workers in goods-producing industries. Canadian data reveal similar trends, with nearly half of the job growth between 1991 and 2001 in highly skilled occupations that normally require a university education; employment in service-producing sectors, which reached parity with goods-producing industries in the late 1950s, had grown to three-quarters of the labour market by the end of the 1990s (Crompton & Vickers, 2000: 7–8; Statistics Canada, 2003a: 7).

Governments, businesses, policy consortia, and other agencies have produced a steady stream of documents and agendas that attempt to guide and monitor the transition to a knowledge-based economy. The prevailing message in these statements is the notion that global competition through knowledge-based economic development is inevitable and generally beneficial, producing a set of conditions to which individuals, firms, and nations must adjust in order to remain competitive and offset any limitations that arise along the way. They also represent a consensus-building exercise, through language that signals an understanding that all individuals and parties stand to gain from these developments, accompanied by exhortations for all participants to take responsibility and act to ensure that the proper adjustments and conditions can be fulfilled.

Statements and recommendations contained within two recent publications—one from the Organisation for Economic Co-operation and Development (OECD, 2001) and the other from the Government of Canada (2002)—are typical of many such documents. The OECD (2001: 97) highlights the importance of information and communications technologies, in conjunction with a broad range of other economic and social policy developments, in capturing the ability to exploit new economic conditions:

Governments today are faced with a new economic environment. ICT has emerged as a key technology with the potential to transform economic and social activity and has led to more rapid growth in countries where the conditions for macroeconomic stability are in place. While it is too early to say how important ICT's transformations will be compared with those of previous innovations, like electricity, government should nonetheless take action to manage adjustment and keep the social costs low. All governments can do more to exploit this new technology further, by accelerating its diffusion, providing the right skills and building confidence. But ICT is not the only factor explaining growth disparities and policies to bolster these technologies will not on their own steer countries on to a higher growth path. Indeed, growth is not the result of a single policy or institutional arrangement, but a comprehensive and co-ordinated set of actions to create the right conditions for future change and innovation.

The OECD report outlines a series of policy recommendations (echoed in similar reports by various business and government agencies or consortia) directed to enhance economic productivity and growth, including several oriented to education and other dimensions of "human capital enhancement":

• Investment in high-quality early education and child care;

• Raising completion of basic and vocational education and improving the quality of the system;

• Improving school-to-work transitions;

• Strengthening the links between higher education and the labour market in a cost-effective way;

• Providing wider training opportunities; and

• Reducing obstacles to workplace changes and giving workers a greater voice. (OECD, 2001: 70)

Statements and recommendations in the report reveal economic logic (evident in the notion that education and child care are "investments" and strategies to enhance and employ labour market developments for economic productivity), mixed with relatively progressive social visions offering participation and opportunity for all social groups (enhancing child care, improving educational participation and attainment, and facilitating employee input) that appear beneficial, reasonable, and politically neutral.

Similar analyses, recommendations, and calls for action are outlined in the federal document *Knowledge Matters*, which was presented as one of the two core papers outlining the Canadian government's innovation strategy. The paper stresses that "further action is required by all" in order "for Canadians to have the skills they need to participate fully in society, and to secure Canada's position as a leader in the world economy" (Canada, 2002: 12). It continues by calling for a unified vision in which "all Canadians work together to develop a common understanding of the challenges we face, articulate a shared vision of where we want to go, and create a plan of action to get us there," including measures to strengthen four main areas of skill and learning development:

• Building a foundation for lifelong learning for children and youth;

• Strengthening accessibility and excellence in post-secondary education;

• Building a world class workforce; and

• Helping immigrants achieve their full potential. (Canada, 2002: 12)

Hale (2002: 23) emphasizes that the innovation agenda to position Canada for successful global competition is accompanied by an inclusion agenda that is oriented toward securing widespread economic participation and managing political and social tensions brought about in the course of economic restructuring:

> The government's evolving innovation strategy is linked to a broader economic paradigm in which government has a distinct, facilitative role in fostering business competitiveness in a dynamic, open economy, organizing both economic and social infrastructure, and facilitating widespread access to and participation in the benefits of the emerging knowledge-based economy. Government policies intended to enhance access to education and to improve incentives for employment-related training are critical to increasing the number of potential "winners" and to reduce the potential "casualties" of continuing economic and technological change.

Hale's account highlights, as well, a recurrent theme that even the most ardent promoters of the benefits of the new economy acknowledge—risks and disparities are likely to be part of the new landscape, so it is better to play to competitive advantage than be left behind. The sections that follow examine how these challenges affect education systems and participants.

CONTEMPORARY EDUCATIONAL REFORMS

Prescriptions for economic innovation come hand in hand with a broader public sentiment that education systems, while contributing significantly to advances in knowledge and skill levels among the population as a whole, must be transformed in order to ensure a better fit and relevance for new economic requirements. The main thrust in the demands for educational reform, signalled in documents such as those cited in the previous section, includes the upgrading of general levels of education, skill, and training across the board; improved participation in higher education; and a better

fit among education, labour market requirements, and job placement.

Measures to reposition education for
competitive performance in new economic
environments are occurring together with
broader transformations in education systems.
Common patterns of educational reform are
evident in Canada and other post-industrial
societies, although the nature and scope of
these changes are somewhat unique in each
context. In addition to the growing emphasis
on lifelong learning, blurring of the boundaries
between academic and vocational education,
and substantial growth in educational programming and participation beyond high
school levels, education systems over the past
two decades have experienced funding
constraint and restructuring; devolution of
decision-making from central to more local
levels; and neo-conservative reforms promoting individualism and choice that attempt to
align education with markets through which
goods and services are produced and
exchanged (Brown, Halsey, Lauder, & Wells,
1997: 19–21). The impetus for educational
reform is grounded in claims that education
must be made more accountable and
responsible to the public, and that it must
better reflect contemporary economic and
labour market conditions. But, while there is
general consensus among most social groups
that coordinated educational planning and
reforms are essential, strong discrepancies are
evident in proposed changes and their outcomes. Job-related education means different
things to different observers, so that employer
demands oriented to training specific types of
workers may be at odds with students' interests
in gaining professional credentials. At the same
time, initiatives to involve parent groups and
local organizations more fully in the educational decision-making process are likely to be
ineffective when they are offset by government
measures to tighten central control over the
terms and limits of educational finance and
other important matters.

Regardless of the images portrayed in
various debates, Canada is positioned well,
relative to most other nations, to embrace the
challenge to become a highly educated,
electronically integrated society. Canada is at
or near the top in most international
comparisons of general educational achievement and educational attainment rates in post-
secondary education (OECD, 2002). Educational attainment continues to expand in both
depth and scope as more and more people
achieve increasingly higher levels of education
and training. About one out of five Canadians
in all age cohorts are engaged in full-time
educational studies; in addition, between
1 and 2 percent of Canadian adults are engaged
in post-secondary studies on a part-time basis,
while about one in four are involved in other
formal adult education and training programs
(calculated from Statistics Canada, 2002b:
48–49). Whereas in 1951 only 1.9 percent of
the Canadian adult population had completed
a university degree, by 2001 that figure had
risen to 15.4 percent, while about half of the
adult population overall had completed at least
some post-secondary education (Statistics
Canada, 2003b: 26). The median levels of
education among Canadians aged 25 to 44
increased from 8.2 years in 1951 to 13.5 in
1996 (Schweitzer, Crocker, & Gilliss, 1995: 23;
Statistics Canada, 2001: 199). Canadians are
also highly engaged in the development,
application, and use of information and
communications technologies. Canada ranks
at or near the top in the world on many
indicators associated with computer access and
availability and use of the Internet at home,
work, and school (Statistics Canada, 2002a).

Within these general trends lie a number of
sources of concern for educators, policy-makers
and policy analysts. Educational participation
rates in Canada are relatively low in comparison with other highly developed nations,
standing at or below the mean participation
rates among OECD countries for nearly all age
cohorts (OECD, 2002, Table C1.2). Amid

mounting rhetoric and initiatives oriented to keep youth in school, the number of high school dropouts remains high: in 1999, about 12 percent of 20-year-olds had left before completing high school, although the comparable proportion was 18 percent in 1991, and many early leavers eventually complete their high school later (Bowlby & McMullen, 2002: 26–27). Substantial proportions of the Canadian adult population have low literacy skills, especially in comparison with many European nations, and considerable inequalities in literacy skills are evident across regions, provinces, socio-economic groups, and age cohorts (Willms 1997). One-quarter or more of Canadian children experience learning and behavioural problems, while the fastest-growing segments of the child and youth population include many groups—such as Aboriginal children and youth, immigrants who speak neither English nor French, and children from low-income families—that are often associated with difficulties with education and integration into labour markets of temporary or longer-term duration (Willms, 2002; Wotherspoon & Schissel, 2001).

Increasing attention is also being directed to the extensive levels of education, skills, and capacity that people have attained in forms that are not officially acknowledged within formal and continuing education. Employers, policy-makers, and some educational institutions are beginning to acknowledge two major dimensions of this phenomenon: non-recognition of foreign credentials, in response to which some agencies are taking steps to address a common problem for immigrants who are not granted full-equivalent credit within Canadian institutions for degrees, certificates, and training attained in other countries; and Prior Learning Assessment Recognition, which refers to procedures established by educational institutions, employers, and other agencies to determine credit equivalency for specific types of non-formal learning and work experiences. There is sub-

stantial additional evidence that our understanding of lifelong learning needs to be broadened extensively to take into account not only the need for more learning, but also to acknowledge the diverse knowledges and skills that emerge through people's social and community experiences. Individuals and groups throughout the population enrich their lives and capacities through regular engagement in informal learning as they engage in deliberate (as opposed to incidental) efforts to learn new knowledge, skills, or understandings related to work, community, home, personal interests, and other social spheres (Livingstone, 1999: 11, 35). Aboriginal people, among other communities, also maintain and disseminate distinct forms of indigenous knowledge expressed through long-standing social, environmental, and spiritual relations. While detractors emphasize its irrelevance to contemporary economic circumstances, indigenous knowledge has numerous applications that are coming to be acknowledged for their bio-medical, ecological, socio-legal, and economic as well as cultural significance. Many persons, both on their own and through interaction with others, also develop highly sophisticated understandings and skills related to their performance of specific tasks or response to practical problems they encounter in their daily lives and work, while others turn to private tutors, Web-based research, or mentors to acquire information and skills they wish to apply in various settings.

The multiple dimensions of intense learning engagement, collectively, suggest that people are simultaneously taking seriously widespread demands to pursue lifelong learning and better job-related training while they encounter a problem that is more fundamental than the issue of knowledge deficit. The concern that many people have limited opportunities to apply and gain recognition for their diverse skills and capacities, however, has not received the same high profile that is accorded questions of educational upgrading and reform. Livingstone (1999: 6), pointing to the uncritical management perspective that dominates much of the analysis of the knowledge economy, highlights the consequence: "*A vicious circle of more learning for fewer jobs is now well established.* More education may generally be personally enriching and learning for its own sake should never be discouraged. But more schooling and training have not created more jobs in any direct sense, nor is much formal education even actually required to perform many current and prospective jobs." The significance accorded knowledge and learning in the knowledge-based economy appears to be oriented more toward specific kinds and applications of knowledge than learning in general.

INEQUALITIES IN EDUCATION AND LEARNING

The benefits of the new economy are widely promoted through attention to high-profile jobs related to the creation and application of sophisticated information technologies and management of information and systems related to those technologies. Clearly, many people are well positioned to benefit from the advantages associated with the knowledge-based economy, especially among those able to translate a combination of education, ingenuity, and organizational or entrepreneurial status into recognized forms of innovation. However, many of the jobs that are being created, especially in the rapidly expanding service sector, do not require advanced levels of formal training or involve job tasks that can be learned relatively quickly. Among the fastest-growing occupations in Canada are customer service and information clerks (notably through employment in telephone call centres) and food counter attendants and kitchen assistants; the top-10 lists also include, for men, grocery clerks and store shelf-stockers, truck drivers, and materials handlers, and, for women, general office clerks, visiting homemakers and housekeepers, and teaching assistants (Statistics Canada, 2003a: 26). In other instances, workers whose jobs are more directly related to their higher-level skills and credentials often have limited scope to exercise discretion and employ the capacities they have. The advent of high-powered computers, wireless technology, sophisticated applications, and Web-based links, for instance, has enhanced the work and productivity of many workers, but these technological innovations along with other types of organizational restructuring have also meant that professional and highly qualified workers can spend much of their time meeting administrative requirements and completing clerical tasks that lie outside their main areas of competence and focus. Information technology can fragment work as well as enhance it, often involving mundane tasks or operations that bypass complex worker skills. Both technology and knowledge enter into economic arrangements more fully for their ability to increase productivity and profit margins than their human benefits. Within the setting of the knowledge-based economy, Lowe (2000: 81) observes labour markets' limited capacity to meet most workers' rising expectations that they will attain meaningful jobs to match their increasing levels of qualifications, and he emphasizes the increasing polarization that occurs "between high- and low-paid jobs, while the rise of a contingent workforce of part-time, contract, temporary, and solo self-employed individuals suggests a further deterioration in the overall quality of work—a trend that is exacerbated by the growing divide between large employers and the small businesses and solo self-employment where most new job creation is taking place."

Nonetheless, the analyses by Livingstone, Lowe, and other observers highlight how these trends are intensified by a compelling logic that, for individuals, drives competition and increases pressure to attain even higher-level credentials and expanding repertoires of skills and training. In the pursuit of these objectives, individual learners and their parents are often inclined to take steps that position them for competitive advantage both in the types of education they engage in and the strategies they adopt to ensure their education and other resources yield desirable employment or entrepreneurial outcomes. Thus, increasing numbers of children are enrolled in early child-care programs and a broad range of extracurricular activities; provided with stimuli to enrich their learning; given access to resources such as tutoring services to ensure their successful progress through schooling; pressured to enter programs and institutions deemed to be high in status and quality; and encouraged to take other actions that will give them an educational advantage.

This competitive logic also intensifies the pressures on schooling, both from below (through rising expectations from parents and students about educational quality and relevance) and above (through the various reforms promoted by governments, businesses, and educational managers). Education is regarded increasingly as a business in which each institution or program is considered a service provider that enters the marketplace offering particular kinds of products to attract and maintain consumer loyalty. The capitalist imperative, apparent not only within specific dimensions of educational funding, organization, and programming, comes to be embedded more deeply in the entire conception and structure of contemporary education systems as lean, flexible agencies producing knowledge and workers for the new economy (Sears, 2003).

The transformations now underway in education systems contain numerous contradictions for learners from diverse backgrounds. Significant boundaries around and within education are widening, so that increasing numbers of people face expanded options related to specific needs and interests that have arisen from emerging issues as well as those

that previously have been ignored by education systems. Students can select courses from different institutions or even within the same institution that emphasize, for instance, Aboriginal cultural programming and nanotechnology studies. Education, understood as part of a continuum of lifelong transitions rather than an isolated institution, has tended to broaden its focus from an orientation on program delivery to ensure that programs are supported by services and resources that recognize the diverse needs and life circumstances of students. Many of these programs and institutions are more inclusive in various ways, enabling greater participation through more open admission criteria; greater diversity in the ways that courses are delivered; enhanced support services for students with special needs; programming initiatives that respond to student interests; and stronger linkages among education institutions, communities, and work settings.

However, the reorganization of education also means that substantial segments of the population face restricted educational options and horizons. Funding cutbacks and institutional restructuring have contributed to the deletion of core courses and services in many educational programs; shifted institutional and research priorities from educational enhancement to revenue generation; left institutions unable to meet student demand for specific programs; and burdened students with additional costs as tuitions and other expenditures related to education have risen. As governments have reduced educational funding or shifted the basis on which it is allocated, corporate sponsorships and other private sources have come to play an increasing part both directly and indirectly in classrooms and educational organizations, influencing everything from the brands of consumer products used or marketed in educational institutions to the types of programs, curricula, resources, and teaching methods available for students, educators and researchers. In many educational institutions, the teachers, professors and other educational workers are monitored and subject to work roles and performance measures based typically on industrial standards rather than on the whole range of characteristics that are essential for effective teaching-learning and scholarly relationships. Educational offerings have become increasingly fragmented and stratified as schools, post-secondary institutions, and other agencies cater to particular clientele, especially when they are no longer regarded as universal services open to all members of a particular neighborhood, community, or region. An ethos of competitiveness has reduced some educational relationships to utilitarian quests for grades, spaces in desirable programs, and credentials, leaving many students to opt or be forced out of desired educational pathways as they become marginalized, overwhelmed, or unable to balance educational requirements and other demands.

Changing educational boundaries and practices have not heralded the disappearance of significant exclusionary dimensions of education despite efforts to address problems for students with initial disadvantage or those confronted with serious life-transition difficulties. Female students have moved into many non-traditional areas, and have increased their educational participation, attainment, and success to such an extent that media and policy attention has come to focus on questions about whether the education system is failing males. However, these trends often overshadow more serious issues related to how and why gender-based differentiation processes continue to channel males and females into education and career paths that are often highly segregated and unequal. Similarly, several encouraging developments suggest the closing of persistent "gaps" in education and employment for Aboriginal people compared to Canadians as a whole, even as critical inequalities in life conditions

and prospects persist and even expand between and within these population groups. Aboriginal people and persons in visible minority groups also experience overt and covert forms of racism and—in common with many other groups, including people with physical and emotional disabilities and those with alternative lifestyles—various forms of discrimination that pose barriers to their educational and occupational success. Educational opportunities, resources, and outcomes also vary by region, with persons living in remote or rural areas, or inner cities, the most likely to experience educational difficulties. All of these factors are influenced by or interact with social class inequalities and related circumstances, such as poverty, that have a significant impact on educational pathways and attainment levels (Guppy & Davies, 1998; Wotherspoon, 2002, 2004). The knowledge-based economy is likely to provide new opportunities for members of some of these groups, but corresponding labour market, educational and policy changes also contribute to an environment that perpetuates and even increases significant socio-economic inequalities.

CONCLUSION

The advent of a knowledge-based society carries mixed implications for education and the people who participate as learners and workers in educational institutions. Many people have unprecedented chances to benefit from significant increases in educational attainment and participation in formal and informal educational learning activities as education and training gain enhanced profiles within new economic arrangements. However, this promise is limited insofar as economic structures that rely on fundamental inequalities are intensified more than they are transformed. In the process, educational relationships that in the broadest sense are about the expansion of human capacities and social interaction become redefined to emphasize productivity, economic growth, and commodity markets.

It is essential to recognize that what has been identified as the capitalist imperative, accompanied by initiatives to transform education into a business or marketplace, are powerful tendencies but they are not all-pervasive, irreversible forces. Education, and the social environments that educational improvement can enhance, are also guided by elements of a democratic imperative that thrives when there are meaningful opportunities for the expression of voices and action representing the full range of diversity among social participants, including children and youth. Education is not merely a business and economic tool, but a social process that at its best contains prospects to foster human growth and social transformation.

Despite widespread demands for educational reform and assurances that schooling will be relevant to emerging job futures, there are diverse visions, linked by general notions of human improvement, about what education systems should become. Debate and dialogue about education are not new, representing instead a fundamental characteristic of cultural, social, and intellectual diversity in a democratic society. A more significant challenge for education and those concerned with its future lies in the need to sustain democratic diversity while simultaneously ensuring that such diversity means more than enduring inequalities, technical problems managed by efficiency experts, or marketplace choices for consumers.

NAVIGATING THE CONCEPTS

1. Wotherspoon suggests that some of the leading drivers for educational change in the knowledge-based society are economic imperatives. What do you feel are the costs and the benefits of having economic forces define and influence educational development?

2. How does the knowledge-based society give an advantage to certain groups while disadvantaging others? Be sure to refer to the article in your answer.

3. Should the education system be designed to provide students with the training they need to find a job? Discuss.

REFERENCES

Bourdieu, P., and J.-C. Passeron. 1990. *Reproduction in education, society, and culture*. Newbury Park, Calif.: Sage.

Bowlby, J. W., and K. McMullen. 2002. *At a crossroads: First results for the 18 to 20-year-old cohort of the youth in transition survey*. Catalogue no. 81-591. Ottawa: Human Resources Development Canada and Statistics Canada.

Brown, P., A. H. Halsey, H. Lauder, and A. Stuart Wells. 1997. The transformation of education and society: An introduction. In *Education: Culture, economy, society*, eds. A. H. Halsey, H. Lauder, P. Brown, and A. Stuart Wells, 1–44. Oxford: Oxford University Press.

Canada. 2002. *Knowledge matters: Skills and learning for Canadians. Canada's innovation strategy*. Ottawa: Human Resources Development Canada.

Carnoy, M., and H. M. Levin. 1985. *Schooling and work in the democratic state*. Stanford, Calif.: Stanford University Press.

Collins, R. 1979. *The credential society: An historical sociology of education and stratification*. New York: Academic Press.

Council of Ministers of Education Canada. 1998. *The transition from initial education to working life: A Canadian report for an OECD thematic review*. Toronto: Council of Ministers of Education Canada.

Crompton, S., and M. Vickers. 2000. One hundred years of labour force. *Canadian Social Trends* (Summer): 1–13.

Guppy, N., and S. Davies. 1998. *Education in Canada: Recent trends and future challenges*. Ottawa: Minster of Industry.

Hale, G. E. 2002. Innovation and inclusion: Budgetary policy, the skills agenda, and the politics of the new economy. In *How Ottawa spends 2002–03: The security aftermath and national priorities,* ed. G. B. Doern, 20–47. Don Mills, Ont.: Oxford University Press.

Livingstone, D. W. 1999. *The education-jobs gap: Underemployment or economic democracy.* Toronto: Garamond Press.

Lowe, G. S. 2000. *The quality of work: A people-centred agenda.* Don Mills, Ont.: Oxford University Press.

Organisation for Economic Co-operation and Development (OECD). 2001. *The new economy: Beyond the hype. The OECD growth project.* Paris: OECD.

———. 2002. *Education at a glance 2002.* Paris: OECD.

Schweitzer, T. T., R. K. Crocker, and G. Gilliss. 1995. *The state of education in Canada.* Montreal: Institute for Research on Public Policy.

Sears, A. 2003. *Retooling the mind factory: Education in a lean state.* Aurora, Ont.: Garamond Press.

Statistics Canada. 2001. *Education in Canada 2000.* Catalogue no. 810-229. Ottawa: Minister of Industry.

———. 2002a. Computer access at school and at home. *The Daily* (October 29).

———. 2002b. Education at a glance. *Education Quarterly Review,* 8(3): 48–53. Catalogue no. 81-003.

———. 2003a. *The changing profile of Canada's labour force. 2001 Census: Analysis series.* Statistics Canada catalogue no. 96F0030XIE2001009. Ottawa: Minister of Industry.

———. 2003b. *Education in Canada: Raising the standard. 2001 Census: Analysis series.* Statistics Canada catalogue no. 96F0030XIE2002012. Ottawa: Minister of Industry.

Willms, J. D. 1997. *Literacy skills of Canadian youth: International adult literacy survey.* Statistics Canada catalogue no. 89-552. Ottawa: Minister of Industry.

———. 2002. The prevalence of vulnerability. In *Vulnerable children: Findings from Canada's national longitudinal survey of children and youth,* ed. J. Douglas Willms, 45–69. Edmonton: University of Alberta Press and Human Resources Development Canada.

Wotherspoon, T. 2002. *The dynamics of social inclusion: Public education and Aboriginal people in Canada.* Toronto: The Laidlaw Foundation, Perspectives on Social Inclusion Working Paper Series (December).

———. 2004. *The sociology of education in Canada: Critical perspectives,* 2nd ed. Toronto: Oxford University Press.

Wotherspoon, T., and B. Schissel. 2001. The business of placing Canadian children and youth "at-risk." *Canadian Journal of Education,* 26(3): 321–39.

Chapter 19

Some Very Good News via Some Very Bad Myths
Reginald Bibby

Source: Bibby, Reginald W. (2002). Some Very Good News via Some Very Bad Myths. In Reginald W. Bibby, *Restless Gods:The Renaissance of Religion in Canada* (Chp. 2, pp.33–54). Toronto: Stoddart Publishing Co. Ltd. Reprinted with permission of the author (2003).

In this chapter from his book *Restless Gods*, Reginald Bibby reviews many of the challenges facing Canada's religious community. He suggests that organized religions need to embrace the changing social landscape if they are to remain relevant in peoples' lives, and yet his analysis of his own *Project Canada* research finds that a surprisingly high number of Canadians still seek answers to life's questions through the religious traditions they were brought up with.

I grew up as a Baptist. Funny thing when you're a Baptist: you don't think of yourself as particularly strange. In fact, you look out at people in other Protestant denominations—friends and neighbours who are United, Anglican, Lutheran, Presbyterian—and see *them* as the ones who are different. And, to be honest, to a ten-year-old Baptist, groups like Catholics, not to mention Mormons or Buddhists, seem *especially* different. Their services are not ones into which Baptists readily wander.

It therefore comes as something of a surprise to Baptists when I tell them about my study of the Toronto Anglican Diocese in the mid-80s—where an Anglican woman who was concerned about changes in liturgy, commented, "We need to be careful, or one day we will end up like the Baptists"! What the Anglican woman probably didn't realize, of course, is that a Baptist in *her* worship service would also feel like the proverbial duck badly in need of some water.

To have conversations with people who are part of other religious groups is to receive a mini-revelation: *everyone thinks that their*

traditions are the norm—their beliefs, their kind of worship, their music, their type of ministry. Consequently, to grow up anything is to feel a measure of comfort with one's own group and a measure of discomfort with other "different" groups. What's true of Baptists and Anglicans can just as readily be seen when a Catholic and a Pentecostal who are dating attempt to alternate pews, or when two United and Jewish friends agree to attend their respective services together on a back-to-back Saturday and Sunday. Sometimes the ecclesiastical trip may be short, such as Anglican to Catholic or Baptist to Alliance; the occasion may also be brief—a wedding, a funeral, or a Christmas service. Regardless, confusion and uneasiness are common. People don't know what they are supposed to do when the music and prayers and rituals and gestures are foreign. What's happening somehow doesn't resonate with the kinds of things that may have moved one in the past, or moves one in the present.

All of this is to say that faith, however personal, invariably has a pronounced social and cultural dimension. To be raised Baptist or

United or Catholic or Mormon is to acquire a religious identity, which is accompanied by ideas and ways of expressing faith that one sees as normative. As basic as such a reality is, it is not one that Canadian religious leaders readily grasped, to the detriment of both their groups and millions of inactive religious people across the country.

A common impression about the attendance drop-off in the post-1960s is that it was associated with millions of Canadians jettisoning their respective religious groups. To borrow some sports jargon, to the extent that people were not involved in the groups of their childhoods, they were seen as having become religious free agents who were shopping their services to new teams. Or, to use the language of the market model, those who wanted to have their religious and spiritual needs met were said to be spending time browsing in an array of "meaning malls" and "spiritual marketplaces." Allegedly, their consumer choices were determined primarily by their personal tastes and whims. In such an environment, people were seen as having little or no regard for the religions of their parents and grandparents. Those, after all, were the "old-time religions." This was a new day—a day of individualism, freedom, and post-denominationalism. Bring on the competition, New Movements, New Age, and all.

It was a poorly informed and extremely naive reading of the times. If all we had been looking at was religion as a set of ideas, then people could have said goodbye to religious groups just as readily as they had reluctantly said goodbye to beliefs about Santa and the Easter Bunny and tooth fairies. If the churches had been no more than religious department stores that had become outdated and no longer competitive, people could have said goodbye to them just as readily as they waved goodbye to Eaton's and headed for Wal-Mart.

But religious groups carry with them cultures and poignant memories. Some two in three Canadians say they attended Sunday schools and services when they were growing up, frequently accompanied by parents, and sometimes by relatives. These were the places where millions of people heard stories, sang choruses, participated in youth groups, were introduced to faith, and made commitments. These were settings in which many of their grandparents and parents, brothers and sisters, aunts and uncles, and closest friends were involved. These places bring back memories of poignant, moving times when they and people they loved were baptized and married, and when they said final farewells to cherished family members and friends.

As we will see, for those who look at the world through theistic eyes, there are signs that the gods are shaking up Canadians from coast to coast, leading them to ask vital questions about life and death, communicating with them directly, and giving them hints of transcendence. In the midst of it all, large numbers of Canadians seem to continue to think that at least some of the answers to what they are experiencing lie in the religious traditions of their parents and grandparents. Most are reluctant to wander very far from their religious homes and many are open to greater involvement—if they can be shown that it is worth their while.

These realities have not been well understood by the country's churches. It's time to clear up the confusion once and for all.

A MONOPOLY VERSUS A MOSAIC

A key to understanding the nature of organized religion in Canada is recognizing that the country's long-established religious groups have had and continue to have a considerable advantage over newer and smaller counterparts in ministering to Canadians. Their longevity has meant that they have sizeable pools of people who have been socialized in their traditions. Their numerical strength has meant, in turn, that they typically gain far more people than they lose through religious intermarriage. This is not to disparage the presence and expansion efforts of newer and smaller religious organizations; it's simply to recognize the competitive facts of Canadian religious life....

There were three key reasons why Canada's religious market broke down. First, contrary to what [Rodney] Stark and many religious leaders had assumed, the country's well-established churches continued to have a considerable competitive advantage because of the latent loyalty of the people who identified with them—those I refer to as "affiliates." People were very reluctant to switch. The market was not as open as everyone had thought. Second, there was a widespread assumption that affiliates who attended sporadically or not at all had dropped out of their groups and had become part of a growing pool of "unchurched" people. Their affiliate religious bodies essentially gave up on them, a fact graphically illustrated by the strange delight many congregations took in cleaning the alleged "deadwood" off their rolls. Because religious groups, and just about everyone else for that matter, were working from these two false assumptions about switching and dropping out, large numbers of people failed to be touched by their churches' ministries and huge amounts of potential resources went untapped. Third, it was widely believed that people who had ceased to be active were not receptive to greater involvement. And if they weren't, neither were their offspring. A prevalent stereotype was that people no longer involved were typically hostile—"poisoned" by bad experiences. Better to turn elsewhere in pursuing recruitment leads.

Ironically, few congregations appear to have carried out systematic studies of their marginal and inactive affiliates. If they had, they would have found that (a) many were, in fact, receptive to greater involvement and (b) especially in urban areas, many were among the Canadians who had moved once in the past five years and simply had not reconnected

Table 19.1	Canada's Religious Families, 2002

	Approximate % of the Canadian Population*
Roman Catholics outside Quebec	23
Roman Catholics in Quebec	19
Mainline Protestants	
United (9), Anglican (6), Lutheran (2),	
Presbyterian (2)	19
Conservative Protestants	
including Baptists, Pentecostals,	
Mennonites, Alliance, Nazarenes	8
Other Faith Groups	
including Jews, Muslims, Buddhists,	
Hindus, Sikhs	6
Religious Nones	20

*A residual 5% or so, mostly Protestants, identify with varied groups that neither fall into any of these six categories nor collectively represent a family with compatible characteristics.

Source: Projection based on *Project Canada* and Statistics Canada data.

with churches after having been involved somewhere else.[1] They needed to be contacted; often no one called. It all added up to a bad misreading of what was happening.

Religious organizations should have known better. For some time they and academics who make a living from studying them had known well how they grow: the primary source of new additions is biological, in the form of family members. An example is a 52-year-old evangelical from Fredericton who playfully told us recently, "I started attending church nine months before I was born, have been carried to church, pushed to church, towed to church, and shoved to church. Now going to church is one of my favourite things."[2] The research is definitive: religious groups grow by growing their own. On national and international scales, growth also takes place through the recruitment of geographically mobile members, whether they arrive from Ontario or Saskatchewan, England or Asia. To the extent that groups recruit people outside their boundaries, the key factors are friendship and marriage—people on the inside befriend them or marry them. Frankly, for all the talk about outreach and evangelism, the research shows that "people from the outside" represent a very limited, bonus source of growth.[3]

This apparent "bad news" about the difficulty Canadian groups have experienced in recruiting outsiders had and continues to have a "good news" flip side with enormously important implications: well-established religious organizations do not lose many people to their competitors. Maybe the Canadian situation is unique, and maybe it's not. But the proverbial bottom line here is that, on the "demand side," Canadians are reluctant to try just any supplier. Most tenaciously stick with the choices of their parents and grandparents' traditions. In the last part of the 20th century, no new or old religious "company" made significant headway in moving in and recruiting Catholics and Protestants who, ostensibly, were no longer involved in their respective groups.[4] What's more, there is little indication that such a preference for the groups of their parents and grandparents is about to change.

Consequently, for well-established religious organizations that want to grow, the starting point should be obvious: they need to relate to those uninvolved Canadians with whom they have the greatest affinity—those millions of people who identify with their traditions, people who "think" they are Roman Catholic, United, Baptist, Lutheran, Jewish, and so on.

As obvious as such a point should have been, it was almost obliterated in recent decades by the debilitating myths of switching, drop-out, and non-receptivity. If these were merely issued to be debated at professional meetings by academics, it wouldn't matter. Unfortunately, however, these have been "very bad myths" because of the practical implica-

tions they have had for how leaders have carried out ministry—who, for example, they have targeted and what they have brought to them. To the extent that leaders have accepted the three myths, explicit strategies for finding affiliates and ministering to them have seldom been formulated and put into place. In the process, they have blown their competitive advantage. The myths that have led to this debacle are so distracting and unproductive that it's worth looking at them more closely.[5]

MYTH NO. 1: PEOPLE ARE SWITCHING

In recent years, some congregational experts and academics in North America—notably, Lyle Schaller and Robert Wuthnow—have led the way in propagating the idea that there has been a sharp decline in the importance being given to religious group loyalties. People are said to be abandoning allegiances to individual Protestant denominations and even to broader religious families such as Protestantism and Catholicism.[6] Congregational gurus tell us that North Americans who continue to want to participate in religious groups are commonly gravitating toward churches that are in touch with their needs, and they are showing little concern for denominational and religious family labels.[7] Such an alleged decline in religious group loyalties is seen as consistent with a more general decline in loyalty to institutions of all types over the last half of this century.[8] Themes such as freedom, inclusiveness, and the dismantling of boundaries are widespread. The saints are said to be circulating freely....

Consistent with what I have been saying, basic learning in sociology suggests there is little reason to expect that large amounts of prounounced religious switching will take place. In view of the pervasive tendency of children to identify with the religion of their parents, switching almost amounts to a form of deviant behaviour.... We all know that the prospect of ... intermarital "defection" is frequently greeted with a wide range of social controls, ranging from stigma to ostracism, particularly when the potential partner is a fair distance removed from one's religious "home."

The inclination to switch is also limited to the reality of cultural commonality. Most people attended services with some regularity when they were growing up. The majority turn to their identification groups when they require rites of passage, want to attend a seasonal service, or feel the need to expose their children to religious activities. That's why people see the religious cultures of their groups as normative. That's why they feel comfortable or uncomfortable in certain worship settings... prefer hymns and pipe organ to songs and a band, appreciate or feel disdain for a written prayer, feel reverence as they look at candles versus laser lights, kneel rather than stand, bow their heads versus raise their arms, pray silently or pray loudly. Culturally, it's a substantial stretch to move from a Jewish to a Pentecostal world—or even from a United to a Baptist world—and vice versa.

Our current emphases on inclusiveness and acceptance of religious diversity should not blind us to another ongoing reality: there are some people who are not interested in turning elsewhere for the simple reason that they favour their groups' versions of truth. So it is that an 82-year-old Catholic from rural Nova Scotia—who, incidentally, has participated in all of our *Project Canada* surveys dating back to 1975 when he was in his late 50s—told us that he was not comfortable going to a Protestant church, not because of bigotry but because "I cannot in good conscience take part in a non-Catholic service. I can go to a funeral of a friend, but I cannot participate in the service." His age notwithstanding, this candid individual is not alone.

As a result of such social and personal factors, there is little reason to believe that Canadians are open to being recruited by other groups, especially those with whom they have

few common theological and cultural ties. To the extent that switching occurs at all, it would be expected both to be limited and to follow fairly predictable lines of affinity. People would be expected to circulate primarily among "the religious families" of their parents.

But don't take my word for it. Let's listen to what Canadians have been saying.

Intergroup Switching

For all the rhetoric about evangelism, outreach, and seeker-sensitive ministries, Canadians who are not actively involved in churches (a) are seldom recruited by such aggressive "outside" groups and (b) if they do become involved, tend to become involved with groups with which they already identify.[9]

Our *Project Canada* surveys show that in the course of acquiring a religious identification, most people continue to more or less "inherit" the religion of their parents, with relatively few switching to other religious families.

• Approximately nine in ten *Catholics in Quebec* and eight in ten *Catholics in the rest of the country* identify with the religion of their parents. To the extent that they don't, the tendency is to say they have no religion.

• The same pattern characterizes some 80% of people from *Mainline Protestant* homes, as well as roughly 70% of Canadians whose parents identified with *Conservative Protestant* or *Other Faith* groups.

• To the extent that people with *Conservative Protestant* backgrounds switch, they tend to move into *Mainline Protestant* denominations.

• The *Religious None* category is characterized by a very high level of switching in and switching out. This category is more like a hotel than a home for many people.

This is not to say that religious switching never takes place. Obviously, some people cross family lines. But proportionately

---

Table 19.2 Extent and Nature of Intergenerational Switching, 2000

Respondent's Religion	RC	MLPROT	CPROT	OTHER	NONE
Mother's Religion					
RCs outside Quebec	80%	4%	1%	3%	12%
RCs in Quebec	89	<1	<1	1	9
Mainline Protestants	6	78	4	3	9
Conservative Protestants	<1	18	71	<1	11
Other Faiths	7	4	<1	71	18
No Religion	11	11	5	<1	73
Father's Religion					
RCs outside Quebec	80	7	<1	2	10
RCs in Quebec	91	<1	<1	<1	8
Mainline Protestants	4	82	4	2	8
Conservative Protestants	<1	14	76	<1	10
Other Faiths	8	4	<1	80	8
No Religion	20	13	4	5	58

Source: Bibby, Project Canada 2000.

Table 19.3 Intergenerational Identification by Religious Families: Panel, 1975 and 1995

			SWITCHED TO:				
1975 IDENTIFICATION	NUMBER	STAYED	MLPROT	CPROT	RC	OTHER	NONE
Mainline Protestant	196	88%		4	3	2	3
Conservative Protestant	31	83	11		<1	6	0
Roman Catholic	102	90	3	4		2	1
Other Faith	15	63	5	22	5		5
No Religion	19	39	33	<1	28	<1	
Totals*	363	85	4	4	3	2	2

*Identification data for 1975 or 1995 missing for 37 respondents.

Source: Bibby, 1999: 157.

---

speaking, switching is the exception rather than the norm, particularly among the largest religious families, Catholics and Mainliners....

In the 2000 *Project Canada* survey, we bluntly asked Canadians two questions pertaining to religious identification: *"How important is your religious tradition to you (that is, being Catholic, United, Buddhist, etc.)?"* and *"Are you open to the possibility of switching to a different tradition?"*

• Some six in ten Canadians who identify with a religious group say that their religious tradition is "very important" or "somewhat important" to them, including 92% of *weekly attenders* and 50% of those who attend less often. Variations between religious families tend to be fairly small.

• More than eight in ten people say they are not open to the possibility of switching to a different tradition, led by 97% of *Quebec*

Table 19.4	Importance of Tradition and Openness to Switching Traditions					
	NAT	RCOQ	RCQ	MLPROT	CPROT	OF
Tradition Important						
"Very" or "Somewhat"	61%	70%	62%	54%	72%	53%
Weekly attenders	92	96	96	93	85	*
Others attending less often	50	57	52	46	55	*
Open to Switching						
"No"	83	87	97	75	81	61
Weekly attenders	92	93	98	86	87	*
Others attending less often	80	83	97	72	72	*

*Numbers insufficient to permit stable percentaging.

Source: Bibby, Project Canada 2000.

Catholics. But here, differences by attendance are small: infrequent attenders are only moderately less likely to be closed to the idea of switching traditions—and in Quebec, there is no difference by attendance! As Ron Graham has observed about the legacy of Catholicism in Quebec, "Three centuries of mysticism do not evaporate in three decades of materialism."[10]

- Although the *Other Faith* sample is small, the preliminary evidence is that this is the category most vulnerable to "defections." Still, even here, resistance to switching characterizes the majority of people.

A Footnote for the Critics

Invariably, some people will say they know of exceptions to the rule. Of course, exceptions exist. I'm not saying that switching never occurs—only that it is relatively rare. And switching typically involves fairly short theological and cultural trips. As American sociologists Dean Hoge, Ben Johnson, and Don Luidens have pointed out, the size of our *tolerance zones* for acceptable religious traditions appears to exceed our personal *comfort zones* with those traditions. They noted in the case of Presbyterian Baby Boomers, for example, that

tolerance zones have expanded over the years, whereas personal comfort zones "are surprisingly narrow and traditional." "For the great majority," they wrote, "the comfort zone extends no farther than Mainline Protestantism, and quite a few draw the line at the Episcopal [Anglican] Church.[11] Sociologists Kirk Hadaway and Penny Marler have concluded that "when Americans do switch, they often remain within the same broad denominational family."[12] It's not that North Americans never switch groups: at least 40% of people in both Canada and the United States have switched denominations at one time or another.[13] However, as Hadaway and Marler have put it, "Americans switch more today than they did in the early 1970s, but when they switch they are more likely to remain in the same larger denominational family."[14]...

The same patterns of limited switching and switching within religious families appear to hold for Canada. The decline in active participation has not been associated with a widespread tendency for Canadians to move to other religious families, or to the No Religion category. In marketing language, the religious economy of Canada continues to be characterized by a very tight market, where the expansion of market shares through the recruitment of people from rival groups is extremely difficult. To the extent that

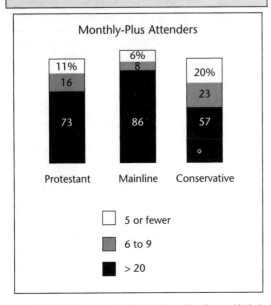

Figure 19.1 Years of Denominational Involvement

Monthly-Plus Attenders

	5 or fewer
	6 to 9
	> 20

Nearly 75% of Protestants, led by Mainliners, have been with their current denominations for more than 20 years. Taking age into account, Mainline Protestants on average have been involved with their current denominations for 80% of their lives, Conservatives for only 57%. Much of the Conservative switching between denominations, however, is within "the family," where choices outnumber those available to Mainliners.

Source: Bibby, Project Canada 2000.

switching does take place, it follows fairly predictable lines of affinity, frequently associated with the breaking down of family-related "social controls." But overall, the market is not particularly open; intergroup movement is very limited.

MYTH NO. 2: PEOPLE ARE DROPPING OUT

Closely related to the loyalty myth is the belief that if people are not attending on a regular basis, they have dropped out. Here it is assumed that identification without involvement simply doesn't count. If, for example, someone says that she or he is an "Anglican" or "Roman Catholic" or "Pentecostal" but seldom attends a service, such a self-designation is typically assumed to mean very little. In part, this is a theological assumption: if people are not involved, they have abandoned the faith. Policy-wise, such individuals are typically viewed by leaders as "unchurched" and, as such, are seen as "up for grabs" in the competitive religious marketplace. Officially, they are the prime targets of groups whose ministries are aimed at evangelism and service.

On the surface, the assumption that people have dropped out seems to be reasonable. If they aren't coming, they must have left. The assumption has led to common dichotomous classifications along the lines of "churched–unchurched," "active–inactive," and "practising–lapsed"—not to mention more pejorative dualities such as "saved–unsaved" and "saint–sinner." Even though this dropping-out myth is older, it has been reinforced by the more recent myth about loyalty decline. People are assumed to be dropping out in part because they have little group loyalty, and it is thought that where they attend next will not, in turn, be guided by group loyalty, but by a consumer-like response to the group that comes up with the most attractive and engaging offer.

Religious Identification

In contrast to radically declining attendance figures, religious identification in Canada stood at 88% in 1991 and at about 85% in 2000. But individuals who indicate that they have "no religion" tend to be disproportionately young. Research shows that such a situation is short-lived for many, who frequently re-adopt the religious group identification of their parents in the course of requesting and receiving religious rites of passage.[15] Their links to their parents' religious groups appear to be sustained not so much by religious content as by family history and these rites of passage.

What is perhaps rather remarkable is not that large numbers of North Americans *identify*

Table 19.5 Accuracy of the Religious Identification Statement: Canadians Identifying and Attending Less Than Monthly, 1985 and 2000

	NAT	RCOQ	RCQ	MLPROT	CPROT	OF
1985	87	84	94	88	86	74
2000	85	89	88	82	86	70

Source: Bibby, Project Can85 and Project Canada 2000.

but are not involved, but rather that they continue to *identify even though they are not involved*. They can be chastised, ignored, and removed from congregational lists—and they frequently are. But still, they don't really leave. Psychologically, emotionally, and culturally, they continue to identify with the traditions of their childhood.

The Meaning of Religious Identification

The *Project Canada* surveys have also asked respondents directly about their inclination to stay versus switching or dropping out, while probing the meaning of their ongoing involvement. Beginning with the 1985 national survey, respondents "not attending religious services regularly" were asked "how well" the following observation describes them:

Some observers maintain that few people are actually abandoning their religious traditions. Rather, they draw selective beliefs and practices, even if they do not attend services frequently. They are not about to be recruited by other religious groups. Their identification with their religious tradition is fairly solidly fixed, and it is to these groups that they will turn when confronted with marriage, death, and, frequently, birth.

Through 2000, about 85% of Canadians who *identify but attend less than monthly* have said that the statement describes them either "very accurately" or "somewhat accurately." Nationally, there has been little change since the mid-80s in the tendency of inactive attenders to acknowledge the accuracy of the description.

It adds up to a situation where, beyond the 20% or so Canadians who attend services almost every week or more, there are another 60%-plus who continue to identify with the country's dominant traditions. Most people in this latter category attend occasionally, believe and practise selectively, are not about to be recruited by alternatives, and are looking to their identification groups for rites of passage. They most definitely have not "dropped out."

As I mentioned at the outset of this chapter, the confusion over switchers and drop-outs involves far more than academic wrangling. It has critically important implications for how religious groups relate to Canadians. If groups see the religious market as essentially wide open, Americans and Canadians will be viewed as religious free agents who can be recruited through effective ministry and evangelism. The problem with such a viewpoint is that it will result in congregations wasting much of their recruitment resources. More seriously, Canadians who might benefit from good ministry will not be identified and pursued.

In contrast, if religious groups would concentrate less on the switcher and drop-out exceptions and more on "the on-going identification rule," they would be in a position to target the very people to whom they have the best chance of ministering—the women and men who already identify with them. Identification represents a measure of affinity; as such, it is the logical place to begin in connecting with people.

Given the pervasiveness of ongoing religious identification, congregations would

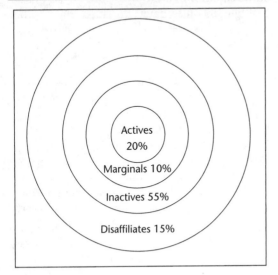

Figure 19.2 "Thinking Concentrically" about Religion Identification

Actives 20%

Marginals 10%

Inactives 55%

Disaffiliates 15%

Source: Bibby, 1995: 49.

be wise to follow Kirk Hadaway's lead in seeing their members and others who identify with their denomination as a series of concentric rings, ranging from active members at the centre through less active individuals to an outer ring of reactive people.[16] Working with such a model, congregations need to develop creative strategies for finding people, exploring their interests and needs, and responding—doing tangible things that I discuss in detail in my 1995 book *There's Got to Be More!*

MYTH NO. 3: PEOPLE ARE NOT RECEPTIVE

One of the most common observations I have heard over the years from religious leaders and from the media is that people "just aren't interested in organized religion anymore." Such a statement is a gross overgeneralization.

As mentioned briefly earlier in the context of Catholicism in Quebec, the latest *Project Canada* national surveys of adults and

teenagers have uncovered a finding that speaks volumes about the opportunity that is staring the country's religious groups in the face. In the adult survey, Canadians who attend services less than once a month were asked, *"Would you consider the possibility of being more involved in a religious group if you found it to be worthwhile for yourself or your family?"* The teen survey posed much the same question, asking young people to respond to the statement, *"I'd be open to more involvement with religious groups if I found it to be worthwhile."*[17] Keeping in mind that only 21% of adults and 22% of teens are currently weekly attenders, it's highly significant that 55% of adults and 39% of teens answered yes.

• Across adult religious families, the receptivity levels are about 55%, even among Quebec Catholics. What's more, one in three Canadians who say they have no religious affiliation maintain that they would be receptive to greater involvement in a religious group "if..."

• Among 15-to-19-year-olds, the receptivity levels are some 40% or more across groups, with about one in five teens with no religious

Table 19.6 Receptivity to Greater Inolvement: People Attending Less Than Monthly, 2000

	Adults	Teens
NATIONALLY	55%	39%
Roman Catholics	56	46
Quebec	55	41
Outside Quebec	56	51
Protestants	64	47
Mainline	63	44
Conservative	73*	55
Other Faiths	67*	4
No Religion	34	21

*Numbers only 16 and 33, respectively; percentages unstable. Included here for heuristic purposes.

Sources: Bibby, Project Canada 2000 and Project Teen Canada 2000.

affiliation saying they are open to more involvement.

Rather than acting either hostile or indifferent to their identification groups, significant numbers of people are obviously receptive to greater participation. The 55% figure for adults represents almost three times the number who indicate they are currently highly involved; the teen figure is almost double the proportion of young people who presently attend weekly.

- Those 55% of adults who say they would consider being more involved in the country's religious groups include some two in three of the people who attend several times a year to yearly; and one in three who say they never attend.

- They are most frequently found in the 18-to-34 and 35-to-44 age cohorts, with receptivity particularly common among younger Protestant adults.

- Males and females are equally likely to indicate that they are open to greater involvement, although there are some variations between groups....

These findings suggest that noteworthy numbers of Canadians are receptive to greater involvement in the country's religious groups. However, the findings also point to a critical qualifier: people have to find that such involvement is worthwhile for themselves and their families. The observation of a mother of three from Saskatchewan illustrates the hurdles that need to be overcome: "We don't attend often and when we do, it leaves much to be desired." The obvious, burning question is, "What do such people see as worthwhile?" A 66-year-old disenchanted Anglican from Vancouver provides us with a key clue: "Their role should be to minister to people who need them."...

One additional piece of information that has emerged from the national adult and youth surveys speaks not only to receptivity but also to accessibility. Canadians young and old are continuing to look to religious groups for rites of passage.

- Almost nine in ten teenagers indicate they anticipate turning to religious groups for future ceremonies relating to marriage and funerals, and seven in ten say the same in the case of births—a response very similar to levels in the mid-1980s.

Table 19.7 Receptivity to Greater Involvement by Select Variables, 2000

	NAT (764)	RCOQ (133)	RCQ (143)	PROT (270)	NONE (160)
TOTALS	57%	56%	55%	64%	34%
Yearly	64	64	57	72	48
Never	36	42	33	42	27
18–34	59	58	61	79	42
35–54	57	64	56	66	27
55+	49	*	52	55	23
Female	56	62	53	71	30
Male	56	57	61	58	39

*Numbers insufficient to permit stable percentaging.

Source: Bibby, Project Canada 2000.

Table 19.8   Desire for Rites of Passage in the Future

"In the future, do you anticipate having any of the following carried out for you by a minister, priest, rabbi, or some other religious figure?"

% Responding "Yes"	Wedding Ceremony	Birth-Related Ceremony	Funeral
Teenagers			
1980s*	87	76	87
2000	89	70	86
Adults			
1980s	19	14	44
2000	24	20	57

*1980s teen data computed from Project Teen Canada 87. "Don't know"s have been included with "no"s; otherwise the respective figures increase to 93%, 85%, and 93%.

Sources: Bibby, Project Teen Canada 2000, Project Can 85, and Project Canada 2000.

- In the case of adults, the levels of anticipated weddings, birth-related ceremonies, and funerals are all up, compared to the mid-80s.

As I have emphasized over the years, these Canadians' choices will not be random. The latent religious identification we have been documenting in this chapter will come to the surface during those times when couples are reflecting on what kind of wedding they want, what should "be done" now that the baby has arrived, or what kind of arrangements should be made for a relative's funeral. And it's not necessarily a case of just bowing to family pressures. Ministers frequently encounter people who, frankly, have little understanding of theology, yet have a sometimes vaguely articulated sense that "God needs to be brought in on the event."[18] With respect to accessibility, think what the desire for rites of passage means: religious groups will not have to go out and find these people; they will be taking the initiative in contacting groups. To put it mildly, such a position would be envied by any number of businesses in the corporate sector.

To sum up, the findings so far show that the "supply side" of religion, the country's churches, have not read the "demand side" very well. At least three major myths have functioned as serious obstacles to effective ministry. The fact that affiliates have refused to switch and haven't dropped out has been bewildering and frustrating to would-be religious competitors who have misread their market opportunity. But more seriously, because misinformed established groups have failed to understand their market advantage, significant numbers of affiliates who need ministry have not been reached by Canada's dominant religious groups....

NAVIGATING THE CONCEPTS

1. From the sociological perspective and with reference to Bibby's findings, how would you explain the apparent contradiction in the observation that few young people are participating in organized religions and yet churches continue to survive year after year?

2. Review and discuss Bibby's research that demonstrates the significant competitive advantages well-established churches have over new churches trying to establish themselves. Is there any evidence from your own community that would help confirm or deny the validity of Bibby's claim?

3. Given Bibby's research, do you believe that church attendance will increase or decrease over the next 25 years? Be sure to refer to the article as part of the justification for your answer.

NOTES

1. Bibby, 1997.

2. *Project Canada* Quota Sample, Winter, 2001–02.

3. For documentation, see Bibby, 1993: 29ff.

4. For a discussion of this failure, see Beyer, 1997: 284ff.

5. Much of the following material dealing with Myths No. 1 and No. 2 is based on Bibby, 1999.

6. See, for example, Schaller, 1987; Wuthnow, 1988; Mead, 1991; Posterski & Barker, 1993; Hoge, Johnson, & Luidens, 1994.

7. See, for example, Barna, 1991; Anderson, 1992; Easum, 1993; Schaller, 1995; Woods, 1996; Bandy, 1997.

8. Americans such as Robert Bellah (1985) and his associates have written that accelerated individualism has been severely threatening group life at all levels, while Allan Bloom (1987) similarly claimed that the individualistic and relativistic legacies of the 1960s have been devastating for relationships and disastrous for institutions. In Canada, Peter C. Newman (1995) maintains that nothing short of a revolution took place between the mid-1980s and 90s, characterized by Canadians moving from a mood of "deference to defiance" in virtually every area of life. I myself (1990) have similarly noted that individualism and relativism have functioned to severely fragment Canadian society, creating unity problems well beyond the threat of Quebec separation.

9. Bibby, 1993: 32, 36–37. According to observers such as Demerath and Yang (1997:5), the situation is similar in the United States as well.

10. Graham, 1990: 123.

11. Hoge, Johnson, & Luidens, 1994: 120.

12. Hadaway & Marler, 1993: 97.

13. Roof & McKinney, 1987: 167; Posterski & Barker, 1993: 51.

14. Hadaway & Marler, 1993: 102.

15. For details, see Bibby, 1993: 157–59.

16. Hadaway, 1990: 46.

17. The adult survey response options were "Yes," "Perhaps," and "No"; receptivity levels combine "Yes" and "Perhaps." In the youth survey, the options were "Strongly Agree," "Agree," "Disagree," and "Strongly Disagree," with receptivity levels being a combination of "Strongly Agree" and "Agree."

18. Bibby, 2001: 118, 197.

REFERENCES

Anderson, L. 1992. *A church for the 21st century.* Minneapolis: Bethany House.

Bandy, T. G. 1997. *Kicking habits: Welcome relief for addicted churches.* Nashville: Abingdon.

Barna, G. 1991. *User friendly churches.* Ventura, Calif.: Regal Books.

Bellah, R., R. Madsen, W. Sullivan, A. Swidler, and S. Tipton. 1985. *Habits of the heart.* New York: Harper and Row.

Beyer, P. 1997. Religious vitality in Canada. *Journal for the Scientific Study of Religion,* 36: 272–88.

Bibby, R. W. 1990. *Mosaic madness: Pluralism without a cause.* Toronto: Stoddart.

———. 1993. *Unknown gods: The ongoing story of religion in Canada.* Toronto: Stoddart.

———. 1997. Going, going, gone: The impact of geographical mobility on religious involvement. *Review of Religious Research,* 38: 289–307.

———. 1999. On boundaries, gates, and circulating saints: A longitudinal look at loyalty and loss. *Review of Religious Research,* 40: 149–64.

———. 2001. *Canada's teens: Today, yesterday, and tomorrow.* Toronto: Stoddart.

Bloom, A. 1987. *The closing of the American mind.* New York: Simon and Schuster.

Demerath, N. J. III, and Y. Yang. 1997. A religious change and changing religions: Who's switching where and why? Paper presented at the annual meeting of the SSSR, San Diego (November).

Easum, B. 1993. *Dancing with dinosaurs.* Nashville: Abingdon.

Graham, R. 1990. *God's dominion: A sceptic's quest.* Toronto: McClelland and Stewart.

Hadaway, C. K.1990. *What can we do about church dropouts?* Nashville: Abingdon.

Hadaway, C. K., and P. L. Marler. 1993. All in the family: Religious mobility in America. *Review of Religious Research,* 35: 97–116.

Hoge, D. R., B. Johnson, and D. A. Luidens. 1994. *Vanishing Boundaries.* Louisville, Ky.: Westminster/John Knox Press.

Mead, L. B. 1991. *The once and future church.* Washington, D.C.: The Alban Institute.

Newman, P. C. 1995. *The Canadian revolution: From deference to defiance.* Toronto: Viking.

Posterski, D. C., and I. Barker. 1993. *Where's a good church?* Winfield, B.C.: Wood Lake Books.

Roof, W. C., and W. McKinney. 1987. *American mainline religion.* New Brunswick, N.J.: Rutgers University Press.

Schaller, L. E. 1987. *It's a different world: The challenge of today's pastor.* Nashville: Abingdon.

———. 1995. *The new reformation: Tomorrow arrived yesterday.* Nashville: Abingdon.

Woods, C. J. 1996. *Congregational megatrends.* Betheseda, Md.: The Alban Institute.

Wuthnow, R. 1988. *The restructuring of American religion.* Princeton, N.J.: Princeton University Press.

PART 6

Urbanization/Globalization

Sociologists examine the forces influencing population movements and consider how global economic and technological changes are altering the very nature of our lives.

Chapter 20

Canada's Rural Population: Trends in Space and Implications in Place

Christopher Bryant and Alun E. Joseph

Source: Reprinted with permission from *The Canadian Geographer,* Vol. 45: 1, 2001, article by Bryant, C. and Joseph, A. E.

In this article, Christopher Bryant and Alun E. Joseph describe the major demographic factors that have shaped rural Canada over the past 20 years. Their exploration uncovers many interesting trends that will continue to influence the population geography of rural Canada.

In 1951, over 38 percent of Canada's population was classified "rural," of which 52 percent lived on farms (Joseph et al., 1988). Nearly 50 years later, the figures are 16 percent and 19 percent respectively (Bourne & Rose, 2001). Rural Canada has moved from a position of national centrality to one of marginality as Canada has urbanized (Troughton, 1995). Complex economic, social, political and technological changes have been ongoing. In this paper, we describe the major demographic processes shaping "rural Canada," especially over the last 20 years. Macro and micro scale processes are strongly linked, so we complement our demographic trends analysis by considering implications for the experience of rural life "in place" and for public policy.

The paper is organized in four sections. First, we describe broad rural population trends. Second, we address population aging and migration, two defining demographic processes for rural Canada. Third, we consider the intersection of economic, social and political processes with demographic trends and discuss how they affect people's lives.

Examples illustrate the importance of understanding the backdrop of institutional restructuring and opportunities for local involvement, especially in terms of the contemporary challenge of sustainability in rural Canada. Finally, we reconsider "diversity" and speculate about the future population geography of rural Canada.

DEFINITIONS, TRENDS AND TYPOLOGIES

Canada's rural population is defined as that which is "not urban," and "rural non-farm" as "rural" minus "farm." Measuring rural population trends is difficult; "urban" and "rural farm" definitions have changed and municipal boundary changes create significant reclassification effects (Keddie & Joseph, 1991a). These problems pale, however, compared to that of the statistical isolation of dispersed farm and non-farm populations from rural service centres when nucleated settlements of 1000 or more are classified as urban. Therefore, we also refer to "rural and small town Canada" (RST Canada), i.e., towns of 1,000–9,999 people, plus the "census rural" population. RST Canada's population share declined from 36 percent in 1971 to 22 percent in 1996. Large inter-provincial variations exist, from 27 percent (Ontario) to 77 percent (PEI) in 1971, and 15 percent (Ontario) to 56 percent (Newfoundland and Labrador) in 1996 (Mendelson & Bollman, 1998), but over six million Canadians still live in RST Canada despite continued metropolitan growth.

Defining "rural" as a residual category paints a homogeneous picture of "rural." Nothing could be further from the truth. Nonetheless, we retain the "rural as residual" approach, addressing the heterogeneity of "rural" through regional commentaries.

Two fundamental trends have affected rural space over the last 50 years: the expansion of the broad area of countryside under urban influence (the urban field) (Dahms, 1998; Bryant et al., 2000); and the decoupling of rural communities from their service centre roles in regions of primary production (Everitt & Annis, 1992; Beesley & Bowles, 1993; Smithers & Joseph, 1999). Two opposing patterns emerged: a meso scale explosion (the urban field); and a macro scale implosion (metropolitan region concentration) (Bryant et al., 1982). These trends have been associated with various functional shifts (Paquette & Domon, 1999), e.g., tourism expansion (Fennell & Weaver, 1997; Dahms & McComb, 1999). In turn, these are reflected in a transformation of rural livelihoods (Fuller & Nichol, 1998) linked to increasing access to metropolitan populations, information and technology (Millward, 1992; Stabler & Olfert, 1994).

These various forces of change have created spatial diversity in rural Canada. Here we focus on the emergence of distinct rural realms. The development of pronounced spatial differentiation can be traced to the 1930s and 1940s, when rural Canada lost its demographic dominance (Joseph & Smit, 1981). Several typologies describe the general outcomes, e.g.,

Bollman's (1994) *(Urban Frontier, Rural Nirvana, Agro-rural, Rural Enclave, Resource Areas* and *Native North)* and Joseph et al.'s (1988) *(Urban Core, Rural Hinterland* and *Remote Hinterland).* Proximity to cities is the defining characteristic of both. Thus, the apparent resurgence of rural population in the 1970s was largely confined to areas adjacent to Census Metropolitan Areas and Census Agglomerations (Keddie & Joseph, 1991b). Subsequent studies have analyzed regional (Davies, 1991; Akwawua, 1999) and local (Joseph & Smit, 1985) dimensions of this countryside re-population.

The coarse differentiation of geographic space into the urban countryside, rural and remote hinterlands provide[s] three distinctive, albeit overlapping sets of policy challenges, discussed below.

MIGRATION AND POPULATION AGING

Migration is the main mechanism through which regional and local populations adjust to changing economic and social circumstances. In rural areas near cities, the process of "dispersed urbanization" (Bryant et al., 1982) or "metropolitan dispersal" (Dahms & McComb, 1999) is reflected in net in-migration to many communities (Beesley & Walker, 1990; Thomson & Mitchell, 1998). Such areas contrast with rural and remote hinterlands still dominated by primary production, where out-migration remains common. In RST Canada, the exodus of rural youth is a recurring theme (Fellegi, 1996), and the "boom-bust" syndrome creates volatility in net migration patterns in remote hinterland towns (Halseth, 1999). The implications for the reconstitution of communities are profound.

Rural population flows are part of a broader, urban-focused whole (Bourne & Rose, 2001), e.g., exurban flows into the "city's countryside" (Bryant et al., 2000). Similarly, in the rural hinterland urban-based, amenity-driven migration flows, especially at retirement, are overlain upon local population flows (Joseph & Hollett, 1992; Dahms, 1996; Bryant, 1999a). The net result of all these flows, with their common focus on small town destinations, is significant population aging in many places (Joseph & Martin-Matthews, 1993). In some regions, aging is even more pronounced in particular population segments, e.g., the Eastern Townships' rural anglophone population (Table Communautaire, 2000).

Moore and Rosenberg (2001) set out the major structural and geographical characteristics of population aging in Canada. Advanced population aging is a defining characteristic of nucleated communities in Canada's rural hinterland. Indeed, in a subset of rural towns, those aged 65 or older constitute over 20 percent of the total, and in some over 30 percent (Hodge, 1991; Joseph & Martin-Matthews, 1993; Everitt, 1996). Partly related to out-migration of younger cohorts, it also invariably reflects the cumulative impact of migration by older cohorts, e.g., rural people seeking housing and services (Joseph & Hollett, 1992) or inter-regional migrants seeking amenity and similar housing and services as local migrants (Dahms, 1996; Everitt & Gfellner, 1996). Concerns about the individual and group dynamics of "growing old in aging communities" (Joseph & Cloutier, 1991; Joseph & Martin-Matthews, 1993) have increased in recent years with progressive restructuring of rural services, especially home-based support for older elderly people (Cloutier-Fisher & Joseph, 2000).

To integrate migration and population aging themes and to link with the discussion of the community "face" of rural population change in the next section, we consider recent trends in several Ontario and Quebec communities. The townships of McKillop, Huron County, and Mono, Dufferin County, provide contrasting examples of dispersed rural settlements, while the town of Harriston and

the village of Erin, Wellington County, provide the same for nucleated settlements. McKillop's population declined by 7.2 percent 1991 to 1996, while Mono's increased by 13.3 percent. Both are relatively youthful, with a 1996 elderly population of 9.5 percent and 8.6 percent respectively. They are also similar in that racial minorities constitute less than 1 percent and less than 3 percent of their respective populations. In contrast, they differ considerably in terms of primary sector employment (32.5% in McKillop versus 5.3% in Mono) and average housing values ($122,835 in McKillop versus $265,972 in Mono).

Harriston's population grew by less than 1 percent 1991 to 1996, while Erin's increased by 5.8 percent. Members of visible minorities account for less than 1 percent of total population in both communities. Harriston displays significant population aging (22.1%) relative to Erin (7.6%). These contrasting age profiles partly reflect in-flows of older people, but they also reflect youth out-migration: in Harriston, the 20–24 cohort in 1996 was only 63 percent of the 15–19 cohort in 1991, while in Erin it was 85.5 percent. These flows, in turn, reflect employment opportunities; Harriston had less of its workforce in secondary activities in 1996 than did Erin (87.1% versus 27.3%). Contrasts are also evident in average house prices ($101,137 in Harriston versus $167,740 in Erin).

The "face" of rural resource hinterlands has also experienced substantial change. In Quebec, the Charlevoix MRC (Municipalité régionale de comté) east of Quebec City on the St. Lawrence north shore has long experienced out-migration and population aging. Sixty percent of the active population is employed seasonally and the 1996 unemployment rate was 16.1 percent. Furthermore, 20 percent of the population lives below the poverty threshold and education levels are among the lowest in the province. As another example,

Rocher-Percé (Pabok) MRC on the Gaspé Peninsula is literally on the "periphery of the periphery." Out-migration is persistent, and its population continues to decrease (by 6.4% 1991 to 1996) and age. Unemployment is rife (30.2% 1996), and schooling and incomes are low. In both cases, economic restructuring in traditional economic sectors has contributed to out-migration, exacerbated by cumulative destabilization of services in areas where rural population density is low and very dispersed.

In contrast, Saint-Sauveur and adjacent communities north of Montreal in the Laurentian foothills constitute a recreational and tourism destination, especially for the "regional tourist" (Bryant & Buffat, 1999). Being only a 30 minute drive from Montreal, the scenic attractiveness of the surrounding hills and the picturesque nature of Saint-Sauveur village have also attracted a substantial influx of residents, including both retirees and commuters to Montreal. These illustrations highlight the socio-economic and socio-demographic diversity of rural population structures in particular places. Mono and Erin are both within Toronto's labour shed. A combination of recreational development and an influx of commuters and retirees have shaped Saint-Sauveur village. McKillop is a relict agricultural community. Harriston, a one-time service centre, is now emerging as a retirement community. Charlevoix is a remote area with a declining traditional economic base; a growing tourism industry has not yet produced a complete reversal in fortunes. Finally, Pabok, despite superb scenic resources, has suffered from a narrow, vulnerable economic base. In 1997, three firms accounted for 82 percent of this MRC's employment. In the forest products sector, Gaspésia Ltée, the regional economy's cornerstone, closed in 1999. With this level of vulnerability, even successful growth in other sectors cannot restore employment and generate stability in the short-to-medium term.

COMMUNITY IMPACTS AND IMPLICATIONS

The broad scale processes of population migration and aging are related to the restructuring of economic activity (e.g., corporate restructuring, technological change) and services (e.g., health care), changing household values (e.g., living standards, family size), and expansion of metropolitan employment opportunities (Bourne & Rose, 2001). They combine in different ways in different contexts; witness the changing faces of communities in the city's countryside, the agricultural hinterlands and the remoter resource hinterlands. The mosaic of structures and change is even more pronounced at the community level. The general patterns are real, but so are the changes being constructed in communities by local actors, through both "natural" and planned decisions (Bryant, 1997; Bryant & Buffat, 1999).

The broad geographic contexts are associated with sets of partially overlapping public policy challenges. All face certain common challenges, such as the provincial level re-organization of many public or quasi-public services in response to changing population needs and cost efficiency objectives. Challenges also vary. In the city's countryside, many services (e.g., education, health care, garbage pick-up and libraries) remain dynamic because populations have stabilized, although providing adequate services to a seasonally expanded population in cottage country may still prove difficult (Bryant, 1999a). In stark contrast, the situation is often severe for farm communities and service centres in the agricultural hinterland, and even more chronic in many remote resource hinterlands, where many essential services have been jeopardized by low and declining populations. School re-organizations, the loss of postal outlets, and the re-organization of religious life (e.g., the part-time priest) are just some of the hardships that have had to be endured.

The fortunes of commercial services (retailing, restaurants) are similar. In the city's countryside, new populations have often permitted market threshold populations to be maintained. Sometimes, this stability is reinforced by "regional tourists" who come from nearby urban centres to purchase goods and services in a "rural small town" setting. Examples exist around all major centres, e.g., Saint-Sauveur north of Montreal and St. Jacobs near Waterloo in southwest Ontario. Again, in agricultural and resource hinterlands, the situation is frequently very difficult, and compounded by the trend towards consolidation of certain services in fewer centres.

For the agricultural and resource hinterlands, the overall pattern of stagnation and cumulative decline is a familiar one, reflecting the deteriorating levels of job opportunities and investment that fuel out-migration. Youth also leave these communities because of lack of higher education opportunities. The exodus of youth is also a withdrawal of potential entrepreneurial resources, particularly given the importance of small and medium sized businesses in the country's economy in the past quarter century (Bryant, 1997). Once again, the situation for many rural communities in the city's countryside is much rosier, although marked differences abound even there.

Even when a rural community appears prosperous, the potential for decline is there. Prosperity can mask considerable vulnerability, economically and socially. Saucan (1999) constructed an Index of Fragility for Quebec's "most rural" regions (MRCs with over 70% of their population classed "rural" 1996). These 28 MRCs (only 23 in 1991) represented 8 percent (122,061 km²) of the area and 8.8 percent (652,229) of the population of Quebec in 1996. The most fragile rural areas included Charlevoix and Pabok. Small populations with narrowly based primary activities have had difficulties maintaining services, retaining youth and spawning new businesses. Apart from significant potential

tourism resources, primary activities vulnerable to depletion or restructuring still occupy a key place in their economic base.

The repercussions socially have been devastating for many: high unemployment; loss of purchasing power; low self-confidence; low solidarity; unwillingness to mobilize; and a dismal track record of failed development programs. In some communities, democratic processes have been eroded, as people give up and opt out. Nonetheless, within this dismal general picture of the hinterlands, and even within the communities depicted as experiencing stagnation and decline, there is some optimism. First, increased attention and emphasis in the last quarter century has been given to local development and control, as central states (federal and provincial governments) have (depending upon the observer's interpretation) withdrawn, reduced or redefined their involvement in managing the economy and society (Bryant, 1997; 1999b). This more explicit attempt by local populations and actors to engage in actually constructing—rather re-constructing—their communities, has actually been present for much longer. It has just not been recognized for its contribution. One could argue that without those past efforts, many rural communities would be in even more difficult situations than they are today. The substantial change is that this effort—increasingly known as sustainable community development—has been recognized and central states have tried to harness local energies. A prime example is the Community Futures program across Canada since the mid-1980s.

CONCLUSIONS

Rural population change in Canada can be described by two major demographic processes, migration and aging. Migration is related to patterns of job opportunity and differentials between urban and metropolitan space and rural space. Aging is related to changing values associated with family size, quality of life, and employment participation by different population segments and life opportunities generally. The macro scale migration process has fueled urban and metropolitan concentration at the expense of many rural areas. In contrast, meso scale processes of urban field development have often compensated for restructuring impacts of traditional rural economic activity as different population segments have infiltrated the countryside (Dahms, 1998; Bryant et al., 2000).

At the micro scale, however, where all processes are juxtaposed, intersect and interact, inter-community differences abound, yielding a remarkable mosaic of structures and dynamics. Local actors and populations have played a not insignificant role in constructing rural space from the start; today, they are being called upon even more to engage in active community re-construction. Central states in Canada have seen in this process a partial solution for managing their own budgetary resources as well as filling the gap that traditional central state regional development programs have been unable to fill.

Significant challenges exist, both for rural communities and central states. First, creating and maintaining adequate service levels requires major efforts in creating employment opportunities. Identifying these and supporting them will require a more creative and open approach to planning and managing change. Such an approach requires an open, transparent democratic process at the community level. The largest obstacle within many communities is the unwillingness of "leaders" to share their "power" even though they would benefit from the creativity and inventiveness of their populations. In many communities, a "culture shift" will be necessary.

Second, important roles still exist for provincial and federal governments. They concern relatively novel functions, such as supporting community capacity building for managing change, recognizing local leadership and creativity and not thwarting innovative change. Programs such as Community Futures in its early years contained the seeds for such innovative, support-oriented public policies and programs for rural areas. Given the great variety of rural spaces and communities, the major challenge is to develop federal and provincial policies that reflect the desire for standards (in terms of services and processes) while simultaneously recognizing the specificities of each locality and the legitimate concerns of citizens for participation. The roots of the geographic patterns that will evolve over the next fifty years are already present today, but considerable uncertainties exist regarding the evolution of technology and values. Probably the only certainty is that tomorrow's rural Canada will be more than ever a mosaic of spaces and places with different population compositions and dynamics.

NAVIGATING THE CONCEPTS

1. From the sociological perspective, how might the experiences of children growing up in a large city differ from those of children growing up in a small town? Do you think that where you grow up influences the adult you become? If so, how; if not, why?

2. In our increasingly complex world, do you sense that some people are attracted to returning to a "simple" life? If so, why do you think they are feeling this way?

3. As a sociologist, do you feel Canadian society will "lose something" if our small rural communities continue to face increasing hardships to retain young people?

REFERENCES

Akwawua, S. 1999. Changing patterns of core-periphery migration in Canada 1961–1991. *Prairie Perspectives*, 2: 1–16.

Beesley, K. B., and R. T. Bowles. 1993. Metropolitan—non metropolitan variations in agriculture and population change. *Rural studies working paper no. 1.* Truro, N.S.: Department of Humanities, Agricultural College.

Beesley, K. B., and G. E. Walker. 1990. Residence paths and community perception: A case study from the Toronto urban field. *Canadian Geographer,* 34, 318–30.

Bollman, R. 1994. A preliminary typology of rural Canada. In *Towards sustainable rural communities,* ed. J. Bryden, 141–44. Guelph, ON: University School of Rural Planning and Development.

Bourne, L., and D. Rose. 2001. The changing face of Canada: The uneven geographies of population and social change. *Canadian Geographer,* 45(1): 105–19.

Bryant, C. R. 1997. The management of processes of change in Canada's small towns and villages. In *Challenge and opportunity: Managing change in Canadian towns and villages,* publication series 48, eds. C. Mitchell, and F. Dahms, 1–28. Waterloo, ON: Department of Geography, University of Waterloo.

———. 1999a. Community-based strategic planning, mobilisation and action at the edge of the urban field: The case of Haliburton County. In *Progress in research on sustainable rural systems,* série estudos 2, eds I. Bowler, C. R. Bryant, and A. Firmino, 211–22. Lisbon: Universidade Nova de Lisboa, Centro de Estudos de Geografia e Planeamento Regional.

———. 1999b. Community change in context. In *Sustainable development series,* vol. 2. *Community perspectives on sustainable development,* eds. A. Dale and J. Pierce, 69–89. Vancouver: Sustainable Development Research Institute, University of British Columbia.

Bryant, C. R., and K. Buffat. 1999. Local development processes in transforming the urban fringe: The case of Saint Sauveur-des-Monts. *Proceedings: New England–St. Lawrence Valley Geographical Society,* 28: 23–31.

Bryant, C. R., P. M. Coppack, and C. Mitchell. 2000. The city's countryside. In *The Canadian city in transition, 2nd ed.: The twenty-first century,* eds. T. Bunting and R. Filion, 333–54. London: Oxford University Press.

Bryant, C. R., L. Russwurm, and A. McLellan. 1982. *The city's countryside.* Harlow, Essex: Longman.

Cloutier-Fisher, D., and A. E. Joseph. 2000. Long-term care restructuring in rural Ontario: Retrieving community service user and provider narratives. *Social Science and Medicine,* 50: 1037–45.

Dahms, F. A. 1996. The greying of south Georgian Bay. *Canadian Geographer,* 40: 148–64.

———. 1998. Settlement evolution in the Arena Society in the urban field. *Journal of Rural Studies,* 14: 299–320.

Dahms, F., and J. McComb. 1999. Counterurbanization, interaction and functional change in a rural amenity area—a Canadian example. *Journal of Rural Studies,* 15: 129–46.

Davies, W. K. 1991. What population turnaround? Some Canadian Prairie settlement perspectives 1971–1986. *Geoforum,* 21: 303–20.

Everitt, J. 1996. A tale of two towns: The geography of aging in southern Manitoba. *Small Town,* 24: 4–11.

Everitt, J., and R. Annis. 1992. The sustainability of Prairie rural communities. In *Contemporary rural systems in transition,* vol. 2, eds. I. Bowler, C. Bryant, and D. Nellis, 213–22. Wallingford, U.K.: CAB International.

Everitt, J., and B. Gfellner. 1996. Elderly mobility in a rural area: The example of southwest Manitoba. *Canadian Geographer,* 40, 338–51.

Fellegi, I. P. 1996. *Understanding rural Canada: Structures and trends.* **http://www. statcan.ca.** Accessed June 2000.

Fennell, D. A., and D. B. Weaver. 1997. Vacation farms and ecotourism in Saskatchewan, Canada. *Journal of Rural Studies,* 13: 467–75.

Fuller, A., and P. Nichol. 1998. *Dynamics of the new rural economy. A workbook of research from Huron County.* School of Rural Planning and Development, University of Guelph.

Halseth, G. 1999. We came for the work: Situating employment migration in B.C.'s small resource-based communities. *Canadian Geographer,* 43. 363–81.

Hodge, G. 1991. *Seniors in small town British Columbia: Demographic tendencies and trends 1961 to 1986.* Burnaby, B.C.: Gerontology Research Centre, Simon Fraser University.

Joseph, A. E., and D. Cloutier. 1991. Elderly migration and its implications for service provision in rural communities: An Ontario perspective. *Journal of Rural Studies,* 7: 433–44.

Joseph, A. E., and G. Hollett. 1992. When I'm 65: The retirement housing preferences of the rural elderly. *Canadian Journal of Regional Science,* 15: 1–19.

Joseph, A. E., P. D. Keddie, and B. Smit. 1988. Unraveling the population turnaround in rural Canada, *Canadian Geographer,* 32: 17–30.

Joseph, A. E., and A. Martin-Matthews. 1993. Growing old in aging communities. *Journal of Canadian Studies,* 28: 14–29.

Joseph, A. E., and B. Smit. 1981. Implications of ex-urban residential development: A review. *Canadian Journal of Regional Science,* 4: 227–24.

———. 1985. Rural residential development and municipal service provision: A Canadian case study. *Journal of Rural Studies,* 1: 321–37.

Keddie, P. D., and A. E. Joseph. 1991a. Reclassification and rural-versus-urban population change in Canada 1976–1981: A tale of two definitions. *Canadian Geographer,* 35, 412–20.

———. 1991b. The turnaround of the turnaround? Rural population change in Canada 1976 to 1986. *Canadian Geographer,* 35: 367–79.

Mendelson, R., and R. Bollman. 1998. *Rural and small town population is growing in the 1990s.* Statistics Canada agricultural division working paper 36. Ottawa: Statistics Canada.

Millward, H. 1992. Public access in the Canadian countryside: A comparative study. *Canadian Geographer,* 36: 30–44.

Moore, E., and M. Rosenberg. 2001. Canada's elderly population: The challenges of diversity. *Canadian Geographer,* 45(1): 145–50.

Paquette, S., and G. Domon. 1999. Agricultural trajectories (1961–1991), resulting agricultural profiles and current sociodemographic profiles of rural communities in southern Quebec (Canada): A typological outline. *Journal of Rural Studies,* 15: 279–95.

Saucan, R. D. 1999. Le développement durable et les zones rurales fragiles au Québec. Master's thesis. Département de Géographie, Université de Montréal.

Smithers, J. A., and A. E. Joseph. 1999. Agricultural and rural community change in Ontario: Understanding complementarity and conflict. In *Sustaining agriculture in the 21st century. Proceedings of the 4th biennial meeting of the International Farming Systems Association,* eds. J. Ogilvie, J. A. Smithers, and E. Wall, 265–74. Guelph, ON: University of Guelph.

Stabler, J. C., and M. R. Olfert. 1994. Saskatchewan's rural communities in an urbanizing world. *Rural Development Perspectives,* 9: 21–27.

Table Communautaire. 2000. *Perspectives de développement économique communautaire.* Huntingdon, Que: Table communautaire du Comité national de développement des ressources humaines pour la communauté minoritaire anglophone.

Thomson, M. L., and C. J. Mitchell. 1998. Residents of the urban-field: A study of Wilmot Township, Ontario, Canada. *Journal of Rural Studies,* 14: 185–201.

Troughton, M. J. 1995. Rural Canada and Canadian rural geography: An appraisal. *Canadian Geographer,* 39: 290–305.

Chapter 21

Africville: The Life and Death of a Canadian Black Community

Donald H. Clairmont and Dennis William Magill

Source: From Clairmont, Donald H., and Magill, Dennis W. (1999). Africville: *The Life and Death of a Canadian Black Community,* Third Edition (pp. 1–19). Toronto: Canadian Scholars' Press. Reprinted by permission of Canadian Scholars' Press Inc.

Donald H. Clairmont and Dennis William Magill review the effects of an urban redevelopment program that relocated 80 black families in Halifax during the 1960s. The program was intended to promote humanitarian ideals, but the experience of Africville demonstrates the many problems associated with forced relocation programs.

To seek social change, without due recognition of the manifest and latent functions performed by the social organization undergoing change, is to indulge in social ritual rather than social engineering.[1]
— *Robert K. Merton*

Halifax, the foundation city of English-speaking Canada, experienced much change during its first two hundred years of existence. Yet the facelift and redevelopment it has undergone since the late 1950s have effected a change as dramatic as the 1917 explosion that levelled much of the city. Stimulated by the Stephenson Report of 1957,[2] urban renewal and redevelopment have resulted in the relocation of thousands of people, the demolition of hundreds of buildings, and the construction of impressive business and governmental complexes. The Africville relocation was part of the larger redevelopment pattern; Africville residents constituted some eight to ten percent of the people affected by approved urban renewal schemes in the city of Halifax during the relocation years.

Africville was a black community within the city of Halifax, inhabited by approximately four hundred people, comprising eighty families, many of whom were descended from settlers who had moved there over a century ago. Tucked away in a corner of the city, relatively invisible, and thought of as a "shack town," Africville was a depressed community both in physical and in socioeconomic terms. Its dwellings were located beside the city dump, and railroad tracks cut across the one dirt road leading into the area. Sewerage, lighting, and other public services were conspicuously absent. The people had little education, very low incomes, and many were underemployed. Property claims were in chaos. Only a handful of families could establish legal title; others claimed squatter rights; and still others rented. Africville, long a black mark against society, had been designated for future industrial and harbour development. Many observers reported that despite these liabilities there was a strong sense of community and that some residents expressed satisfaction with living in Africville.

In 1964 the small black ghetto of Africville began to be phased out of existence. By that time most residents of Halifax, black and white, had come to think of Africville as "the slum by the dump." Most Haligonians, including some Africville residents, did not regard the community as viable and recognized a need for planned social change. The relocation plan announced by the city of Halifax, which purported to be more than simply a real estate operation, appeared to be a response to this need. The plan emphasized humanitarian concern, included employment and education programs, and referred to the creation of new opportunities for the people of Africville. To the general public, the proposed relocation was a progressive step.

In addition to official pronouncements, there were other indications that the Africville program would be more humane and progressive than the typical North American urban relocation. Halifax city council had adopted recommendations contained in a report submitted by a noted Canadian welfare specialist experienced in urban renewal. There was much preliminary discussion of the relocation by city officials among themselves, with Africville residents, and with a "caretaker" group of black and white professionals associated with the Halifax Human Rights Advisory Committee. Relocation plans were not *ad hoc* and haphazard. City officials were required to articulate their policies well and in detail; many implications and alternatives were considered.

There were also indications in the relocation decision-making structure that the Africville program might realize its official rhetoric. A social worker was appointed by the city to take front-line responsibility for the varied aspects of the relocation and to act as liaison between the city administration and the relocatees. The social worker, who was on loan from the Nova Scotia Department of Public Welfare, had a measure of autonomy vis-à-vis the city and an independent contingency fund to meet day-to-day emergencies and opportunities with a minimum of bureaucratic delay. In negotiating the real estate aspects of relocation, the social worker brought proposed agreements before a special advisory committee consisting of aldermen and several members of the Halifax Human Rights Advisory Committee.

In terms of its rationale, public rhetoric, and organizational structure, the Africville relocation seemed worthy of study. The plan was *liberal-oriented* (that is, aimed at ending segregation and providing improved opportunities for the disadvantaged), *welfare-oriented* (that is, it hoped to coordinate employment, educational, and rehabilitative programs with the rehousing of people), and run by experts (that is, the planning, execution, and advice were provided by professionals). An examination of the Africville relocation could be expected to yield greater fundamental insight into planned social change than would a study of typical relocation programs that were accomplished by administrative fiat and stressed primarily the physical removal of persons. It seemed important to study and evaluate the Africville relocation both in its particularity and against the background of general relocation issues.

There were additional reasons for studying the Africville relocation. First, Africville was part of a trend in the 1960s for governmental initiative in relocation programs, and there was reason to expect that other tentative relocations in Nova Scotia and elsewhere would be patterned after the Africville experience. Second, Africville had attracted national and even international notice, and there was broad public interest in the relocation. Third, accounts of pre-relocation social conditions and attitudes were available. Two surveys had been conducted[3] and other material was available in city records. Finally, in 1968 the Africville relocation had already been acclaimed locally as a success. One city alderman noted:

The social significance of the Africville program is already beginning to show positive results as far as individual families are concerned. The children are performing more satisfactorily in school and they seem to take more of an interest in their new surroundings. This report is not intended to indicate that the program has been 100 percent successful; however I believe it can be said that it has been at least 75 percent, judging by the comments of the relocated families.[4]

Private communication with city officials and relocation officials in the United States and Canada brought forth praise for the organization and rhetoric of the Africville relocation.

Was the Africville relocation a success? If so, from whose perspective? To what extent? What accounted for the success or lack of it? It is hoped that answers to these and related questions will contribute to an appreciation of the Africville relocation and of relocation generally.

THE RELOCATION PHENOMENON

Relocation must be seen in the context of a general North American mobility pattern, and certain distinctive features should be noted. The most important distinction is that relocation is part of planned social change carried out, or at least approved, by public agency. The initiation of relocation, as seen by the relocatees, is usually involuntary and an immediate function of the political process. Our present concern is with relocation as it pertains to private residences, involves neighbourhoods or communities, and is a function of comprehensive programs of social change. This kind of relocation accounts for but a small measure of the mobility noted in Canada and the United States, but it was

significant because it was distinctive. It was noted earlier that the Africville relocation was itself part of a much larger redevelopment project in the city of Halifax. In terms of the sweep of lifestyle change, even such large urban projects have been dwarfed by post–Second World War Canadian relocation projects in the Arctic and in Newfoundland. In 1953, Newfoundland, with 6000 miles of coastline and approximately 1150 settlements, undertook a program to move people from the small outposts to larger viable communities which could be serviced efficiently. Between 1965 and 1970 over 3250 households were moved.[5]

As many low-income Americans and Canadians can testify, urban renewal is a prime example of forced relocation. Urban renewal legislation began in the 1940s in both countries. By 1968 approximately forty-five Canadian urban redevelopments had been initiated at a cost of 270 million dollars for 1500 cleared acres.[6] While the scope of urban renewal in Canada was quite small in the light of American experience, the Canadian program was significant enough that one can complain that there were too few Canadian studies looking into the politics, issues, and human consequences of renewal programs. To overcome this lack of knowledge and to place the Africville relocation in perspective, more comprehensive themes will be discussed in this [selection].

From a political-administrative perspective there are four relocation models: the traditional, development, liberal-welfare, and political. The Africville project is the best Canadian example of the liberal-welfare type of relocation.... [T]hese models vary along six dimensions: (1) ideological premises; (2) formulation of policy; (3) implementation of policy; (4) intended beneficiaries; (5) central actors and organizational units; and (6) key problems. These models are ideal types to which actual relocation programs correspond to a greater or lesser degree.

THE DEVELOPMENT MODEL

The development model was the most prevalent political-administrative approach to relocation in North America. This type of relocation was usually justified in terms of supposed benefits for the system as a whole, whether the system is society, the city, etc. It was usually initiated by order of political authorities and administered by bureaucrats; it was not anticipated that relocatees would benefit other than indirectly. The underlying ideology of the development model was system-oriented and neo-capitalist; an accurate statement of its premise in urban renewal has been offered by Wallace: "[it considers] renewal, as a public activity, to be intervention in a market and competitive system and to be justified by the need to make up for imperfections in the market mechanism that impede the adjustment process, to eliminate conditions which are economic or social liabilities."[7] In the context of contemporary urban renewal, the development model incorporated the usual city-design approach, focusing on questions of beautification, zoning, and structure,[8] and was usually intended to increase the city tax base and achieve civic pride or attract industry.

The development model can be illustrated by past urban renewal programs in Toronto. Ignoring relocatees as viable interest groups the programs operated implicitly on the basis of certain ideological premises: to correct imperfections in the social system (removal of so-called slums) and overall system development (economic growth), or both. As is the case in many Canadian cities, Toronto's past development policy was closely linked to the businesses and commercial-property industry which provided homes, apartment buildings, shopping centres, and industrial complexes. Thus the elimination of "blight areas" and construction of highrise apartment and office buildings generated an important source of urban revenue. Referring to this policy of "dollar planning," Fraser observed:

As long as Toronto [in 1972], like all other municipalities in Canada has to depend upon property taxes as its sole source of income, the overwhelming power of development interests in determining the direction and quality of Toronto's growth will remain unchallenged.

...[T]he key to a municipality's prosperity remains its rate of growth; Toronto planners have been consistently ignored by city councils that have been over the years almost exclusively uninterested in any discussions about the quality of that development.[9]

A non-urban example of the development model of relocation has been described by John Matthiasson, in his study of the forced relocation of a band of Cree Indians in Northern Manitoba. The Cree were relocated to make way for a gigantic power project; they were not involved in the project planning and despite their displeasure "they accepted in a fatalistic manner the announcement of the relocation. They believed that the decision had been made by higher authorities, and that they had neither the right nor power to question it."[10]

The development model of relocation had its limitations. In particular, its econocentric and "undemocratic" features were criticized. The assumption that relocatees benefit indirectly from relocation was challenged, as was the premise that the system as a whole somehow redistributed fairly the benefits accruing from forcing people to move and facilitating the development of private industry. Some critics argued that if one included social-psychological factors in one's conception of costs, the relocatees could be seen as subsidizing the rest of the system. The criticism had some effect, and the liberal-welfare model became increasingly common.[11] One official explained:

In the fifteen years since [urban renewal's] inception, we have seen a progressive broadening of the concept and a strengthening of tools. We have seen, increasingly, both the need for, and realization of, rapprochement between physical and social planning, between renewal and social action. But the fully effective liaison of the two approaches has almost everywhere been frustrated by the absence of the tools to deal as effectively with the problems of human beings as with the problems of physical decay and blight.[12]

Another writer has observed,

social welfare can no longer be treated as the responsibility of private and more or less bountiful ladies and gentlemen or as the less respected branch of the social welfare community and the city government. Tied as it is to the concerns as dear to the heart of the country as economic prosperity it merits a place in the inner sanctum, particularly of planning commissions.[13]

THE LIBERAL-WELFARE MODEL

The "rediscovery" of poverty,[14] the war on poverty, the increasing pressure "from below" upon the development model, and the broadening definition of urban renewal led to the widespread emergence of the liberal-welfare-oriented approach. The liberal-welfare model, like the development model, emphasized expertise and technical knowledge in its operation and administration, and invariably was initiated by public authority. The principal difference is that the liberal-welfare model purported to benefit the relocatees primarily and directly. Under this model, welfare officials often saw themselves as "caretakers" for the relocatees; one relocation official has said, "the department of relocation is the tenants' advocate."[15] The liberal-welfare model of relocation was characterized by a host of social welfare programs supplemental to housing policies and was regarded as an opportunity for a multifaceted attack on poverty and other problems. It was this liberal-welfare model and its assumptions that shaped the rhetoric underlying the 1963–64 decision to relocate Africville.

Ideologically, the liberal-welfare model was much like the development model in that it tended to operate with a consensus model of society and posited a basic congruency between the interests of relocatees and those of society as a whole, it was "undemocratic" in the same sense as the development model; the low-status relocatees were accorded little attention, either as participants in the implicit political process or as contributions to specific policies or plans of action. There was an effort, however, to persuade rather than to ignore the relocatees. Criticism of the liberal-welfare model of relocation was related primarily to the ideological level. Some writers noted that liberal welfarism had become part of the establishment of contemporary North American society.[16] Its proponents were presumed to be handmaidens of strong vested interests, reconciling the disadvantaged and patching up the symptoms of social malaise. Critics pointed out that the special programs associated with the liberal-welfare model of relocation tended to be short-term and unsuccessful. The welfare rhetoric often diverted attention from the gains and benefits accruing to the middle-income and elite groups in society. The critics attacked the liberal-welfare model on the premise that the social problems to which it is ostensibly directed could be solved only through profound structural change effecting a redistribution of resources, and by providing relocatees with the consciousness and resources to restructure their own lives.

The liberal-welfare model is best illustrated by the Africville relocation.... The community of Africville was defined as a social problem, and relocation was regarded as an intervention strategy designed to help solve the "social and economic problems of Africville residents." The central actors in the formation and implementation of relocation policy were politicians, bureaucrats, experts, and middle-class caretakers; there was no meaningful collective participation by Africville residents. The relocatees were to be major beneficiaries through compensation, welfare payments, and rehabilitative retraining programs. The major problem with the relocation was that, although rooted in liberal-welfare rhetoric, it failed to achieve its manifest goals.

THE POLITICAL MODEL

The liberal-welfare model of relocation was revised and developed both as a response to criticism at the ideological level and in reaction to its lack of operational success. There was a growing interest in citizen participation in all phases of relocation; in the firmer acceptance, structurally and culturally, of the advocacy function of relocation officials; in the coordination of relocation services; and in the provision of resources. It is difficult to assess how far this interest has been translated into fact. There appeared to be a shift in the 1970s, at least conceptually, to the political model of relocation and a frank recognition that relocation usually entailed a conflict of interest, for example, between the relocatees and the city. There was an attempt to structure the conflict by providing relocatees with resources to develop a parallel structure to that of the government. Although society and the relocatee were considered to benefit equally, this political perspective assumed that relocatees benefited both directly and indirectly; directly in terms of, say, housing and other welfare services, and indirectly by participating in the basic decision-making and the determination of their life situation. The political model of relocation was based on the premise that social problems were political problems and emphasized solutions through political action; relocation was approached primarily as a situation in which problems were solved not by the application of expertise but by the resolution of conflicting interests.

Beyond the considerable costs (the dollar cost is less hidden than in the other relocation model) and administrative difficulties entailed, there were other grounds for criticism of the political model. There was a tendency to overemphasize the solidarity and common interests of relocatees, to exaggerate the multiplying effects of political participation in relocation,[17] and to raise serious questions about how far government could proceed or would proceed in fostering extra-parliamentary political action.

Citizen participation, a core element in the political model, was institutionalized in the United States by the community action programs of the 1964 Economic Opportunity Act. Numerous books and articles, far too many to cite, have discussed the reasons, operations, and failures of "maximum feasible participation" of the poor in the war on poverty.[18] Citizen participation was also part of the United States model city programs, which required that local residents be involved in the planning process and implementation of changes in their neighbourhoods. Contrasted with the United States, Canada has relatively few examples of related social-animation projects. The rise of "militant" citizen groups was a phenomenon which developed later in Canada. The public outcry against the community work of the Company of Young Canadians and the subsequent governmental intervention to close this organization may be an indication of the limits of this perspective. The only Canadian publication illustrating the political model of a relocation is Fraser's study of Toronto's Trefann Court. Trefann Court residents successfully fought off a development-type relocation project; subsequently, the conflict arising from different interests was recognized as an integral part of the city's social organization. Despite internal community conflict between homeowners and tenants, a number of community residents, leaning heavily on outside: "resource people," developed a cohesive organization and set up a working committee (a parallel structure) to establish a conceptual scheme for community change in conjunction with the existing city bureaucracy. The Trefann Court case also pointed to a key problem in the political model, that of assessing the representativeness of any one group of citizens to speak, argue, or vote for an entire community. With the establishment of "parallel structures," many citizens grow frustrated with the tedious detail involved in committee work. In Fraser's words:

The fact that the Working Committee operated under formal rules of order, dominated by minutes, reports, rules of procedure and legislative decorum widened the gap between the committee and the community. As debates became more lengthy, detailed and technical, the meetings became harder to follow for the ordinary Trefann resident who might drop in.[19]

THE TRADITIONAL MODEL

Finally, there is the traditional model of relocation in North American society. This is a limiting type of relocation carried out under governmental auspices, for it is a form of planned social change characterized by self-help and self-direction. It is the neighbourhood or community leaders, often indigenous minority-group leaders working through indigenous social organizations, who plan and carry out the relocation, generally with official support and some resource commitment by government agencies. The traditional model entails a largely laissez-faire strategy whereby the relocatees benefit directly and technical expertise is used to advise rather than to direct. Criticism of this approach contends that, without political action, neither the available resources nor the generation of initiative can be effective in the case of low-status groups.

There are numerous examples of the traditional model of relocation. Group settlement and resettlement in various parts of Canada have been common. The relocation of Beechville, a black community on the outskirts of Halifax, is an example within the Halifax metropolitan area. Community leaders, anticipating a government attempt to relocate the residents, organized themselves into a co-operative housing association, received

funds from Central Mortgage and Housing Corporation, and reorganized their community partly on their own terms. The scope available for traditional relocation models lessens as society becomes more technocratic and centralized.

CONCEPTUAL FRAMEWORK

...[O]ur emphasis will be on the liberal-welfare model of planned social change and its implementation during the Africville relocation. During the analysis we focus on questions of power and exchange among the various participants of the relocation. Thus, from the perspective of power and exchange,[20] we can examine the power resources and relationships among the individual persons and groups involved in the relocation, the historical evolution of these social facts, the goals held by the different parties, and the strategies and tactics employed in establishing the terms of the relocation "contract." We can also analyse the role of outsiders, experts, and community "leaders" and focus on questions such as the mobilization of advocacy, relocation resistances and alternatives, and the relation of rhetoric to action. It is vital in the Africville case to have a larger historical view, observing the historical exchange patterns between the city and the Africville people and tracing the implications of these patterns in making Africville "ripe for relocation" and in influencing the relocation decision-making and mechanics.

An aspect of this perspective concerns the context of negotiations and the bargaining strategies developed by the parties involved. Accordingly, attention was devoted to probing the relocatees' knowledge about the relocation; their strategies (use of lawyers, co-operation with fellow relocatees, and development of special arguments in dealing with city officials), and their perceptions of the city's goals, strategies, and resources. The relocation social worker completed a questionnaire concerning each re   mily which paid considerable attenti   negotiations with relocatees and his p   .ion of their goals, strategies, and resc   .es. This perspective included the concept .f rewards, costs, profits, and distributive just 'e. It would appear, for instance, that relocatees would have been satisfied with the relocation if rewards exceeded costs and if they thought that the city and other relocatees would not "get a better deal." Information concerning rewards, costs, sense of distributive justice, and satisfaction was obtained through the questionnaires, the interviews, and the case studies.

Despite problems in measuring each relocatee's perception of the relative profit accruing to himself or herself, other relocatees, and the city of Halifax, and problems occasioned by differences between long-term and short-term effects, this power and exchange approach is significant for the relocation literature which often appears to keep aloof from the "blood and guts" of relocation transaction. Equally important, by placing the Africville relocation within a typology of relocation models, it is possible to explore the domain consensus (that is, the basic terms of reference held in common and prerequisite to any exchange) associated with the liberal-welfare approach, and especially how such domain consensus (for example, "disadvantaged communities or people have few intrinsically valuable resources and need to be guided by sympathetic experts") develops and how it sets the limits and context of bargaining and reciprocity.

RESEARCH STRATEGIES

The methods employed in this study were varied: questionnaires, in-depth interviews, historical documents, newspapers, case studies, and "bull sessions" with relocatees. A useful baseline source of data was the survey of Halifax blacks, including Africville [residents],

conducted in 1959 by the Institute of Public Affairs, Dalhousie University. The original questionnaires were available for re-analysis, an important consideration since many of the data were not published and the published material contained several significant inaccuracies.[21] The 1959 survey questionnaire provided basic demographic data as well as information concerning mobility aspirations, employment, education, and social life.

The collection of data for this study began in 1968. The researchers arranged for two students from the Maritime School of Social Work to prepare twenty case studies.[22] A review of the students' case studies and field notes, guided by the perspective developed by the researchers, aided the drafting of a questionnaire. In 1968 current addresses of the relocatees were also traced and brief acquaintance interviews were conducted.

The most intensive data collection period was June to December 1969. One of the researchers (D.W.M.) conducted in-depth, tape-recorded interviews with individual people associated with the relocation decision-making and implementation: politicians, city officials, middle-class caretakers, the relocation social worker, consultants, and Africville relocatees involved in the decision-making. During these interviews an open-ended interview guide[23] was used to explore knowledge of Africville and awareness of pre-1964 relocation attempts and also the actual relocation decision-making and mechanics. Each of the approximately two-hour interviews was transcribed and analysed for patterns. Many quotations used in this book are taken from these tape-recorded interviews.

Concurrently, the other researcher (D.H.C.), with two assistants, was meeting informally with the relocatees, individually and in "bull sessions." On the basis of these experiences and the case studies, we all drafted and pretested an extensive questionnaire. From September to December, 1969, the questionnaire was employed by interviewers hired and trained by the researchers. The lengthy questionnaire[24] asked about the relocatee's background characteristics: life in Africville, personal knowledge of relocation decision-making processes, relocation strategies, nego-tiations, costs, rewards, and post-relocation conditions. The questionnaire was given to all household heads and spouses who had lived in Africville and had received a relocation settlement of any kind. Approximately 140 persons were interviewed, several in places as far distant as Winnipeg and Toronto.

In June, 1969, the relocation social worker spent eight days answering a questionnaire[25] on the relocatees' background characteristics, his relocation bargaining with each relocatee, and his perception of the latter's rewards, costs, and strategies. Such data enabled us to analyse more precisely the relationships among parties to the relocation, for similar data from the relocatees and their perception of the reloca-tion social worker were obtained from the relocatee questionnaire.

Two other research tactics were employed at the same time as the interviews were con-ducted. One of our assistants was conducting in-depth, tape-recorded interviews with black leaders in the Halifax area concerning their assessment of Africville and the implications of relocation. Another assistant was gathering historical data and interviewing selected Africville relocatees concerning the historical development of the community. Important sources of historical data were the minutes of Halifax City Council (read from 1852 to 1969), reports of the Board of Halifax School Commissioners, the Nova Scotia Public Archives, files in the Registry of Deeds, the Halifax *Mail-Star* library, and the minutes of the Halifax Human Rights Advisory Commit-tee. In all phases of research, the Africville files in the Social Planning Department, City of Halifax were of special value.

PHASES OF THE AFRICVILLE STUDY

The Africville Relocation Report, in addition to being an examination of relocation and planned social change and a contribution to the sparse literature on blacks in Nova Scotia, represents a fusion of research and action. The researchers did not begin the study until virtually all the Africville people had been relocated, and the research strategy resulted in the study being more than an evaluation.[26] The process of obtaining collective as well as individual responses, and of establishing a meaningful exchange with relocatees, fostered collective action from former Africville resi-dents. Some local government officials objected to what they have referred to as the researchers' "activist" bias. The researchers maintain, how-ever, that exchanges had to be worked out with the subjects of research as well as with the funding agencies. The liberal ethic posits informed voluntary consent as fundamental to adult social interaction; informed voluntary consent requires, in turn, meaningful exchange among the participants.

The study began in October, 1968 with a meeting of relocated Africville people. This was the first time since relocation that former residents of Africville had met collectively. This stormy meeting, called by the researchers, was a public airing of relocatee grievances and led to relocatee support of the proposed study. Subsequent talk of forming committees to press grievances with the city of Halifax was an important result of the meeting. The research-ers encouraged this tendency, for the expressed grievances appeared legitimate, and the researchers considered that it would be both possible and important to tap a collective or group dimension in the relocation process as well as to study the usual social-psychological considerations.

Later in the same week, at a meeting that the researchers had arranged with city officials, relocation caretakers, and civic leaders, the researchers related the expressed grievances of the relocatees and urged remedial action. General support for the proposed study was obtained at this second meeting, and the pending reconsideration of relocation by the city's newly created Social Planning Department was crystallized.

During the winter and spring of 1969, as the present study was being planned in detail, the action-stimulus of the researchers' early efforts was bearing fruit. Social Planning Department officials were meeting with the relocatees and, as it were, planning the second phase (not initially called for) of the Africville relocation. With provincial and municipal grants totalling seventy thousand dollars, the Seaview Credit Union was organized to assist relocatees experiencing financial crises; in addition, plans were formulated to meet housing and employment needs, and special consideration was to be given to former Africville residents whose needs could be met within the city's existing welfare system. A relocatee was hired to manage the credit union and to assist with other anticipated programs.

During the main data-gathering period, the summer of 1969, and in line with a decision to obtain collective as well as individual responses, the researchers met with informed groups of Africville relocatees to discuss current and future remedial action, it became apparent that the so-called second phase of the relocation would be inadequate to meet the people's needs. There was little identification with the credit union and it was floundering, for many relocatees who became members were either unable or unwilling to repay loans. Other anticipated programs and action promised by the city were delayed or forgotten due to bureaucratic entanglements and to lack of organization and pressure on the part of the relocatees.

The relocatees still had legitimate grievances related to unkept promises made at the time of relocation and later. With the formation of the Africville Action Committee, a third phase of the relocation began in the fall of 1969 and winter of 1970. The task of this new committee, developed from group discussions held between the researchers and relocatees, was to effect governmental redress through organized pressure. Several position papers were developed by the Africville Action Committee and negotiations were reopened with the city of Halifax. Although numerous meetings of relocatees were held during the first half of 1970, problems within the Africville Action Committee and the absence of resource people until the fall of 1970 hindered progress. With the committee stumbling along, and the credit union and other city-sponsored projects either ineffectual or nonexistent, the relocation process appeared to have petered out. The action committee was reactivated when one of the authors (D.H.C.) returned to Halifax permanently in the fall of 1970 and groups of relocatees were subsequently reinvolved in reading and criticizing a draft of the present study and in evaluating the relocation and the remedial action taken. Since the fall of 1970, the Africville Action Committee was active. Widespread support for its claims was obtained from community organizations, subcommittees were established to deal with questions of employment, housing, and financial compensation; and city council authorized the establishment of a city negotiating team to meet with representatives of the action committee.

In 1974, at the time of publication of the first edition [of the book from which this chapter is excerpted], the Africville Action Committee, to all intents and purposes, had ceased to function. Although it could claim some credit for a special employment train-ing program through which a number of unemployed Africville relocatees had found jobs, the action committee fell far short of its goals.

The city's lack of a positive imaginative response and the internal organizational problems of the action committee hindered other proposals. What remained in 1974 was a reorganized credit union, a modest base for further redress and group action. However, by 1999 the Seaview Credit Union was no longer in existence; it had collapsed over two decades ago. However, the community is not dead.... Africville still thrives in the hearts and minds of many of the relocatees. In addition, Africville still has rich symbolic value for fostering black consciousness in Nova Scotia.

POSTSCRIPT

Throughout the study, we consciously and deliberately attempted to achieve a viable fusion of research and social responsibility. The research focussed on the collective responses of the group as well as on individual responses. At each stage in the study (conception, data gathering, data analysis, and preparation for publication) the collective and individual inputs that gave the study an action potential were obtained from relocatees. Drafts of appropriate chapters were sent for critical comment to officials and others involved in the relocation. The study became a stimulus to action because the normal researcher-subject exchanges could be worked out in concrete, actual terms. This was preferable to the usual research situation where, in effecting exchanges with the people being studied, the researcher typically makes vague references to the possible benefit of the study and does little or nothing to follow up implied promises of action.[27] But of course, our research strategy has its weakness too. It is difficult to feel satisfied that the kind of exchange relations that we established had productive consequences. Despite our involvement (in the early 1970s) with petitions, committee work, and attempts at rational problem solving, little redress of the inadequacies of the relocation program was achieved and the manifest

goals of the liberal-welfare rhetoric of the relocation remain, in large measure, unrealized.

NAVIGATING THE CONCEPTS

1. Have there been any relocation/revitalization programs in your own community? If so, which relocation model appears to have provided the justification for the move? Are the people who were relocated still in the community today?

2. With reference to the article, when, if ever, do you feel forced relocation programs are justified?

3. What role, if any, do you feel that racial discrimination played in the Africville relocation program? Discuss.

NOTES

1. *Social Theory and Social Structure* (Glencoe, Ill.: The Free Press, 1949), p. 80.

2. Gordon Stephenson, *A Redevelopment Study of Halifax, Nova Scotia* (Halifax, N.S.: City of Halifax, 1957).

3. *The Condition of the Negroes of Halifax City, Nova Scotia* (Halifax: Institute of Public Affairs, Dalhousie University, 1962); and G. Brand, *Interdepartmental Committee on Human Rights: Survey Reports* (Halifax, N.S.: Nova Scotia Department of Welfare, Social Development Division, 1963).

4. Minutes of the Halifax City Council, Halifax, N.S., September 14, 1967.

5. The Government of Newfoundland initiated the program in 1953. In 1965 a joint federal-provincial program was initiated under a resettlement act. In 1970 the program was placed under the direction of the Federal Department of Regional Economic Expansion. For an overview of the resettlement program, see Noel Iverson and D. Ralph Matthews, *Communities In Decline: An Examination of Household Resettlement in Newfoundland*, Newfoundland Social and Economic Studies, No. 6, (St. John's, Nfld.: Memorial University of Newfoundland, Institute of Social and Economic Research, 1968). For a critical assessment of studies of the resettlement program, see Jim Lotz, "Resettlement and Social Change in Newfoundland," The *Canadian Review of Sociology and Anthropology* 8 (February, 1971): 48–59.

6. See Table 4, "Completed Redevelopment Projects" in *Urban Renewal* (Toronto: Centre for Urban and Community Studies, University of Toronto, 1968). Reprinted from *University of Toronto Law Journal*, 18. No. 3 (1968): 243.

7. David A. Wallace, "The Conceptualizing of Urban Renewal," *Urban Renewal* (Toronto: Centre for Urban and Community Studies, University of Toronto, 1968), 251.

8. An example of such a project is one reported by Thurz in southwest Washington, D.C. Little was done for the relocatees, but the relocation was widely acclaimed for its futuristic redevelopment design. For a critique of this approach, see Daniel Thurz, *Where Are They Now? (*Washington, D.C.: Health and Welfare Council of the National Capital Area, 1966). See also Jane Jacobs, *The Death and Life of Great American Cities* (New York: Random House, 1961).

9. Graham Fraser, *Fighting Back: Urban Renewal in Trefann Court* (Toronto: Hakkert, 1972), p. 55.

10. John Matthiasson, "Forced Relocation: An Evaluative Case Study," paper presented at the annual meeting of the Canadian Sociology and Anthropology Association, Winnipeg, 1970.

11. In recent years some minor progressive modifications have been introduced with reference to the development model; these deal with advance notice and public hearings, relocation compensation, and the availability of housing stock. See, Robert P. Groberg, *Centralized Relocation* (Washington, D.C.: National Association of Housing and Redevelopment Officials, 1969).

12. William L. Slayton, "Poverty and Urban Renewal," quoted in Hans B. C. Spiegel, "Human Considerations in Urban Renewal," *Urban Renewal,* op. cit., 311.

13. Elizabeth Wood, "Social Welfare Planning," quoted in Spiegel, op. cit., 315.

14. For a discussion of this, see Kenneth Craig, "Sociologists and Motivating Strategies," M.A. thesis, University of Guelph, Department of Sociology, 1971.

15. Groberg, op. cit., p. 172.

16. See Alvin W. Gouldner, *The Coming Crisis of Western Sociology* (New York: Basic Books, 1970), pp. 500–02.

17. Relocation is a short-term consideration, for most services brought to bear on relocatee problems rarely extend beyond rehousing. A more general critique of the multiplying effect of citizens' involvement in relocation is given by S. M. Miller and Frank Riessman, *Social Class and Social Policy* (New York: Basic Books Inc., 1968).

18. The historical antecedents and reasons for the legislation are discussed in Daniel Moynihan, *Maximum Feasible Misunderstanding* (New York: Free Press, 1970). For an alternative interpretation, see Francis Fox Piven and Richard A. Cloward, *Regulating the Poor: The Functions of Public Welfare* (New York: Random Vintage Books, 1972), pp. 248–84. The operation of the program is discussed by Ralph M. Kramer, *Participation of the Poor: Comparative Community Case Studies in the War on Poverty* (Englewood Cliffs, N.J.: Prentice Hall, 1969).

19. Fraser, op. cit., p. 262.

20. For a discussion of this theoretical perspective, see Peter M. Blau, *Exchange and Power in Social Life* (New York: Wiley, 1964); and George Caspar Homans, *Social Behavior: Its Elementary Forms* (New York: Harcourt, Brace and World, 1961).

21. *The Condition of the Negroes of Halifax City,* Nova Scotia, op. cit.

22. Sarah M. Beaton, "Effects of Relocation: A Study of Ten Families Relocated from Africville, Halifax, Nova Scotia," Master of Social Work Thesis, Maritime School of Social Work, Halifax, N.S., 1969; and Bernard MacDougall, "Urban Relocation of Africville Residents," Master of Social Work Thesis, Maritime School of Social Work, Halifax, N.S., 1969.

23. The interview guide is published in Donald H. Clairmont and Dennis W. Magill, *Africville Relocation Report* (Halifax, N.S.: Institute of Public Affairs, Dalhousie University, 1971), pp. A131–A135.

24. Ibid., pp. A97–A128.

25. Ibid., pp. A83–A96.

26. Some relocation studies have been carried out as part of the relocation decision-making, see William H. Key, *When People Are Forced to Move* (Topeka, Kansas: Menninger Foundation, 1967), mimeographed, others have been concurrent with the relocating of people, see Herbert J. Gans, *The Urban Villagers: Group and Class in The Life of Italian Americans* (New York: The Free Press, 1962). The present study is unique in that it fostered collective action carried out after the relocation.

27. See Craig, op. cit.

Chapter 22

The Information Age: Apartheid, Cultural Imperialism, or Global Village?

R. Alan Hedley

Source: Hedley, R. Alan. (1999). The information age: Apartheid, cultural imperialism, or global village? *Social Science Computer Review,* 17(1): 78–87. Reprinted by permission of Sage Publications, Inc.

R. Alan Hedley examines the impact of the information revolution on the developed nations in the North and the developing nations in the South. His analysis of the information revolution demonstrates some potential for new technology to encourage dialogue on economic development issues, but it also reveals that the benefits are mainly felt in the developed nations of the North.

INTRODUCTION

The concept of development does not have a long history. It dates back to the industrial revolution, which first produced global differences among the peoples of the world in terms of socioeconomic development. The most profound result of this revolution was the huge gain in human productivity, which in turn significantly raised individual income (Hedley, 1992, pp. 63–97). Between 1801 and 1901, total national income in Britain increased more than 600% (Mitchell, 1962, p. 366). By 1870, workers in industrial nations earned 11 times more than their counterparts in nonindustrial countries. Moreover, the advantages of industrialization have been cumulative: Today, as we embark on the so-called information revolution, per capita income is 52 times greater in developed than less developed countries (World Bank, 1995,

p. 53), thus magnifying what one author has termed a *Global Rift* (Stavrianos, 1981).

The term *sustainable development* is even more recent. It gained widespread currency as a result of the report produced by the World Commission on Environment and Development (1987). Established in 1983 by the United Nations due to the growing realization that "the development paths of the industrialized nations are clearly unsustainable" (p. xii), the Brundtland Commission defined sustainable development as "development that meets the needs of the present without compromising the ability of future generations to meet their own needs" (p. 43). According to Michael Jacobs (1991, pp. 60–61), the "core meaning" of sustainable development as defined by the Brundtland Commission involves three key elements: (a) the necessity of considering the biosphere in making

Author's Note: This article is a revised version of a presentation that was given at the 14th International Conference of the World Association for Case Method Research and Application, Madrid, 1997.

economic policy, (b) commitment to more equitable distribution of economic and natural resources to present as well as future generations, and (c) concern for nonfinancial aspects of human welfare in the determination of development (e.g., health and education).

We are thus learning that to ensure the development of humankind and, indeed, to safeguard our very existence on this planet, we must heed the environmental context in which development occurs, distribute the products of human labor and the Earth's resources more equitably now and in the future, and modify our values to emphasize the quality of human life. In this article, I focus on two of these aspects of sustainable development—the distribution of resources and the quality of life. Specifically, I examine the structure of the emerging information revolution and assess what implications it has for reducing the gap between rich and poor nations, providing greater balance among cultures, and improving the quality of life for all peoples.

THE INFORMATION REVOLUTION

Marc Porat (1977) made one of the first efforts to define and measure the information economy. Using the Standard Industrial Classification Codes, Porat found that information goods and services accounted for approximately half of both gross national product and employment in the United States in 1967. However, Porat's classification grouped both modern and traditional information activities. Most of the industries he identified either predated the original industrial revolution (e.g., real estate, insurance, banking, law, accounting, and architecture) or grew out of the transportation and communication revolution occurring at the turn of the 20th century (e.g., publishing, telephone, radio, and photographic and motion picture industries).

Consequently, Porat simply reconfigured the existing economy to emphasize its information component. Although this is a legitimate endeavor, as it illustrates a general transformation from physical to intellectual activities, it does not reveal the direct impact of the modern information revolution. Porat's analytical strategy, and others like it (Bell, 1976), adopt an inclusive view of an information society.

A more exclusive approach focuses on that part of the economy that emerged directly as a result of the microelectronic revolution of the late 1960s (Gilder, 1989). For the purposes of this article, information technology refers primarily to computer hardware, components, software, services, and also the new telecommunications infrastructure essential to computer networking. The Organisation for Economic Co-operation and Development (OECD, 1996, p. 3) adopts a similar approach in defining the information sector. Although admittedly conservative in its specification of what to include and exclude in the information revolution, this strategy offers two definite advantages: (a) It permits a clear analytical distinction between "old" and "new" information technology, and (b) it provides an explicit empirical base for comparative research.

A major problem in measuring the modern information revolution is that economic and labor force data are classified into traditional industrial categories. Thus, although we can identify the manufacturing component of this technological innovation in terms of computers produced and numbers employed in producing them, it is next to impossible to measure the applications of this innovation within the economy. These data are hidden throughout all the standard industrial and occupational codes. As a result, we are limited to those applications specifically identified as computer services. Commenting on this problem, a *Business Week* article notes that "government statistics track goods and jobs, not flows of information... [which] means... [there is] a large and vibrant 'ghost economy' that traditional economic indicators don't measure" (Mandel, 1994, p. 26). Consequently, the actual impact of computers in the world economy is vastly underreported. However, until data are organized into categories more indicative of the microelectronic transformation, this is the only reliable way to measure it.

Table 22.1 presents a number of dimensions that reflect what an information revolution entails. For example, there must be a discernible body of information workers who are organized in some fashion to produce innovative goods and services. In turn, this requires infrastructural support. Finally, to the extent that a revolution does take place, its effects should be noticeable in the larger society. Table 22.1 specifies each of these dimensions along with available empirical indicators that can be used to measure them. Employing these multidimensional empirical indicators, a researcher could conceivably collect cross-national data over time to plot both individual and aggregate change. These data would permit estimates to be made of information and communications technology (ICT) development both within countries over time and comparatively between nations (or world regions) at particular points in time. This kind of research design would provide the necessary empirical foundation for more careful analyses of the worldwide effects and impact of ICT.

Applying the empirical indicators in Table 22.1, we may conclude that the information revolution is still very much in its beginning stages and is limited primarily to the developed countries. Just five G-7 nations (United States, Japan, Germany, France, and United Kingdom) accounted for 80% of the information technology market in 1994, and American and Japanese corporations dominate the industry (OECD, 1996, pp. 7, 37). By July 1996, developed countries had 201 personal computers per 1,000 people compared to only

6.2 per 1,000 in the rest of the world (World Bank, 1997, p. 286). Analysis of the Internet, the worldwide network of personal computers connected to host computers, indicates that it is overwhelmingly American based, English speaking, and Western focused. In January 1997, 63% of the estimated 16.15 million host computers connected to the Internet were in the United States, 74% in English-speaking nations, and fully 90% of the Internet operated out of Western countries (Network Wizards, 1997). To date, despite claims to the contrary, the nascent yet burgeoning information revolution is not a worldwide phenomenon.

These data hold few surprises. Similar to the previous two industrial revolutions, the information revolution has its origins in the West. However, because it is just beginning, it does not necessarily have to follow the same trajectory. Although the information revolution could well exacerbate existing economic and cultural fault lines, thus widening the global rift between North and South, it also offers the possibility of a truly interconnected global village. In the following section, I examine these possibilities, paying particular attention to the concept of sustainable development.

THREE DEVELOPMENT SCENARIOS

1. *Apartheid.* Left to grow unchecked in the global marketplace, the information revolution will more than likely solidify and reinforce existing cleavages. Indeed, a current world map displaying the location of the four largest computer networks (including the Internet) divides the world along the same North-South axis originally drawn in the 1980 Brandt Report (Matrix Information and Directory Services, 1997). This "do-nothing" approach to development is basically a strategy of exclusion or apartheid; it is also inherently unstable and therefore unsustainable. Given that the income gap between North and South continues to

increase and that the South represents a growing proportion of the world's population, it is only a matter of time before those in the South perceive these disparities as intolerable (Hedley, 1985). In fact, signs of increasing world disorder are already apparent: escalating acts of terrorism and civil disobedience, rising illegal migration and refugee flows, spiraling crime rates, widespread famine and disease (including AIDS), and many local disputes that erupt into international conflicts. Clearly this is not the path to sustainable development. As the United Nations Commission on International Development warned us almost three decades ago, "Before long, in our affluent, industrial, computerized jet society, we shall feel the wrath of the wretched people of the world. There will be no peace" (Pearson Report, 1969).

2. Cultural imperialism. Given the statistics already cited, another likely development outcome could see the world becoming increasingly Westernized. Although the theory of cultural convergence (Kerr, Dunlop, Harbison, & Meyers, 1964) has been heavily criticized, it appears particularly applicable to the emerging information and communications revolution. The central thesis of convergence theory states that upon the introduction of technologically superior techniques, structural adaptations are made that in turn affect other aspects of society until eventually all societies, no matter how

---

Table 22.1   Dimensions and Measures of an Information Society

1. Economic activity/labor
   a) Percentage of labor force in computer hardware, software, and services industry
2. Economic output/productivity
   a) Percentage contribution of computer industry to gross domestic product (GDP)
   b) Percentage share of value added in computer manufacturing to GDP
3. Organization/structure
   a) Computer companies as a percentage of total business corporations
   b) Number of employees per company in the computer industry
   c) Use of information technology in business
   d) Computer literacy among employees
4. Technological infrastructure
   a) Computer power (MIPS) per capita
   b) Investment in telecommunications as a percentage of GDP
   c) Internet hosts per 1,000 inhabitants
   d) Digital main lines as a percentage of total main lines
5. Technological innovation
   a) Computing R&D as a percentage of total manufacturing R&D
   b) Computing professional and technical workers as a percentage of all professional and technical workers
   c) Information technology patents granted as a percentage of total patents
6. Technological diffusion
   a) Computers per capita
   b) Percentage of households with personal computers
   c) Information technology spending as a percentage of GDP

Source: Organisation for Economic Co-operation and Development (1996) and *World Competitiveness Report 1995* (1995).

dissimilar they were initially, converge in certain patterns of social organization and behavior. Concerning the introduction of computer and telecommunications technology, unlike previous technological revolutions, a significant part of the technical process is itself cultural. Even though computer software commands computers in binary code, the software originates in words, the effective currency of culture. According to Einstein (1941/1954), "The mental development of the individual and his way of forming concepts depend to a high degree upon language. This makes us realize to what extent the same language means the same mentality" (p. 336). And Gilder (1989) further adds that we are now reaching the stage where "the distinction between hardware and software will all but vanish" (p. 328).

Although earlier technologies incorporated aspects of culture in their designs in the form of standards and regulations, these were more limited in scope. But information technology, by its very nature, is cultural. "The notion that information and communication are, in fact, culturally neutral is the greatest myth of our time" (Mowlana, 1996, p. 179). Consequently, to the extent that only one culture or one linguistic group produces the bulk of software, as is presently the case, and "as hardware designs increasingly embody software concepts" (Gilder, 1989, p. 329), then certainly the possibility exists for cultural imperialism on a massive scale.

Microsoft CEO Bill Gates (1995) speaks directly to the evolution of ICT and the prospect of (American) cultural convergence:

American popular culture is so potent that outside the United States some countries now attempt to ration it. They hope to guarantee the viability of domestic-content by permitting only a certain number of hours of foreign television to be aired each week. In Europe the availability of satellite and cable-delivered programming reduced the potential for government control. The information highway is going to break down barriers and may promote a world culture, or at least a sharing of cultural activities and values. (p. 263)

What will this "world culture" look like? Which "cultural activities and values" will be adopted? According to recent newspaper reports (Weise, 1997), it could be a "Bill Gates" world. In a bid to position himself for the next phase of the information revolution, Gates has formed a new company, Teledesic Corporation, which is investing $9 billion to ring the planet with 840 satellites to provide worldwide Internet access (see **http://www.teledesic .com/**). Although a truly global Internet could bring about a new age in which all human beings have access to the same information (see below), it is also possible that this heavenly infrastructure could increase Western cultural and economic dominance on a scale never before even imagined. Should this development approach take precedence, it would by definition also be accompanied by strategies of exclusion and therefore be unsustainable for the same reasons advanced earlier.

3. Global village. As already indicated, a third development option exists. Given that the Internet (and its likely successor) is a configuration of two-way, horizontally connected computers accessed mainly by individuals via personal computer, its technology represents a significant break with previous one-way, top-down, mass communication media and, consequently, the potential for mass indoctrination. Although the Internet still permits the exercise of widespread power, as argued in the cultural imperialism scenario, its multiple interactive, real-time capability combined with its potential for universal access are novel features never before experienced on a world scale. According to Brown and Brown (1994), the information revolution "will provide a virtually seamless world communications network capable of reaching every inhabitant on earth" (p. 3). For the first time ever, a true global village in which all people have the opportunity to interact and to voice their individual concerns is possible, if not yet realized. For the hitherto disenfranchised of the world, the information revolution could thus provide the means to organize and to articulate their needs, such that they could eventually participate in a more just and humane and, therefore, sustainable world society.

How likely is this development outcome? Given the first two scenarios, and the fact that entrenched interest groups are committed to maintaining the status quo, it does not seem at all probable. However, to the extent that we can find empirical support for this third option on the Internet, we would at least have some grounds for cautious optimism. Such evidence comes from a content analysis of one Internet discussion group, established prior to a 1997 conference on Knowledge for Development in the Information Age (Global Knowledge 97). Sponsored by the United Nations Development Programme and the World Bank, it was set up "to facilitate broad discussion of the Conference themes at all levels of civil society" (Majordomo, 1997). Participants were informed

that the List offers a major forum for the exchange of ideas as well as an important channel for input into the Conference itself. The UNDP and other Conference sponsors encourage those from around the world, especially those in the South, to use the list to express their own needs, experiences, and suggestions related to Conference themes. (Majordomo, 1997)

Although my analysis is not based on a comprehensive survey of the Internet (if indeed that is possible), it does provide limited information on the extent to which the global village option is available on the Internet and the kinds of access that marginalized groups have to it. Notice of the availability of this particular on-line discussion was published widely on the Internet by the United Nations, the World Bank, and the Canadian government (Global Knowledge 97, 1997).

My period of observation began on March 24, 1997 (the time of the first e-mail posting), and ended 1 month later (April 23). During this time, 98 discussants (65% male) from 23 countries (43% from the North) posted 170 messages on a variety of development issues. (Altogether, there were approximately 700 subscribers to the GKD97 list discussion; J. Brodman, e-mail communication from the master moderator of the GKD97 list, May 7, 1997.) Although more Southern than Northern countries were represented, the vast majority of individual discussants (80%) were from the North. However, it should be noted that some people writing from the South were in fact Northern development workers and that several Northern writers were originally from the South. Because I could determine only where messages originated (and not the nationality of the authors), it is impossible to provide a breakdown by nationality. Most of the discussants ($n = 77$) made reference to their work in their messages; they constituted four major occupational groups: government-affiliated professional development workers, 30% (of whom close to half worked for UN agencies); academics, 22%; private development and information technology consultants, 21%; and nongovernmental organization (NGO) representatives, 18%. Graduate students occupied the remaining group (9%). Finally, it is interesting to note the major issues discussed. As requested in the information for participants, they related broadly to the themes of the forthcoming conference: the North-South gap, global information flow, communications infrastructure development, universal (scientific) knowledge versus local indigenous knowledge, development and empowerment initiatives, overseas and distance education programs, brain drain, and implications of the information revolution for global development.

These data are not remarkably different from what could be found in a traditional face-to-face development conference, except for the fact that on-line, many individuals from all over the world can engage in extensive real-time discussion at just a fraction of the cost of physically bringing these people together. Because of this, some on-line discussants were not the traditional development workers and researchers usually found at conferences; they were part of the group targeted for development. Although they made up only a small proportion, these people offered viewpoints not usually voiced at conventional conferences. For example, one stressed the need to wire the rural South with appropriate technology (e.g., conventional and cellular telephones and community radio) "to enable the majority to learn what is going on and air their views too.... [As a result,] the North would be able to receive more accurate information about the situation in the South." Thus, both the Internet in particular and electronic communication in general provide the technological means to broaden the constituency of discussion.

A particularly distinctive feature of on-line discussion is the references made to various sites on the Internet. Table 22.2 provides a listing of the 54 sites directly mentioned by these discussants (although in some cases the actual electronic addresses were not provided). Of these, 50 are located on the central Internet as Web sites, whereas 4 are e-mail addresses. Concerning the Web sites, it is important to note that each one in turn provides direct hyperlinks with other related Web sites. From these 50 Web sites, therefore, it is possible to link up with literally hundreds of other sites (and e-mail addresses) that are in some way involved with development. As a result, Table 22.2 provides the means to tap into conceivably all that exists about development on the Internet. For example, a visit to the Global Knowledge Internet site in 1998 revealed a listing of 192 Web sites pertaining to development, which in turn are linked to hundreds of other electronic addresses.

Table 22.2 reveals a wide variety of development resource centers available on the Internet. Although the list is not representative, given the particular issues addressed and discussants involved, it does reflect great diversity in terms of focus, sponsorship, language, and point of origin. For example, in addition to major development organizations, there are national government agencies, not-for-profit information centers, charitable foundations, educational institutions, research centers, environmental enterprises, private consultancy firms, and large and small NGOs that offer everything from technical advice and information to solidarity, protection, assistance, and "community."

There is also substantial representation from the South in terms of communications infrastructure development (Grameen Communications), electronic networks (Isis, QuipuNet, Red Caldas), and NGOs (ABANTU for Development, Research Network on Sustainable Structural Adjustment Policies). These organizations were established by people of the South to address particular development concerns as they defined them. They are currently engaged in a wide variety of innovative projects. Furthermore, much of their work is complemented by the more numerous development agencies operating from the North.

The list in Table 22.2 constitutes evidence of at least the nucleus of a global village, especially to the extent that one realizes it is illustrative of a much larger and more diverse development network. For example, the SD Gateway (**http://sdgateway.net**), operated by the UN International Institute of Sustainable Development, contains an archive of 88 electronic mailing lists, including GKD97, covering "topics ranging from ecology to economics to ethics to community initiatives." Consequently, thousands of concerned people (experts and laypersons alike) from both the North and the South are communicating with

Table 22.2	Internet Development Resource Centers Identified on the GKD97 Internet List Discussion and Global Knowledge Website*

Communications infrastructure development

Association for Progressive Communications (**http://www.apc.org/english/**)

Bellanet International Secretariat (**http://home.bellanet.org**)

Grameen Communications (**http://www.grameen-info.org/gc/**)

Internet Society (ISOC) (**http://www.isoc.org/**)

National Telecommunication Cooperative Association (NTCA) (**http://www.ntca.org**)

Network Startup Resource Center (NSRC) (**http://www.nsrc.org/**)

Partnerships for ICTs in Africa (**http://www.uneca.org/aisi/picta**)

UNDP Special Unit for Technical Cooperation Among Developing Countries (**http://tcdc.undp.org**)

World Bank InfoDev Program (**http://www.infodev.org**)

Electronic networks/building community

Association for Community Networking (AFCN) (**http://www.afcn.org**)

Centre for Community & Enterprise Networking (**leesing@sparc.uccb.ns.ca**)

Isis—Women's International Cross-Cultural Exchange (**http://www.isis.org**)

Letslink (**http://www.letslinkuk.org**)

QuipuNet (**http://www.quipunet.org**)

Red Caldas (**http://www.colciencias.gov.co/redcaldas/**)

Web Networks (**http://community.web.ca/**)

World Association of Community Radio Broadcasters (**http://www.web.apc.org/amarc/**)

Distance education

COL Knowledge Finder (**http://www.col.org/kf/**)

Global Distance Education Network (GDENet) (**http://www.ouhk.edu.hk/cridal/gdenet**)

Rivers of Life (**http://cgee.hamline.edu/rivers/**)

School Net Africa (**http://www.schoolnetafrica.org.eg**)

Virtual University (**http://www.vu.org/campus.html**)

Development assistance and research Government organizations

Canadian Bureau for International Education (**http://www.cbie.ca/**)

Canadian International Development Agency (**http://www.acdi-cida.ca/**)

Centre for International Research and Advisory Networks (**http://www.nuffic.nl/ciran**)

International Development Research Centre (**http://www.idrc.ca**)

Netherlands Directorate General for International Co-operation (**http://www.os.minbuza.nl/**)

Swedish International Development Agency (SIDA) (**http://www.sida.se/**)

UN Development Programme (**http://www.undp.org/**)

UN Economic Commission for Africa (**http://www.un.org/depts/eca**)

UN Food and Agricultural Organization (**http://www.fao.org/**)

UN International Institute for Sustainable Development (**http://www.iisd.org**)

UNESCO Early Childhood and Family Education Section
  (**http://www.unesco.org/education/educprog/ecf/**)

continued

Table 22.2 continued

Nongovernmental organizations

ABANTU for Development (**http://www.abantu.org**)

Alliance for Democracy (**http://www.thealliancefordemocracy.org**)

Environment & Development of the Third World (Enda Third World) (**http://www.enda.sn/indexuk.htm**)

International Co-operative Alliance (ICA) (**http://www.coop.org/**)

Research Network on Sustainable Structural Adjustment Policies (**http://www.jp.or.cr/catedra/**)

Urban Popular Economy Programme (**ecopop@enda.sn**)

World Information Transfer (**http://www.worldinfo.org**)

World University Service of Canada (**http://www.wusc.ca**)

Charitable foundations

Benton Foundation (**http://www.benton.org**)

Rockefeller Foundation (**http://www.rockfound.org/**)

The MacArthur Foundation (**http://www.macfdn.org/**)

Private organizations

African Management Services Company (AMSCO) (**http://www.amsco.org**)

Consultant, Global Information Analysis (**rlabelle@web.net**)

Global Village for Future Leaders of Business and Industry (**http://www.lehigh.edu/~village**)

Management Systems International (**rwebster@msi-inc.com**)

Development Information centers

Development Gateway (**http://www.developmentgateway.org**)

Enterprise Development Website (**http://www.enterweb.org**)

Global Digital Opportunity Initiative (GDOI) (**www.markle.org**)

Global Information Infrastructure Commission (GIIC) (**http://www.giic.org/**)

UN Global Urban Observatory Network (GUONet) (**http://www.unhabitat.org/guonet/**)

Union of International Associations (**http://www.uia.org**)

*This table was revised in January 2004 for inclusion in this book. It reflects current names and Web contact information for the organizations concerned.

each other on a wide variety of development issues. Thus, we may conclude that the Internet can provide an interactive forum for many different kinds of groups to disseminate particular points of view and to engage in dialogue with interested others. It also represents a widely varied information resource available to all who have access to it. Although the issue of access remains a serious problem, there are indications even now that strategic access to the Internet is currently being gained by a small core of those traditionally without voice. Moreover, as the electronic communications infrastructure becomes more broadly established, largely as a result of the efforts of organizations such as those listed in Table 22.2, we may expect even greater and more diverse representation on the Internet. And with the establishment of a virtual global village, truly inclusive discussion and debate on development could finally take place—a necessary precondition to achieving sustainable development.

CONCLUSION

The development scenarios just examined are not mutually exclusive; yet to the extent that apartheid and cultural imperialism, that is, processes of exclusion, continue to gain in ascendancy, there is diminishing likelihood of the inclusive global village option. However, analysis of the Internet reveals that technologically greater opportunity exists now for the previously excluded to participate. Is this sufficient? Some who are deeply committed to the concept of inclusion have grave reservations. Consider the following excerpt from a (Northern) discussant in my case study:

Poverty is a choice the world has made. It is a political choice. The information revolution will be another instrument to implement that choice. Only a governance revolution would represent a real change. And to link the information revolution with democratization is naive in the extreme, parallel to the current leap of faith linking democratization and open markets.

Given the history of humankind since the industrial revolution, it may well be naive to expect that we can tear down the many institutionalized structures of exclusion that are currently in place. However, if we do not try, all of us will eventually lose. At stake is the very survival of our species (Piel, 1992). My case study and other data I presented on development via the Internet indicate that both the technological infrastructure and the will to make a difference are growing. It is possible to reduce the North-South gap, to provide greater cultural balance, and to improve the quality of life for all human beings—but then again, it always has been.

NAVIGATING THE CONCEPTS

1. Do you feel that information technology in general, and the personal computer in particular, enhance or confine global democratic movements and economic development? Discuss with reference to Hedley's findings.

2. One could argue that the information revolution has influenced how students learn and are taught. On the other hand, while the ability to surf the Web has made accessing information easier, are you a better student because of these technological advances? Discuss.

3. Hedley quotes the comment: "Poverty is a choice the world has made. It is a political choice. The information revolution will be another instrument to implement that choice." Discuss.

4. What are the benefits and the costs associated with the information revolution? Do you feel that the benefits outweigh the costs? Defend you answer with reference to Hedley's analysis.

REFERENCES

Bell, D. 1976. *The coming of post-industrial society.* New York: Basic Books.

Brandt Report. 1980. *North-South: A program for survival.* Cambridge, Mass.: MIT Press.

Brown, F. B., and Y. Brown, 1994. Distance education around the world. In *Distance education: Strategies and tools,* ed. B. Willis, 3–39. Englewood Cliffs, N.J.: Educational Technology.

Einstein, A. 1954. The common language of science. In *Ideas and opinions by Albert Einstein,* ed. C. Seelig. New York: Wing Books. Reprinted from *Advancement of Science,* 2(5), 1941.

Gates, B. 1995. *The road ahead.* New York: Viking.

Gilder, G. 1989. *Microcosm: The quantum revolution in economics and technology.* New York: Simon and Schuster.

GKD97. 1998. The GK virtual conference: Recommendations and cases from the GKD97 list. [Online] Available: **http://www.globalknowledge. org/english/ search/index.html.**

Global Knowledge 97. 1997. International conference on knowledge for development in the information age, Toronto (June 22–25). [Online] Available: **http://www.globalknowledge.org.**

Hedley, R. A. 1985. Narrowing the gap between the rich and the poor nations: A modest proposal, *Transnational Perspectives,* 11(2/3): 23–27.

———. 1992. *Making a living: Technology and change.* New York: HarperCollins.

Jacobs, M. 1991. *The green economy: Environment, sustainable development and the politics of the future.* London: Pluto.

Kerr, C., J. T. Dunlop, F. Harbison, and C. A. Meyers. 1964. *Industrialism and industrial man.* New York: Oxford University Press.

Majordomo. 1997. Welcome to the Global Knowledge for Development Conference Internet list discussion. Information provided for Internet discussion group participants by **Majordomo@tristram.edc.org.**

Mandel, M. J. 1994. The digital juggernaut. *Business Week* special issue, *The Information Revolution*: 22–29.

Matrix Information and Directory Services. 1997. Current world map of the Matrix and the Internet (March 28). [Online] Available: **http://www.mids .org/.**

Mitchell, B. R. 1962. *Abstract of British historical statistics.* Cambridge, U.K.: Cambridge University Press.

Mowlana, H. 1996. *Global communication in transition: The end of diversity?* Thousand Oaks, Calif.: Sage.

Network Wizards. 1997. Internet domain survey (January). [Online] Available: **http://www.nw.com/.**

Organisation for Economic Co-operation and Development (OECD). 1996. *Information technology outlook 1995.* Paris: Author.

Pearson Report. 1969. *Partners in development: Report of the Commission on International Development.* New York: Praeger.

Piel, G. 1992. *Only one world: Our own to make and keep.* New York: Freeman.

Porat, M. 1977. *The information economy: Definition and measurement* (Special Publication 77-12, U.S. Department of Commerce, Office of Telecommunications). Washington, D.C.: U.S. Government Printing Office.

Stavrianos, L. S. 1981. *Global rift: The Third World comes of age.* New York: William Morrow.

Weise, E. 1997. Plan would launch 840 satellites to deliver Internet. *New York Times* (March 18).

World Bank. 1995. *World development report 1995.* Oxford, U.K.: Oxford University Press.

———. 1997. *1997 world development indicators.* Washington, D.C.: International Bank for Reconstruction and Development.

World Commission on Environment and Development. 1987. *Our common future.* Oxford, U.K.: Oxford University Press.

World competitiveness report 1995. 1995. Lausanne, Switzerland: IMD and World Economic Forum.

Chapter 23

Globalisation

Anthony Giddens

Source: Copyright (© 2002) From *Runaway World: How Globalization Is Reshaping Our Lives* by Anthony Giddens. Reproduced by permission of Routledge/Taylor & Francis Books, Inc.

Anthony Giddens suggests that the true influences of globalization are only starting to become evident. Globalization is far more than an economic revolution; for Giddens, it is a dynamic and multi-faceted process that is changing the very nature of our lives.

A friend of mine studies village life in central Africa. A few years ago, she paid her first visit to a remote area where she was to carry out her fieldwork. The day she arrived, she was invited to a local home for an evening's entertainment. She expected to find out about the traditional pastimes of this isolated community. Instead, the occasion turned out to be a viewing of *Basic Instinct* on video. The film at that point hadn't even reached the cinemas in London.

Such vignettes reveal something about our world. And what they reveal isn't trivial. It isn't just a matter of people adding modern paraphernalia—videos, television sets, personal computers and so forth—to their existing ways of life. We live in a world of transformations, affecting almost every aspect of what we do. For better or worse, we are being propelled into a global order that no one fully understands, but which is making its effects felt upon all of us.

Globalisation may not be a particularly attractive or elegant word. But absolutely no one who wants to understand our prospects at century's end can ignore it. I travel a lot to speak abroad. I haven't been to a single country recently where globalisation isn't being intensively discussed. In France, the word is *mondialisation*. In Spain and Latin America, it is *globalización*. The Germans say *Globalisierung*.

The global spread of the term is evidence of the very developments to which it refers. Every business guru talks about it. No political speech is complete without reference to it. Yet even in the late 1980s the term was hardly used, either in the academic literature or in everyday language. It has come from nowhere to be almost everywhere.

Given its sudden popularity, we shouldn't be surprised that the meaning of the notion isn't always clear, or that an intellectual reaction has set in against it. Globalisation has something to do with the thesis that we now all live in one world—but in what ways exactly, and is the idea really valid? Different thinkers have taken almost completely opposite views about globalisation in debates that have sprung up over the past few years. Some dispute the whole thing. I'll call them the sceptics.

According to the sceptics, all the talk about globalisation is only that—just talk. Whatever its benefits, its trials and tribulations, the global economy isn't especially different from that which existed at previous periods. The world carries on much the same as it has done for many years.

Most countries, the sceptics argue, gain only a small amount of their income from external trade. Moreover, a good deal of economic exchange is between regions, rather than being truly world-wide. The countries of the European Union, for example, mostly trade among themselves. The same is true of the other main trading blocs, such as those of Asia–Pacific or North America.

Others take a very different position. I'll label them the radicals. The radicals argue that not only is globalisation very real, but that its consequences can be felt everywhere. The global market-place, they say, is much more developed than even in the 1960s and 1970s and is indifferent to national borders. Nations have lost most of the sovereignty they once had, and politicians have lost most of their capability to influence events. It isn't surprising that no one respects political leaders any more, or has much interest in what they have to say. The era of the nation-state is over. Nations, as the Japanese business writer Kenichi Ohmae puts it, have become mere "fictions." Authors such as Ohmae see the economic difficulties of the 1998 Asian crisis as demonstrating the reality of globalisation, albeit seen from its disruptive side.

The sceptics tend to be on the political left, especially the old left. For if all of this is essentially a myth, governments can still control economic life and the welfare state remain intact. The notion of globalisation, according to the sceptics, is an ideology put about by free-marketeers who wish to dismantle welfare systems and cut back on state expenditures. What has happened is at most a reversion to how the world was a century ago. In the late nineteenth century there was already an open global economy, with a great deal of trade, including trade in currencies.

Well, who is right in this debate? I think it is the radicals. The level of world trade today is much higher than it ever was before, and involves a much wider range of goods and services. But the biggest difference is in the level of finance and capital flows. Geared as it is to electronic money—money that exists only as digits in computers—the current world economy has no parallels in earlier times.

In the new global electronic economy, fund managers, banks, corporations, as well as millions of individual investors, can transfer vast amounts of capital from one side of the world to another at the click of a mouse. As they do so, they can destabilise what might have seemed rock-solid economies—as happened in the events in Asia.

The volume of world financial transactions is usually measured in US dollars. A million dollars is a lot of money for most people. Measured as a stack of hundred-dollar notes, it would be eight inches high. A billion dollars—in other words, a thousand million—would stand higher than St Paul's Cathedral. A trillion dollars—a million million—would be over 120 miles high, 20 times higher than Mount Everest.

Yet far more than a trillion dollars is now turned over *each day* on global currency markets. This is a massive increase from only the late 1980s, let alone the more distant past. The value of whatever money we may have in our pockets, or our bank accounts, shifts from moment to moment according to fluctuations in such markets.

I would have no hesitation, therefore, in saying that globalisation, as we are experiencing it, is in many respects not only new, but also revolutionary. Yet I don't believe that either the sceptics or the radicals have properly understood either what it is or its implications for us. Both groups see the phenomenon almost solely in economic terms. This is a mistake. Globalisation is political, technological and cultural, as well as economic. It has been influenced above all by developments in systems of communication, dating back only to the late 1960s.

In the mid-nineteenth century, a Massachusetts portrait painter, Samuel Morse, transmitted the first message, "What hath God wrought?," by electric telegraph. In so doing, he initiated a new phase in world history. Never before could a message be sent without someone going somewhere to carry it. Yet the advent of satellite communications marks every bit as dramatic a break with the past. The first commercial satellite was launched only in 1969. Now there are more than 200 such satellites above the earth, each carrying a vast range of information. For the first time ever, instantaneous communication is possible from one side of the world to the other. Other types of electronic communication, more and more integrated with satellite transmission, have also accelerated over the past few years. No dedicated transatlantic or transpacific cables existed at all until the late 1950s. The first held fewer than 100 voice paths. Those of today carry more than a million.

On 1 February 1999, about 150 years after Morse invented his system of dots and dashes, Morse Code finally disappeared from the world stage. It was discontinued as a means of communication for the sea. In its place has come a system using satellite technology, whereby any ship in distress can be pinpointed immediately. Most countries prepared for the transition some while before. The French, for example, stopped using Morse Code in their local waters in 1997, signing off with a Gallic flourish: "Calling all. This is our last cry before our eternal silence."

Instantaneous electronic communication isn't just a way in which news or information is conveyed more quickly. Its existence alters the very texture of our lives, rich and poor alike. When the image of Nelson Mandela may be more familiar to us than the face of our next-door neighbour, something has changed in the nature of our everyday experience.

Nelson Mandela is a global celebrity, and celebrity itself is largely a product of new communications technology. The reach of media technologies is growing with each wave of innovation. It took 40 years for radio in the United States to gain an audience of 50 million. The same number was using personal computers only 15 years after the personal computer was introduced. It needed a mere 4 years, after it was made available, for 50 million Americans to be regularly using the Internet.

It is wrong to think of globalisation as just concerning the big systems, like the world financial order. Globalisation isn't only about what is "out there," remote and far away from the individual. It is an "in here" phenomenon too, influencing intimate and personal aspects of our lives. The debate about family values, for example, that is going on in many countries might seem far removed from globalising influences. It isn't. Traditional family systems are becoming transformed, or are under strain, in many parts of the world, particularly as women stake claim to greater equality. There has never before been a society, so far as we know from the historical record, in which women have been even approximately equal to men. This is a truly global revolution in everyday life, whose consequences are being felt around the world in spheres from work to politics.

Globalisation thus is a complex set of processes, not a single one. And these operate in a contradictory or oppositional fashion. Most people think of globalisation as simply "pulling away" power or influence from local communities and nations into the global arena. And indeed this is one of its consequences. Nations do lose some of the economic power they once had. Yet it also has an opposite effect. Globalisation not only pulls upwards, but also pushes downwards, creating new pressures for local autonomy. The American sociologist Daniel Bell describes this very well when he says that the nation becomes not only too small to solve the big problems, but also too large to solve the small ones.

Globalisation is the reason for the revival of local cultural identities in different parts of the world. If one asks, for example, why the Scots want more independence in the UK, or why there is a strong separatist movement in Quebec, the answer is not to be found only in their cultural history. Local nationalisms spring up as a response to globalising tendencies, as the hold of older nation-states weakens.

Globalisation also squeezes sideways. It creates new economic and cultural zones within and across nations. Examples are the Hong Kong region, northern Italy, and Silicon Valley in California. Or consider the Barcelona region. The area around Barcelona in northern Spain extends into France. Catalonia, where Barcelona is located, is closely integrated into the European Union. It is part of Spain, yet also looks outwards.

These changes are being propelled by a range of factors, some structural, others more specific and historical. Economic influences are certainly among the driving forces—especially the global financial system. Yet they aren't like forces of nature. They have been shaped by technology, and cultural diffusion, as well as by the decisions of governments to liberalise and deregulate their national economies.

The collapse of Soviet communism has added further weight to such developments, since no significant group of countries any longer stands outside. That collapse wasn't just something that just happened to occur. Globalisation explains both why and how Soviet communism met its end. The former Soviet Union and the East European countries were comparable to the West in terms of growth rates until somewhere around the early 1970s. After that point, they fell rapidly behind. Soviet communism, with its emphasis

upon state-run enterprise and heavy industry, could not compete in the global electronic economy. The ideological and cultural control upon which communist political authority was based similarly could not survive in an era of global media.

The Soviet and the East European regimes were unable to prevent the reception of Western radio and television broadcasts. Television played a direct role in the 1989 revolutions, which have rightly been called the first "television revolutions." Street protests taking place in one country were watched by television audiences in others, large numbers of whom then took to the streets themselves.

Globalisation, of course, isn't developing in an even-handed way, and is by no means wholly benign in its consequences. To many living outside Europe and North America, it looks uncomfortably like Westernisation—or, perhaps, Americanisation, since the US is now the sole superpower, with a dominant economic, cultural and military position in the global order. Many of the most visible cultural expressions of globalisation are American—Coca-Cola, McDonald's, CNN.

Most of the giant multinational companies are based in the US too. Those that aren't all come from the rich countries, not the poorer areas of the world. A pessimistic view of globalisation would consider it largely an affair of the industrial North, in which the developing societies of the South play little or no active part. It would see it as destroying local cultures, widening world inequalities and worsening the lot of the impoverished. Globalisation, some argue, creates a world of winners and losers, a few on the fast track to prosperity, the majority condemned to a life of misery and despair.

Indeed, the statistics are daunting. The share of the poorest fifth of the world's population in global income has dropped, from 2.3 per cent to 1.4 per cent between 1989 and 1998. The proportion taken by the richest fifth, on the other hand, has risen. In sub-

Saharan Africa, 20 countries have lower incomes per head in real terms than they had in the late 1970s. In many less developed countries, safety and environmental regulations are low or virtually non-existent. Some transnational companies sell goods there that are controlled or banned in the industrial countries—poor-quality medial drugs, destructive pesticides or high tar and nicotine content cigarettes. Rather than a global village, one might say, this is more like global pillage.

Along with ecological risk, to which it is related, expanding inequality is the most serious problem facing world society. It will not do, however, merely to blame it on the wealthy. It is fundamental to my argument that globalisation today is only partly Westernisation. Of course the Western nations, and more generally the industrial countries, still have far more influence over world affairs than do the poorer states. But globalisation is becoming increasingly decentred—not under the control of any group of nations, and still less of the large corporations. Its effects are felt as much in Western countries as elsewhere.

This is true of the global financial system, and of changes affecting the nature of government itself. What one could call "reverse colonisation" is becoming more and more common. Reverse colonisation means that non-Western countries influence developments in the West. Examples abound—such as the latinising of Los Angeles, the emergence of a globally oriented high-tech sector in India, or the selling of Brazilian television programmes to Portugal.

Is globalisation a force promoting the general good? The question can't be answered in a simple way, given the complexity of the phenomenon. People who ask it, and who blame globalisation for deepening world inequalities, usually have in mind economic globalisation and, within that, free trade. Now, it is surely obvious that free trade is not an unalloyed benefit. This is especially so as concerns the less developed countries.

Opening up a country, or regions within it, to free trade can undermine a local subsistence economy. An area that becomes dependent upon a few products sold on world markets is very vulnerable to shifts in prices as well as to technological change.

Trade always needs a framework of institutions, as do other forms of economic development. Markets cannot be created by purely economic means, and how far a given economy should be exposed to the world marketplace must depend upon a range of criteria. Yet to oppose economic globalisation, and to opt for economic protectionism, would be a misplaced tactic for rich and poor nations alike. Protectionism may be a necessary strategy at some times and in some countries. In my view, for example, Malaysia was correct to introduce controls in 1998, to stem the flood of capital from the country. But more permanent forms of protectionism will not help the development of the poor countries, and among the rich would lead to warring trade blocs.

The debates about globalisation I mentioned at the beginning have concentrated mainly upon its implications for the nation-state. Are nation-states, and hence national political leaders, still powerful, or are they becoming largely irrelevant to the forces shaping the world? Nation-states are indeed still powerful and political leaders have a large role to play in the world. Yet at the same time the nation-state is being reshaped before our eyes. National economic policy can't be as effective as it once was. More importantly, nations have to rethink their identities now the older forms of geopolitics are becoming obsolete. Although this is a contentious point, I would say that, following the dissolving of the Cold War, most nations no longer have enemies. Who are the enemies of Britain, or France, or Brazil? The war in Kosovo didn't pit nation against nation. It was a conflict between old-style territorial nationalism and a new, ethically driven interventionalism.

Nations today face risks and dangers rather than enemies, a massive shift in their very nature. It isn't only of the nation that such comments could be made. Everywhere we look, we see institutions that appear the same as they used to be from the outside, and carry the same names, but inside have become quite different. We continue to talk of the nation, the family, work, tradition, nature, as if they were all the same as in the past. They are not. The outer shell remains, but inside they have changed—and this is happening not only in the US, Britain, or France, but almost everywhere. They are what I call "shell institutions." They are institutions that have become inadequate to the tasks they are called upon to perform.

As the changes I have described in this chapter gather weight, they are creating something that has never existed before, a global cosmopolitan society. We are the first generation to live in this society, whose contours we can as yet only dimly see. It is shaking up our existing ways of life, no matter where we happen to be. This is not—at least at the moment—a global order driven by collective human will. Instead, it is emerging in an anarchic, haphazard, fashion, carried along by a mixture of influences.

It is not settled or secure, but fraught with anxieties, as well as scarred by deep divisions. Many of us feel in the grip of forces over which we have no power. Can we reimpose our will upon them? I believe we can. The powerlessness we experience is not a sign of personal failings, but reflects the incapacities of our institutions. We need to reconstruct those we have, or create new ones. For globalisation is not incidental to our lives today. It is a shift in our very life circumstances. It is the way we now live.

NAVIGATING THE CONCEPTS

1. Do you feel that you are a part of the "global village"? Why, or why not?

2. In your opinion, is a global culture emerging? If so, what are the key features of this culture and where is it originating from? If not, why have instantaneous global telecommunications not had more of an impact on defining a global sense of community?

3. What are the benefits and the costs associated with globalization? Do you feel the benefits outweigh the costs? Defend you answer with reference to Giddens's analysis.